# Celtic
# Myth & Legend

AN A–Z OF PEOPLE AND PLACES

*Companion volume by Mike Dixon-Kennedy:*

ARTHURIAN MYTH & LEGEND
An A–Z of People and Places

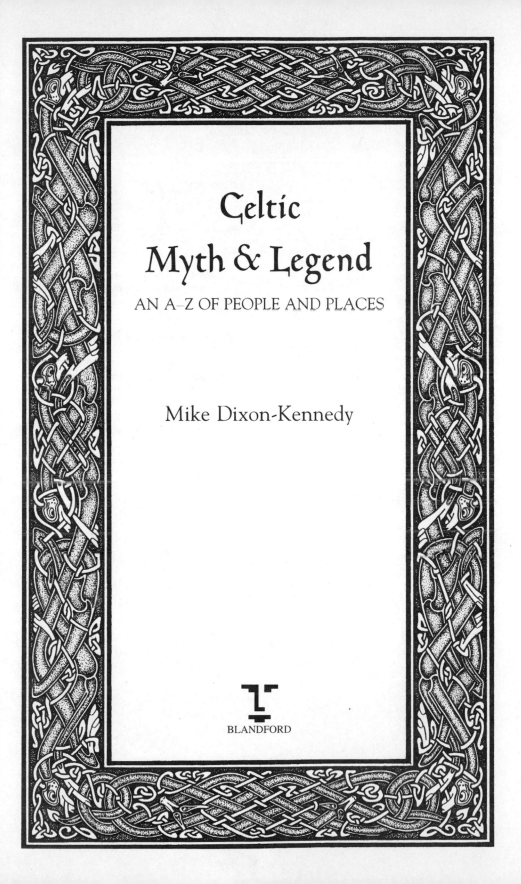

# Celtic
# Myth & Legend

## AN A–Z OF PEOPLE AND PLACES

Mike Dixon-Kennedy

BLANDFORD

A BLANDFORD BOOK

First published in the UK 1996 by Blandford
A Cassell Imprint
Cassell Plc, Wellington House,
125 Strand, London WC2R 0BB

Distributed in the United States by Sterling Publishing Co., Inc.,
387 Park Avenue South, New York, NY 10016–8810

Distributed in Australia by Capricorn Link (Australia) Pty Ltd
2/13 Carrington Road, Castle Hill, NSW 2154

British Library Cataloguing-in-Publication Data
A catalogue entry for this title is available from the British Library

ISBN 0–7137–2571–0 (hardback)

ISBN 0–7137–2613–X (paperback)

Celtic artwork by Chris Down
Typeset by Keystroke, Jacaranda Lodge, Wolverhampton
Printed and bound in Great Britain by Hartnolls Limited, Bodmin, Cornwall

# Contents

In loving memory of my mother.
Missed but not forgotten.

# Introduction

When I was asked to write this book as a follow-up to *Arthurian Myth & Legend: An A–Z of People and Places* (Blandford, 1995) my initial thought was 'no problem'. However, as I sat down to consider the mass of Celtic literature, both ancient and modern, it soon struck me that this was not going to be as easy as I first thought. In the end I had to apply strict rules about what was included in the text, and what was not.

The main problems with the study of Celtic mythology and legend are, first, when did the Celts first appear and, second, when did they disappear? The answer to the first question is almost impossible to find, as no one has so far determined the date of origin of the Celts with any degree of accuracy. Some say they date from the twelfth century BC, others from the ninth and so on. The second question is quite easy to answer, for in truth the Celts have never really died out.

That, however, left me with having to determine a date after which things would definitely have to be omitted. In Ireland I made this date the arrival of Christianity. In Britain I made it the arrival of the Anglo-Saxons, although I have treated the British entries with a fair degree of flexibility. However, having already written a book about the Arthurian myths and legends, I immediately decided to all but exclude those myths and legends from this book, even though many of them undoubtedly have Celtic origins, or connections.

In this book, which is the result of over fifteen years of research (though not solely concentrating on the Celts, for the whole subject of world mythology fascinates me), you will find that the majority of the entries refer to Irish mythology and legend. This is not a bias towards that noble race, but rather a fact of history. Britain and the continent have been invaded so many times that the Celtic tradition has been all but annihilated. However, Ireland fared somewhat better, and today Ireland is possibly the only truly Celtic stronghold left.

I hope that I have made this book as complete and authoritative as I can. No such book could be completed without the help of a great many people, but to list them all here would take far too much space. I will simply say a great big 'thank you' to them all, for they will know who they are. I will undoubtedly have omitted something or made some false assumption within this book. Should you want to bring anything to my attention, please address your comments to me via the publisher, and they will make sure your letters reach me.

There are, however, several people whom I cannot neglect. First, I should like to thank Stuart Booth at Cassell for commissioning this book. The other five people who merit attention are very close to me – my wife Gill and our four children; Christopher, Charlotte, Thomas and Rebecca. I thank them for their tolerance and patience while I have been locked away working on the research that has led to this book and then again while preparing the text.

Mike Dixon-Kennedy
Lincolnshire

# how to Use This Book

Even though the book is basically arranged as a simple, straightforward dictionary, several conventions have been adopted to make cross-referencing much easier and to make the text more decipherable.

Where headwords have alternative spellings that consist solely of the omission or addition of letters, those letters affected within the headword are enclosed in brackets. For example, **Dag(h)d(h)a** would lead to *Daghdha*, *Dagda*, *Daghda* or *Dagdha* all being acceptable variants. Where variants are created by different spellings, the entry is given under the most correct form of the word, the variant endings being given in the form of, for example, **Bor~mo, ~vo** which gives the alternate spellings of *Bormo* and *Borvo*. This is also sometimes used for complete words that might vary; e.g. **Gronw ~Bebyr, ~Pebyr**. Where names have a part of their full form normally omitted, that part is enclosed in brackets, e.g. **Conchobar (mac Nessa)**.

Words that appear in SMALL CAPITALS indicate there is a separate entry for that word.

The use of *italics* indicates that the reference is to a text.

Where more than one entry appears under a headword, each entry is preceded by a number. Further references to these words within the text of the book are followed by the appropriate number in superscript – e.g., LODAN[2].

When a country is indicated under each headword, it does not imply that the character, myth or legend concerned was solely restricted to that country. Rather it indicates the country of origin, and it may well be that the myth or legend was known further afield.

# Spelling and Pronunciation Guide

When the legends of the Celts were being recorded, standardized spelling was not common. As a result there are a great many variations within the many works I have consulted during the preparation of this book. I have tried – and I must stress tried – to adopt the commonest, or most correct form of each name. I apologize if you consider I have made mistakes in my choices. This system, however, does lead to one small problem, that being multiple entries under variant spellings.

As far as is humanly possible I have tried to weed out these entries, but some are sure to have slipped through my net. Again I apologize. The main problem here is one of association, for how does one recognize a true variant, if the stories related under the variants differ? Here I make no apologies, for the fault here is not mine, but that of those who first put pen to paper to preserve these stories for our enjoyment. The translators of the nineteenth century did little to improve the situation, for these show amazing variations, even within the same work!

Although many of the names within this book may look peculiar to modern readers, they are not difficult to pronounce. A little effort and the following guide will help you to ensure that these names are pronounced correctly. Please bear in mind, however, that the same vowels can be pronounced differently depending on regional accents.

*Consonants: as in English, but with a few exceptions:*

|       |                                                                    |
|-------|--------------------------------------------------------------------|
| c:    | hard, as in c_at (never soft as in c_entury)                       |
| ch:   | Gaelic – v, as in v_an                                             |
| ch:   | Welsh – hard, as in Scottish Lo_ch (never soft as in ch_ur_ch)    |
| dd:   | th as in th_en (never as in th_istle)                             |
| f:    | v, as in o_f                                                       |
| ff:   | f, as in o_ff                                                      |
| g:    | hard, as in g_irl (never as in g_em)                              |
| gh:   | silent, as in English                                              |
| ll:   | a Welsh distinctive, sounded as 'tl' or 'hl' on the sides of the tongue |
| r:    | trilled, lightly                                                    |
| rh:   | as if hr, heavy on the 'h' sound                                  |
| s:    | always as in s_ir (never as in hi_s)                              |
| th:   | as in th_istle (never as in th_en)                               |

*Vowels: as in English, but with the general lightness of short vowel sounds:*

a: as in f_a_ther
e: as in m_e_t or sometimes long, as in l_a_te
i: as in p_i_n or sometimes long, as in e_at
o: as in n_o_t
u: as in p_i_n or sometimes long, as in e_at
w: a 'double-u', as in vac_uu_m, or t_oo_l; but becomes a consonant before vowels, such as in the name Gwen
y: as in p_i_n, or as in e_at, but sometimes as 'u' in b_u_t

There is virtually no difference, for the beginner, between i, u and y.


*Accent*
Welsh: normally on the next to last syllable.
Gaelic: as indicated. A circumflex (^) indicates length, thus dûn is pronounced *doon* not *dewn*.
Diphthongs: none in Welsh, each vowel is pronounced individually.

# The Celts

## THE PEOPLE, THEIR ART AND LANGUAGES

Although a true history would require a volume of its own, the following is intended to give a very brief insight into the Celts.

## THE PEOPLE

The Celts originated, so it is widely accepted today, in central Europe *c*.1200 BC in the basin of the Upper Danube, the Alps, and parts of France and south Germany. Classical legend accounts for the naming of the people through the story of Celtina, daughter of Britannus, who had a son by Hercules named Celtus who became the progenitor of the Celtic people.

The Celts developed a transitional culture between the Bronze and Iron Ages, the ninth to fifth centuries BC, a culture known as the Halstatt culture from the excavations carried out at Halstatt, southwest of Salzburg. They farmed and raised cattle, and were pioneers of iron working, reaching their peak in the period from the fifth century BC to the Roman conquest, this latter culture being known as the La Tène culture from the archaeological site in Switzerland.

In the sixth century BC they spread into Spain and Portugal and were known as the Celtiberi ('Iberian Celts'). Over the next three hundred years they also spread into the British Isles, north Italy (sacking Rome in 390 BC), Greece and the Balkans, although they never established a united empire, probably because they were divided into numerous tribes. Their various conquests were made by emigrant bands, which made permanent settlements in these areas, as well as in that part of Asia Minor that was later to be known as Gallatia. In the first century BC the Celts were defeated by the Roman Empire, and by Germanic tribes, and confined to western Europe, especially England, Wales and Ireland. Even here they were not safe, for the Romans invaded Britain in 43 AD and sought to annihilate Celtic beliefs. This they failed to do, and it was not until the arrival of the Anglo-Saxons in the fifth century AD that the Celts were pushed into the furthest corners of Britain. By that time the continental Celts had all but disappeared, and those left as true Celts were confined to the southwest of England, parts of Wales and almost all of Ireland. The advent of Christianity was the final nail in the Celtic coffin, although Ireland has managed to retain most of its Celtic beliefs, customs and traditions right up to modern times.

## ART

Celtic art originated as a style *c*.500 BC, possibly on the Rhine, and spread west-wards to Gaul and the British Isles, and southwards to Turkey and Italy. Metalwork using curving incised lines and inlays of coloured enamel and coral survived at La Tène, Switzerland. The most remarkable example of Celtic art has to be the Gündestrup Cauldron that was discovered in a peat bog in Vesthimmerland, Denmark, in 1891. Dating possibly from the first or second century BC, this remark-able vessel clearly demonstrates the advances the Celts made in their artistic style from the primitive origins as demonstrated by the finds at Halstatt.

## LANGUAGES

Celtic languages are a branch of the Indo-European family and are divided into two groups: the Brythonic or P-Celtic, which covers Welsh, Cornish, Breton and Gaulish, and the Goidelic or Q-Celtic, which covers the Gaelic languages of Irish, Scottish and Manx. Celtic languages once stretched from the Black Sea to Britain, but have been in decline for centuries, limited to small areas of western Europe, the so-called 'Celtic Fringe'.

As their names suggest, a major distinction between the two groups is that while Brythonic has 'p' (as in Old Welsh *map*) Goidelic has a 'q' sound (as in Gaelic *mac*). Gaulish is the long-extinct language of Gaul, while Cornish died out as a natural language in the late eighteenth century, and Manx in 1974. All surviving Celtic languages have experienced official neglect in recent centuries, and have suffered from emigration.

# Dictionary

## Abandinus
*British*

A local deity of unknown attributes and characteristics, whose name occurs only at Godmanchester in Cambridgeshire.

## Abartach
*Irish*

The son of ALCHAD, a magician who mysteriously made a number of the FIAN disappear. They were rescued by GOLL and OSCAR, and a levy, which was to include his wife, was imposed on him for his trickery. Abartach, however, simply used his magic to disappear and thus escape the fine.

## Abcan mac Bicelmois
*Irish*

The harper of the TUATHA DÉ DANANN when LUGH arrived at TARA.

## Acallamh na Senórach
*Irish*

*Colloquy with the Ancients*, one of the most attractive and interesting pieces of Irish mythological literature. A long narrative, dating from about the thirteenth century, the *Colloquy* is a collection of stories set in a mythical framework and thus contains much primitive material.

## Achtland
*Irish*

One of the daughters of DOEL who appears in the *Longes mac nDuil Dermait*. She is the husband of CONNLA[1], a giant who sleeps with his head on a rock in the west of his island home and his feet in the east. When CÚ CHULAINN came to this island, Achtland agreed to help him locate her brothers who had mysteriously disappeared. She led Cú Chulainn to another island where he released her brothers from the enchantment placed on them by EOCHO ROND.

## Acorn
*General*

Celtic symbol of life, fecundity and immortality.

## Addanc
*Welsh*
Also AFANC

A legendary Welsh monster whose name, in modern Welsh, means 'beaver'. The word *addanc*, when employed as a noun rather than a proper name, can also be used to refer to a water-dwelling spirit, which is not, in this case, an animal, but has a more human appearance.

There is no description of the Addanc. Welsh legend says that PEREDUR overcame an Addanc with manipulative skills, for it threw spears and other

11

missiles at him. Later legend attached this occurrence to the Arthurian knight Perceval, and even credited King ARTHUR himself with defeating such a creature at Llyn Barfog.

## Addaon
*Welsh*

The son of TALIESIN. Noted for his wisdom, he was killed by LLONGAD GRWRM FARGOD EIDYN. Sources do not make it clear whether Addaon was the only son of Taliesin, nor do they name his mother.

## Aed
*Irish*

1 The son of the King of CONNACHT and husband of the beautiful IBHELL.
2 The son of the DAGHDHA who was killed by CONCHEANN for seducing his wife. The Daghdha punished Concheann by making him carry Aed's corpse until he found a stone long enough to cover his grave. Some sources make Aed an alternative name for the Daghdha himself, which would, in this case, mean 'fire'.
3 The husband of AIDE. His wife and family were drowned by DUB, who sank their boat.

## Aed Abrat
*Irish*

The father of LI BAN, FAND² and OENGHUS.

## Aed Finn
*Irish*

Possibly an historical person who is thought to have been responsible for writing down the *Immram Curaig Maíle Dúin*. The final passage of this text describes Aed Finn as the chief sage of Ireland, but he remains unknown from any other source.

## Aed Ruadh
*Irish*

A tyrannical king, whose champion invoked the powers of the sea, sun, wind and firmament against him. The sun grew so hot that Aed Ruadh was forced to bathe in the sea. A great wind blew up, which whipped the sea into a frenzy and drowned Aed Ruadh.

## Aeda
*Irish*

1 A dwarf, the FILI of FERGUS MAC LEDA. He accompanied EISIRT to FAYLINN, the realm of IUBDAN, a land inhabited by an elfin race. There, even though he was smaller than the average four-year-old child, Aeda caused panic, for to the inhabitants of Faylinn he was a veritable giant.
2 A prince to whom the giantess BEBHIONN had been betrothed by her father TREON against her wishes. In an attempt to escape her forthcoming marriage, Bebhionn sought the protection of FIONN MAC CUMHAILL. No sooner had Fionn mac Cumhaill pledged to protect her, however, than a male giant appeared and ran her through with his spear before Fionn mac Cumhaill could respond. This giant was Aeda, who had heard of Bebhionn's flight from her commitment and swore that he would avenge the dishonour she had brought on him. Even though Fionn mac Cumhaill and his men chased Aeda, they could not catch him as he strode out to sea and climbed into a huge ship and sailed away.

## Aedán mac Gabráin
*Irish*

A King of DÁL RIADA and the father of the appropriately named ARTHUR OF DÁL RIADA. He was helped in his fight against the SAXONS by his ally FIACHNA LURGAN, King of DÁL NARAIDI, and the magical intervention of MANANNÁN MAC LIR.

## Aedd
*Welsh*

Sometimes given the epithet 'the Great', Aedd was the father of PRYDEIN, the eponym of BRITAIN[1] in Welsh tradition.

## Aedh
*Irish*

The son of the King of LEINSTER who was enticed into a síDH by the daughters of BODB. For three years Aedh was cared for by the inhabitants of the síDH, but eventually he and fifty other youths managed to escape, whereupon they met St PATRICK who had just arrived in IRELAND. He told his story to St Patrick who must have converted him on the spot, for Aedh is reputed to have told the saint that he would eventually die as God willed, the TUATHA DÉ DANANN having no further power over him.

## Aeife
*Irish*

Appearing in the *Acallamh Na Senórach* Aeife and her sisters, CLIODNA and EDAEIN, eloped from TÍR TAIRNGIRI with CIABHAN, LODAN[1] and EOLUS. When they reached IRELAND a huge wave rolled in from the sea and engulfed the boat they had been travelling in.

## Aen-eas, -eus
*Graeco-Romano-British*

In classical Graeco-Roman mythology, Aeneas was the son of Anchises by the goddess Aphrodite (Roman Venus). According to Virgil (70–19 BC), Aeneas, a member of the Trojan royal family, was reported to have survived the sack of Troy and to have made his way to Italy with a group of Trojan refugees. There, again according to Virgil, Aeneas became the legendary founder of the Roman people and a direct ancestor of the Emperor Augustus.

His great-grandson BRUTUS brought a group of Trojan descendants to ENGLAND. Landing at TOTNES in Devon, Brutus and his followers overcame a race of giants before travelling north and east to found their capital city of TROIA NOVA (New Troy), which is today known as LONDON. Through this relationship Aeneas is regarded not only as the legendary founder of the Roman people but also of the British people and the supposed ancestor of King LEIR. GEOFFREY OF MONMOUTH categorically states that Aeneas was the ancestor of the ancient British kings, while John Dryden (1631–1700) specifically names Aeneas as a direct ancestor of King ARTHUR. Both associations may have some historical background, but it has never been conclusively proved that Brutus ever came to England, and thus the connection to Aeneas seems suspect.

## Aengaba
*Irish*

One of the TUATHA DÉ DANANN who fought against the FIR BHOLG at the first Battle of MAGH TUIREDH. Curiously, Aengaba is usually referred to as 'Aengaba of Norway', but no explanation for this association can be found in the ancient texts. It may well be that Aengaba is actually a foreign interloper into the Irish myths, and has no real role to play.

## Aenghus
*Irish*

1 A variant of OENGHUS, and one from which the anglicized version of Oenghus, Angus, may be seen to be derived.
2 The name of an ULSTER warrior who challenged CET in the *Scéla Mucce Maic Dá Thó*.

## Aeracura
*Gaulish*

The name given to an ancient earth goddess whose image is known only from an altar stone found at Oberseebach in Switzerland. It appears that she was later displaced in her role by 'DIS PATER', although this is by no means certain and the goddess known as Aeracura may have been a tutelary goddess.

## Aes síd(l)h
*Irish*

The collective name for the TUATHA DÉ DANANN. It means 'hill folk'.

## Aesus
*Romano-Gaulish*

One of a triad of deities recorded by Lucan (AD 39–65), the other two members being TARANIS and TEUTATES. Aesus appears to be a latinized form of ESUS, the normal spelling of the deity usually included in this triad.

## Afagddu
*Welsh*
Also AVAGDDU

A son of TEGID VOEL and his goddess wife CERRIDWEN, brother of MORFRAN AB TEGID and CREARWY. He is described as the most ill-favoured man in the world, dark and ugly, in direct contrast to his light and beautiful sister Crearwy, the fairest maiden to have ever lived. Some sources say that Afagddu was a nickname applied to Morfran ab Tegid rather than a personal name. Cerridwen attempted to brew him a divine potion of inspiration, but the three essential drops fell on GWION BACH. Cerridwen chased and caught GWION BACH, who was later reborn as TALIESIN, but whether she brewed Afagddu a fresh potion is not recorded.

## Afanc
*Welsh*
See ADDANC.

## Afollonau
*Welsh*

A Welsh MYRDDIN poem that names the little known CHWIMLEIAN as a flower-maiden. This characterization has led to the later association of Chwimleian with both BLODEUWEDD and GUENDOLOENA.

## Aganippus
*British*

A King of the FRANKS. According to GEOFFREY OF MONMOUTH he was the husband of CORDELIA, the youngest daughter of the then King of BRITAIN[1], the semi-mythical King LEIR, who came to live with them in France after REGAN and GONERIL, Leir's two eldest daughters, along with Regan's husbands HENWINUS and MAGLAURUS, had seized Leir's kingdom. Aganippus raised an army, routed Leir's two sons-in-law and reinstated Leir as king for the last three years of his life.

## Agnoman

*Irish*

1 A son of SERA, the brother of STARN and PARTHOLÁN and the father of NEMHEDH.

2 The father of CRUNDCHU.

## Agricola

*Welsh*

Called a good king by GILDAS, Agricola was the ruler (*c.* AD 500) of DEMETIA, the ancient name for the Welsh kingdom of DYFED. Some sources claim that he liberated Demetia from the UÍ LIATHÁIN, the Irish dynasty that had ruled the kingdom before his reign. Later sources connect him with King ARTHUR, saying that he may well have been one of Arthur's commanders or that he and Arthur were in frequent contact.

## Ahes

*Gaulish*

A MARI-MORGAN, a class of supernatural beings peculiar to BRITTANY. Ahes was held responsible for the destruction of the legendary city of YS, though later tradition connects her with Morgan Le Fay, the connection simply stemming from the classification of being, the Mari-Morgans, of which Ahes was but one. See also DAHUT.

## Ai

*Irish*

A FILI of the TUATHA DÉ DANANN.

## Aide

*Irish*

The wife of AED[3]. She and her children were drowned by DUB, who caused the seas to swell and engulf her boat.

## Aided Chlainne Lir

*Irish*

*The Children of Lir*, an ancient text that tells the story of the children of LIR. Lir was disgusted at the choice of BODB DEARG as King of the TUATHA DÉ DANANN, and he would have been punished had Bodb not intervened and given Lir his own daughter, AOBH, as his wife. Aobh bore Lir four children, two boys and two girls, although some sources vary the numbers of both sexes, before she died. Bodb compensated Lir by giving him his other daughter AOIFE, but she was jealous of her step-children and transformed them into swans, a shape they kept for 900 years, even though they retained the powers of speech and reason and were blessed with the most exquisite song. Bodb punished Aoife by changing her into a demoness. The children of Lir resumed their human form during the time of St PATRICK, accepted the Christian faith and died.

## Aided Chlainne Tuirenn

*Irish*

*The Children of Tuirenn*, a text that gives one version of the story of the arrival of LUGH at TARA, although this is not the usual story of that god's appearance at the court of the TUATHA DÉ DANANN. This version says that Lugh arrived riding AONBARR, the horse of MANANNÁN MAC LIR, his countenance being so bright that none could look upon him. He killed many of the FOMHOIRÉ when they came to claim their tribute, an act that led BALAR's wife, CÉTHLIONN, to acknowledge that it had been prophesied that, after the arrival of Lugh, the power of the Fomhoiré would be no more. BRES[1] saw Lugh riding towards the Fomhoiré as the 'sun rising in the west'. He begged for his life in return for delivering the Fomhoiré into the hands of the Tuatha Dé Danann.

This account is contrary to the normally accepted story of the arrival of Lugh at Tara and the subsequent Second Battle of MAGH TUIREDH which this story simply seems to replace with the meeting between Lugh and Bres.

## Aideen
*Irish*

The wife of OSCAR, she died of grief after the death of her husband at the Battle of GABHRA and was buried on BEN EDAR by OISÎN, Oscar's father, who built the great dolmen that still stands over her grave.

## Aíf-e, -a
*Irish*

The rival of SCÁTHACH, Aífe is described as the fiercest and strongest woman-warrior in the world. She was fought and conquered by CÚ CHULAINN, although at one stage in the fight she shattered his sword and appeared to have the upper hand. Cú Chulainn then took Aífe as his concubine, and after he had returned to IRELAND she bore him a son, CONALL or Conlaí.

## Aige
*Irish*

An unfortunate maiden, who was transformed into a fawn by the SIABHRA and forced to wander around IRELAND. Later she was killed, and all that remained of her was a bag of water, which was thrown into a river that carried her name from that time onwards.

## Ail-ill, -ell
*Irish*

The consort of MEDHBHA, Queen of CONNACHT, and the father of ÉDÁIN ECHRAIDHE, the most beautiful woman in all IRELAND. Ailill and Medhbha were the great legendary enemies of CONCHOBAR MAC NESSA, against whom they bid for ownership of MAC DÁ THÓ's dog and boar and against whom they fought in Medbhba's attempt to obtain the DONN CUAILNGÈ.

## Ailill
*Irish*

The father of MAÍL DÚIN. Having been killed and buried under the rubble of a destroyed church, Maíl Dúin set off on a long voyage to avenge the death of his father, a voyage that is recounted in the *Immram Curaig Maíle Dúin*.

## Ailill Aine
*Irish*

A King of LEINSTER. The son of LOEGHAIRE LORC, King of IRELAND, Ailill Aine was killed by his uncle COBTHACH COEL, the brother of Loeghaire Lorc, when Cobthach Coel usurped his throne. Ailill Aine's son, LABHRAIDH LOINGSECH, was driven into exile but used this time to gather together an army with which he later returned, killed Cobthach Coel and his supporters, and so regained the kingdom of Leinster.

## Ailill Anglonnach
*Irish*

The brother of EOCHAID AIREMH, he fell in love with ÉDÁIN ECHRAIDHE, his brother's wife. They arranged a tryst on three occasions, but on each occasion Ailill Anglonnach was given a sleeping draught by MIDHIR, who was seeking to reclaim Édáin for himself. Édáin refused to leave her husband for Midhir, and, when she recounted what had happened to Ailill Anglonnach, he was cured of his illicit love.

## Ailill Olum
*Irish*

A King of MUNSTER who ravished AINÉ[2] and was subsequently killed by her magic.

## Aillén mac Midhna
*Irish*

A terrible being of whom there is no complete description. He came to TARA every year at SAMHAIN and, having first bewitched all the warriors with enchanting music, burned down the court. When the eight-year-old FIONN MAC CUMHAILL came to Tara, he pressed the point of his spear into his forehead and thus remained immune when Aillén mac Midhna started his enchantment. Then, when Aillén mac Midhna advanced, breathing fire, Fionn mac Cumhaill calmly stepped out and beheaded him.

## Ainé
*Irish*

1 A variant of Ana, which is itself a variant of DANU.
2 A daughter of EOGABAL, Ainé dwelt on CNOC AINÉ in MUNSTER. Originally a fertility deity, she was ravished by AILILL OLUM, whom she killed by use of magic. Ainé persisted well into the Christian era when she was said to have been captured by Lord Desmond, whom she married, and subsequently bore a son. Soon afterwards she and her son disappeared, but they made many visits, until Lord Desmond died and the son, Gerald, became the fourth Earl of Desmond. He disappeared, so it is said, in 1398, but legend says that he may still be seen once every seven years riding around the banks of Loch Gur beneath whose waters he lives.

Although the Lord Desmond legend is fairly recent, Ainé is obviously a very early figure, for her father, Eogabal, is a member of the TUATHA DÉ DANANN. He was killed by FERCHESS while he was leading his cattle to pasture outside his SÍDH. Ainé, who accompanied him, was outraged or raped by OILILL, whom she struck so hard that there was no flesh left on his right ear, which earned him the mocking epithet 'Bare Ear'.

Ainé swore vengeance against Ferchess and Oilill. Some years later EOGAN, the son of Oilill, and LUGAID MAC CON heard sweet music drifting from a yew tree. When they went to investigate, they found inside the tree a small harper, whom they took to Oilill. However, as both Eogan and Lugaid mac Con claimed the harper as theirs, Oilill was forced to choose who should be the rightful owner. He naturally chose his son, a choice that led to the Battle of MACH MUCRIME in which all seven of Oilill's sons were killed.

3 A daughter of CULANN and sister to MILUCHRADH. Both she and her sister fell in love with FIONN MAC CUMHAILL, but Ainé let it slip that she would never marry a man with grey hair. On hearing this, Miluchradh caused a lake to appear, the waters of which would turn anyone who bathed in them grey in an instant. Miluchradh then turned herself into a hind and allowed herself to be hunted by Fionn mac Cumhaill, drawing him towards the lake into which she leapt. Fionn mac Cumhaill followed her into the water, whereupon Miluchradh disappeared. When Fionn mac Cumhaill emerged from the lake as a grey-haired man, Ainé lost her love for him, but Miluchradh was shunned by him.

## Ainge
*Irish*

A daughter of the DAGHDHA, who features in a short parable about the magical creation of woodland. She had gathered together a bundle of twigs to build herself a tub to bathe in. These twigs were stolen by GAIBLE, son of NUADHA, who threw them to the wind. When they landed, they immediately became trees.

## Ainnle
*Irish*

A son of UISNECH and one of the two brothers of NAOISE, the other being ARDÁN, both of whom fled with Naoise and DEIRDRU to ALBA (or SCOTLAND). They were killed on their return from exile by CONCHOBAR MAC NESSA, even though they had been promised safety.

## Airem
*Irish*

One of the three leaders of the Sons of MÍL ÉSPÁINE who killed the three kings of the TUATHA DÉ DANANN. Airem killed MAC CÉCHT, while EBER killed MAC CUILL and AMHAIRGHIN killed MAC GRÉINE.

## Airmed
*Irish*

A daughter of DIAN CÉCHT and sister of MIDACH. After the death of Midach, Airmed sorted the medicinal herbs collected by her brother, but Dian Cécht muddled them up again because he feared that their potency would diminish his position as a divine healer.

## Aislinge Oenguso
*Irish*

*The Dream of Oenghus*, one of the earliest sections of the BOOK OF LEINSTER, which was written prior to 1160.

## Alaisiagae
*British*

A generic name given to four war goddesses, who were originally worshipped in the Teutonic heartland but whose worship was brought to BRITAIN[1] by the Romans. Named as BEDE[1], FINNILENE, BAUDIHILLIE and FRIAGABI, they had similar characteristics to the Norse-Teutonic Valkyrie. Their worship in Britain appears to have been localized in the area immediately south of Hadrian's Wall, and they were possibly invoked as protection against the marauding PICTS. Their names have been found, along with that of the Roman god Mars, on a stone at Housesteads on Hadrian's Wall.

## Alaron
*British*

The consort of BLADUD, whom she helped to build the therapeutic baths at KAERBADUS or BATH.

## Alaw
*Welsh*

A river on the island of ANGLESEY, on whose banks BRANWEN, the sister of BENDIGEID VRAN, was alleged to have died of a broken heart. Close to the river lies BEDD BRANWEN, the traditional site of her burial.

## Alba
*Irish*

An archaic term, of Irish origin, that

was used to refer to SCOTLAND. It is still sometimes used poetically today. In the post-ANGLO-SAXON period the name developed into the better known and more widely used form of ALBANY.

## Albanact(us)
*British*

Named by GEOFFREY OF MONMOUTH as a son of BRUTUS, and thus a great-great-grandson of the Trojan AENEAS. He had two brothers, LOCRINUS and KAMBER. After Brutus had died, the three sons shared the country between them, Locrinus becoming king of ENGLAND, Kamber king of WALES, and Albanact the king of SCOTLAND. Geoffrey of Monmouth says that this is how each of those countries derived their early names: LOCRIS for England, CAMBRIA for Wales and ALBANY for Scotland. This is false etymology, for Locris comes from the Welsh LLOEGR, Cambria comes from CYMRY, which means 'fellow countrymen', and Albany from ALBA or ALBION. According to Geoffrey of Monmouth, Albanact was killed by invading Huns, but this is once more pure fiction, for the Huns never invaded BRITAIN[1].

## Alban(y)
*British*

The post-ANGLO-SAXON British term for SCOTLAND, which derived from the older ALBA, itself of Irish origin, although it might equally have derived from ALBION.

## Albine
*British*

According to the fifteenth-century *Chronicles of Great Britain* by John de Wavrin, Lady Albine and her three, some say fifty, sisters came to the island that was to be named ALBION in her honour, having been banished from their own country for killing their husbands. This story has a parallel in the classical Greek myth of the fifty Danaides, the daughters of Danaus, who killed their husbands, the fifty sons of Aegyptus, on their wedding night. John de Wavrin places the time of their arrival as coinciding with the rule of Jahir, third judge of Israel after Joshua. A demon who took the form of a man came to live with the four women, and their offspring were giants, who continued to multiply until the arrival of BRUTUS. It is possible that one of these giants was none other than Albion himself.

## Albion
*British*

A legendary giant who was reputed by GEOFFREY OF MONMOUTH to have been the eponymous first ruler of BRITAIN[1], the island itself being referred to as Albion before the arrival of BRUTUS. Some accounts say that he was the son of an unnamed sea god, while others say that he might have been one of the giant offspring of ALBINE and her sisters. Later Romano-Celtic tradition states that Albion travelled south to help his brothers fight Hercules during that hero's tenth labour and was killed as a result. Albion's career was outlined in Holinshed's *Chronicles* (1577), and his name is still used to refer poetically to Britain or, more correctly, ENGLAND, in much the same way as ALBA or ALBANY is still sometimes used to refer to SCOTLAND.

## Alchad
*Irish*

A king of TÍR TAIRNGIRI and father of ABARTACH.

## Aldan
*Welsh*

An historical daughter of a South WALES nobleman who was, according to tradition, the mother of MYRDDIN.

## Aldroenus
*Gaulish*

A King of BRITTANY, also known as Audrien, and brother of CONSTANTINE[1]. He sent his brother to rule the Britons, at their own request, after he had himself turned down the offer of becoming the King of BRITAIN[1].

## Alisanos
*Gaulish*

A generic name for deities of rocks and rock formations.

## Alloit
*Irish*

A mysterious deity, who is sometimes named as the father of MANANNÁN MAC LIR, although presumably without his usual epithet. This association would seem to suggest that Alloit was a sea deity who was later replaced by LIR.

## Alspradoc
*British*

The legendary enemy of the equally legendary COEL. Unlike Coel, however, nothing further is known of Alspradoc.

## Amaethon
*Welsh*

A son of DÔN and brother to the likes of GWYDION FAB DÔN, GILFAETHWY, GOFANNON and ARIANRHOD. Amaethon seems to have been an agricultural deity, for his name appears to be derived from the Welsh *amaeth*, 'ploughman'. Amaethon brought OTHERWORLDLY animals to earth from ANNWFN, which led to the mythical Battle of CATH GODEU at which he defeated ARAWN with the help of his brother Gwydion fab Dôn.

## Amaite Aidgill
*Irish*

'Hags of Doom'. During the First Battle of MAGH TUIREDH the voices of the Amaite Aidgill, along with those of the BADBA and BLEDLOCHTANA, were raised on command of the DAGHDHA against the FIR BHOLG.

## Ama(i)rg-en, -in
*Irish*
See AMHAIRGHIN.

## Ambrosius Aureli(an)us
*British*

A character of undoubted historicity, who was also known as AURELIUS AMBROSIUS and who lived in the fifth century. His career was chronicled by GEOFFREY OF MONMOUTH. The brother of UTHER and CONSTANS, Ambrosius Aurelius was smuggled to BRITTANY following the murder of his brother Constans by the usurping VORTIGERN. Later he returned from his exile, together with Uther, intent on taking back the throne that was rightfully his. Aurelius Ambrosius landed at TOTNES, Devon, where he was proclaimed king. He laid seige to Vortigern and succeeded in burning down the usurper's tower while Vortigern was still inside. He then went on to defeat the SAXONS. PASCHENT, Vortigern's son, later had Ambrosius Aurelius poisoned by a Saxon woman named Eopa. He was supposedly buried within the boundaries of STONEHENGE.

These meagre facts are all that can be said about the historical life of Ambrosius Aurelius. The remaining 'facts' are pure fabrication. To celebrate his victory over the Saxons he was said to have commissioned MYRDDIN to build a great monument on Salisbury Plain. This monument was none other than Stonehenge. Legend calls it the Giants' Ring and says that Myrddin brought it from IRELAND, when in fact the stone ring had already been in position for 3,000 years or more.

GILDAS uses what was possibly the most correct form of his name, Ambrosius Aurelianus, and supports the claim of Geoffrey of Monmouth that it was he who instigated the fighting that finally put an end to the advance of the Saxons. Gildas goes on to call him the 'last of the Romans', obviously a reference to his ability to halt the Saxons where others had failed. NENNIUS[1], however, says that Ambrosius Aurelius was the son of a Roman consul, but then contradicts himself by saying that he was the fatherless son Vortigern intended to sacrifice when his tower kept on falling down. Geoffrey of Monmouth connects the name of Ambrosius Aurelius with the legendary King ARTHUR by saying that he was Arthur's nephew. Other sources even suggest that he was the origin of Arthur. The fifteenth-century poet Rhys Goch Eryri says that following his death at the hands of Eopa his head was buried beneath DINAS EMRYS, but this is simply poetic licence.

**Amergin**
*Irish*
See AMHAIRGHIN.

**Amhairghin**
*Irish*

Also Amairgen and Amairgin. A son of MÍL, a FILI who was one of the leaders of the Sons of MÍL ÉSPÁINE, or GAELS, who came from Spain to IRELAND, landing on 1 May, the feast of BELTANE. *En route*, his wife SKENA fell overboard and was drowned. Defeating an army of the TUATHA DÉ DANANN, the invaders set out for the capital TARA and met the three goddesses BANBHA, FÓDLA and ÉRIU, the wives respectively of the Tuatha Dé Danann's three kings, MAC CUILL, MAC CÉCHT and MAC GRÉINE. The invaders promised each goddess in turn that the land should bear her name if she would favour them. Finally Ériu told Amhairghin that the Sons of Míl Éspáine would conquer all of Ireland and rule there forever. However, she warned DÔNN, their discourteous king, that neither he nor his heirs would enjoy the land. Soon afterwards Dônn was drowned and buried on the island of TECH DUINN, to which he still welcomes the spirits of dead warriors.

When they reached Tara, the three kings of the Tuatha Dé Danann disputed the right of the Sons of Míl Éspáine to Ireland. As a compromise, they asked Amhairghin to judge their claims, and he ruled that the invading Sons of Míl Éspáine should put out to sea again to beyond a magical boundary referred to as the ninth wave. They did so, but when they turned and attempted to return to the land, the Tuatha Dé Danann sent an enchanted wind against them. Amhairghin called upon the SPIRIT OF IRELAND to help them and the wind dropped, allowing the Sons of Míl Éspáine to land. They then defeated the Tuatha Dé Danann at the Battle of TAILTIU, all three kings being killed in the battle, Mac Cuill by EBER, Mac Cécht by AIREM, and Mac Gréine by Amhairghin himself.

The Tuatha Dé Danann were still determined not to be exiled, however, and they used their magical powers to deprive the conquerors of both milk and grain. Eventually the Sons of Míl Éspáine agreed to divide the land with them, the Tuatha Dé Danann receiving the underground half. Their leader, the DAGHDHA, gave each of their chiefs a síDH for his dwelling place. There the Tuatha Dé Danann still live.

## Amlawdd Wledig
*Welsh*

The husband of GWENN[2] and the father of EIGYR. Amlawdd Wledig is also credited with being the father of GOLEUDDYDD, the mother of CULHWCH. 'Wledig' is a title rather than a name. Roughly translated it means 'chief' and would seem to indicate Amlawdd's position within the community.

## Amorgin
*Irish*

The father of CONALL CERNACH.

## Amren
*Welsh*

The son of BEDWYR[2]. His name later passed into the Arthurian cycle as the son of Bedivere.

## An Ghlas Ghaibhleann
*Irish*

The wondrous milk-bearing cow of GOIBHNIU, which was stolen by BALAR but magically disappeared and returned to its master.

## Ana
*Irish*
See DANU.

## Andarta
*Gaulish*

A bear goddess who, along with her counterpart ARTIO, had a classical parallel in the Greek goddess Artemis. Like the Greek goddess, she could assume the form of a bear, her totem animal, at will.

## Andate
*British*

A deity of unknown characteristics and attributes. It has been suggested that Andate may simply be an alternative spelling for ANDRASTE or a British adoption of the Gaulish bear goddess ANDARTA.

## A(n)draste
*British*

A fierce goddess of victory to whom her opponents were sacrificed in a sacred grove. Described in Dio Cassius' *Annals* XIV, Andraste was said to be both mysterious and terrible. At one stage she was reputed to have been invoked by Queen BOUDICCA when she revolted against Roman tyranny during the first century AD. She is of the same type as the Irish goddess the MÓRRÍGHAN, and it is possible that she may also have been known as ANDATE. This leads to a further assumption that she may have originated in the Gaulish bear goddess ANDARTA, since Andate has also been mooted as a British variant of that goddess.

## Andrivete
*Welsh*

The daughter of King CADOR[2] of NORTHUMBRIA. After her father's death, AYGLIN, Andrivete's uncle, usurped the throne and tried to marry her off to an unnamed man of his choosing. She escaped and married CEI, who advanced on Northumbria prepared to fight for his wife's inheritance. The people, however, forced Ayglin to step down, and Andrivete regained her kingdom. This local Northumbrian story later passed into the Arthurian cycle, in which Andrivete's husband was better known as Sir Kay.

## Androgeus
*British*

The son of LUD and brother of TENUANTIUS. When Lud died, neither of his sons was old enough to become king, so CASSIVELLAUNUS, Lud's brother, assumed the crown, making Androgeus Duke of KENT and Tenuantius Duke of CORNWALL in an attempt to forestall potential trouble. During JULIUS CAESAR's first foray into BRITAIN[1], Cassivellaunus, Androgeus and Tenuantius fought together and forced the Romans to withdraw, NENNIUS[2], Cassivellaunus' brother, managing to take the sword from Julius Caesar himself but dying shortly afterwards from the wounds he received.

Two years later Julius Caesar tried again to invade Britain and was again repulsed. During the victory celebrations, however, an argument arose over a fatal blow that had been foully struck in a boxing match by a nephew of Androgeus. So severe was the disagreement that civil war broke out. Androgeus betrayed his uncle and brother to Caesar, whom he arranged to help when he landed for the third time. Led by Androgeus, the Romans besieged Cassivellaunus at CANTERBURY. Androgeus now changed colours again and mediated a peace between the two sides before leaving with Caesar to live, and later die, in Rome.

## Angharhad (Golden-hand)
*Welsh*

A maiden who appears in the MABINOGION as the lover of PEREDUR[1]. At first she refused Peredur's advances, which forced him to state that he would not speak to any Christian until she changed her mind. Eventually, she did. It has been suggested that her epithet 'Golden-hand' indicates her generous nature.

## Angles
*General*

A Germanic tribe, originating in the Schleswig-Holstein region of northern Europe, which along with their neighbours, the SAXONS, invaded BRITAIN[1] during the fifth century AD and settled in East Anglia (hence its name), MERCIA and NORTHUMBRIA.

## Anglesey
*General*

A large island off the northwest coast of WALES, separated from the mainland by the Menai Straits. The island has a long Celtic history, and it is reputed to be the last resting place of BRANWEN, who died there after she had been brought back from IRELAND, her alleged grave being BEDD BRANWEN, close to the banks of the River ALAW.

## Anglo-Saxon
*General*

The collective name for the ANGLES and SAXONS who, together with the JUTES, conquered much of BRITAIN[1] between the fifth and seventh centuries. The Angles settled in East Anglia, MERCIA and NORTHUMBRIA; the Saxons in ESSEX, SUSSEX and WESSEX; and the Jutes in KENT and southern Hampshire, most notably on the Isle of Wight. The Angles and Saxons came from the Schleswig-Holstein region and may have united before the invasion; the Jutes are usually said to have originated in JUTLAND. There was probably considerable intermarriage with the romanized Celts, although the latter's language and culture almost totally disappeared.

Following the invasion and conquest, a number of independent kingdoms were established, commonly referred to as the Heptarchy ('seven kingdoms'). These survived until the early ninth century, when they were amalgamated and united under the overlordship of WESSEX.

### Anglo-Saxon Chronicle, The
*British*

A history of England from the time of the Roman invasion to the eleventh century. It was started in the ninth century, during the reign of King Alfred, and written as a series of chronicles in Old English by monks, and the work was still being executed in the twelfth century.

The *Chronicle*, which consists of seven different manuscripts, forms a unique record of early English history and of the development of Old English prose up to its final stages in the year 1154, by which time it had been superseded by Middle English.

### Anguis-h, -el
*Irish*

A King of IRELAND, whose name is a form of OENGHUS. An historical King Oenghus is believed to have reigned in southern Ireland during the fifth century, and his name may therefore be an error in the translation from Gaelic into Old English. His variant name, Anguisel, has led to his being sometimes confused by GEOFFREY OF MONMOUTH with King AUGUSELUS of SCOTLAND.

### Ankeu
*Gaulish*

An obscure god of death in BRITTANY. He is described as the 'master of the world', and is sometimes known as the harbinger of death. Ankeu usually appears as a skeleton in a white shroud, driving a cart with squeaky wheels.

### Anluan
*Irish*

The son of MAGA and brother of CET, Anluan is sometimes known as Hanlon. With his brother he appears in the *Scéla Mucce Maic Dá Thó*, when they are invited by MEDHBHA and AILILL to participate in the hunt for the DONN CUAILNGÈ (brown bull), the story of MAC DÁ THÓ and his boar forming one of the preambulatory stories to this much longer work. At the feast where the honour of carving the boar had been taken by Cet, none dared to challenge him for that honour. When Conall Cernach arrived, however, Cet yielded the honour to him but taunted him by saying that his brother, Anluan, would challenge him. Conall Cernach thereupon threw the bloody head of Anluan onto the table.

### Annw(f)n
*Welsh*

The name given to the Welsh OTHERWORLD, which was ruled over by ARAWN. PWYLL, Lord of DYFED, agreed to spend a year in Annwfn after he had insulted Arawn by driving his hounds from a stag. During his time in Annwfn, Pwyll disposed of HAFGAN, Arawn's sworn enemy. For the year that Pwyll was to spend in the Otherworld, he and Arawn assumed each other's appearance and each ruled the other's domain. Arawn later sent PRYDERI. Pwyll's son, a herd of swine, animals that had never before been heard of, let alone seen, on earth.

Although it is usually considered to be the Welsh UNDERWORLD, the domain of the dead and a dark, shadowy realm, it is described in the MABINOGION as a recognizable kingdom that appears to have had several regions along the same lines as Hades, the Underworld of classical Greek mythology. The early Welsh poem *Preiddeu Annwfn* perhaps gives the best description of the realm, although this poem embroiders the traditional view by weaving its story around King ARTHUR. The narrator of the poem is TALIESIN, a member of the party whose expedition to Annwfn to capture a magic cauldron is the theme of the poem.

Sailing overseas to reach its goal, the party first comes to CAER WYDYR, a glass fort, but cannot induce the watchman to talk, thus suggesting a land of the silent dead, a land that is also referred to in the *Historia Britonum* of NENNIUS[1]. The party next comes to CAER FEDDWIDD (the fort of CAROUSAL), which is also known as CAER RIGOR or CAER SIDDI, in which case it is said to be ruled over by ARIANRHOD. Here a fountain runs with wine and no one ever suffers from illness or reaches old age; it is an idyllic realm to which most men would hope to pass after their life on earth had come to an end.

*Preiddeu Annwfn*, which would appear to have later developed into the Quest for the Holy GRAIL, clearly owes its existence to the earlier story of the expedition of BENDIGEID VRAN to IRELAND. Both expeditions numbered Taliesin among the party of explorers and in both only seven survived, Taliesin again numbering among both sets of survivors.

**Answerer, The**
*Irish*

A translation of Fragarach, the name given to the divine sword of LUGH.

**Anu**
*Irish*

The earth mother, who is better known as DANU. Some sources seek to say that the goddess's true name was Anu, and that Danu was the corruption of this name, rather than vice versa. This may, indeed, be the case, for the myths tell us that Danu was the daughter of DELBAETH, the brother of the DAGHDHA. Anu may, therefore, represent the true form of the Irish MOTHER GODDESS.

**Anu, Paps of**
*Irish*

A pair of hills in Kerry, southern IRELAND, which resemble a woman's breasts. They derive their name from ANU and are said to be one of the homes of the TUATHA DÉ DANANN. See also DA CHICH NANANN.

**Aobh**
*Irish*

A daughter of BODB. She became the wife of LIR in an attempt to resolve Lir's differences with the TUATHA DÉ DANANN after he had been overlooked for the kingship. She bore Lir four children, two sons and two daughters, before she died. Her sister AOIFE became Lir's next wife, but she grew jealous of her step-children and changed them into swans.

**Aodh**
*Irish*

1 According to quite a late tradition, Aodh is mentioned in the genealogy of

St BRIDE. He is said to be the son of ART and the father of DUGAL the Brown, who was better known as the DAGHDHA.

2 The son of MORNA. He lost an eye in a battle during which he killed CUMHAILL and was thenceforth known as GOLL ('One-eyed'), the name by which he is usually known.

3 A member of the TUATHA DÉ DANANN whose unnamed wife fell in love with DONN and turned him into a stag when he did not respond.

## Aoife
*Irish*

A daughter of BODB and second wife of LIR. She grew jealous of Lir's four children by his first wife, her sister AOBH, and, during a trip to visit Bodb, she turned them into four swans. They were fated to remain in that form for 900 years, after which they would revert to their human form. Bodb turned Aoife into a raven, or 'demon of the air', for her evil. Later tradition said that she had been turned into a crane, which was killed by MANANNÁN MAC LIR who used the skin to make a bag in which he kept all his treasures.

## Aonbarr
*Irish*
Also ENBARR

The horse of MANANNÁN MAC LIR, which was said to be able to travel, like the wind, over both land and sea, while no rider on his back could be killed. Some accounts say that LUGH rode Aonbarr when he came to TARA. See also *Aided Chlainne Tuirenn*.

## Apollo Cunomaglus
*Romano-British*

Although this deity, whose name is found only at Nettleton, is a derivation of the classical Graeco-Roman god Apollo, his epithet, or surname, is Celtic, meaning 'Horned Lord'. It would appear to be an attempt by the Romans to combine the attributes of their deity with those of CERNUNNOS.

## Apples, Isle of
*British*

The name used by GEOFFREY OF MONMOUTH to refer to the paradisal land of the dead, better known as AVALON. The use of this name possibly derives from the Irish EMHAIN ABHLACH, an island that is associated with the Irish god of the sea MANANNÁN MAC LIR and whose name means 'Emhain of the Apple Trees'. Irish tradition makes this island the Isle of ARRAN.

## Aquae Sulis
*Romano-British*

The Roman name for the city of BATH, whose temples were dedicated to the Romano-Celtic goddess SULIS MINERVA, an amalgam of the Roman goddess Minerva and the local British deity SULIS.

## Aranrhod
*Welsh*

A variant of ARIANRHOD.

## Arav-ia, -ius
*Welsh*

The mountain, better known today as SNOWDON, which was the home of the giant RIENCE or RHITTA.

## Arawn
*Welsh*

The king of ANNWFN, the Welsh OTHER-

WORLD, and thus, by the association of his realm with the land of the dead, god of the dead. PWYLL and Arawn agreed to change places for a year after Pwyll had driven Arawn's hounds from a stag, the exchange being Pwyll's apology for the insult. During his year in Annwfn, Pwyll killed HAFGAN, Arawn's sworn enemy, and behaved honourably towards Arawn's wife for, although he resembled Arawn, Pwyll refused to lie with Arawn's wife even though they shared a bed and she assumed him to be her husband. When Pwyll returned home at the end of the year he found that Arawn had ruled his realm of DYFED with unprecedented wisdom. Contact between Pwyll and Arawn continued for many years. After Pwyll's death Arawn sent a gift of a herd of swine to PRYDERI, the son of Pwyll, animals that had never been seen on earth before. Arawn was alleged to have been defeated by AMAETHON at the mythical battle of CATH GODEU, although whether he was actually killed – if, indeed, it is possible to kill the lord of Annwfn – is not made clear.

In a Welsh version of GEOFFREY OF MONMOUTH, the name Arawn is used to translate AUGUSELUS, the brother of URIEN, while the *Trioedd Ynys Prydein* also mention an Arawn, this time making him the son of KYNFARCH. In both instances it is the lord of the dead, the ruler of Annwfn, who is the undoubted original.

## Ard-Mhac-Léinn
*Irish*

The name used by CÚ CHULAINN, in the cycle of tales that surround that hero, to refer to the OTHERWORLD, the world to which he will travel after death.

## Ard-Rieship
*Irish*

'High Kingship', the position that a King of all IRELAND would assume, his title being ARDRÍ or 'High King'.

## Ard Righ
*Irish*

A variant of Ardrí.

## Ardán
*Irish*

A son of UISNECH and one of the two brothers of NAOISE, the other brother being AINNLE, who fled with him and DERDRIU to ALBA. He and his brothers, all of whom had once held positions of importance and favour at the court of CONCHOBAR MAC NESSA, were killed by that king after they had returned from exile, although they had been promised safety by the three emissaries sent by the king to ask them to come back.

## Ardrí
*Irish*

'High King', the title assumed upon attaining the ARD-RIESHIP, although the title is sometimes recorded as ARD RIGH.

## Arduinna
*Gaulish*

A goddess, possibly of the hunt, or a protectress of wild animals, who is depicted seated on a wild boar.

## Ar(f)derydd
*Welsh*
Also ARTHURET

A battle, fought c.575 for a 'lark's nest' (*sic*), between the British prince

GWENDDOLEU and his cousins GWRGI and PEREDUR. Gwenddoleu was killed during the battle by RHYDDERCH HAEL, and MYRDDIN, having fought in the battle and having won a golden torc (an armband or necklace of twisted metal), lost his reason and became a hermit in SCOTLAND. The fact that the battle was for a 'lark's nest' appears to indicate that the fight was actually for ownership of the important harbour of Caerlaverlock, which translates as Fort Lark.

## Ar(i)anrhod
*Welsh*
Also ARANRHOD

One of the main characters in the *Mabinogion* story of *Math fab Mathonwy* ('Math, Son of Mathonwy'). Arianrhod clearly belongs to a pre-Christian tradition. She is not simply a local or national deity who has been preserved in myth and legend, but is also a stellar figure, a goddess of time, space and energy, associated with the observation of a particular group of stars. Her stellar role is supported by the fact that in Welsh the constellation of corona borealis is known as CAER ARIANRHOD, 'Arianrhod's Castle', although this name is also applied to the aurora borealis, the northern lights. Her name means 'queen of the wheel', 'silver wheel' or 'high fruitful mother', which has led to her being referred to as the goddess of the starry wheel.

The sister of GWYDION FAB DÔN, Arianrhod was put forward for the position of footholder (a royal position held by a virgin) by her brother to Math fab Mathonwy. However, as she performed the rite of stepping over the wand to attest her virginity, two bundles fell from her. The first was a golden-haired boy, who was christened DYLAN. He immediately set forth for the sea,

whose nature he assumed, thenceforth being known as DYLAN EIL TON.

The second bundle was also a baby boy. Gwydion fab Dôn quickly concealed him in a chest and later adopted him. Four years passed before Gwydion fab Dôn showed the boy to his mother, but, embarrassed by the reminder of her shame, Arianrhod cursed the boy, saying that he should have no name until she herself gave him one, something she had no intention of doing. Gwydion fab Dôn evaded this curse by disguising both himself and the boy and tricking his sister into naming her son LLEU LLAW GYFFES. Furious at the trick, for Gwydion fab Dôn could not resist taunting his sister with the fact that she had named her son, Arianrhod again cursed the boy saying this time that he would never bear arms until she herself bestowed them upon him. Again her brother found a way around the curse, this time by magically laying siege to her castle, Caer Arianrhod, on ANGLESEY. In her horror at being attacked, Arianrhod gave weapons to her son and begged him to protect her, although as he was in disguise there was no way she could know who he was. Once more Gwydion fab Dôn could not resist taunting his sister, so Arianrhod cursed the unfortunate Lleu Llaw Gyffes for a third time, this time saying that he should never marry a mortal woman. This final curse was again overcome by Gwydion fab Dôn, although this time he needed the help of the magician Math fab Mathonwy. Together they manufactured Lleu Llaw Gyffes a wife from the flowers of oak, broom and meadowsweet and named BLODEUWEDD ('Flower Face').

Even though the rationalization and extension of the mythology of Arianrhod is confused, it cannot disguise her true nature as a goddess. The theme of twin brothers borne magically by a virgin or, in the case of Arianrhod, by one who claimed to be a virgin, is repeated in various forms throughout Celtic mythology and folklore. It also resonates through world mythology and into Christianity. Arianrhod is the ruler of CAER SIDDI, a magical realm in the north, although later poetic works, such as the *Preiddeu Annwfn*, place this realm in the OTHERWORLD, ANNWFN, where it was visited by ARTHUR and TALIESIN, among others. The medieval MYRDDIN texts use the Greek goddess Ariadne to suggest a connection with Arianrhod. This is no mere coincidence, for their names, and even their attributes, are remarkably similar, for Ariadne is an earth goddess who also has stellar significance. It has also been suggested that Arianrhod's name gave rise to Argante, the elfin Queen of AVALON.

## Armes Prydein
*Welsh*

The *Prophecy of Britain*, an heroic Welsh poem, probably written between 900 and 930. Unique in being the first work to refer to the magician MYRDDIN, the *Armes Prydein* can be regarded as a work of propaganda, for it calls upon the British to unite against the SAXON invaders and foretells that CYNAN and the last British king, CADWALLADER, son of CADWALLON, will once more rise to lead a great army that will include the men of Dublin, the Irish Gaels, and the men of CORNWALL and Strathclyde, and drive the Saxons back into the sea from whence they came.

## Armorica
*Gaulish*

An ancient name for the region of GAUL that is today known as BRITTANY.

## Arran, Isle of
*Irish*

Situated in the Firth of Forth, this island is usually identified as the paradisal island of EMHAIN ABHLACH, an island associated with the Irish sea god MANANNÁN MAC LIR. Later, GEOFFREY OF MONMOUTH seems to have connected the earlier paradise of Emhain Abhlach with AVALON, which he calls the Isle of APPLES.

## Art (Aoinfhear)
*Irish*

The son of CONN CÉTCHATHLACH, a legendary king who was thought to have reigned in prehistoric times and might have his origin in a forgotten deity. A late genealogy of St BRIDE supports this relationship, saying that Art (here without the epithet) was the son of CONN[1] and the father of AODH[1], which in turn would make him the grandfather of the DAGHDHA, who is called DUGAL the Brown in the genealogy. A later Irish romance develops the character Art Aionfhear and makes him a son of ARTHUR, possibly simply substituting Arthur for Conn.

## Artai-os, -us
*Romano-British*

A deity of unknown characteristics and attributes who, some suggest, was the original of King ARTHUR, although this would appear to be based on etymology alone. In GAUL Artaios was equated with Mercury, which has led some to speculate that Artaios is simply a derivative of ARTIO.

## Arthgen
*Gaulish*
Also ARTOGENUS

A name known from the Roman period. It simply means 'son of the bear' or, perhaps, 'son of the bear God'.

## Arthur
*British*

A semi-legendary, mythologized King of BRITAIN[1], whose name is possibly a form of *Artorius*, a Roman *gens* name, although it might have Celtic origins, coming from *artos viros* meaning 'bear man', or from ARTAIOS, or even from Artos, an obscure deity who also has connections with a bear cult. He clearly dominates late Celtic mythology, although the legends that surround him undoubtedly come from the post-Christian era and draw on a multitude of different sources. The period immediately after the withdrawal of the Roman legions early in the fifth century is called the Dark Ages because so little is known about it. It is during this period that it is thought that a powerful leader, or chieftain, or even a series of such leaders or chieftains, commanded the Celtic troops of the West Country and held the invading SAXONS at bay. However, the time is so shrouded in mystery that the truth of the matter is that no one knows for certain.

The Arthur whose legends concern the Knights of the Round Table, Queen GUINEVERE and the Holy GRAIL is almost certainly a composite figure, combining the attributes and achievements of more than one person. One hypothesis says that he is to be identified with the Celtic king RIOTHAMUS, but the more contemporary view is that Arthur was a professional soldier, never a king, in the service of the British kings during the period between the departure of the Roman armies and the influx of the Saxon invaders.

True Celtic references to Arthur do not exist. Indeed, there are no contemporary references to him, either historical or legendary. Those sources that have a Celtic connection, namely through his supposed relationship as the cousin of CULHWCH, date from a period far removed from the final days of Celtic influence in Britain. The *Mabinogion* remains the nearest source of reference to a Celtic Arthur, but traditionally even the *Mabinogion* carries no Arthurian references.

Many people wrongly cite Arthur as a Celtic king. It seems more likely that he was nothing more than a powerful general, whose ability in battle won him the respect of his peers. Time and the imagination of later writers elevated him in rank to that of a king, but even then the exploits of those surrounding him surpass his own deeds.

Arthur will remain a fascinating area of study, but to consider him as a Celtic king, or even deity, would be wrong until some concrete evidence has been uncovered that inextricably links him with the Celtic period. He most likely originated in the dying days of the Celtic peoples in Britain, the stories surrounding him growing as the people were forced farther and farther away from their native lands. Eventually Arthur will rise again, or so the legends say, and restore the Celtic people to their dispossessed lands, a legend that raises Arthur far above the level of a mere king and places him among the elite race of gods. Perhaps that is the truth behind the stories of Arthur. In essence he seems a godlike figure. Therefore, as the Celtic people were driven from their lands, a long-forgotten god may have been brought out, dusted down and given a new name and persona, a persona that would allow the defeated

Celts to retain a pride in their own race and a hope that one day they would return.

Readers who wish to study the entire scope of the Arthurian legends should refer to *Arthurian Myth and Legend: An A–Z of People and Places* by Mike Dixon-Kennedy, Blandford, 1995.

## Arthur of Dál Riada
*Irish*

The son of AEDÁN MAC GABRÁIN, King of DÁL RIADA. It has often been argued that he is the historical figure about whom the legends of King ARTHUR have grown. This Arthur was said to have fallen in a battle against the forces of Aethelfrith, his death allegedly being foretold to his father by St COLUMBA.

## Arthuret
*Welsh*

The latinized form of the Welsh word ARFDERYDD.

## Artio
*Gaulish*

The goddess of the bear cult who was worshipped by the continental Celts in the area of the present-day Berne, Switzerland. A figurine of a goddess feeding a bear was found at Berne ('Bear-City'), the inscription on the box pedestal reading *Deai Artioni Licinia Sabinilla* ('Licinia Sabinilla [dedicated this] to the goddess Artio'). The box pedestal has a slit in it through which coins could be dropped in offering. She appears to bear a striking resemblance to the classical Greek goddess Artemis, with whom she shares the ability to change into a bear at will, and has a counterpart in ANDARTA.

## Artogenus
*Gaulish*
See ARTHGEN.

## Arviragus
*British*

An historical King of BRITAIN[1] who, according to GEOFFREY OF MONMOUTH, succeeded his brother GUIDERIUS, who had been killed during the Roman invasion led by CLAUDIUS in AD 43. Arviragus and Claudius formed a peaceful relationship when Arviragus married Claudius' daughter GENVISSA, the wedding taking place on the banks of the River Severn, where Arviragus and Claudius jointly founded the city of Gloucester. Arviragus later revolted against the Roman oppression, but peace was restored through the intervention of Genvissa.

Some sources name Arviragus as the king who gave JOSEPH OF ARIMATHEA the twelve hides of land at GLASTONBURY on which he allegedly founded the original abbey. Others tenuously link him with Arthurian legend, because some sources claim that Arviragus, CARATACUS and ARTHUR are all different names for the same person. A more likely supposition seems to be that Arviragus was a local Somerset prince who managed to maintain his independence after the invasion of Claudius, possibly through marriage but more likely by capitulation in return for keeping his kingdom.

## Asal
*Irish*

The original owner of the seven magical swine of LUGH. The swine could be killed and eaten one day, and yet be alive, ready and willing to be killed and eaten again the following day. Asal is simply described as the King of the Golden

Pillars, an obviously OTHERWORLDLY kingdom, as the seven magical swine would indicate, for swine originated in the Otherworld. Asal may, therefore, be seen as an Irish form of ARAWN, the ruler of ANNWFN, in Welsh legend, for he, too, owned a herd of magical swine, which he gave to PRYDERI.

## Ascapart
*British*

A giant, possibly one of the companions of ALBION. He was killed by BEVIS and buried under Bevis Mound near Southampton, Hampshire.

## Asclepiodotus
*British*

According to GEOFFREY OF MONMOUTH, a King of BRITAIN[1] during the time of Diocletian (245–313). Maintaining his autonomy against Rome cost him the crown, for he was so preoccupied with staving off the attentions of the Roman empire that COEL easily deposed him. History records an Asclepiodotus, but he was a Roman, as his name would seem to suggest, and Geoffrey of Monmouth's assertion that he was a British king is a pure flight of fancy.

## Atepomaros
*Gaulish*

A deity whose name means 'possessing great horses' and who possibly dates from the Roman period. This connection leads to the supposition that he was originally a native horse or solar deity who became assimilated with the classical Apollo along with his chariot and horses, which daily traversed the sky bearing with them the light of the sun.

## Athrwys
*Welsh*

The son of MEURIG, King of GLENVISSIG. It is possible that Athrwys was himself the King of Gwent, although when dealing with early Welsh history this cannot be said for certain.

## Audrien
*Gaulish*

An alternative name sometimes given to ALDROENUS.

## Auguselus
*British*

The brother of URIEN and, according to GEOFFREY OF MONMOUTH, King of SCOTLAND. It seems likely that his name is a variant of ARAWN, the ruler of ANNWFN, with whom he is sometimes identified.

## Aurelius Abrosius
*British*
See AMBROSIUS AURELI(AN)US.

## Aurelius -Conan, -Caninus
*British*

According to GILDAS, who uses the name Aurelius Caninus, a local king who enjoyed making war and plundering the spoils. GEOFFREY OF MONMOUTH makes him the successor of CONSTANTINE[1].

## Avagddu
*Welsh*
See AFAGDDU.

## Avallach
*Welsh*

The name sometimes used to refer to

AVALLOCH, the son of BELI MAWR and father of MODRON. Within the Arthurian legends the name Avallach is used as a variant for the Isle of AVALON.

## Avallo(c(h))
*Welsh*

Originally a deity of rather obscure origins and attributes, he is named, according to tradition, as the son of BELI MAWR and the father of the goddess MODRON. WILLIAM OF MALMESBURY said that he lived on the Isle of AVALON with his daughters, thus supporting his entry into the Arthurian cycle, although his variant name of AVALLACH is sometimes used to refer to AVALON.

## Avalon
*British*

A mythical paradise, known as the 'Fortunate Isle', that is most widely known from the Arthurian legends as the place to which ARTHUR was taken after his final battle to recover from his mortal wounds. The realm has much older origins than the fifth century from which Arthur dates, however, and has, since early times, been regarded as a place fit for only the bravest and most virtuous of mortal beings.

Early Celtic legends say that the island could be reached only on a boat guided by the sea god BARINTHUS, a point that was later to resurface in the Arthurian tales. The island itself was co-ruled by ten maidens, one of whom, MORGEN, undoubtedly the origin of Morgan Le Fay, is referred to as the shape-changing mistress of therapy, music and the arts. Other sources say that it was ruled by the mysterious BANGON about whom nothing more is known. GEOFFREY OF MONMOUTH calls Avalon the Isle of APPLES or INSULA POMORUM, although he also calls it Avallo, which appears to be a corruption of AVALLOCH, the son of BELI MAWR who was said to live on the island with his daughters.

The name Avalon originates in Welsh legend, in which it is the kingdom of the dead, although some authorities maintain that the name, and therefore also the place, is of Irish origin. Others add still further to the confusion, saying that the name has biblical origins in the place Ajolon, where the sun was made to remain in the sky to enable the Israelites to win a great battle (Joshua 10:12). As with so much that is Celtic, the origins of the name have disappeared, and all that is left is speculation, usually based on etymology.

## Ayglin
*Welsh*

The usurping uncle of ANDRIVETE. When he usurped the throne of NORTHUMBRIA he wanted Andrivete to marry a man of his choosing in order to keep her in check. She flouted his wishes, escaped and married CEI, who helped her regain her inheritance.

## Badba

*Irish*

'Furies', supernatural spirits who were said to have been employed by the DAGHDHA during the First Battle of MAGH TUIREDH. They were invoked on the fourth day of the battle along with the BLEDLOCHTANA and AMAITE AIDGILL.

## Bad(h)b(h)

*Irish*

The goddess of war, whose name appears to mean 'scald-crow'. She is depicted as a raven or a hooded crow. Bird-shaped, red-mouthed and with a sharp countenance, the Badhbh was one aspect of the triad goddess the MÓRRÍGHAN, her other aspects being MACHA and NEMHAIN. There are countless triple goddesses in Celtic and other pagan systems. Some authorities consider them as three aspects of the same thing, such as the waxing, fullness and waning of the moon, or as youth, maturity and old age, but more commonly they are seen as agricultural deities whose aspects reflect the sowing, ripening and reaping of crops.

In common with her sisters, the other aspects of the Mórríghan, the Badhbh sometimes appeared as a foul hag, sometimes as an alluring maiden, but most commonly as a bird. She was often to be seen on the battlefield near those she had selected to die, for it was her duty to preside over the battlefield. Before a battle the Badhbh would usually be encountered beside a stream in which she was washing the armour and weapons of those who were about to die.

The Badhbh not only selected those to die in battle, but could also, by the use of powerful magic, alter the course of a battle to suit her own ends. This is a trait she shared with her sisters. Other shared traits were an affinity with water, an ability to alter her form at will and an insatiable lust for both men and gods.

CÚ CHULAINN once encountered the Badhbh as a red woman wrapped in a red cloak riding in a chariot drawn by a one-legged red horse. The pole connecting the horse to the chariot passed through the animal and emerged from its forehead, where it was fixed with a wooden peg. The Badhbh was accompanied by a man who drove a cow using a forked hazel switch. Cú Chulainn asked their names, a question that the Badhbh answered in a series of riddles. Infuriated by this, Cú Chulainn leapt onto the chariot, which immediately disappeared, leaving the hero sprawling on the ground. Above him the Badhbh circled in the form of a carrion crow.

In combination with her sisters, the Badhbh became one of the most fearsome of all Celtic deities. There was no known protection against her charms, and, once selected, all that the chosen one could hope for was a quick and painless death.

## Bal-ar, -or

*Irish*

Known as Balar of the Dreadful, Baleful or Evil Eye, this hero, god and monster, a one-eyed giant, was the king of the FOMHOIRÉ. His power lay, not in his size, but in his single eye. Even though it took four men to lift his eyelid, once his eye was exposed, a single glance could unman a host.

A supposed direct ancestor of LUGH, whom some name as Balar's grandson by his daughter ETHLINN, Balar was killed by that very god as the final conflict of the Second Battle of MAGH TUIREDH. Lugh dispatched a slingshot with such accuracy and force that not only did it penetrate Balar's single eye but continued through the giant's head to wreak havoc amongst the Fomhoiré hordes assembled behind their king. Some sources say that the slingshot killed twenty-seven of the Fomhoiré who had been too slow in taking cover, although the actual number killed is open to speculation, many going so far as to say that only a few of the Fomhoiré escaped to flee the country. Balar's corpse was hung on a sacred hazel, which dripped poison and split asunder.

In some respects, Balar is similar to the giant of Welsh mythology YSPADDADEN, the giant father of the maiden OLWEN, although it is unclear whether there is any direct connection between the two giants. See also AIDED CHLAINNE TUIRENN.

## Baldudus

*British*
See BLADUD.

## ball-seirc

*Irish*

The beauty spot said to have been placed on the forehead of DIARMAID UA DUIBHNE by a young maiden who revealed herself to him as the personification of youth.

## Banánachs

*Irish*

Spirits of an unknown nature, who were reputed to have shrieked in the air around CÚ CHULAINN while the hero fought with FERDIA, their cries being joined by those of the BOCÁNACHS and the GENITI GLINNE. They would seem to be a representation of the battle fury of Cú Chulainn and may be a partial origin of the BANSHEE.

## Banb(h)a

*Irish*

One of the triad of goddesses known collectively as the SPIRIT OF IRELAND or the SOVEREIGNTY OF IRELAND, her other aspects being FÓDLA and ÉRIU. Like that other Irish triad, the MÓRRIGHAN, she and her sisters have bird characteristics. Early myth says that she was the leader of a company that came to IRELAND in a time before the biblical Flood, although this company is also said to have been led by CESAIR. Of these people all but one, FINTAN[1], drowned in the Flood, and Banbha passed into the realms of deification.

She later reappears as the wife of MAC CUILL. Now she is an eponymous goddess and primal figure of sovereignty, and is combined in trio with Fódla and Ériu, whom some call her sisters. They, with their three husbands, opposed the invasion of Ireland by the Sons of MÍL ÉSPÁINE with magic. After the invaders had landed and had defeated a TUATHA

DÉ DANANN army, they marched towards TARA. *En route* they encountered and wooed Banbha and her sisters, each promising victory to the invaders if the bribe they were offered was sufficient. That offered to Ériu was the best, for that promised the naming of the country after her. Since that time Ireland has been known as EIRE.

## Banblai
*Irish*

The father of BUIC.

## Bangon
*British*

A mysterious character who is named in a few sources as the ruler of AVALON. However, nothing more is known about this deity, and it remains questionable whether he is Celtic or simply a later invention.

## Banshee
*Irish*

A fairy being in Irish folklore whose wailing lament is supposed to warn of an impending death. Their origin may lie with the BANÁNACHS, BOCÁNACHS and GENITI GLINNE, supernatural beings who were reported to have filled the air with their screams during the battle between CÚ CHULAINN and FERDIA.

## Bardsey
*Welsh*

Known as YNYS ENLLI in Welsh, the small island of Bardsey lies just off the tip of the beautiful Lleyn Peninsula in GWYNEDD, at the northern entrance of Cardigan Bay. Now a bird sanctuary and observatory, the island was an important holy site to the Celts who built a monastery there,

now ruined, in the sixth century. The island later became known as the Island of Twenty Thousand Saints, the reputed last resting place of PADARN who lies there in the company of 20,000 saints. Later still it became one of the alleged resting places of MERLIN as he awaits the return of King ARTHUR.

## Barinthus
*Welsh*

A mysterious OTHERWORLDLY sea deity about whom very little is known. He does, however, make an appearance in the later Arthurian legends as the boatman who ferried the mortally wounded King ARTHUR on his final journey to AVALON.

The character of Barinthus remains shrouded in mystery. Why he should appear only in late legends is a mystery, as he is clearly a very early deity. One possible explanation for the existence of Barinthus is the widespread belief that the land of the dead, the OTHERWORLD, lay across a vast sea, and Barinthus was duly accorded the honour of ferrying the dead to the eternal land. See also MANANNÁN MAC LIR.

## Baruch
*Irish*

One of the RED BRANCH and a close ally of CONCHOBAR MAC NESSA. When FERGUS MAC ROICH arrived back in IRELAND with NAOISE, DERDRIU, ARDÁN and AINNLE, Baruch placed Fergus mac Roich under an obligation to spend the night with him, thus keeping him away from EMHAIN MHACHA where Conchobar mac Nessa intended to kill the three sons of UISNECH. See also GESSA.

## Bascna
*Irish*

The leader of one of the two clans that made up the FIAN, the other being Clan MORNA. Both Bascna and Morna fought alongside their chief FIONN MAC CUMHAILL.

## Bath
*British*

City in the county of Avon, England. Legend says that the city was founded on the site of the healing waters that cured BLADUD, the magical son of King HUDIBRAS. The Roman name for the city was AQUAE SULIS, so named after the goddess SULIS to whom the hot springs found in the city were dedicated. The Romans obviously thought it politically wise to incorporate the local deity into their name for the city as the site was quite obviously one of important religious significance to the indigenous population.

## Baudihillie
*British*

The name of one of the ALAISIAGAE, the others being BEDE[1], FINNILENE and FRIAGABI, to whom an altar was dedicated at Housesteads on Hadrian's Wall. It is thought that her name means 'Ruler of Battle'. Her worship, which appears to have been brought to BRITAIN[1] during the Roman period, seemingly continues well after the withdrawal of the Roman armies, although whether it was the Celts or the PICTS who continued this worship is uncertain.

## Bav
*Irish*
See MÓRRÍGHAN.

## Bave
*Irish*

The shape-shifting daughter of CALATIN. Having assumed the shape of NIAMH[1], she coaxed CÚ CHULAINN to leave his place of safety, thus instigating the series of events that were to lead to his death. Some think that Bave is a simple variant of Bav, an alternative name given to the MÓRRÍGHAN. This may indeed be the case, for it was Cú Chulainn's ignorant behaviour towards the Mórríghan that ultimately caused his death.

## Bé Find
*Irish*

The generic name given to water-sprites, semi-divine women who live by, or in, streams, lakes and fountains, or in forests and woods. Later tradition included mermaids under this name.

## Beälcu
*Irish*

The warrior from CONNACHT who found CONALL CERNACH hideously wounded and dying after he had killed CET. Conall Cernach pleaded with him to kill him, but Beälcu would not kill a man so close to death. Instead he carried the dying warrior home and cured him of his wounds, fully intending to kill Conall Cernach in single combat. However, fully recovered, Conall Cernach was set upon by the three sons of Beälcu, but by some unrecorded ploy Conall Cernach managed to have them kill their own father before he killed and beheaded them and carried their heads back to ULSTER in triumph.

## Beann Ghulban
*Irish*
Also BEN BULBEN

The owner of a magical boar with no ears or tail that was the foster brother of DIARMAID UA DUIBHNE. The boar itself is usually referred to as Beann Ghulban, although it was actually unnamed. Even though it had been prophesied that Diarmaid ua Duibhne would be killed by the boar, he still went ahead and hunted it. During the hunt Diarmaid ua Duibhne was mortally gored, seconds before he managed to dispatch the beast with his broken sword.

## Bebhionn
*Irish*
Also VIVIONN

A giantess, the daughter of TREON from TÍR INNA MBAN, who sought the protection of FIONN MAC CUMHAILL after her father had betrothed her to AEDA[2] against her will. While sitting with Fionn mac Cumhaill, Bebhionn's intended strode ashore, killed her with a single cast of his huge lance and then strode back out to a huge waiting boat before Fionn mac Cumhaill or his men could respond.

## Bébind
*Irish*

The sister of BOANN and the mother of FRAOCH.

## Bebo
*Irish*

The Queen of FAYLINN and wife of IUBDAN, whom she accompanied to ULSTER to visit the giant humans who lived there, for she and her husband are commonly referred to as the 'Wee Folk' or fairies. She and her husband were held captive for a short while until, after a series of plagues imposed by IUBDAN's subjects, they were released for a ransom of magical items.

## Béchuille
*Irish*

A member of the TUATHA DÉ DANANN. She is described as a witch and is also sometimes described as a foster mother to the gods, although this role is not developed in the legends.

## Bécuma
*Irish*

The enchantress who was banished by the TUATHA DÉ DANANN for seducing the son of MANANNÁN MAC LIR. She later returned and caused CONN CÉTCHATHLACH to exile his son ART, and then lived with the king for a year during which time no corn grew and no cows gave milk. Conn Cétchathlach's advisers told him that the sacrifice of the son of a 'sinless couple' would be needed to break the enchantment of Bécuma. Just such a child was found, but his mother arrived with a wondrous cow that was accepted in the child's place. Bécuma now turned her attentions to Art, but left the Tuatha Dé Danann forever after Art had succeeded in returning from the land of dead with DELBCHAEM.

Some authorities have sought to connect Bécuma with the similarly named BÉCHUILLE but, although both are enchantresses, there is nothing further to support this assimilation.

## Bedd Branwen
*Welsh*

The alleged burial place of BRANWEN. Situated on the banks of the River ALAW 1 mile northeast of the church in

Treffynnon on ANGLESEY, the burial chamber beneath this cromlech was excavated in 1813 and an urn containing the cremated bones of a woman discovered.

## Bedd Taliesin
*Welsh*

Northeast of Talybont, on the slopes of Moel-y-Garn, DYFED, is a CAER reputed to contain the remains of TALIESIN. The barrow consists of a large stone slab and cairn, the other stones having been removed over the years as building materials.

In the nineteenth century an attempt was made to discover the bones of Taliesin, and to remove them for reburial in a Christian rather than pagan site. During the excavation a sudden terrible thunderstorm arose. Lightning struck the ground nearby, and, fleeing for their lives, the men abandoned their tools, never returning to collect them or to try again.

## Bede

1 (*British*). The name of one of the four ALAISIAGAE, Teutonic war goddesses whose worship was brought to BRITAIN[1], most probably by the Romans. An altar to these four goddesses, the other three being FINNILENE, BAUDIHILLIE and FRIAGABI, was dedicated at Housesteads on Hadrian's Wall.
2 (*General*). ANGLO-SAXON scholar, theologian and historian (c.673–735), who is usually referred to as the Venerable Bede. He was born near the town of Monkwearmouth, County Durham, and at the age of seven he was placed in the care of Benedict Biscop within the monastery of Wearmouth, and in 682 moved to the new monastery of Jarrow, Northumberland. He was ordained as a priest there in 703 and remained a monk for the rest of his life. A prolific writer, he produced homilies, lives of saints and of abbots, hymns, epigrams, works on chronology, grammar and physical science, as well as commentaries on the Old and New Testaments. His greatest work was his Latin *Historia Ecclesiastica Gentis Anglorum* ('Ecclesiastical History of the English People'), which he completed in 731. It remains the single most valuable source for early English history.

## Bed-wyr, -vyr
*Welsh*

1 The father of PEDRAWD and thus grandfather of BEDWYR[2]. Like his namesake, he reappeared in the later Arthurian legends with the name Bedivere.
2 A member of the party formed to help CULHWCH in his quest to locate and secure the maiden OLWEN. The other members of the party were CEI, CYNDDYLIG the Guide, GWRHYR the Interpreter, GWALCHMAI FAB GWYAR and MENW FAB TEIRGWAEDD. Each was chosen for their own specialist skills. Bedwyr was chosen because, even though he only had one hand, he was still faster with his sword than three others who fought together.

Bedwyr's father was named as PEDRAWD, whose own father was also known as BEDWYR[1]. He had two children by an unnamed wife, a son AMREN and a daughter ENEUAVC. Bedwyr re-emerged in the later Arthurian legends as Bedivere.

## Bel(en-os, -us)
*Gaulish and British*

One of the most widespread of all Celtic gods, whose variant name, Belenos, was mostly used in Alpine regions, particularly NORICUM, of which Belenos was the tutelary deity. The representation of the power of light, the word *bel* meaning 'bright' or 'brilliant', Bel has many solar attributes. It was these that led him to be identified, on both sides of the Channel, with the Roman god Apollo during the time of the Roman occupation.

The patron of the festival of BELTANE, Bel was said to have been the son of Light rather than being a solar deity himself. He was also known as the Lord of Therapy, a distinction that again directly links Bel with the Roman god Apollo, although it is quite possible that this is a later idea, and was simply added to Bel's solar attributes to make him even more comparable to Apollo. It is quite probable that Bel was later personified in the legendary early Briton BELI MAWR.

## Belatucadros
*British*

'Fair shining one', a horned Celtic god of war, whose cult was active in Cumbria and who has been often equated with the Roman god of war, Mars. A number of stones dedicated to Mars Belatucadros have, in fact, been found in Cumbria. Belatucadros was obviously a popular deity among the northern Celts because he was worshipped by both soldiers and civilians, a trait not often found in the worship of warlike deities.

## Beli (Mawr)
*British and Welsh*

A legendary early Briton who is thought to have originated as the god BEL, although this connection is by no means certain. His two famous sons were LLUDD and LLEFELYS, while his daughter, or possibly sister, was PENARDUN who, by

LLYR, was the mother of BENDIGEID VRAN. According to Henry of Huntingdon (c.1084–1155), Beli Mawr was the brother of the first-century British king CUNOBELINUS. Welsh legend makes him the father of AVALLOC, grandfather of MODRON, and Lord of the OTHERWORLD.

Beli Mawr appears in the later Arthurian legends by two means. First, through the pedigree of Bendigeid Vran; second, through etymological connections.

## Belisima
*Irish*

A late title afforded to BRIGHID. It seems quite possible that the word is of Italian derivation, for in Italian the word *bellissima* means 'beautiful', an apt description for Brighid.

## Bel(l)inus
*British*

A son of MOLMUTIUS and TONWENNA, the brother of BRENNIUS and, according to GEOFFREY OF MONMOUTH, the legendary founder of CAERLEON-ON-USK. His name is possibly a derivation of BEL or BELI MAWR. Belinus traditionally succeeded his father after a blood feud between him and his brother was settled by arbitration. Five years later Brennius broke the peace and sailed to Norway where he married the king's daughter and raised an army. However, Belinus routed them on their return to ENGLAND. Brennius fled to GAUL, and Belinus became the undisputed sovereign. Some time later Brennius returned with a Gaulish army, but Tonwenna interceded, and the two brothers were reconciled. The two brothers now invaded Gaul, which they subdued before pressing on into Italy. Following their successful sacking of Rome, Brennius decided to remain in Italy while Belinus returned to

England and ruled in peace for the rest of his life, adding greatly to the fortifications surrounding TROIA NOVA (LONDON), and founding several new cities.

The sacking of Rome, which appears in Geoffrey of Monmouth, took place in 390 BC. However, the leader of the Celtic army was a Gaul by the name of BRENNOS[2]. It would seem that Geoffrey of Monmouth simply altered the name and gave him a semi-divine brother to claim the sacking of Rome for the British.

## Belt-ane, -ene, -ine
*General*

A Celtic festival, held on 1 May, which marked the beginning of the Celtic summer. It was presided over by, and named after, BEL. Fires lit on the night preceding the festival were held to purify the land after the ravages of winter and to herald a time of regeneration and regrowth. Formerly one of the Scottish quarter days, Beltane was said to have been the date on which the first of the human race, the Sons of MÍL ÉSPÁINE, landed on Irish soil. To this day, the rites of purification with spring-water and the lighting of purifying bonfires are connected with the ancient festival of Beltane.

## Beltené
*Irish*

One of the many names applied to the god of death. However, even though an etymological connection to the feast of BELTANE is obvious, there is no connection, for that festival was one of rebirth and not, therefore, something in which a god of death would be involved.

## Ben Bulben
*Irish*
See BEANN GHULBAN.

## Ben Edar
*Irish*

The burial place of AIDEEN, the wife of OSCAR. She died of a broken heart when her husband was killed and was buried by OISÍN, who built a huge dolmen over her grave.

## Bendigeid Vran
*Welsh*

The giant son of LLYR and PENARDUN and brother of BRANWEN and MANAWYDAN FAB LLYR. Some sources, however, make Bendigeid Vran and Branwen the children of Llyr by IWERIADD, while Manawydan fab Llyr was the son of Llyr by Penardun. He is more commonly referred to as BRÂN THE BLESSED, and his story is told in the *Mabinogion*. The god of fertility and patron of craftsmen, warrior, harpist and poet, his name can sometimes mean 'raven'. His ranking among the gods was downgraded to that of folk hero after the advent of Christianity, but early stories illustrate his great importance.

Bendigeid Vran, whose court was alleged to be at Harlech, had a son named CARATACUS who has been identified with the British leader of that name who opposed the Romans in AD 43, when CLAUDIUS landed with his invasion forces. It has even been mooted, in direct contradiction of his own godly status, that Bendigeid Vran introduced Christianity to BRITAIN[1]. The *Mabinogion* says that Bendigeid Vran gave his sister Branwen to MATHOLWCH, King of IRELAND, together with a magic cauldron. However, while Matholwch was in Britain he was insulted by EFNISIEN, Bendigeid Vran's half-brother, and on his return to Ireland he took his revenge on Branwen. Learning of the suffering of Branwen, Bendigeid Vran crossed from WALES to Ireland by walking on the seabed and, once he was there, a mighty battle ensued. At first the forces of Matholwch held the upper hand, for every night they took their dead and wounded and placed them in the magic cauldron that Bendigeid Vran had given to Matholwch, an act that restored them to full health and vigour. However, after EFNISIEN had succeeded in destroying the cauldron, Bendigeid Vran and his men quickly exterminated the entire Irish population, save for five pregnant women who hid in a cave, their resulting children becoming the forefathers of the new Irish race.

So fierce was the fighting that only seven of his men survived to return to Wales, and Bendigeid Vran himself was mortally wounded in the foot with a poisoned dart. During his absence CASWALLAWN, the son of BELI, disinherited Manawydan fab Llyr, the brother and heir of Bendigeid Vran. The seven survivors of the expedition were PRYDERI, Manawydan fab Llyr, GLIFIEU, TALIESIN, YNAWAG, GRUDDIEU and HEILYN. Bendigeid Vran ordered these seven to cut off his head and carry it to the WHITE MOUNT in LONDON, there to bury it with the face towards FRANCE as a magical guardian over Britain. Bendigeid Vran also told the seven that they would be a long time travelling to their goal, adding that his head would be pleasant company for them during their long journey. For seven years, he told them, they would remain in Harlech, where they would feast in splendour while being detained by the magical singing of the birds of RHIANNON. He told them that they would live in PENVRO for eighty years, only leaving after they had opened a door that looked towards CORNWALL.

Everything passed exactly as Bendigeid Vran foretold, until finally the seven carried out his last wish and buried his head as ordered. Later stories say that King ARTHUR dug up his head, for he alone wanted to be the sole guardian of Britain. Popular belief still holds that the head of Bendigeid Vran is buried within the boundaries of the Tower of London, possibly beneath the White Tower.

Branwen, whom the seven brought home with them, looked back towards Ireland and, thinking about the destruction that had been brought about for her sake, died of a broken heart. She was buried near the River ALAW on ANGLESEY, her grave being known as BEDD BRANWEN.

Bendigeid Vran has undoubtedly given much to the later Arthurian legends. His magical cauldron was, so it has been suggested, refined to reappear as none other than the Holy GRAIL, and his mortal wound has also been likened to the wound inflicted on the Fisher King.

The translation of Bendigeid Vran's name as 'raven', although this is normally the translation of Brân, is particularly significant when the presence of ravens at the Tower of London is considered. These ravens, sacred birds to the Celts, are never permitted to leave the confines of the Tower of London, for if they do, so it is said, the White Tower will fall into ruin and Britain will fall to invaders. It is perhaps just as well that today the birds have their wings clipped and that Bendigeid Vran's head remains just where he ordered it to be buried.

Bendigeid Vran should not be confused with the Irish hero BRÂN[1], who is an entirely different character, a hero rather than a god.

## Bersa
*Irish*

The husband of MAIR.

## Bevis
*British*

The traditional killer of the giant ASCAPART, whom he buried under a mound near Southampton, Hampshire, that is, appropriately, known as Bevis Mound.

## Bilé
*Irish*

According to some sources, the son of BREGON or ITH, and father of MÍL, though in these instances Míl is usually referred to as MILÉ.

## Birôg
*Irish*

The Druidess who accompanied CIAN to TORY Island and enabled him to avenge himself on BALAR by seducing Balar's daughter ETHLINN, who was kept locked away in a solitary tower after it had been prophesied that her child would kill Balar. Ethlinn subsequently gave birth to three boys. Two were killed by Balar, but the third, LUGH, survived and later fulfilled the prophecy at the Second Battle of MAGH TUIREDH.

## Bith
*Irish*

The son of NOAH and father of CESAIR. He was said to have been one of the possible leaders of the fifty-three people who came to IRELAND in a time before the Flood. Of these fifty-three, only three were men: Bith himself, FINTAN[1] and the pilot LADRA. Alternatively, these invaders were led by BANBHA who later become one of the triad of goddesses known as the SPIRIT OF IRELAND.

## Black Arcan
*Irish*

According to Irish folk tradition the killer of FIONN MAC CUMHAILL, although the mythological cycles name this person as FINNÉCES, a character who was at one time his mentor.

## Black Book of Carmarthen, The
*Welsh*

LLYFR DU CAERTYDDIN, an important source of Welsh mythological and legendary belief. Dating from *c*.1105, although possibly copied from much earlier works, *The Black Book of Carmarthen* is so called because it was written by the black-robed monks of CARMARTHEN. The original manuscript is today housed in the National Library of Wales at Aberystwyth.

## Blackbird of Cilgwri
*Welsh*

An ancient bird with whom GWRHYR the interpreter communicated during the expedition mounted by CULHWCH. The bird directed them to the STAG OF RHEDYNFRC, which in turn sent them to the OWL OF CWN CAWLWYD, which took them to the EAGLE OF GWERNABWY, which guided them to the SALMON OF LLYN LLW.

## Bladud
*British*
Also BALDUDUS

The magical son of HUDIBRAS, the founder of the hot springs and temple at BATH and a great master of the Druidic arts, including necromancy and magical flight.

According to GEOFFREY OF MONMOUTH, he was directly descended from AENEAS and BRUTUS. Geoffrey of Monmouth develops what was obviously an earlier belief by adding that Bladud was an ancestor of King ARTHUR. The association between Bladud and the Druidic arts possibly draws on Welsh or Breton bardic tradition. He is again mentioned in the *Vita Merlini* as a guardian of therapeutic springs and wells. His story clearly derives from a local Somerset folk tradition, although it is the version given by Geoffrey of Monmouth that gives us the most commonly told version of the life of this king.

This story says that Bladud was sent by Hudibras to study philosophy in Athens, but, while he was there, his father died. Bladud returned home, sources say in the year 873 BC, to claim his throne, bringing with him some of the learned Greeks he had met in Athens. Together they founded a university at Stamford in Lincolnshire, which flourished until the coming of St Augustine, when Celtic learning was suppressed in favour of Catholicism. Skilled in magic, Bladud conjured up the hot springs at Bath and built a temple to Minerva over them, and in this he placed devices of his own invention to provide a perpetual flame. He also famously invented a means of flying with artificial wings. He flew on these to LONDON but crashed onto the temple of Apollo, which stood where ST PAUL'S CATHEDRAL stands today, and was killed. He had reigned for twenty years, and during that time is credited with founding the city of KAERBADUS or Bath. He was succeeded by that other famous mythical king, King LEIR.

However, a legend that was extant in the Somerset and Bath area from early times tells a slightly different version, although the similarities between the two are evident, and it is obvious that Geoffrey of Monmouth drew on and refined this version for his own. This early story says that, during the reign of Hudibras, Bladud contracted leprosy and was banished from the royal court. Before his departure he was given a ring by his mother so that he would be instantly recognizable to her again. Bladud travelled to Greece and, following receipt of the news of his father's death, returned to ENGLAND where he took up a lowly job tending a herd of swine, for no blemished king could ascend the throne, and his leprosy ruled him out. This job is traditionally said to have been at Swainswick near Bath. While he was tending the herd he noticed that there was a favourite place in which they liked to wallow, and he noticed especially that those that had blemished skin were restored to full health by the mud. He tried the same treatment and was immediately cured, enabling him to claim his rightful throne. Over the spot where he was miraculously cured he and his consort ALARON built a temple that was the foundation of the city of Bath.

A less well-known story concerning the therapeutic waters at Bath and their connection with Bladud claims that they are the result of Bladud's experiments. During his time in Greece Bladud acquired advanced scientific knowledge. Using this skill he buried two tuns (a tun being a barrel with a capacity of 252 gallons) containing burning brass, and two more, this time of glass, containing seven types of salt, brimstone and wild fire. All four tuns were said to be the source of the heat within the waters of Bath, their contents spilling over into the water itself. Consequently the waters were regarded as being poisonous and were not to be drunk under any circumstances. The habit of 'taking the waters' did not, apparently, begin until the reign of Charles II in the seventeenth century.

Some commentators, using the information concerning Bladud's skill in the Druidic arts, have connected the king with the OTHERWORLD. Indeed, in the cosmology of the *Vita Merlini*, Bath is placed in the centre of BRITAIN[1], which is, in turn, placed in the centre of the world, thus providing a portal to the Otherworld, of which the swine is a native animal, and over which Bladud presides. This connection appears only in later works, and is a simple decoration of the earlier stories that give no reference to the Otherworld at all.

## Blai
*Irish*

1 One of the five people responsible for raising CÚ CHULAINN. The other four were FINDCHOÉM, his aunt; SENCHA, described as 'the pacifist'; FERGHUS MAC ROICH; and AMHAIRGHIN. Blai is reputed to have defended the honour of the men of IRELAND, even during their pillaging.
2 An alternative name sometimes given to SAAR, the wife of FIONN MAC CUMHAILL and mother of OISÍN.

## Bláthna-d, -t
*Irish*

A beautiful OTHERWORLDLY maiden. On the occasion when CÚ CHULAINN and his men were raiding the Otherworld, here depicted as SCOTLAND, CÚ ROÍ MAC DÁIRI appeared to the great hero in disguise and offered to help him. Thanks to his intervention, Cú Chulainn and his men captured a magical cauldron – a familiar icon in tales of the Otherworld – three magic crows and the beautiful Bláthnad. Cú Chulainn and his men broke their promise to share the spoils, however, and the enraged CÚ ROÍ MAC DÁIRI seized the lot and married the maiden.

Cú Chulainn planned his revenge and conspired with Bláthnad on the feast of SAMHAIN. Cú Roí mac Dáiri was murdered, and Bláthnad passed into the ownership of Cú Chulainn. Cú Roí mac Dáiri was avenged by FERCHERDNE his FILI, who, noticing Bláthnad standing close to the edge of a cliff, ran at the girl, caught her around the waist, and threw them both to their deaths on the rocks below.

## Bleddyn
*Welsh*

The name given by MATH FAB MATHONWY to the boy born as a wolf-cub to GILFAETHWY and GWYDION FAB DÔN during the third year of their punishment for the rape of GOEWIN. The first year they had spent as a stag and hind, and had borne a fawn, which Math fab Mathonwy turned into a boy to whom he gave the name HYDWN. The second year was spent as a boar and sow, in which guise they bore a wild piglet, who was likewise transformed and named HWYCHDWN. At the end of the third year, Gilfaethwy and Gwydion fab Dôn were returned to their human form, and found themselves the parents of three boys.

## Bledlochtana
*Irish*

Monsters or supernatural beings who were envoked on the fourth day of the First Battle of MAGH TUIREDH by the DAGHDHA. They were accompanied on this occasion by the BADBA and AMAITE AIDGILL.

## Blodeu(w)edd
*Welsh*

A flower-maiden whose name means 'Flower Face'. She was created from the flowers of oak, broom and meadowsweet by MATH FAB MATHONWY and GWYDION FAB DÔN as a wife for LLEU LLAW GYFFES to circumvent the third curse put on him by his mother ARIANRHOD, that curse being that he would never have a mortal wife until she herself gave him one, a thing she, naturally, never intended to do. Regrettably, Blodeuwedd was unfaithful to Lleu Llaw Gyffes with the hunter GRONW BEBYR. She and her lover contrived to kill Lleu Llaw Gyffes, who could be killed by a spear that had been worked for a year at Mass time on Sundays, and then only if he were standing with one foot on the back of a billy goat and the other in a bathtub.

Blodeuwedd persuaded her husband to demonstrate this curious position to her while Gronw Bebyr hid in the bushes armed with the appropriate spear. As Lleu Llaw Gyffes adopted the required stance, Gronw Bebyr cast the spear but only managed to wound him. Lleu Llaw Gyffes immediately changed into an eagle and flew away. Blodeuwedd was changed into an owl by Gwydion fab Dôn for her infidelity, and Gronw Bebyr was killed by Lleu Llaw Gyffes after he had been found and healed by Gwydion fab Dôn. Some authorities consider that Blodeuwedd was the original of GUENDOLOENA, who is, in turn, considered by some as the forerunner of the Arthurian GUINEVERE.

## Blunderboar
*British*

The giant who once managed to capture JACK THE GIANT-KILLER. Jack later escaped and killed Blunderboar and his brothers.

## Boadicea
*British*

Popular version of BOUDICCA.

## Boann(a(n))
*Irish*
Also BÓINN

The sister of BÉBIND, goddess of the river BOYNE, wife of NECHTAN[1] and mother of OENGHUS MAC IN OG, the result of a secret union with the DAGHDHA. The story of their illicit union is told by the tenth-century poet Cináed úa hArtacáin. Boann travelled to stay with her brother ELCMAR, a vassal of the DAGHDHA, with whom she sought an affair, but Elcmar discovered this and swore never to stay away long enough to give them time to consummate their lust for each other. The Daghdha easily circumvented this by causing the sun to stay still for nine months, so Elcmar did not know he had been away for that long. On his return he realized that something had been going on because of the changes he saw in the flowers and trees. Shortly before Elcmar's return, Boann had given birth to a boy whom she left outside the SÍDH of MIDHIR, who took the infant in and raised him as his own, although later he told the boy of his parentage.

## Bocánachs
*Irish*

Spirits of an unknown nature who were reputed to have shrieked in the air around CÚ CHULAINN, while the hero fought FERDIA, their cries being joined by those of the BANÁCHS and the GENITI GLINNE. They would seem to be a representation of the battle fury of Cú Chulainn, and may be a partial origin of the BANSHEE.

## Bodb
*Irish*

The Goddess of battle. Following the Second Battle of MAGH TUIREDH, Bodb gave a prophecy of doom after recounting the heroic struggle.

## Bodb (Dearg)
*Irish*

A King of MUNSTER, sometimes known as Bôv, who was employed by the DAGHDHA to seek out the dream woman with whom OENGHUS MAC IN OG had fallen in love. After a year he reported that he had found the maiden at a lake. Bodb and Oenghus Mac in Og travelled to the lake, where they saw the maiden with her 149 sisters. Bodb informed Oenghus Mac in Og that her name was CAER[2], the daughter of ETHAL ANUBAL, a prince of CONNACHT, and he told Oenghus Mac in Og that he must enlist the help of AILILL and MEDHBHA if he wished to meet the maiden. This he did, and after following their magical instructions, was united with Caer as a swan, and together they flew back to Oenghus Mac in Og's home at BRUGH NA BÓINNE.

Bodb Dearg was chosen to be the king of the TUATHA DÉ DANANN after the death of the Daghdha, although this choice upset LIR, who had been neither consulted nor considered. To compensate Lir, Bodb Dearg gave Lir one of his daughters, AODH, to be his wife. She bore him four children, two boys and two girls, before dying. Bodb Dearg then gave Lir his other daughter AOIFE, but she grew jealous of her step-children and changed them into swans, a form in which they would remain for 900 hundred years. Bodb Dearg cursed Aoife and turned her into a raven or, as some say, a 'demon of the air'. Some sources name a third daughter of Bodb Dearg as SAAR, and make her the wife of FIONN MAC CUMHAILL and mother of OISÎN.

## Bodhmhall
*Irish*

The daughter of TADG and sister of MUIRNE. According to the LEABHAR NA HUIDHRE, FIONN MAC CUMHAILL was born at her home. She subsequently became the guardian of the young Fionn mac Cumhaill and raised the boy, at that time called DEIMNE, in seclusion for the child's own safety.

## Bóinn
*Irish*
See BOANN.

## Book of Leinster, The
*Irish*

An important source text, dating from the twelfth century. It contains one version of the *Taín Bó Cuailngè*, which possibly dates from the eighth century. It also contains the *Dinnshenchas*, an early Christian tract.

## Bor mo, vo
*Gaulish*

A deity who is associated with seething or boiling waters and who is yet another god of the Apollo type. He is usually paired with the goddess DAMONA or 'Divine Cow'.

## Boscawen-un
*British*

A stone circle in a particularly remote location approximately 4 miles west of Penzance. A nearby rocky outcrop displays an impression said to be the footprint of one of the old Cornish giants, possibly CORMORAN himself. Boscawen-un stone circle is mentioned in the Welsh *Trioedd Ynys Prydein* as one of the three main

GORSEDDS (assembly places for bards and augurs) in BRITAIN[1]. Although it certainly predates the Celtic era by some considerable time, this stone circle was, like many other similar structures around the country, used by the DRUIDS for their worship.

## Boudicca
*British*

The first-century queen of the ICENI in Norfolk, England. Her husband PRASUTAGUS had tried to retain some independence from the invading Romans by remaining on good terms with Rome as a client king. After he died, however, the Romans took charge and plundered the royal household. Boudicca was flogged and her daughters raped. Boudicca then roused her people and the people of the neighbouring TRI-NOVANTES, invoked the goddess ANDRASTE, and led a campaign against the Romans. At first successful, she razed Camulodunum (Colchester) late in AD 60, then LONDON and finally the new city of Verulamium (St Albans) in AD 61. Finally, the Romans recovered from the surprise of Boudicca's attack, and defeated her army. Boudicca took poison.

The location of Boudicca's grave remains one of the many unsolved mysteries of the era. For a while STONEHENGE was considered her monument. Others say that she lies under Platform 10 at King's Cross Station or is buried under a mound in Parliament Hill Fields, Hampstead. Her ghost, however, appears to be able to move freely around, for it is often sighted near the earthworks of Amesbury Banks in Epping Forest, and in 1950 she was sighted driving her war chariot out of the mist near Cammeringham, Lincolnshire.

Boudicca's name may be an assumed one, for it appears to mean 'Victory', a name she may have adopted after her invocation of Andraste. She is generally portrayed as tall, fierce-looking and harsh-voiced, with a mass of flaming red hair that hung down to her waist.

## Bôv
*Irish*
See BODB DEARG.

## Boyne
*Irish*

The Irish river of which BOANN was the patron goddess. The river rises in Westmeath and spills into the Irish Sea at Drogheda on the east coast to the north of Dublin. One of the most important and richly decorated of all the European megalithic monuments is to be found on the northern banks of the river at NEW GRANGE. This tumulus has an important rôle in the Irish mythological cycles. Known as BRUGH NA BÓINNE, it is the home of OENGHUS MAC IN OG, the son of the DAGHDHA, whom some hold responsible for its construction.

## Braciaca
*Gaulish*

The goddess of ale, although ale to the Celts was not the brew known today, but a divine drink, consumed by the gods.

## Brân
*Irish*

1 Not to be confused with BRÂN THE BLESSED, or correctly BENDIGEID VRAN, Brân is a hero of an OTHERWORLDLY adventure that is typically Irish in flavour and content.

The son of FEBAL, Brân was lured away by a beautiful spirit to TÍR INNA MBAN, an OTHERWORLDLY realm, which the spirit described as a paradisal land. Brân set sail with twenty-seven companions and, *en route*, encountered the sea god MANANNÀN MAC LIR driving a chariot. As they came together, Manannán mac Lir changed the sea into a flowery plain, the fishes into flocks of sheep and the leaping salmon into frisking calves, before driving away over the now solid surface of the sea. As he disappeared the sea returned to normal.

Sailing on, Brân and his companions reached the magical island, but were afraid to land. However, the leader of the women threw a ball of string out to him which stuck to his hand, and by this method their ship was hauled to the shore. As soon as they landed, a strange euphoria spread across the adventurers, who were led through Tír inna mBan to a great hall where they were told there was a bed and a wife for every man, along with an unlimited supply of food and drink. The entire island was inhabited by beautiful women, and soon Brân and his companions had settled into a life of comfort and happiness. After what seemed like just a year, Brân and his men returned to IRELAND. As their ship neared the shore a crowd of people gathered on the shore and called out to the ship, asking his name. Brân replied, telling them both his name and that of his father. After a short while they shouted back to him that the only Brân they knew of was from one of their ancient stories called 'The Voyage of Brân'.

A strange apprehension gripped the adventurers, the truth of their absence becoming clear when one of them, eager for home, leapt ashore. The instant his foot touched the beach, his body collapsed in a heap of dust. They had been absent not for just a year, but for many hundreds of years, and Brân and his companions were as dead men, alive only aboard their ship due to the enchantment of Tír inna mBam. Brân

called out the details of their adventure to the people on the shore, then turned the ship back out to sea and sailed away, never to be heard of again.

2 One of the hounds of FIONN MAC CUMHAILL, the other being called SGEOLAN. These dogs were nephews of Fionn mac Cumhaill, for they were born to TUIREANN, Fionn mac Cumhaill's sister, who had married ILLAN and had been transformed into a wolf-hound by her husband's supernatural mistress, a form she retained until Illan renounced her.

As a boast, OENGHUS MAC IN OG stated that neither of these hounds would be capable of killing a single swine in his herd but, rather, that his black boar would kill them. A year later, Fionn mac Cumhaill released his hounds against a herd of a hundred swine that had appeared outside Oenghus Mac in Og's home and killed them all, Brân killing the prized black boar. Oenghus Mac in Og complained that the swine had in fact been his children in disguise. A quarrel followed, during which Fionn mac Cumhaill readied himself to attack Oenghus Mac in Og, but he sued for peace.

## Brân (the Blessed)
*Welsh*

The literal translation of BENDIGEID VRAN.

## Brangaled
*Welsh*

The owner of a drinking-horn, CORN BRANGALED, that was said to have been capable of providing any drink desired, and numbered among the THIRTEEN TREASURES of BRITAIN[1].

## Brangwaine
*Welsh*

The name given to BRANWEN in later Welsh tradition from the post-Celtic epoch.

## Branwen
*Welsh*

The daughter of LLYR, brother to BENDIGEID VRAN, and half-sister to EFNISIEN and NISIEN. Branwen was given to MATHOLWCH, the King of IRELAND, by her brother Bendigeid Vran, along with a magical cauldron. However, during the wedding celebrations in WALES, Efnisien insulted Matholwch so badly that, once he had returned to Ireland, he vented his anger on his new bride. Learning of this ill-treatment, Bendigeid Vran led an army to Ireland and, having first been on the losing side thanks to the very cauldron he had given Matholwch, he finally laid Ireland to waste after Efnisien had destroyed the cauldron. However, so great was the destruction that only seven of the invading Welsh survived, and only five pregnant Irish women lived on, for they had taken refuge in a cave. Bendigeid Vran himself was mortally wounded and, before he died, ordered the seven survivors to remove his head and bury it under the WHITE MOUNT in LONDON, face towards FRANCE, there to serve as a guardian to the island.

The seven – TALIESIN, PRYDERI, MANAWYDAN FAB LLYR, GLIFIEU, YNAWAG, GRUDDIEU and HEILYN – brought Branwen back to Wales, but, on their arrival in ANGLESEY, she sat down and looked back towards Ireland. Thinking of the destruction that had been brought about on her behalf, she died of a broken heart, and was buried at BEDD BRANWEN on the banks of the River ALAW, a site that was excavated in 1813, when the cremated remains of a woman were discovered in a contemporary urn.

The five Irish survivors all gave birth to sons. When they were of age, each of the five women took one of them for husband, founded the five provinces of Ireland, and set about repopulating the decimated island.

## Branwen ferch Llyr
*Welsh*

*Branwen, Daughter of Llyr*, one of the four main stories of the *Mabinogion*, concerns the fate of BRANWEN and the destructive expedition mounted by BENDIGEID VRAN to IRELAND.

## Brea
*Irish*

A contemporary of PARTHOLÁN, who is named as the first man ever to build a house or make a cauldron.

## Bregia
*Irish*

A giant whose three herdsmen attempted to attack CÚ CHULAINN but were killed.

## Bregon
*Irish*

The descendant of a Scythian noble expelled from Egypt who settled in Spain. Bregon built a high tower from which his son, ITH, sighted the far-off land of IRELAND. This sighting led to the invasion of Ireland by the Sons of MÍL ÉSPÁINE, although not directly, for the story that tells of this sighting says that Ith was the first to land in Ireland, having travelled there with ninety followers. At first he was received warmly by the TUATHA DÉ DANANN, but, after he had so richly praised the fertility of the land, the

Tuatha Dé Danann suspected him of having designs on the island and killed him. His body was taken back to Spain by his companions, and it was this event that led to the subsequent invasion.

## Breng
*Irish*

'Lie', one of the three names of the wife of the DAGHDHA. Her other names were MENG and MEABEL.

## Brennius
*British*

A son of MOLMUTIUS and TONWENNA and the brother of BELINUS. After their father's death the two brothers quarrelled over who should reign in his place. The quarrel was settled by arbitration, and Belinus became king with Brennius, subject to him, as the overlord of the region north of the Humber. After five years of peace, Brennius was persuaded to rebel and travelled to Norway where he married the king's daughter and sailed back with a large army. Belinus, who had received intelligence of the impending attack, was ready to meet his brother as he attempted to land in NORTHUMBRIA. Belinus routed the Norwegians, and Brennius was forced to flee to GAUL. There he married for a second time and again raised an army against his brother. He crossed the Channel at the head of a Gaulish army, but Tonwenna intervened, and the two brothers were reconciled, the Gaulish army staying in BRITAIN[1]. Sometime later the two brothers crossed the Channel, the Gaulish army with them, subdued the Gauls and marched on Italy where they sacked Rome. Brennius stayed in Rome, while Belinus came home and ruled in peace for the rest of his life.

Brennius appears to have been a figment of GEOFFREY OF MONMOUTH's imagination, for the Celtic sack of Rome, which occurred in 390 BC, was led by a Gaul by the name of BRENNOS[2]. The slight change in name and definite change in nationality appear to have been Geoffrey of Monmouth's way of claiming the victory for the British.

## Brenn-os, -us
*Gaulish*

1 An ancient god to whom the Celts attributed their success in the battles of Allia and Delphi, and who was mistaken by Roman and Greek chroniclers for a human leader.
2 The Gaulish leader of the Celtic forces that sacked Rome in 390 BC. He is usually confused with BRENNOS[1].

## Bres
*Irish*

1 During the First Battle of MAGH TUIREDH, NUADHA, the king of the TUATHA DÉ DANANN, lost an arm, and, because the king had to be physically unblemished, he could no longer reign and abdicated in favour of Bres, who had been raised among the Tuatha Dé Danann, his mother's people, even though his father, ELATHA, was a FOMHOIRÉ leader.

Bres was not a good ruler, even though his alternative name of GORMAC means 'dutiful son', being both tyrannical and mean, offering no form of entertainment to his followers and making even the greatest of them toil like common slaves. He married BRIGHID, the daughter of the DAGHDHA, but compelled her father to build him a fort. He treated OGHMA with contempt and made him collect firewood. Unable to stand the tyranny any longer, COIRBRE, the FILI of the Tuatte Dé

Danann, cursed Bres in a magical satire that made his face erupt in boils. Forced to abdicate, he defected to the Fomhoiré and mustered an army against his former people.

During the Second Battle of Magh Tuiredh, Bres was captured and pleaded for his life, promising in return four harvests a year and continual supplies of milk from the Tuatha Dé Danann's cows. These offers were rejected, but his life was spared in return for essential advice on the best times to plough, sow and reap.

2 The brother of MEDHBA, CLOTHRU, Ethne, LOTHAR and NÁR.

3 The emissary of the TUATHA DÉ DANANN who met with the emissary of the FIR BHOLG before the First Battle of MAGH TUIREDH. He proposed that the two factions should divide the land equally, but this was not to be and he was killed in the resulting battle. See also SRENG.

## Bresal Echarlam mac Echach Baethlaim
*Irish*

A hero at TARA whose name was given by the door-keeper to LUGH when that god was attempting to gain entry to the royal court. How he became a hero or why he was regarded as one is not recorded.

## Brí
*Irish*

The daughter of MIDHIR who was loved by LIATH. When Liath attempted to meet with Brí, her father's attendants kept him at bay with a barrage of slingshots. Liath was forced to retreat after his servant had been killed, and Brí died of a broken heart.

## Brí Leith
*Irish*

The SÍDH in County Longford, IRELAND, that was the home of MIDHIR, a god of TÍR TAIRNGIRI. Although the sídh was an OTHERWORLDLY home, a home of the dead, Midhir had, like MANANNÁN MAC LIR, associations with rebirth.

## Brian
*Irish*

A son of TUIRENN and brother of IUCHAR and IUCHARBA. Some name his mother as DANU, and it is thought that the three brothers are, in true Celtic style, really three aspects of the same person, Brian being a form of the Gaulish BRENNOS[1], the god to whom the GAULS attributed their success at the battles of Allia and Delphi.

For a long time the three brothers had been involved in a blood feud with CIAN, the father of LUGH. While Cian was travelling to ULSTER to muster an army, he was intercepted and killed by the three brothers. Lugh discovered this and punished them by setting increasingly difficult tasks that would arm him for the forthcoming Second Battle of MAGH TUIREDH. The first task consisted of collecting three apples that were as large as a baby's head and that could cure all wounds and ailments. The second was to obtain a magical pigskin that had the same properties. The third was to collect a spear whose point was so hot that it had to be housed in a block of ice. The fourth was to procure a chariot and its horses that could outrun the wind over both land and water. The fifth was to collect the seven magical swine of King ASAL, which could be eaten one day but reappear again the next, ready and willing to be eaten again. The sixth was to obtain a young dog that was so awful it terrified every other beast in the world.

The seventh was to collect a cooking spit from the sunken island of FINCHORY. The eighth and final task was to shout three times from the top of a hill owned by MIODCHAOIN, a king who was a close friend of Cian, and who was, with his sons, under a bond never to allow any man to raise his voice on the hill.

The three brothers completed the first seven tasks with relative ease, but were almost killed as they attempted to carry out the last task. Finally, they feebly gave the three required shouts, but lay mortally wounded. Lugh refused to heal them using the pigskin they had obtained for him and thus they died.

## Briccne
*Irish*

The name of the monk who advised MAÍL DÚIN of the identity of the murderers of his father.

## Bricriu
*Irish*

'Poisoned Tongue', a malicious hero who built a wonderful hall and gave a feast for all the men of ULSTER and CONNACHT, threatening untold strife if either party refused to attend. As it was customary for the most notable warrior present to carve the roast, there was much competition for the honour. Bricriu secretly persuaded three heroes, LOEGHAIRE BUADHACH, CONALL CERNACH and CÚ CHULAINN, all to claim this honour. A brawl ensued, which resulted in the three being sent to Connacht to seek the judgement of MEDHBHA. She awarded the victor's palm to Cú Chulainn. However, when the three returned, Loeghaire Buadhach and Conall Cernach refused to acknowledge the verdict, saying that Cú Chulainn had undoubtedly bribed the queen. Bricriu then sent the three to the King of MUNSTER, CÚ ROÍ MAC DÁIRI, who also awarded the honour of carving the roast to Cú Chulainn. Again, the other two refused to accept the verdict, but Cú Roí mac Dáiri proved his verdict to be correct, and finally the right of Cú Chulainn was accepted. Following the débâcle nobody would have anything to do with Bricriu, and he remained a social outcast for the rest of his life.

## Brid(e)
*Irish*

A virgin deity who later became known as BRIGHID, or Bride, and then St Bride. Her attributes were light, inspiration and the skills associated with fire, such as metal-working and purification. Like Vesta of classical Roman mythology, a perpetual flame was kept burning in her honour. A genealogy, of sorts, for St Bride exists in a chanted protective prayer.

## Bridei
*Welsh*

The son of MAELGWYN who became King of the PICTS after he had been invited to assume the crown. A formidable figure, he conquered most of the western Highlands. St COLUMBA was reported to have visited him, travelling to him along the valley that is today filled with the waters of Loch Ness. Within this great valley there was a well that never dried up and whose waters had to be contained by a heavy lid. One day a woman left the cap off and the valley filled with water, at which the people cried 'Tha loch nis ann!' ('There is a lake there now!'), which is why the lake is called Loch Ness. This event was supposed to have happened while Columba was on his way to Bridei at Inverness.

## Brigantes
*British*

An ancient and powerful Celtic people of northern England whose tutelary goddess was BRIGANTIA, hence their name. CARATACUS, king of the CATUVELLAUNI, was traditionally handed over to the Romans with whom he was at war by CARTIMANDUA, Queen of the Brigantes.

## Briganti(a)
*British*

Almost certainly to be identified with the Irish BRIGHID, Brigantia was the tutelary goddess of the BRIGANTES. A pastoral and river goddess, whose name means 'High One', Brigantia was inextricably connected to flocks and cattle, for she was said to have been reared on the milk of a white, red-eared cow, a beast that came from the OTHERWORLD.

The powerful queen CARTIMANDUA worshipped Brigantia almost exclusively over other Celtic deities. Brigantia, the highest goddess of English Celtic belief was depicted in several ways, although all seem to have some aspect of the warrior within them. She was crowned on top of a globe, the symbol of victory; armed and wearing a breast-plate; or bare-breasted in the company of the war god and a ram-headed serpent. Her therapeutic aspects came through her associations with water, both the rivers Briant and Brent being named after her. A third-century inscription on Hadrian's Wall identifies Brigantia with DEA CAELISTIS.

## Briggidda
*Irish and British*

An early form of BRIDE/BRIGHID, but, so it would appear, slightly later in date than the earliest form of all, BRID.

## Brig(h)id
*Gaulish, Irish and British*

1 Goddess of poetry, handicrafts and learning. The daughter of the DAGHDHA, she had two sisters, BRIGHID[2] and BRIGHID[3]. She was especially worshipped by the FILIDH who were under her direct inspiration. Brighid was Christianized as Brighid or BRIDE, her popularity in both pagan and Christian times being attested to by the many sites that bear her name. The worship of Brighid survived well into the Christian era in both IRELAND and SCOTLAND, where pagan-Christian prayers and ceremonies in her honour were carried out until at least as recently as the nineteenth and early twentieth centuries. Sometimes equated with BRIGANTIA, which is possibly an early form of her name, it was reported by the medieval chronicler GIRALDUS CAMBRENSIS that an eternal sacred fire was kept burning at her shrine at Kildare, southern Ireland.

It is not unusual for Brighid, whose name means 'exalted one', to be amalgamated with her two sisters into a single goddess, who was said to be the goddess of smiths and metal-working, poetry, inspiration, healing and fertility, the name Brighid being used as a generic name for the goddess. Her primal function, as the burning of an eternal flame would suggest, was that of fire and illumination. In many Romano-Celtic temples she was frequently amalgamated with the goddess Minerva. As the patroness of *filidhecht*, or poetry, she was of great importance to the DRUIDIC tradition, which also made her the goddess of divination.

2 Sister of BRIGHID[1] and BRIGHID[3], hence a daughter of the DAGHDHA, this Brighid was the goddess of smiths and metal-working.

3 Sister to BRIGHID[1] and BRIGHID[2], hence a daughter of the DAGHDHA, this Brighid was the goddess of healing and fertility.

## Brighid, St
*Irish*

The Christianized version of the old Celtic goddess BRIGHID[1], although her attributes seem to suggest that she is in fact the amalgamation of all three of the Brighids who were daughters of the DAGHDHA. Legend says that she was born at sunrise on the threshold of the house, being fed on the milk of a supernatural cow. This would appear to incorporate the nourishment of the goddess BRIGANTIA, herself thought to be an early version of Brighid[1], into the Christian saint. Christian folk tradition says that she was the midwife and foster mother of the baby Jesus.

It was said that any house in which she stayed was filled with light. She was attended by nineteen nuns who helped her to guard a perpetual fire in a grotto surrounded by a hedge, a precinct into which no man was permitted to enter. Her feast-day was 1 February, the old Celtic feast of IMBOLC, and her primal function was that of fire and illumination.

## Brigindo
*Gaulish*

A variant of BRIGHID, which is found on a few inscriptions in GAUL.

## Brigit
*British*

A variant of BRIGHID. It is also possible that Brigit was the origin of the goddess BRIGANTIA, the tutelary deity of the powerful BRIGANTES.

## Britain

1 (*General*). An island in northwest Europe, which is thought to derive its name from *Priteni*, the name the PICTS used for themselves, and which consists of the countries of ENGLAND, SCOTLAND and WALES. The country has had a long and chequered history of invasion and conquest, a history that has all but destroyed the Celtic tradition in England, although it remains in fragmentary form in the west country, especially CORNWALL, and in Wales. Scotland was never a true Celtic domain, although a number of Celtic stories involve that country.

In legend the island was first ruled over by a giant named ALBION, whose name was subsequently poetically applied to the island and whose career was outlined in Holinshed's *Chronicles* of 1577. Surprisingly, GEOFFREY OF MONMOUTH does not mention Albion, instead simply saying that giants predated men in Britain. He continues to say that Britain was colonized by BRUTUS, a descendant of the Graeco-Roman AENEAS, and that the island then maintained its independence until the Roman invasion.

The *White Book of Rhydderch*, which dates from the fourteenth century, gives an entirely different – and decidedly Welsh – early history, saying that the country was first called Myrddin's Precinct, MYRDDIN being latinized to the more famous variant of MERLIN in the text. It was then known as the Isle of Honey before becoming Britain, the country allegedly being named after PRYDEIN, son of AEDD (who may be cognate with the Irish sun god AEDH), had conquered it. Unsurprisingly Geoffrey of Monmouth makes no mention of this concept.

Other traditions say that Prydein

came from Cornwall and conquered Britain after the death of PORREX, the latter appearing as one of the successors of Brutus in Geoffrey of Monmouth. Irish tradition says that the country was named after BRITAIN[2], the son of NEMEDIUS, who settled on the island. Still others say that Britain simply derives from the Latin name for the island – *Britannia*.

Histories of Britain before the Roman invasion and occupation tell us little more than the legendary concepts. Archaeology is perhaps the best guide. Prior to 2800 BC the inhabitants were Neolithic hill farmers. These were followed by people who worked both copper and gold, and who were, in all probability, true Celts. At some stage Celts who were able to work iron became the dominant people, but even archaeologists find it difficult to put a date to the start of their pre-eminence. JULIUS CAESAR made exploratory expeditions to Britain, but it was not until the reign of CLAUDIUS that the Roman occupation began. Eventually Rome abandoned Britain and left it to fend for itself against the PICTS from the north, the Irish from the west, and the ANGLES, SAXONS and JUTES from the east.

2 (*Irish*). The son of NEMEDIUS who is considered, by some, as the eponym of BRITAIN[1], the country in which he settled. His name is sometimes spelt Britan.

## Britan
*Irish*
See BRITAIN[2].

## Brittany
*General*

A province of northwestern FRANCE that, following the Roman occupation of BRITAIN[1], was largely inhabited by an immigrant British population. GEOFFREY OF MONMOUTH says that the Breton royal family was closely related to the British one, that the kingdom was formed when the Roman emperor MAXIMIANUS (reigned 383–388) bestowed the crown on Conan Meriadoc, a nephew of Octavius, who is elsewhere called EUDAF, King of Britain. When the British needed, and indeed wanted, a king, ALDROENUS, the successor of Conan Meriadoc, gave the Britons his brother CONSTANTINE[1].

## Britto
*British*

A variant of BRUTUS, found in the writings of NENNIUS[1].

## Britu
*British*

The son of VORTIGERN by SEVIRA.

## Broadb
*Irish*

The brother of OENGHUS MAC IN OG.

## Brochmail
*Welsh*

A legendary king of the Welsh kingdom of POWYS, who is said to have reigned some time during the fifth or sixth centuries. His name appears on a pillar near the ruins of Valle Crucis Abbey in CLYWD. This pillar was erected by CYNGEN FAB CADELL, the last King of Powys, who died in Rome in 854. The pillar, which is now known as the Pillar of ELISEG, contains an inscription that appears to give the descent of the kings of Powys. The inscription makes Brochmael the son of Eliseg and the father of CADELL.

## Brogan
*Irish*

The scribe to St PATRICK by whom he was employed to write down the legends surrounding FIONN MAC CUMHAILL and the FIAN.

## Brugh na -Bóinne, -Boyna
*Irish*

The home of OENGHUS MAC IN OG, the son of the DAGHDHA. It is located in an area formed by a twist in the River BOYNE between the present-day towns of Slane and Oldbridge. This mound is, after TARA itself, the most important Bronze Age relic in IRELAND.

Brugh na Bóinne, or NEW GRANGE, is an earth mound some 36 feet high and shaped like an inverted saucer. An entrance hall, lined with slabs of stone, runs 60 feet into the mound before opening out into a spacious chamber approximately 20 feet high. The roof of this chamber is corbelled – that is, it is made of overlapping stones with a circular stone to finish it off at its centre. It is so well constructed that the interior was bone dry when it was discovered in 1699 by Edward Lhwyd.

Excavations at Brugh na Bóinne have revealed an unusual opening above the entrance that allows the morning sun on the winter solstice to illuminate the central chamber, shining directly onto three linked spirals carved into the wall. By itself this is not particularly remarkable, but the entrance hall is slightly curved, and yet the sun manages to slice through at a precise angle and light up the design. This feat of engineering, coupled with the excellence of the construction and ornamentation, indicates that Brugh na Bóinne was constructed by a highly refined people.

The entrance stone to the tumulus is perhaps the finest example of megalithic art in western Europe. It is finely carved with a complex pattern of arcs, spirals and diamonds, the entire surface being finely textured with dots which gives it a rich green colour.

The date of the construction of Brugh na Bóinne is still open to question. Radiocarbon dating places this at about 2500 BC, but current thinking makes the tumulus at least 500 years earlier, thus making it contemporary with the construction of the pyramids in Egypt. Regrettably, the exact purpose of Brugh na Bóinne, other than its legendary connection with Oenghus Mac in Og, will never be known as the Danes plundered the site in the ninth century.

## Bruighean Caorthuinn
*Irish*

*The Fairy Palace of the Quicken-trees*, an ancient text that tells the story of FIONN MAC CUMHAILL when he defeated and killed the King of LOCHLANN but spared his son MIDAC whom he brought up in his own household. Later Midac had his revenge by inviting the FIAN to visit him at his palace, a magically created place known as the Palace of the Quicken-trees. Once inside, the FIAN found themselves fastened to their seats and unable to move. DIARMAID UA DUIBHNE arrived and fought the army of Midac and, entering the palace, released the trapped members of the fian using the blood of three kings. A later addition to the story recounts how the blood ran out before Diarmaid ua Duibhne got to CONAN MAC MORNA. Conan mac Morna chided Diarmaid ua Duibhne for leaving him to last, whereupon Diarmaid ua Duibhne took a firm hold of Conan mac Morna and wrenched him free of the seat, leaving a large patch of his skin behind.

## Brutus
*Graeco-Romano-British*

The legendary founder of the British people, the great-grandson of the Trojan AENEAS, he traditionally conquered BRITAIN[1] from the giants and founded LONDON, naming it TROIA NOVA ('New Troy').

Expelled from Italy for accidentally killing his father SILVIUS, Brutus first went to Greece where he found a group of Trojan exiles enslaved by King PANDRASUS whom he fought and defeated. He claimed the reluctant hand of Pandrasus' daughter, IGNOGE (anglicized as IMOGEN), and compelled Pandrasus not only to release his prisoners but also to supply them with ships, provisions and bullion. Well-equipped, Brutus and the Trojans sailed west and discovered another group of Trojan exiles under the leadership of CORINEUS. They joined forces and sailed to ENGLAND, landing at TOTNES, Devon, where they were attacked by the giants who at that time inhabited England. The giants were led by GOGMAGOG whom Corineus defeated in single combat at Plymouth. Brutus then marched to the banks of the River Thames where he founded his capital city, Troia Nova, and where he was eventually buried.

GEOFFREY OF MONMOUTH, who recounts his story, makes Brutus the traditional founder of the British people, the progenitor of a line of kings and the eponym of Britain itself.

## Brychan (Brycheiniog)
*Welsh*

An early legendary king of POWYS, although some sources make him a fifth-century British chieftain. He is alleged to have been the father of as many as sixty-three saints, including St Gwladys. He was also said to have been the grand-father of URIEN of RHEGED by way of his daughter NEFYN. His alleged grave is marked by an old stone with a ring cross on it in Llanspyddid Church, near Brecon, Powys.

## Bryn Gwyn
*Welsh*

'White Mount', the Welsh for the mount in LONDON on which the White Tower within the Tower of London now stands. Legend says that this is the place where the severed head of BENDIGEID VRAN was buried by the seven survivors of the disastrous expedition to IRELAND to avenge the cruelty shown to Bendigeid Vran's sister BRANWEN by her Irish husband MATHOLWCH.

## Buan
*Irish*

The daughter of SAMERA. She fell in love with CÚ CHULAINN but died when her head hit a rock as she fell in an attempt to leap onto Cú Chulainn's chariot.

## Buda
*Irish*

A shrewd old man who sometimes appears in translations of the *Fledd Bricrenn* as one of the many judges of the right to be called Champion of all IRELAND that was being contested by CÚ CHULAINN, LOEGHAIRE BUADHACH and CONALL CERNACH. Buda arranged the contest by which a giant should cut off the heads of each of the three contestants, after they had first cut off his own head. Loeghaire Buadhach and Conall Cernach obviously believed that the giant would be dead if they cut off his head, for they refused the giant his turn, but Cú Chulainn duly knelt down, and the giant proclaimed him the champion by right.

This story is usually associated with the judgements of AILILL, MEDHBHA and CÚ ROÍ MAC DÁIRI, although it may be that the usually accepted version of the *Fledd Bricrenn* is an abridged version and that this portion of the story belongs in the full rendition.

## Budic(ius)
*Gaulish*

According to GEOFFREY OF MONMOUTH, the name of two early kings of BRITTANY. One is purely Arthurian in nature and was said to have married ARTHUR's sister. The other was said to have raised the exiled AMBROSIUS AURELIUS and UTHER. Budic is, in all probability, identifiable with King Budic I of Cornouaille, who traditionally reigned in Brittany some time before 530.

## Buic
*Irish*

The son of BANBLAI who was killed by CÚ CHULAINN as he escorted the captured DONN CUAILNGE to the camp of AILILL and MEDHBHA.

## Buichet
*Irish*

The foster mother to the six foster children of DERBRENN who had turned them into six swine. Buichet craved to eat them, so they fled to OENGHUS MAC IN OG for help. He refused until a year later, but by that time five had been killed, and the sole survivor lived a life of solitary grief.

## Buino
*Irish*

A son of FERGUS MAC ROICH and brother of ILLAN. When his father was obliged to

feast with BARUCH on his return from SCOTLAND with DERDRIU and the sons of UISNECH, he and his brother escorted the four to EMHAIN MHACHA. He was persuaded to desert his charges by CONCHOBAR MAC NESSA, who bribed him with a great estate, a desertion that led to the death of his brother when Conchobar mac Nessa attacked and killed the sons of Uisnech.

## Bwlch-y-Groes
*Welsh*

A pass through the mountains on the highest road in north WALES above Tan-y-Bwlch. Here lived the giant RHITTA who had a penchant for collecting beards from the men he killed in order to make a cloak. One day, however, the man he picked on killed him and threw him down the hillside, where he was buried, presumably because he was too heavy to be carried off and buried elsewhere. A path leads down the hill to Tan-y-Bwlch, which is known as RHIW BARFE, 'The Way of the Bearded One'. The giant's grave consists of a long, narrow trench surrounded by large boulders.

The alternative site for this battle, and for the giant's grave, is YR WYDDFA FAWR, or Mount SNOWDON. This tale was later embroidered to make the vanquisher of Rhitta none other than King ARTHUR, who obviously had no desire to part with his own beard.

## Byanu
*Irish*

A controversial name, which is only found in one OGHAM inscription on the eastern seaboard of the USA. It is possibly a derivation of DANU, but it is the location of the inscription that proves so controversial. To date, there has been no conclusive evidence that the Celts ever conquered the Atlantic, but existence of the Ogham inscription in America would seem to suggest that this was, indeed, the case. The problem remains, however, that, if the Celts did make the passage, why did they change the name of the goddess from Danu to Byanu? Until conclusive proof comes to light, the question of the Celts sailing the Atlantic will provide scholars with food for endless discussion and argument.

## Cadair Idris
*Welsh*

A mountain in GWYNEDD. The name means the chair or seat of IDRIS, a legendary Welsh giant, although this may refer to his intellect rather than his physical size, for he was reputed to have been a poet, astronomer and philosopher. A chamber formed by massive rocks on the summit was thought to have been his 'observatory', while the hollow formed by LLYN CAU, a small lake on the south side of the mountain, was his 'chair'. Popular legend holds that anyone who dares to sleep on the summit of Cadair Idris, or, come to that, of Mount SNOWDON, will be found the next morning as a corpse, a madman or a brilliant poet.

Another small lake on the mountain is called Llyn-y-tri graienyn, 'The Lake of the Three Pebbles'. Its name is derived from three boulders standing near it, boulders that Idris found in his shoe, which he emptied out where they now stand. One of these boulders is 24 feet long, 18 feet wide and 12 feet high, a measure of the size of Idris.

## Cadair, neu car Morgan Mwynfawr
*Welsh*

The chair of MORGAN MWYNFAWR, which had the power to carry a person seated in it anywhere they desired to go. It numbered among the THIRTEEN TREASURES of BRITAIN[1].

## Cadell
*Welsh*

A legendary king of the Welsh kingdom of POWYS, who was said to have reigned sometime during the fifth or sixth centuries. His name appears on a pillar known as the Pillar of ELISEG, near the ruins of Valle Crucis Abby in CLYWD. This pillar, which was allegedly raised by CONCENN or CYNGEN FAB CADELL, the son of Cadell, gives a list of the legendary kings of Powys, although not all of the inscription was readable when the pillar was examined in 1696 by Edward Llwyd. According to this inscription, Cadell was the son of BROCHMAIL and the father of Concenn.

## Cador

1 (*British*) A ruler of CORNWALL, variously described as a king or a duke. He played a major part in the defeat of the SAXONS. Later tradition made him an ally of King ARTHUR, his son CONSTANTINE[2] succeeding that legendary monarch.
2 (*Welsh*) A King of NORTHUMBRIA, whose daughter ANDRIVETE circumvented the usurping plans of her uncle AYGLIN by marrying CEI.

## Cadwallad(e)r
*Welsh*

An historical seventh-century hero, the

son of CADWALLON, king of the VENDOTI. He defeated and killed Edwin of NORTHUMBRIA in 633 but, approximately one year later, was himself killed in battle. Cadwallader features in the *Armes Prydein*, which foretells that he will rise again and lead an army that will drive the SAXONS back into the sea. Welsh tradition makes him a saint who was active in and around ANGLESEY and CARMARTHEN.

## Cadwallon
*Welsh*

The father of CADWALLADER, according to GEOFFREY OF MONMOUTH, and king of the VENDOTI who lived in north WALES.

## Caer

1 (*Welsh*). The Welsh for an earthen barrow, the equivalent of the Irish SÍDH. Where Caer appears as part of a name, either on its own or incorporated into a longer word, it is usually a reference to an OTHERWORLDLY abode.
2 (*Irish*). The daughter of ETHAL ANUBAL, a TUATHA DÉ DANANN prince of CONNACHT. OENGHUS MAC IN OG fell in love with her after she had appeared to him in a dream, but no matter how hard he searched he could not find her. Turning for help to BODB, Oenghus Mac in Og had to wait a year before Bodb reported that he had found his 'dream maiden' on the banks of a lake along with her 149 sisters. Ethal Anubal refused to hand over his daughter, and he was taken prisoner by AILILL and the DAGHDHA. Still he refused to hand over his daughter, as he feared her magical powers. Finally, Oenghus Mac in Og travelled to the lake and explained to Caer his love for her. She consented, her father was released, and the two, in the form of swans, flew away to BRUGH NA BÓINNE.

## Caer Arianrhod
*Welsh*

The palace of ARIANRHOD, which legend locates on ANGLESEY, although folk tradition makes it a sunken and lost land in the centre of Caernarvon Bay. This folk tradition places the castle three-quarters of a mile offshore, near Dinas Dinlle, GWYNEDD, on the northwest side of the Lleyn Peninsula. It appears as a reef of stones that is laid bare at low tide, the sea having smothered her castle in revenge for her harsh treatment of LLEU LLAW GYFFES. A couple of miles further south MAEN DYLAN stands on a stretch of gravel. This marks the alleged grave of Arianrhod's first-born son, DYLAN EIL TON.

## Caer Dathyl
*Welsh*

The court of MATH FAB MATHONWY, although some sources say it is the home of GWYDION FAB DÔN.

## Caer Feddwid(d)
*Welsh*

The Fort of CAROUSAL, which is located in ANNWFN. Caer Feddwidd is a paradisal kingdom in which a fountain runs with wine and no one ever knows illness or old age. Later tradition says it was visited by King ARTHUR and his company. See also CAER SIDDI.

## Caer L(l)ud(d)
*Welsh*

'Lludd's Fort', the ancient name for the city of LONDON after LLUDD had rebuilt it, though some say that the name is derived from LUGH, the god of light. Later it became known as CAER LUNDEIN and still later as LUNDEIN or LWNDRYS.

## Caer Luel
*British*

The name of the ancient Celtic city that is today known as CARLISLE. The Romans under Agricola seized the town in AD 80 and made it their regional capital, naming it *Luguvallium*. Caer Luel was located at the convergence of three rivers, the Eden, the Calder and the Petteril. Such places have a magical quality that tend to make them the centre of legendary landscapes. Legends abound in the region surrounding Carlisle about a former kingdom, known as RHEGED, which flourished in the seventh century.

## Caer L(l)undein
*Welsh*

A later name for CAER LLUDD, or ancient LONDON. It is quite easy to see that London is a simple derivative of Lundein.

## Caer Rigor
*Welsh*

An alternative name for CAER FEDDWIDD. This variant, which shares the same attributes as Caer Feddwidd, suggests a paradisal realm of the dead from which there is no return.

## Caer Siddi
*Welsh*

An alternative name for CAER FEDDWIDD, the OTHERWORLDLY Fort of CAROUSAL, which shares the same attribute of a fountain that runs with wine. Under this name the realm was said to have been ruled by ARIANRHOD.

## Caer Wydyr
*Welsh*

A glass fort, which is located in ANNWFN, the Welsh OTHERWORLD. Later tradition says that, like CAER FEDDWIDD, it was visited by King ARTHUR and his company.

## Caerleon-on-Usk
*Welsh*

An important Celtic city on the River Usk in GWENT, southern WALES. It is the site of a Roman amphitheatre and fort. GEOFFREY OF MONMOUTH calls it the 'City of the Legions' and claims that it was founded by a King BELINUS, who is perhaps the ancient legendary king BELI MAWR. Later tradition connected the city with King ARTHUR.

## Cai
*Welsh*
See CEI.

## Caibell
*Irish*

A supernatural king who had a beautiful daughter, a trait he shared with his ally ÉTAR. Two earthly kings sought the hands of the daughters and were offered battle for them. The battle took place at night so that there could be no distinction between earthly warriors and those of the two kings, who inhabited neighbouring SÍDH. The battle was so ferocious that four hillocks were made from the antlers of those killed, for the two kings and their followers appeared as deer. Finally a lake had to be formed to quell the fighting. Caibell was killed, as were the two earthly kings. Only Étar survived.

### Cailleach Beara
*Irish*

'Hag of Beare', an ancient deity whose name is more recent. She appears to be a remembrance of an earlier MOTHER GODDESS or guardian spirit whose haunt is the wilds of the Beare peninsula from which she takes her name.

### Cairbr-e, -y
*Irish*

The son of CORMAC MAC AIRT, whom he succeeded as King of IRELAND. The hand of his daughter SGEIMH SOLAIS was sought by a son of the King of the DECIES. The FIAN then claimed a tribute, which, so they claimed, was customarily paid to them on these occasions, but Cairbre refused to pay and went to war against the fian. At the Battle of GABHRA, when the majority of the fian were wiped out, Cairbre killed OSCAR, the son of OISÎN, in single combat, but received mortal wounds from which he quickly died.

### Cairbre
*Irish*
See CAIRPRE NIAPER.

### Cairenn
*Irish*

A SAXON from BRITAIN[1] who married EOCHU MUGMEDÓN and, by him, became the mother of NÍAL NOÍGIALLACH.

### Cairpre (Niaper)
*Irish*

The father of ERC[2]. Cairpre Niaper was killed, along with CÚ ROÍ MAC DÁIRI, during a fight with CÚ CHULAINN. Erc then marched against Cú Chulainn, one of the events that was to lead to the death of Cú Chulainn.

### Calad-bolg, -cholg
*Irish*

The magical sword carried by CÚ CHULAINN. Its name derives from *calad*, 'hard', and *bolg*, 'lighting', and has been linguistically linked with CALADVWLCH, which is mentioned in the *Mabinogion* story of *Culhwch and Olwen*.

### Caladvwlch
*Welsh*

Linguistically linked to CALADBOLG, this sword appears in the story of *Culhwch and Olwen*. See also EXCALIBUR.

### Calatin
*Irish*

The father of twenty-seven sons who were, together with their father, killed by CÚ CHULAINN. His unnamed wife posthumously bore three monstrous sons and three daughters, who were cared for by MEDHBHA when they studied the magic arts in order to find a way to defeat Cú Chulainn. They later marched with ERC and his companions against Cú Chulainn and took part in the battle that was to lead to Cú Chulainn's death. See also BAVE.

### Caledon
*British*

An ancient name for SCOTLAND. Many authorities believe that this word was simply latinized by the invading Romans (who, of course, never conquered Scotland), to give their name for the country, Caledonia.

## Cambria
*General*

An ancient name for WALES. It is still widely used to refer to items that come from, or are to be found, in Wales, such as the Cambrian Mountains.

## Camulos
*British and Gaulish*

A war deity whose name is to be found in inscriptions in SCOTLAND and GAUL. It is thought that he was the patron deity of COLCHESTER, after whom the Romans named the city Camulodunum. Camulos has been equated with the Roman Mars, and some commentators have sought to make him the original of CUMHAILL, but there is no evidence to suggest that Camulos was worshipped in IRELAND.

## Cano
*Irish*

An historical figure whose death is recorded as having occurred in 688. The son of the Scottish king GARTNÁN, Cano was exiled to IRELAND, where he was entertained by the elderly MARCÁN, whose beautiful young wife CRÉD had fallen in love with Cano even before she first saw him. During a feast given in Cano's honour, Créd drugged the entire company and begged Cano to take her as his mistress, but he refused to do this while he was still in exile. However, so taken with Créd was Cano that he pledged his undying love to her and gave her a stone that embodied his life.

Eventually, Cano was recalled to SCOTLAND following the death of his father, and he became king. Every year he and Créd attempted to meet at Inber Colptha (the BOYNE estuary), but they were always forestalled by her step-son, COLCU, with a guard of one hundred warriors. Frustrated, the pair decided to give it one last go, this time arranging to meet at Lough Créde in the north. As they came within sight of each other, Colcu once again appeared and drove Cano away. Unable to withstand her suffering any longer, Créd jumped from her horse and dashed her brains out on a rock. During the fall from her horse Créd dropped the stone that Cano had given her. It smashed into tiny pieces, and three days later Cano died.

## Canola
*Irish*

A mysterious Irish woman who appears in a story concerning the magic of the Irish harp. She fled from her husband, for reasons unknown, and was lulled to sleep by the sound of sinews clinging to the skeleton of a whale. Her husband found her on the beach and built a framework in which to house the sinews, the very first harp, whose music reconciled the couple.

## Canterbury
*General*

A cathedral city in KENT, which was called Durovernum by the Romans, and was the SAXON capital of Kent. The Celtic church was established at Canterbury in Roman times, but in the fifth century, when the Romans left and the heathen Saxons and JUTES replaced them as the rulers of southeast England, Christianity was extinguished in the city.

Around 580 the local king, Aethelbert, married Bertha, a Christian princess. She brought a chaplain with her, and, although Aethelbert retained his pagan beliefs, he allowed his queen to restore an ancient Christian church to the east of the city. This church, St Martin, is still there and claims to be the oldest Christian church in England.

Canterbury became the home of British Christianity after 597 when Pope Gregory sent St Augustine to ENGLAND. Bertha welcomed the missionary to Canterbury, and before long her husband had accepted Christianity and was baptized in the church of St Martin. Augustine built an abbey in 598, to the east of the city wall, around Aethelbert's pagan temple, which became the Church of St Pancras. A former Celtic Christian church was remodelled as a cathedral, and on his death Augustine was buried in his abbey.

## Cantre'r Gwaelod
*Welsh*

Also known as MAES GWYDDNO, Cantre'r Gwaelod is one of the three lost lands of popular Welsh tradition, the other two being LLYS HELIG and CAER ARIANRHOD. Cantre'r Gwaelod, or 'Lowland Hundred', lies in Cardigan Bay, and was supposedly inundated by the sea in the fifth century, when GWYDDNO GARANHIR, who was also known as DEWRARTH WLEDIG, was Prince of the Hundred.

## Caoilte mac Ronan
*Irish*

One of the warriors, described as the 'fleetest of foot who could overtake the March wind', at the wedding feast of FIONN MAC CUMHAILL, his uncle, and GRÁINNE. He and four others, OISÍN, OSCAR, GOLL MAC MORNA and DIARMAID UA DUIBHNE, were not given the sleeping draught that Gráinne administered, and so witnessed the bond under which she placed Diarmaid ua Duibhne to elope with him, and were instrumental in making sure that he complied, as he was honour bound to do. Later tradition says that Caoilte mac Ronan lived for many hundreds of years after the destruction of the FIAN and is reputed to have told their exploits to St PATRICK.

## Capalu
*Gaulish*

The continental name for the CATH PALUG.

## Caradaw-c, -g

1 (*Welsh*) A son of BENDIGEID VRAN. He headed the council left by his father when he and his troops invaded IRELAND to avenge the mistreatment of BRANWEN at the hands of MATHOLWCH. He was ousted during his father's absence by CASWALLAWN, who usurped Bendigeid Vran's kingdom.

2 (*British*). The son of BRENNIUS who, according to GEOFFREY OF MONMOUTH, lived with his father in Rome after Brennius and BELINUS had sacked the city. It is quite likely that this Caradawc is the same as CARADAWC[1], for Brennius is often regarded as a variant of BRÂN THE BLESSED, the popular name of BENDIGEID VRAN.

## Caradoc Vreichvras
*Welsh*

The son of LLYR MARINI, husband of TEGAU EUFRON, father of MEURIC and owner of the horse LLUAGOR. The legendary ancestor of a ruling dynasty, it is thought that he may have founded the kingdom of GWENT during the fifth century. The epithet *vreichvras* ('strong-armed') is usually misinterpreted as *briefbras* ('short arm'), and it is by this mistranslated epithet that he is most commonly known. Caradoc Briefbras was later to reappear in the Arthurian romances, but his character and lineage were completely altered.

## Caratacus
*British*

The son of CUNOBELINUS and brother of TOGODUMNUS, Caratacus was the King of the CATUVELLAUNI, a tribe of Britons who lived near what is now known as St Albans at the time of the Roman invasion. His historicity is unquestioned. Having led a hard-fought guerilla campaign against the Roman invaders from his stronghold with the support of two Welsh tribes, the SILURES and the ORDOVICES, he was handed over to his enemy by CARTIMANDUA, Queen of the BRIGANTES, but was pardoned by the Emperor CLAUDIUS after he had been taken to Rome. It has been suggested that his story became legendary and that he should be considered as the original King ARTHUR. However, other commentators say that Caratacus should be regarded as identical with ARVIRAGUS, or with Arviragus' cousin.

## Carell
*Irish*

A late ruler of IRELAND and a contemporary of St PATRICK. He is not called 'King', but rather 'Chieftain'. His wife was said to have eaten whole the salmon that was the then incarnation of TUAN MAC STERN, the sole survivor of the invasion of Ireland led by PARTHOLÁN. The salmon turned into a baby within the woman, and nine months later Tuan mac Stern was reborn, thenceforth known as TUAN MAC CARELL.

## Carlisle
*General*

A city of Cumbria, on the confluence of the rivers Eden, Calder and Petteril, which derives its name from CAER LUEL, the Celtic town that was situated on the knoll where the castle now stands. The entire area around the city is shrouded in legends concerning the ancient kingdom of RHEGED, which later passed into the Arthurian cycle.

## Carmac
*Irish*

A legendary ancestor of St BRIDE. He appears in her genealogy as the son of CARRUIN and father of CIS, and thus also an ancestor of the DAGHDHA.

## Carman
*Irish*

The mother of three sons who came from Athens, her home, to blight the TUATHA DÉ DANANN, who sent out AI, CRIDENBÉL, LUGH LAEBACH and BÉCHUILLE to do battle with them. The three were soundly beaten and left Carman behind as surety that they would never return. She died in captivity.

## Carmarthen
*Welsh*

The town in DYFED that can rightly claim to one of the oldest towns in WALES. Probably beginning life as a Celtic hillfort that was obliterated by the Romans who built a wooden fort on its site in AD 75. This was the most westerly of their large forts, but few traces remain. However, the discovery of an amphitheatre with a seating capacity of 500 would seem to suggest that the garrison at Carmarthen was not insignificant.

The town was the alleged birthplace of MYRDDIN and is actually known in Welsh as *Caerfyrddin*, 'the city of Myrddin'. Some suggest that Myrddin took his name from the town, while others say that it was named after him. Whatever the truth, the town certainly has many connections with this famous wizard, better known as

MERLIN, and his prophecies. Probably the best known of these is that concerning the PRIORY OAK or MERLIN'S TREE. Myrddin prophesied that the town would fall if this particular tree ever fell. Its remains now stand in the foyer of St Peter's Civic Hall, because the tree was moved in 1978 by the local authority from its site in the town, since it consisted mainly of concrete and iron bars and this constituted a traffic hazard. Carmarthen, however, is still awaiting the fulfilment of the prophecy, but perhaps simply moving the tree was not enough to bring about the town's downfall.

## Carnedd y Cawr
*Welsh*

'The Giant's Carn', an alternative name for YR WYDDFA FAWR or Mount SNOWDON.

## Carnute
*Gaulish*

The ancient Celtic name for the city of Chartres, FRANCE. JULIUS CAESAR reported that the DRUIDS used to meet at Carnute, while Aventius added that when they were expelled from GAUL by the Emperor Tiberius their sacred groves were felled. However, Carnute retained its holy and mystical connections, which the new Christian faith was eager to absorb, and the site was thus chosen for the building of Chartres Cathedral, which some say covers the earlier meeting place of the DRUIDS.

## Carousal, Fort of
*Welsh*

A literal translation of the OTHER-WORLDLY castle of CAER FEDDWIDD.

## Carrawburgh
*British*

A Roman fort on Hadrian's Wall between Chester and Housesteads. In Roman times a well was sunk and a shrine erected and maintained there to a goddess whose name was revealed as COVENTINA during excavations at the site in 1876. It is unknown whether she was a local or imported deity, but she was obviously a deity of some importance from the sheer quantity of votive offerings discovered in her well.

## Car(r)idwen
*Welsh*

See CERRIDWEN.

## Carruin
*Irish*

The earliest ancestor of St BRIDE to be mentioned in a genealogy that makes Carruin the father of CARMAC.

## Cartimandua
*British*

The queen of the powerful BRIGANTES, who was alleged to have handed CARATACUS, King of the CATUVELLAUNI, over to his enemies, the Romans.

## Cascorach
*Irish*

The minstrel of the TUATHA DÉ DANANN. He is alleged to have lulled St PATRICK and his retinue to sleep with his music, a fact recorded by BROGAN, St Patrick's scribe.

## Casnar
*Welsh*

A British prince who is described as

belonging to the same lineage as GWYN GOHOYW, whose daughter, CIGFA, married PRYDERI.

## Cassivelaunus
British

The brother of LUD and NENNIUS[2], whom the Welsh call CASWALLAWN and make the brother of LLUDD, LLEFELYS and NYNNIAW[3]. Because Lud's sons were too young to succeed their dead father, the throne passed to Cassivelaunus, who made the two young men, ANDROGEUS and TENU-ANTIUS, the Dukes of KENT and CORNWALL respectively. Twice Cassivelaunus repelled the Romans under the leadership of JULIUS CAESAR, but was defeated in a battle near CANTERBURY after ANDROGEUS had betrayed his uncle to the Romans. Cassivelaunus capitulated and agreed to become a vassal king. After he died and was buried at YORK, he was succeeded by Tenuantius, as Androgeus had travelled to Rome where he remained until he died.

History reveals that Cassivelaunus was the king of the CATUVELLAUNI, although his power drew respect from much further afield. His capital was later called Verulamium by the Romans, a city that is today known as St Albans.

## Caswallawn
British

The son of BELI and the conqueror of the ISLAND OF THE MIGHTY, thus disinheriting MANAWYDAN FAB LLYR, the brother and heir of BENDIGEID VRAN, and cousin of PRYDERI.

A separate Welsh tradition makes Caswallawn the brother of LLUDD, LLEFELYS and NYNNIAW[2], thus having his origin in CASSIVELAUNUS, the historical king of the CATUVELLAUNI at the time of the first Roman incursion led by JULIUS CAESAR.

## Cath Fi(o)nntrá(ga)
Irish

The Battle of Ventry, a story in which the TUATHA DÉ DANANN helped the members of the FIAN in battle against an unnamed enemy, referred to simply as 'big men', presumably giants. Magical weapons were conveyed to FIONN MAC CUMHAILL by LABHRAIDH LAMFHADA, weapons that had been made by Tadg and which are recorded as shooting balls of fire. Other weapons were forged for the fian by the one-eyed, one-legged ROC, a smith god who only appears in this story.

## Cath Godeu
Welsh

A mythical battle in which ARAWN was defeated by AMAETHON, one of the sons of DÔN, who was helped by the magic of his brother GWYDION FAB DÔN. The battle came about after Amaethon had brought up several animals up from ANNWFN, the OTHERWORLD, the realm of Arawn.

## Cath Maighe Tuiredh
Irish

The Battle of Magh Tuiredh, an important part of the BOOK OF LEINSTER, which recounts the First and Second Battles of MAGH TUIREDH, and thus records much of the early mythological history of IRELAND.

## Cath Palug
Welsh

A monstrous member of the cat family, whose name means 'clawing cat'. It was one of the vile offspring of the pig HÊN WEN and was thrown into the sea from whence it was saved and raised by the sons of PALUG on ANGLESEY, where it grew to an enormous size and proceeded to devour at least 180 warriors. The Welsh poem *Pa Gur* tells how CEI travelled to Anglesey with a view to killing lions and especially prepared himself for a meeting with the Cath Palug. Unfortunately, this poem is incomplete, but it may have told how Cei defeated the animal. Another tradition says that the Cath Palug was the offspring of CERRIDWEN, who was also sometimes known as Hên Wen. The continental name for the Cath Palug was CAPALU.

## Cathb(h)a(d)(h)
*Irish*

The DRUID who foretold that DERDRIU, the daughter of FEDLIMID, FILI to CONCHOBAR MAC NESSA, would be exceptionally beautiful but the cause of much suffering and torment within ULSTER. He is also reputed to have told the youth SÉDANTA that his life would be short but glorious. Shortly afterwards, this youth killed the hound of CULANN, and thence became known as CÚ CHULAINN. Cathbhadh is the grandfather of Cú Chulainn according to a traditional genealogy, which shows that DEICHTINE was his daughter by MAGA.

## Catigern
*British*

A son of VORTIGERN. He fell in battle near Aylesford, KENT, in the fifth century and is supposedly buried in a Neolithic cromlech known as Kit's Coty House, though this cromlech pre-dates the death of Catigern by some considerable time.

## Catuvellauni
*British*

A tribe of Britons who inhabited a large area between the Thames and Cambridgeshire at the time of the Roman invasion in AD 43. At the time of the first invasion led by JULIUS CAESAR, their king was CASSIVELAUNUS, who led a fierce fight against the invaders before being captured and handed over to the Romans by CARTIMANDUA, Queen of the BRIGANTES. He was pardoned by CLAUDIUS.

## Céatach
*Irish*

The warrior who captured a maiden, who then mysteriously disappeared. He set off in search of her and became embroiled in a lengthy battle on the side of her three brothers, who daily fought a foe that came back to life at night. That night Céatach remained with the dead and watched as a hag restored them to life with a potion from a small pot. He killed the hag and all those she had restored to life, but before she died the hag placed him under a bond to report his actions to a neighbouring king. He did this and was forced to fight the king, whom he killed, but not until the king had also placed Céatach under an oath to report what he had done. Again Céatach had to fight to prove his worth, which again he did, and again he was placed under oath to report his deeds, but this time to a monstrous cat. The cat killed Céatach but fell onto the warrior's sword and died as well. Some time later, the maiden and her three brothers came looking for Céatach and, finding him dead, poured the potion from the cauldron of the hag onto him, and so restored him to life.

## Cei
*Welsh*

Later to re-emerge under the guise of Sir Kay in the Arthurian legends, Cei was among the party assembled by CULHWCH in his quest to locate the maiden OLWEN. Each of the party was chosen for a particular skill. Cei's talents were his ability to stay for nine days and nights without breathing or sleeping and to change his height at will. In addition, his body temperature was so high that he never got wet, and during the cold his companions could kindle a fire from him. The other members of the party were BEDWYR[2], CYNDDYLIG the Guide, GWRHYR the Interpreter, GWALCHMEI FAB GWYAR and MENW FAB TEIRGWAEDD.

## Ceithin
*Irish*

The uncle of LUGH and brother of CÚ and CIAN.

## Cell-y-Dewiniaid
*Welsh*

'The Grove of the Magicians', a grove of oak trees, long since felled, near DINAS EMRYS. Within this grove, VORTIGERN'S counsellors were said to meet to discuss the events of their times. They were buried in an adjoining field with each grave, at one time, marked by a stone. These, too, have long since vanished.

## Celtchar
*Irish*

The son of UTHECAR, the father of NIAMH[1], and one of the ULSTER warriors who belatedly came to the aid of CÚ CHULAINN towards the end of his epic defence of Ulster against the forces of MEDHBHA and AILILL. He was also one of the warriors who half-heartedly opposed the right of CET to carve the roast pig of MAC DÁ THÓ.

## Celyddon
*Welsh*

An ancient Welsh name for SCOTLAND. Many believe that the Welsh name gave rise to the more common Old English variant of CALEDON, which latter form possibly gave the Romans their name for Scotland, Caledonia.

## Cenchos
*Irish*

One of the FOMHOIRÉ. His name means 'The Footless', thus presumably indicating that, while he still had the single leg that was a feature of the Fomhoiré, his limb terminated in a stump.

## Ceneu
*Welsh*

According to Welsh tradition, the son of COEL GODEBOG, father of MOR[1] and great-great-great-grandfather of MYRDDIN.

## Cenn Crúiach
*Irish*

'Head of the Mound', a deity, also known as Crom Cruach, who was said to have been introduced to IRELAND by TIERNMAS. Cenn Crúiach was undoubtedly a solar deity, but no trace of a being remotely like him has, as yet, been discovered in pagan literature or in the writings of St PATRICK. His purpose appears to have been the protection of the SÍDH. Offerings of children and animal firstlings were sacrificed to him. St Patrick was alleged to have come across a statue of Cenn Crúiach, which bowed down before him moments before the earth opened up and swallowed the pagan image.

## Cerne Abbas
*British*

A village approximately 8 miles north of Dorchester, in the south of England, that is famous for the gigantic figure carved on the side of a hill above the village that is, predictably, known as the Cerne Abbas Giant. The outline of the giant, which stands 180 feet tall, is formed by trenches cut through the turf to reveal the white chalk beneath. On the summit of the hill above the giant is a rectangular earthwork called the Trendle, or Frying Pan, which may have been the site of a temple dedicated to the giant that stands on the hillside below.

The date and origin of the giant remain unknown, but he was undoubtedly a fertility deity, as his huge erect phallus, some 30 feet in length, would indicate. Stylistically, the giant is ascribed to the first century AD and is thought, by some, to represent the Roman hero-god Hercules. This representation is supported by archaeological research, which has revealed the outline of what might be a lion's skin, one of the usual attributes of Hercules, beneath the giant's outstretched left arm.

The ancient name of the giant is recorded in a thirteenth-century text by Walter of Coventry, which says that Cerne Abbas is in the pagan district of Dorset where the god HELITH was once worshipped, although later this god was referred to as HELIS and HEIL. Helith was a solar deity, his name possibly being derived from the Celtic word for 'sun', and as such this connection would fit the Cerne Abbas Giant, possibly the most striking representation of a fertility deity to be found in Europe.

## Cernunnos
*Widespread*

The Lord of the Animals, the 'Horned One', whose image is found throughout the Celtic lands in Romano-Celtic worship sites, and whose role as an animal god and hunter is preserved in Celtic folklore and legend. As the guardian of the portal leading to the OTHERWORLD, Cernunnos became associated with wealth

and prosperity, although his earlier function had been of a nature deity, the ruler of the active forces of life and death, regeneration and fertility. The name Cernunnos is known only from one damaged carving found at Notre Dame in Paris. This carving, which shows a deity with short horns, carries the incomplete inscription 'ERNUNNO'. Since that discovery the name has been used as a generic term for all occurrences of the 'Horned One'. Cernunnos was, in all probability, a deity of Gaulish origin, and his worship was prominent in the areas settled by Belgic tribes that imported him to BRITAIN[1].

Cernunnos was of such importance to the Celts that the Christian church made him a special target of abuse, taking his image to be that of the Devil, *deo falsus* or 'false god'. He was much maligned, even by his own worshippers, his cult opponents and even today by those who claim to be his revivalist supporters. The cult of Cernunnos was especially encouraged by the DRUIDS in their attempt to regularize the local Celtic deities into some form of pantheon and thus to establish Cernunnos as a national, rather than a local, deity. Cernunnos was possibly the nearest the Celts got to a universal father god within their fragmented system of worship.

His status as a fertility god is of much later origin, for Cernunnos has much less to do with sexuality than is held in popular belief. He is the god of hunting, culling and taking. His purpose is to purify through selection and sacrifice in order that the powers of fertility, regeneration and growth may progress unhindered. His image still survives in the figure of HERNE THE HUNTER, an antlered woodland being who dwells in Windsor Forest. He is also possibly the god originally worshipped in the surviving Abbots Bromley horn dance.

Cernunnos is usually represented holding a ram-headed serpent in his left hand, or a serpent with a ram's horn, while he himself sits, cross-legged. He has both animal and human ears, and carries a magnificent set of antlers from which hangs one torc, sometimes two. To his right stands a stag whose antlers are comparable to those of the god himself. Around him other woodland animals gather. The stag was, according to Celtic tradition, the oldest of all animals, and it played a major role in their culture as an Otherworld creature, luring hunters into the tangled masses of the forests, the land of the gods, where it would allow itself to be eaten and then resurrected. One of the most remarkable images of Cernunnos is to be found on the GÜNDESTRUP CAULDRON. It is quite possible that the Irish CONALL CERNACH is a representation of Cernunnos.

The ram-headed serpent, representing the chthonic aspect of Cernunnos, is the totem creature of fire from within the earth, a creature that held special significance to the Celts as an emblem of power. Later Romano-Celtic images of the god, after he had adopted the role of god of wealth, sometimes show him with a sack of coins, which he pours out onto the ground.

## Cer(r)idwen
*Welsh*
Also CARRIDWEN

The corn goddess and wife of TEGGID VOEL. She is usually represented as a crone, the goddess of dark, prophetic powers, whose totem animal is the sow, which represents the fecundity of the OTHERWORLD. She is the keeper of the cauldron of the Otherworld, in which inspiration and divine knowledge are brewed, and it is this aspect that features most prominently in her story.

Like many Celtic goddesses, Cerridwen had two opposing children. One was the maiden CREARWY, the most beautiful girl ever to have been born, her very person radiating light and warmth. The other was the boy AFAGDDU, the ugliest boy to have lived, whose soul was dark and cold. A second son is also sometimes added to the list of Cerridwen's children. Named MORFRAN AB TEGID, some say that he is none other than AFAGDDU, for Afagddu may possibly be a derisive nickname for Morfran ab Tegid. Others say that they are two separate children, but no source gives any indication of Morfran ab Tegid's attributes. It seems most likely that Afagddu and Morfran ab Tegid are one and the same, for mythology tends to follow set patterns, and it would be extremely unlikely for a goddess such as Cerridwen to have had more than two children representing opposing forces.

To compensate her son for his misfortune, Cerridwen decided to brew a potion that would empower him with the gifts of inspiration and knowledge and would give him the ability to know all things past, present and future. Collecting together the magical herbs required, she placed them in her cauldron and set GWION BACH, the young son of GWREANG, to stir the potion for the required year and a day and the blind man MORDA to stoke the fire. At the end of the allotted time three drops of the hot liquid splashed onto Gwion Bach's thumb. As the little boy sucked his thumb to cool it, he was filled with the potency of the brew. Having now given up its essence, the remainder of the potion became poisonous, the cauldron spilt asunder and the contents poisoned the local waterways and killed the horses of GWYDDNO GARANHIR which drank the contaminated water. The sucking of the thumb by Gwion Bach may enshrine an ancient Celtic divinatory practice that involved chewing the thumb. This practice was known in early IRELAND as IMBAS FOROSNAI, and seems to have relied on the notion that chewing the raw flesh of the thumb imparted sagacity.

Gwion Bach immediately knew that his life was in danger and fled the site. When Cerridwen found the cauldron in pieces, she flew into a rage and beat Morda so cruelly about the head with a billet of wood that one of his eyes fell out onto his cheek. Realizing that it was Gwion Bach who was responsible for the loss of her potion, Cerridwen dashed off after the boy in the guise of a fearful black hag and soon started to gain on him. Seeing Cerridwen gaining, Gwion Bach used his new-found powers to change himself into a hare so that he might run faster, but Cerridwen countered by changing herself into a greyhound. Gwion Bach saw Cerridwen gaining again and leapt into a river, changing into a fish as he did so. Cerridwen dived in after him and became an otter. Gwion Bach left the river and flew up into the air as a bird, with Cerridwen following as a hawk. Finally Gwion Bach saw a barn and, dropping onto the threshing floor, turned himself into a grain of wheat thinking that he would be safe among the thousands of other grains that lay scattered all around. Cerridwen changed herself into a hen and, scratching around the floor, swallowed the hapless Gwion Bach.

Resuming her human form, Cerridwen discovered that she was pregnant. Nine months later she gave birth to Gwion Bach as a boy so beautiful that she could not bring herself to kill him. Instead she sewed him up inside a leather bag and threw him into the river. The bag caught on the fish weir of GWYDDNO GARANHIR, whose son ELPHIN found and opened it. The first thing he saw was the forehead of the child inside and immediately exclaimed 'Radiant Brow', thus naming

TALIESIN, for the name Taliesin means 'Radiant Brow'.

Cerridwen, whose name means 'White Grain', was also known as HÊN WEN, or 'old white one', the sow that supposedly gave birth to several monstrous offspring, one of which was the CATH PALUG, although this animal also has another tale of its birth (see below). She was also the patroness of poetry, a just connection considering that the birth of the great bard Taliesin is a part of her story. She was, through her totem animal, connected with the sow goddess, as well as with ALBINE, the eponym of ALBION. Cerridwen lived at CAER SIDDI, also known as CAER FEDDWIDD, an Otherworldly kingdom that was represented in the stars as a spiral, although this realm is also sometimes associated with ARIAHRHOD.

Not content with all these attributes and associations, Cerridwen was also said to have been given a kitten that grew up to be the Cath Palug. This connection led to Cerridwen being associated with a cat cult, although, quite perversely, she also had connections with wolves and was said, by some, to have been the centre of a Neolithic cult.

## Ces(s)air

*Irish*

Also KESAIR

The daughter of BITH, son of NOAH, who led the first invaders to the shores of IRELAND in a time before the Flood. Her party consisted of fifty women and just three men; Bith, LADRA and FINTAN[1]. These three men shared the women among them, but, after Ladra had died, Bith and Fintan took twenty-five women each, Cesair falling to Fintan. Bith died shortly before the Flood, which killed all the women and left Fintan as the sole survivor, for he had hidden in a cave that the waters of the Flood never reached. He lived on for many centuries as a shape-shifting immortal and witnessed all the subsequent invasions of IRELAND.

## Cet
*Irish*
Also KET

The brother of ANLUAN. A warrior of CONNACHT, Cet claimed the right to carve the boar of MAC DÁ THÓ and cruelly derided all those who sought to challenge him until CONALL CERNACH arrived to whom he quickly gave way. However, Cet taunted Conall Cernach saying that had his brother Anluan been present he would have given him a run for his money. Conall Cernach then removed the bloody head of Anluan from a pouch and threw it onto the table in front of Cet.

## Cethern
*Irish*

A companion of CÚ CHULAINN who fought the combined armies of AILILL and MEDHBHA. He received numerous wounds in the conflict and retired to his camp for treatment. However, Cethern was a churlish man, and killed several of the physicians for saying that his wounds were fatal. Finally, one physician told him he could either lie around and await death or pull himself together and die with honour on the battlefield. Cethern chose the latter. In preparation, he lay for two days in a tub of bone marrow. He was then fortified with the ribs of a chariot wrapped around him to secure his own broken ribs and finally armed to the hilt. So frenzied was his attack that, on seeing him drawing close, the men of CONNACHT placed the crown of Ailill on a standing stone, which Cethern simply split in half. So angry was he at the subterfuge that he made a captive Connacht warrior wear the crown as he split him in half. Cethern killed many hundreds of the Connacht warriors before he was outnumbered and killed.

## Céthlionn
*Irish*

The wife of BALAR, who told her husband that the arrival of his grandson LUGH among the ranks of the TUATHA DÉ DANANN would, as had been prophecied, bring about the downfall of the FOMHOIRÉ. See also AIDED CHLAINNE TUIRENN.

## Chwim-leian, -bian
*Welsh*

The flower-maiden mentioned in the MYRDDIN poem *Afullonau*. She is thought to be identifiable with GUENDOLOENA and BLODEUWEDD.

## Ciabhan
*Irish*
Also KEEVAN

Appearing in the *Acallamh na Senórach*, Ciabhan, one of the FIAN, journeyed over the seas to the land of MANANNÁN MAC LIR with LODAN[1] and EOLUS. There the three persuaded the sisters CLIODNA, AEIFE and EDAEIN to elope with them, Cliodna travelling with Ciabhan. They had just reached shore, when a huge wave rolled in and engulfed the lovers, drowning the three maidens, as well as ILDÁTHACH and his sons who, themselves in love with Cliodna, had set off in pursuit of her. Some sources, however, say that the wave did not drown the sisters, but rather carried them back to TÍR TAIRNGIRI.

## Cian

*Irish*

Also KIAN

The Brother of CÚ and CEITHIN and the earthly father of LUGH. He had been involved in a long-standing blood feud with the sons of TUIRENN – BRIAN, IUCHAR and IUCHARBA – by whom he was killed. His death was avenged by his son Lugh, who made the three murderous men collect a number of items required by the TUATHA DÉ DANANN for the forthcoming Second Battle of MAGH TUIREDH. Brian, Iuchar and Iucharba completed all the tasks set them, but died as a result of the injuries they received performing the last task.

## Cigfa

*Welsh*

Also KICVA

The daughter of GWYN GOHOYW and the wife of PRYDERI. She was left alone with MANAWYDAN FAB LLYR after Pryderi had been magically imprisoned within a CAER.

## Cimbaoth

*Irish*

Also KIMBAY

According to the eleventh-century historian Tierna of Clonmacnois, Cimbaoth ruled *c.*300 BC and was responsible for the foundation of the kingdom of ULSTER and the building of EMHAIN MHACHA. Legend says that Cimbaoth was the son of RED HUGH and the brother of MACHA and DITHORBA. On the death of their father, Macha refused to yield the throne to Dithorba who went to war with her. He was killed, and Macha then compelled Cimbaoth to marry her, and so ruled as queen of all IRELAND. The five sons of Dithorba were captured by Macha and made to build the ramparts of her fortress, which has since that time been known as Emhain Mhacha.

## Cis

*Irish*

An ancestor of St BRIDE, according to an oral genealogy of that saint that forms part of a protective prayer. This genealogy makes Cis the son of CARMAC and the father of CREAR.

## Clas Myrddin

*Welsh*

'Merlin's Precinct or Enclosure', which is, according to the *Trioedd Ynys Prydein*, one of the earliest names for ENGLAND.

## Claudia

*British*

Claudia has the distinction of being the only Briton to be mentioned in the Bible (2 Timothy 4:21). She is described as the child of blue-painted parents (Celts), yet in Rome, where she lived, she had acquired every civilized grace.

## Claudius

*General*

The fourth Roman emperor (40 BC – AD 54) who was born in Lyon. He was the younger son of Drusus senior and brother of the emperor Tiberius. He inaugurated the conquest of BRITAIN[1], taking part in the opening campaign in person (AD 43). GEOFFREY OF MONMOUTH claims that ARVIRAGUS became the King of Britain after the death of his brother GUIDERIUS during the Roman invasion. Peace was established between Arviragus and Claudius, when the former married GENVISSA, Claudius' daughter. Arviragus later revolted, but Genvissa interceded and peace was once again established.

## Cleena
*Irish*

A queen of the SÍDH of south MUNSTER. Her name is sometimes said to be a variant of CLIODNA.

## Cliach
*Irish*

A harper who is mentioned in an incidental reference as having sought the hand of a daughter of BODB but was kept at bay for a year by the magic powers of that deity and then died when a DRAGON appeared from beneath the ground.

## Cli(o)dna
*Irish*

The most beautiful woman in the world. A divine maiden who is accompanied by three brightly coloured magical birds, whose song is so sweet that they soothe the sick and wounded to sleep, and feed on the fruit of the apple trees of the LAND OF PROMISE, TÍR TAIRNGIRI.

Another story concerning Cliodna appears in the *Acallamh na Senórach*. CIABHAN, one of the FIAN, journeyed over the seas to the land of MANANNÁN MAC LIR with LODAN[1] and EOLUS. There they persuaded the sisters Cliodna, AEIFE and EDAEIN to elope with them, Cliodna travelling with Ciabhan. They had just reached shore when a huge wave rolled in and engulfed the lovers, drowning the three maidens, as well as ILDÁTHACH and his sons who, themselves in love with Cliodna, had set off in pursuit of her. Some versions of the story say that, rather than drowning the three sisters, the wave simply carried them back to the land of Manannán mac Lir. Yet another version says that she left the Land of Promise with IUCHNA to travel to OENGHUS MAC IN OG, and it was on that occasion when the wave carried her back to the realm of Tír Tairngiri.

## Cliton
*Welsh*

One of the nine sisters of MORGEN.

## Clogwyn Carnedd yr Wydffa
*Welsh*

'The Precipice of the Carn of Yr Wyddfa', a name sometimes used to refer to YR WYDFFA FAWR or, alternatively, to the cairn that used to be situated on the top of the mountain that is today known as Mount SNOWDON.

## Cloten
*British*

The ruler of CORNWALL after the death of PORREX, and the father of MOLMUTIUS.

## Clothru
*Irish*

The sister of MEDHBHA and Ethne. Her brothers were BRES[2], NÁR and LOTHAR. All three sisters were at one stage the wife of CONCHOBAR MAC NESSA, Clothru and Ethne becoming successive wives after Medhbha had left the king for AILILL. Clothru remained childless until she had an incestuous affair with each of her three brothers. From each affair she bore a son named LUGAID[1], although some sources name but one son with this name, and give him the three brothers as his father. She subsequently had an affair with one of her sons and bore him a son named CRIMTHANN NIA NAÍR.

## Clud
*Welsh*

A shortened and popular form of GWAWL
FAB CLUD.

## Clutarius
*Welsh*

The father of MAELGWYN.

## Clwyd
*General*

An ancient Welsh kingdom that is the
equivalent of the county of the same name
today. The kingdom was once closely
aligned with POWYS, as is illustrated on
the Pillar of ELISEG, which is situated in
Clwyd and yet gives a list of the early
kings of Powys.

## Clydno Eiddyn
*Welsh*

The owner of a cauldron that was considered one of the THIRTEEN TREASURES
of BRITAIN[1].

## Cnoc Ainé
*Irish*

A small hillock in MUNSTER, said to be the
home of the supernatural woman AINÉ[2].

## Coba
*Irish*

The trapper to EREM, son of MÍL. He was
the first to prepare a trap and pitfall in
IRELAND. However, he tested it by putting
his leg into it and, having broken his shin
bone and his arms, he died.

## Cobthach Coel
*Irish*

In order to usurp the Irish throne,
Cobthach Coel killed his brother
LOEGHAIRE LORC, King of IRELAND, along
with his nephew, AILIL AINE, King of
LEINSTER. At the same time he drove
LABHRAIDH LOINGSECH, Ailil Aine's son
into exile. With the help of the Men of
MUNSTER, Labhraidh Loingsech regained
his kingdom and went on to make peace
with Cobthach Coel, even inviting the
usurper to his court, although this was a
trick. Labhraidh Loingsech had an iron
house prepared for his visitor and his
thirty vassal knights, who accepted the
invitation in all innocence. When they
were all inside the iron house, Labhraidh
Loingsech had the door fastened and
ordered fires to be kindled all around it,
thus roasting Cobthach Coel and his
supporters to death. See also COVAC,
LOEGHAIRE[1].

## Codal
*Irish*

The foster father of ÉRIU. He appears in a
very early story concerning the creation
of the landscape of IRELAND. One day he
was feeding Ériu on the side of a small
hillock, and as she grew, so too did the
hillock on which she was standing. It
would have continued to grow until it
had swamped Ireland had not Ériu
complained to her foster father of the
heat of the sun and the coolness of the
wind. He immediately led her off what
was by now a mountain, which stopped
growing the moment she left its slopes.

## Coel
*British*

Possibly an historical figure flourishing in
the north country in the early fifth

century, who successfully defended his kingdom against the PICTS and Scots. He is almost certainly the Old King Cole of nursery-rhyme fame, as the adjective *hen* ('old') was applied to him. A fourth-century manuscript says that Coel was King of all BRITAIN[1], dying in AD 267, while a sixteenth-century manuscript draws him into the Arthurian cycle saying that, through his mother, he was an ancestor of ARTHUR.

Tradition names his wife as STRADAWL and his daughter as GWAWL, who may have been the wife of CUNEDDA. Regarded as the founder and ruler of COLCHESTER, legend says that this city was besieged by the Roman Emperor Constantius Chlorus for three years and that, after peace had been restored, the emperor married Coel's daughter HELENA, who is better known as St Helena. Their son, Constantine the Great, was born in AD 265.

## Coel Godebog
*Welsh*

The father of *Ceneu* and great-great-great-great grandfather of MYRDDIN in Welsh tradition.

## cóigedh
*Irish*

The collective name for the five provinces of IRELAND into which the country was divided by the invading FIR BHOLG. Literally meaning 'one-fifth', these five provinces were ULSTER, LEINSTER, MUNSTER, CONNACHT and MEATH.

## Cóir Anmann
*Irish*

'Fitness of Names', which gives an account of the adventures of CONNLA[2], although it differs from the normal by saying that Connla was slain by his enemies rather than departing in a boat to a divine kingdom from which he never returned.

## Coir-bre, -pre
*Irish*

The FILI of the TUATHA DÉ DANANN who so skilfully and magically satirized BRES[1] that that tyrannical king broke out in boils, abdicated the throne and defected to the FOMHOIRÉ, the people of his father.

## Coirpre
*Irish*

The son of DOEL. He once fought with CÚ CHULAINN but was forced to yield and, having carried Cú Chulainn into his castle, gave the hero his daughter, who remains unnamed.

## Colcu
*Irish*

The stepson of CRÉD who was always on hand when she attempted to meet with CANO. Eventually his intervention led to the suicide of Créd and the death, three days later, of Cano.

## Collen, St
*Welsh*

An early Welsh saint who once lived in a hermitage on the slopes of GLASTONBURY TOR. One day he heard two men speaking of GWYNN AP NUDD, and he reproached them for speaking of pagan beliefs. They replied that he had offended Gwynn ap Nudd and would have to suffer the consequences. The following day a messenger arrived from Gwynn ap Nudd and invited Collen to visit the king, but Collen refused. The messenger arrived again the following day, this time making thinly disguised threats. For several more days the messenger arrived, each day increasing the severity of the threats. Finally, Collen consented to visit Gwynn ap Nudd and, armed with holy water, climbed Glastonbury Tor, where he entered a magical castle on its summit. Gwynn ap Nudd offered him food, but Collen refused, knowing that if he ate he would be condemned to spend the rest of his days in the OTHERWORLD. Collen sprinkled the holy water all around him and in an instant the castle and all its inhabitants vanished, leaving Collen quite alone on the summit of the hill. From that day to this the fairy castle of Gwynn ap Nudd has never been seen again.

This story, although based on a seventh- or eighth-century tradition, was not written down until the sixteenth century, and it appears to have been much altered over the years. See also TOLLEN.

## Colmcille
*Irish*
See COLUMBA.

## Colum Cualleinech
*Irish*

A smith, described as 'of the three processes', employed by the TUATHA DÉ DANANN at the time of the arrival of LUGH. It seems quite probable that Colum Cualleinech is a composite figure representing the three smith gods GOIBHNIU, CREIDHNE and LUCHTAINE, although this is by no means certain.

## Columba, St
*Irish*

The famous early Irish monk, who is said to have lived from 521 to 597. Born in Gartan in County Donegal, Columba attended a school that was run by St Finnian at Moville on Strangford Lough. He founded numerous monasteries in IRELAND, before leaving to preach to the PICTS in 563 following a dispute with his old mentor.

Numerous legends exist surrounding the character of St Columba, who is also known as St Colmcille. One particular legend says that Columba was responsible for driving the last remnants of the FOMHOIRÉ from their home on TORY Island with the aid of his cloak, which spread out from underneath him as he sat on it, causing the Fomhoiré to flee in case they were smothered. They leapt off the island and were never heard of again.

Columba left Ireland in a curragh with twelve followers and landed first on the island of IONA. The king of DÁL RIADA gave Columba the island, and he founded a monastery there that was to become one of the most famous and influential in all Christendom. It was from this base that Columba and his disciples set out on missions among the Picts and Scots.

On one occasion he was travelling to visit BRIDEI, a son of MAELGWYN, who had become king of the Picts. As he travelled down the Great Glen, he stopped to rest for the night on the slopes of one side of the valley. While he slept a local woman forgot to recap an inexhaustible well that lay in the valley, and when Columba and the local people awoke the following morning the valley had become a deep lake. The locals exclaimed 'Tha loch nis ann!' ('There is a lake there now!'), which is how Loch Ness came into being and got its name. Shortly afterwards a huge monster surfaced in the lake and chased the boat carrying his disciples. Columba commanded it to do them no harm, and the monster slid beneath the surface of the lake. This is the first alleged report of the Loch Ness Monster.

## Conaire Mór
*Irish*

The incestuously conceived son of EOCHAIDH AIREMH and his daughter ÉDÁIN. His conception occurred after MIDHIR gave Eochaidh Airemh the choice of fifty women, all of whom appeared to be his wife ÉDÁIN ECHRAIDHE. The one Eochaidh Airemh chose was in fact his own daughter, and it was not until after Conaire Mór had been born that the girl's true identity was revealed. However, some sources say that Conaire Mór Eochaidh Airemh's grandson by MESS BUACHALLA, the daughter of Eochaidh Airemh and his own daughter ESS, for it was Ess whom he had chosen thinking that she was his wife Édáin Echraidhe.

## Conall
*Irish*
Also CONLAÍOR CONLAOCH

The son of CÚ CHULAINN and his mistress AÍFE. Born in SCOTLAND, Conall remained there after his father had returned to IRELAND. Under the tutorage of SCÁTHACH, Conall grew to be a mighty warrior and sorcerer. Finally, he was sent to Ireland with strict instructions that he should not reveal his true identity to any who challenged him. As Conall approached the coast of Ireland in his bronze boat, the heroes of that land were so amazed by his magical deeds that they sent a champion, CONALL CERNACH, to challenge the newcomer. Conall Cernach was quickly defeated, so Cú Chulainn himself went out to meet the lad, despite the pleas of EMER, Cú Chulainn's wife, who warned him that the boy could only be his own son.

When Conall refused to give his name, Cú Chulainn attacked him. They fought long and hard, and it was only with great difficulty that Cú Chulainn at last managed to inflict a mortal wound. As Conall lay dying he revealed his identity to his father. Cú Chulainn was filled with remorse and, taking his son's corpse, showed the men of ULSTER his son.

## Conall Ce(a)rnach
*Irish*

The son of AMORGIN and one of the three champions who were persuaded by BRICRIU to claim the champion's right to carve the roast at a feast. (The other claimants were LOEGHAIRE BUADIIACH and CÚ CHULAINN; some sources make Cú Chulainn the foster son of Conall Cernach.) The right to carve the roast was awarded to Cú Chulainn twice, firstly by MEDHBHA of CONNACHT, and subsequently by CÚ ROI MAC DÁIRI. On both occasions the judgement was refused by the two losers, but they were finally made to accept it.

Conall Cernach also appears in the story of MAC DÁ THÓ's boar, in which he is portrayed as the champion. On this occasion the Connacht champion CET was about to carve the pig when Conall Cernach appeared. Cet grudgingly gave way to the superiority of Conall Cernach, but not before he had taunted him by saying that if ANLUAN (Cet's brothers) were present he would give Conall Cernach a sound thrashing. At this Conall Cernach removed the severed head of Anluan from a pouch and threw it onto the table in front of Cet. He then set about carving and devouring the pig.

Conall Cernach met his end at the hands of CONALL, whom he challenged as that magical youth approached the shores of IRELAND in search of his father Cú Chulainn. When Conall Cernach asked Conall his name, the youth refused, following the instructions of SCÁTHACH, so Conall Cernach attacked him, but was quickly overcome. The youth was finally killed by his own father.

## Conan mac Lia
*Irish*

The son of LIA, Lord of LUACHAR. After his father had been killed by FIONN MAC CUMHAILL, Conan mac Lia took his revenge by harrying the FIAN for seven years. Finally, he was captured and brought before Fionn mac Cumhaill, to whom Conan mac Lia swore an oath of allegiance and served faithfully for the next thirty years.

## Conan mac Morna
*Irish*

A son of MORNA. A fat, bald character, Conan mac Morna was derisively known as 'Conan the Bald'. On one occasion he and several other members of the FIAN entered a SÍDH where they found a wondrous feast. They sat down to devour the food, but, as they did so, the door started to shrink. Realizing that they had been tricked by the gods, Conan mac Morna's comrades bolted for the exit, but Conan mac Morna simply continued to eat. Eventually he was alerted to their predicament, but he found himself stuck fast to his chair. Several of the fian grabbed hold of him and tugged him lose, but he left a large portion of his flesh behind. To cover the open wound, the skin of a black sheep was hurriedly slapped into place, where it stayed until Conan mac Morna died.

The cowardice of Conan mac Morna is clearly demonstrated on the occasion when the fian put him forward to fight LIAGAN. Liagan mocked the choice of Conan mac Morna, who retorted that Liagan was in more peril from the man that stood behind him that from the one who stood in front of him. Liagan turned around, and Conan mac Morna cut off his head, an act of cowardice that amused the rank and file of the fian, but annoyed FIONN MAC CUMHAILL. See also MIDAC.

## Conán (Maol)
*Irish*

A member of the FIAN and a close friend of DIARMAID UA DUIBHNE. He was present with his friend, together with OSCAR and GOLL MAC MORNA, when Diarmaid ua Duibhne received the mark on his forehead, his BALL-SEIRC or 'love-spot', from a young lady that would thenceforth cause any maiden who saw it to fall in love with him.

## Conann
*Irish*

One of the two kings of the FOMHOIRÉ during the time of the people of NEMHEDH. He was the ruler on the occasion of the revolt of Nemhedh and his people, and was killed during their storming of TORY Island.

## Conaran
*Irish*

A king of the TUATHA DÉ DANANN in the time of FIONN MAC CUMHAILL. He had his three hag-like daughters punish Fionn mac Cumhaill for hunting the deer he considered to be his exclusive property. However, two of the daughters were killed by GOLL before they could exact their punishment on Fionn mac Cumhaill. The third appeared to restore her sisters to life, but Goll took her prisoner and burned Conaran's SÍDH.

## Concenn
*Welsh*

An alternative name for the last king of POWYS, who is more usually known as CYNGEN FAB CADELL. This name appears on the Pillar of ELISEG, which was erected by Cyngen fab Cadell near the ruins of Valle Crucis abbey in CLYWD. The inscription on this pillar gives a short genealogy of the kings of Powys, in which Concenn is the son of CADELL and thus great-grandson of Eliseg, to whom he erected the pillar.

## Concheann
*Irish*

After Concheann's wife had been seduced by AED[2], a son of the DAGHDHA, Concheann killed the youth, whereupon the Daghdha made Concheann carry the corpse until he found a stone large enough to cover the grave.

## Conchenn
*Irish*

A daughter of BODB. When the harper CLIACH came to her father's home to court her, Bodb's magic kept him at bay for a whole year, after which the earth opened, a DRAGON appeared and Cliach died of fright.

## Conchobar (mac Nessa)
*Irish*

The son of NESSA by the giant FACHTNA and one of the greatest Kings of ULSTER, whose reign is alleged to have been at the very beginning of the Christian era. Conchobar mac Nessa was the father, brother or half-brother of DEICHTINE, the mother of CÚ CHULAINN, although some accounts make Conchobar mac Nessa that hero's father, yet these sources do not hint at an incestuous relationship. Conchobar mac Nessa's traditional genealogy shows a bloodline connection between Conchobar mac Nessa and the sons of UISNECH, whom he was to have treacherously murdered.

Conchobar mac Nessa held his court at EMHAIN MHACHA where, as his first heroic deed, Cú Chulainn defeated all fifty youths in the king's service. His FILI, FEDLIMID, was the father of the maiden DERDRIU. At her birth it was prophesied that she would be very beautiful, but would cause untold suffering in Ulster. Some wanted to kill her at birth, but Conchobar mac Nessa refused to do this, saying that he would marry her when she came of age. However, as Derdriu reached maturity she fell in love and eloped with NAOISE. Conchobar mac Nessa took his revenge some time later by killing Naoise and his brothers, after which Derdriu committed suicide. Conchobar mac Nessa also plays a role in the ribald story of MAC DÁ THÓ's boar, although only as an observer to the events, and also in the later version of this story known as *Fledd Bricrenn*.

Conchobar mac Nessa's death occurred after he had made an unjust and cruel attack on MESGEDRA, King of LEINSTER, who was killed by CONALL CERNACH. Conall Cernach removed the dead king's brain and mashed it up and mingle it with lime to form a small ball known as a 'brain ball', one of the deadliest of all weapons. It was kept in the treasure house of EMHAIN MHACHA, from where it was stolen by CET. Some time later, Cet used the 'brain ball' in battle and struck Conchobar mac Nessa full in the forehead. His physicians advised him that to remove it would mean his death, and they sewed up the wound with golden thread. Conchobar mac Nessa was told that he had nothing to fear provided he managed to keep his cool. Unfortunately he was unable to do this. In the excitement of battle the 'brain ball' exploded, and Conchobar mac Nessa died.

## Condatis
*Gaulish*

A generic name given to the deities of river confluences.

## Condery
*Irish*

The messenger sent by CÚ CHULAINN to ask the name of the magical youth approaching Ireland. The youth refused to answer the question, so CONALL CERNACH was sent out against him, but was quickly killed. Cú Chulainn then fought the youth himself and, having inflicted a mortal wound on the young man, discovered that it was none other than his son CONALL.

## Conl-aí, -aoch
*Irish*

Alternative name(s) for the magical warrior CONALL, the son of CÚ CHULAINN and AÍFE.

## Conmarch
*Welsh*

The painter or sculptor in the employ of CONCENN, who inscribed the Pillar of ELISEG at the command of his employer.

## Conn
*Irish*

1  An ancestor of St BRIDE according to the genealogy recorded in an early protective prayer, which makes Conn the son of CREAR and father of ART. One legend tells of the time he was bewitched by BÉCUMA who eventually left him after his son Art had returned from the dead with DELBCHAEM.
2  The son of LIR and AOBH, and brother to FIONUALA, HUGH and FIACHTRA.

## Conn Cétchathlach
*Irish*

'Conn of One Hundred Battles', the father of CONNLA[2] and grandfather of CORMAC MAC AIRT. His son went to live with an OTHERWORLDLY maiden and was never seen again.

One day, while Conn Cétchathlach stood on the ramparts of TARA with his DRUIDS and FILIDH, a horseman approached out of the swirling mists and invited the company to visit his home. The horsemen led them to MAGH MELL. There, in a house built next to a golden tree and having a golden ridge pole, they found the god LUGH and the SOVEREIGNTY OF IRELAND. Beside the deities, there was a golden bowl and cup, and a silver vat. As the vision faded, these items remained, and Conn Cétchathlach returned to Tara with the godly gifts.

## Connacht
*Irish*

One of the five CÓIGEDH, or provinces, into which the leaders of the invading FIR BHOLG divided IRELAND, the other four being ULSTER, LEINSTER, MUNSTER and MEATH. Traditionally Connacht and Ulster were great rivals. Connacht is the ancient name for the county that is today known as Connaught.

## Connla
*Irish*

1  The husband of ACHTLAND. A giant, he slept on his island home with his head on a stone in the west, and his feet against another in the east.
2  The son of CONN CÉTCHATHLACH. He fell in love with an OTHERWORLDLY maiden who came from TÍR NA MBÉO, went to live with her there and was never seen again.

## Constans
*British*

According to GEOFFREY OF MONMOUTH,

Constans was the son of King CONSTANTINE[1] and the brother of both AMBROSIUS AURELIUS and UTHER. After CONSTANTINE had died, Constans was installed as a puppet king by VORTIGERN, though first he had to be persuaded to leave the monastery in which he had taken refuge. Finally, Vortigern had himself proclaimed king after having Constans killed by PICTS in his pay. Later tradition makes Constans the uncle of King ARTHUR through his brother UTHER who was, of course, Arthur's father.

## Constantine
*British*

1 The brother of ALDROENUS, King of BRITTANY, he became the King of BRITAIN[1] and had three sons; CONSTANS, AMBROSIUS AURELIUS and UTHER. He was succeeded by Constans, who was persuaded to take up the crown by VORTIGERN, after Constantine had been murdered by a PICT.

   Welsh genealogies give Constantine a father named KYNNVOR, while another makes him the son of SOLOMON, King of Brittany, and brother of ALDROENUS. Constantine is more usually known as King Constantine II, to save confusion between him and CONSTANTINE[2]. Some have sought to connect Constantine with the Roman Emperor Constantine III (reigned 407–411). The connection between the Roman Constantine and the King of Britain rests on two points. First, Constantine was said to have come from Brittany, an area that was under the rule of the Roman Constantine. Second, they both had sons named Constans who lived for a while within the sanctuary of a monastery.

2 An historical sixth-century king of DUMNONIA. Tradition calls him King Constantine III, the son of CADOR[1],

ruler of CORNWALL, and the recipient of the crown of ENGLAND from the dying King ARTHUR, this event being recorded as happening in the year 542.

## Cooley
*Irish*

The southern half of the province of ULSTER. It was the home of a bull known as the DONN CUAILNGÈ, or 'Dark One of Cooley'. The quest of MEDHBHA and AILILL to capture this bull is told in the *Taín Bó Cuailngè*.

## Cophur in dá muccida
*Irish*

*The Two Swine-Herds*, an introductory story to the *Taín Bó Cuailngè*. It tells of friendly relationships between two swine-herds, one from CONNACHT and one from ULSTER, whose friendship was spoiled by the people. They go through a shape-shifting saga and end up as worms which are eaten by two cows. These cows subsequently give birth to FINDBHENNACH and the DONN CUAILNGÈ.

## Coran-ieid, -iads
*British*

A mysterious people, said to have infected (*sic*) BRITAIN during the reign of LLUDD. They could overhear every conversation, and they used magical money to undermine the fragile economy, because, although the money appeared to be real, it would turn into mushrooms if kept for any time. They were killed after Lludd had discussed the matter out at sea with his brother LLEFELYS. Llefelys gave Lludd large numbers of an insect, never before seen in Britain, that should be crushed and fed to everyone. Normal humans would feel only a slight discomfort, but the Coranieid would be poisoned.

The Coranieid may be Breton in origin, for their name is similar to KORRIGANED, a Breton name for supernatural beings. However, one of the *Trioedd Ynys Prydein* states that the Coranieid came from Arabia.

## Cordelia
*British*

The youngest daughter of King LEIR and the sister of GONERIL and REGAN. Cordelia married AGANIPPUS, King of the FRANKS, after she had been dispossessed by her two scheming elder sisters. Her husband later restored Leir to the throne for the last three years of his life. Cordelia buried her father in an underground chamber beneath the River Soar in Leicestershire. This chamber, to which all the local craftsmen used to come at the beginning of each year to perform their first act of labour, was later dedicated to the Roman god Janus.

## Corineus
*Graeco-Romano-British*

An exiled Trojan leader, who came to BRITAIN in the company of BRUTUS. Renowned as a soldier and a giant killer, he was Brutus' champion as they landed and defeated the giant GOGMAGOG, the battle between Gogmagog and Corineus occurring, according to legend, on Plymouth Hoe. Even though Gogmagog managed to break three of Corineus' ribs, this served only to madden him, and he finally flung Gogmagog to his death. Two huge figures commemorating the giants, for Corineus was himself thought of as a giant, were carved in the white limestone overlooking Plymouth harbour. These were destroyed in 1671. In return for ridding the country of the giants, Brutus gave Corineus the land of CORNWALL, which he named after himself.

## Cormac mac Airt
*Irish*

Possibly an historical character and traditionally the King of IRELAND in 227–266, Cormac mac Airt, son of ART and thus a grandson of CONN CÉTCHATHLACH, ascended to the throne after having his predecessor MAC CON stabbed. He was not able to become king immediately, however, because a relative of Mac Con had set fire to his hair, and he had to wait for it to grow again. He died in 266 after a salmon bone caught in his throat, and he was buried at RELIGH NA RIGH. Legend makes Cormac mac Airt the father of GRÁINNE.

One particular story concerning this king says that Cormac mac Airt was lured to visit TÍR TAIRNGIRI by MANANNÁN MAC LIR, who assumed the guise of a warrior and appeared to the king so disguised at dawn on May Day morning as the king stood on the ramparts of TARA. Manannán mac Lir told the king that he came from a realm where decay, falsehood, old age and death were unknown. So entranced was Cormac mac Airt with the warrior's description that he readily agreed to exchange three wishes with the stranger for a bough of three golden apples that produced a healing music when shaken.

Exactly a year later Manannán mac Lir reappeared to claim his three wishes, and in so doing stole away with Cormac mac Airt's wife and family. The king set off in hot pursuit, even though he had no idea where he was heading. *En route* he was overtaken by a strange, thick mist, which seemed to guide him. As it cleared, Cormac mac Airt came to a wondrous palace standing in the middle of a beautiful plain. Entering, he was entertained by a handsome warrior and a charming girl to whom he told his story and of the loss of his wife and children. Lulled to sleep by the wonderful singing of the warrior, Cormac mac Airt awoke the following morning to find his wife and children restored to him.

The warrior then revealed himself as Manannán mac Lir, saying that he had lured the king to Tír Tairngiri to reward him, upon which he gave Cormac mac Airt a wonderful golden cup. Next morning Cormac mac Airt, his wife, and his children awoke to find themselves lying on the grass outside their home at Tara. Beside them were the golden apples and the cup presented to him by Manannán mac Lir. This cup would break into three pieces if three lies were spoken over it, but three truths told over the pieces would make it whole again. It is this cup that led to the wisdom of Cormac mac Airt, but it mysteriously vanished upon his death. An annalist records that Cormac mac Airt disappeared for seven months in 284, which is supposedly when he visited Manannán mac Lir.

This story bears obvious comparison with that of CONN CÉTCHATHLACH, although in that story the godly gifts were given by LUGH and the SOVEREIGNTY OF IRELAND.

## Cormac mac Cuilennáin
*Irish*

An historical medieval Irish writer (fl.900), who states that MANANNÁN MAC LIR was a wonderful navigator and a merchant of incomparable ability, who hailed from the Isle of MAN. Because of these skills he had, according to Cormac, become regarded as a god by both the Irish and the Welsh. While the story itself is undoubtedly a fabrication, it obviously lends weight to the possibility that the Irish Manannán mac Lir and the Welsh MANAWYDAN FAB LLYR are simply the Irish and Welsh aspects of the same deity.

## Cormac mac Dubthach
*Irish*

The son of DUBTHACH – his name literally means 'Cormac son of Dubthach'. He was sent to SCOTLAND with his father and FERGHUS MAC ROICH by CONCHOBAR MAC NESSA to guarantee the safety of NAOISE, DERDRIU, ARDÁN and AINNLE if they returned to IRELAND from their self-imposed exile. Unaware of the treachery that awaited their return, the exiles travelled back to Ireland with the three messengers. When Derdriu and the sons of UISNECH arrived at EMHAIN MHACHA, Conchobar mac Nessa went back on his word and had the young men killed by EOGHAN MAC DURTHACHT and his company. Furious at this act, FERGHUS MAC ROICH, Dubthach and Cormac mac Dubthach attacked and burned Emhain Mhacha, killing three hundred of the Men of ULSTER before they deserted to AILILL and MEDHBHA of CONNACHT, the enemies of Conchobar mac Nessa.

## Corm-oran, -ilan
*British*

A uniquely Cornish character, the most famous of all English giants. He was popularly disposed of by JACK THE GIANT-KILLER who, in Sir Thomas Malory's *Morte d'Arthur* and earlier in GEOFFREY OF MONMOUTH's *Historia Regum Britanniae*, fought the prototype of the later popular giant whose home was on ST MICHAEL'S MOUNT, off Penzance, CORNWALL. Jack the Giant-killer, who in English rather than Cornish, illustrates the popularization of the tale as it spread from its origins in Cornwall to the rest of the country. He remains, uniquely, the only European hero to triumph over a giant by his own natural dexterity and wit rather than relying on force of arms. Later legends replace Jack the Giant-killer as the killer of Cormoran with King ARTHUR.

Cormoran has become immortalized in the fairy-tale of 'Jack and the Beanstalk', for he is none other than the giant who lives in the wonderful land Jack stumbles across when he climbs the beanstalk that has magically appeared outside his house. Cormoran is, in this instance, possibly based on an earlier tradition, which would replace 'Englishman' with 'Cornishman', said to have rejoiced in the familiar cry:

> Fee, fi, fo, fum,
> I smell the blood of an Englishman!

## Corn Brangaled
*Welsh*

A drinking-horn owned by BRANGALED and numbered among the THIRTEEN TREASURES of BRITAIN[1]. It was said to be able to provide any drink that its holder desired.

## Cornubia
*Romano-British*

The name given by the Romans to CORNWALL, then the western portion of the kingdom of DUMNONIA.

## Cornwall
*British*

A county in the west of southern ENGLAND. Legend says that it gained its name from CORINEUS, upon whom the land was bestowed by BRUTUS. Part of the county was, at one time, within the ancient realm of DUMNONIA, and called CORNUBIA by the Romans. The tribal rulers of Cornwall were united under a high king, but from the fifth to the ninth centuries it was gradually taken over by the invading SAXONS. It is the resistance of the Cornish people to these invaders that has led to the many legends associated with

the county, none more potent than the belief that King ARTHUR held the Saxons at bay and will one day return from the dead to drive them from the land. To this day the county is remarkably Celtic in nature, and visiting the ancient sites to be found dotted all over the county is a worthwhile and satisfying experience.

## Covac
*Irish*

The son of UGAINY and brother of LOEGHAIRE[1]. When Ugainy died, Loeghaire inherited the throne, which consumed Covac with envy. His DRUID advised him to feign death and then took news of his death to Loeghaire. When Loeghaire arrived and bent over the supposed corpse to kiss his brother, Covac stabbed him through the heart and thus ascended to the throne. As a young boy MAON, son of AILILL AINE, was brought into the presence of Covac, who made him eat a portion of his father's and his grand-father's hearts, along with a mouse and all her young. The disgust Maon felt left him dumb and, fearing nothing from a boy who had lost the power of speech, Covac let him go. Many years later Maon returned and killed Covac. Having recovered his powers of speech, he was known as LABRAIDH LOINGSECH. See also COBTHACH COEL.

## Coventina
*British*

The goddess of springs and waters, who is depicted as floating on a leaf with a water plant in one hand and a flowing cup in the other. Her most famous association is with the spring at CARRAWBURGH. Her shrine here, near a fort on Hadrian's Wall, has revealed large numbers of coins, bronze votive offerings and even a human skull, although it is unlikely that the latter was the result of a human sacrifice.

## Craftiny
*Irish*

The harper of King SCORIATH, who was sent by the king's daughter, MORIATH, to Gaul with a magic harp that restored the speech of MAON, who was thenceforth known as LABRAIDH LOINGSECH, which means 'The Mariner who speaks'.

## Crann Bethadh
*Irish*

The 'Tree of Life', an icon found in many pagan cultures. The human world lies amid the tree, beside its trunk, while the OTHERWORLD lies within its roots, and the heavens within its branches. The best known tree of this nature is the Norse-Teutonic version, Yggdrasil.

## Crann Buidhe
*Irish*

The deadly, yellow-shafted spear of DIARMAID UA DUIBHNE, although it was not powerful enough to save him from being killed by the boar BEANN GHULBAN.

## Crear
*Irish*

An ancestor of St BRIDE, found in a genealogy of that saint contained within a chanted protective prayer that makes Crear the son of CIS and father of CONN[1].

## Cre-arwy, -irwy
*Welsh*

The daughter of the goddess CERRIDWEN and TEGID VOEL, and sister to AFAGDDU. She is described as the fairest women in the world, light and beautiful, in contrast to her brother, the darkest and ugliest of all men. It is common for goddesses to have two children who reflect both sides of nature, a notion that has carried through into Christian times in the concept of good and evil.

## Créd
*Irish*

The daughter of King GUAIRE of CONNACHT, and the beautiful young wife of the ageing MARCÁN. She fell in love with the exiled CANO even before she had set eyes on him, and at a feast drugged all those present so that she might implore Cano to take her as his mistress. Cano refused to do so while he was still in exile from his native SCOTLAND, but he pledged his undying love for Créd and gave her a stone that embodied his life. Eventually, Cano was recalled to Scotland where he was made king. Remembering their pledge, Cano and Créd attempted to meet each year at Inber Colptha (the BOYNE estuary). However, each attempt was foiled by Créd's stepson COLCU with a guard of 100 warriors. Finally, frustrated by their numerous failures, the two illicit lovers decided to meet at Lough Créde in the north (the Lough gained its name from Créd and the events that were about to occur there). As the two came within sight of each other, Colcu once again appeared and drove off Cano. In desperation, Créd threw herself from her horse and dashed out her brains against a rock, although some say that this was accidental. In falling she dropped the stone that Cano had given her. It smashed into tiny pieces, and three days later Cano himself died.

## Creiddyl-ad, -ed
*Welsh*

The daughter of LLUD LLAW EREINT,

although some name her father as the god LLYR, and the original of CORDELIA, the youngest daughter of King LEIR who has his origins in Llyr, thus suggesting that the god was her most likely father. Her hand was fought over by GWYNN AP NUDD, and GWYTHR, son of GREIDAWL. First one, then the other, would have the upper hand, the contest being fated to continue at each May Day until Doomsday. The story is undoubtedly inspired by some earlier, now lost, legend concerning divine combatants. Later stories say it was King ARTHUR who ruled how the contest was to be fought.

## Cre(i)d(h)ne
*Irish*

A god of metal-working, a brazier or *cerd*, one of the brothers, or aspects, of the great GOIBHNIU, the divine smith, his other brother/aspect being LUCHTAINE, the divine wheelwright. As a triad deity the three smiths were collectively known as the TRÍ DÉ DÁNA. Together they worked at the speed of light to keep the TUATHA DÉ DANANN supplied with weapons for the Second Battle of MAGH TUIREDH, weapons from which none who were wounded would ever recover.

Creidhne, on this occasion on his own, helped the great leech DIAN CÉCHT to fashion NUADHA an artificial arm from silver after he had lost one during the First Battle of MAGH TUIREDH. Once the arm had been fitted Nuadha became known as Nuadha Airgedlámh, or 'Nuadha of the Silver Hand'. See also COLUM CUALLEINECH.

## Creirwy
*Welsh*
See CREARWY.

## Creudylad
*Welsh*

A little used variant of CREIDDYLAD.

## Cridenbél
*Irish*

A lampooner. He occupied the house in which the DAGHDHA was forced to live by BRES[1] and demanded the best of the ration every night. OENGHUS MAC IN OG heard of this and told the Daghdha to put three gold coins in Cridenbél's portion, for these would kill him. Before this, Cridenbél had been employed by the TUATHA DÉ DANANN when he was sent out to help rid IRELAND of the monstrous children of CARMAN. At that stage he appears to have been an accepted member of the TUATHA DÉ DANANN, but his head appears to have been turned by Bres, with whom he possibly thought he might curry favour.

## Crimmal
*Irish*

The uncle of DEIMNE, whose fortunes were restored after Deimne, later known as FIONN MAC CUMHAILL, killed LIA and gave his uncle the treasure of the FIAN he had stolen from Lia.

## Crimthan(n) (Nia Náir)
*Irish*

An historical King of IRELAND who reigned for a solitary year (*c.* AD 74). Legend says he was the son of LUGAID[1] and was married to a supernatural woman by the name of NÁIR, whom he met on a military campaign. Among the gifts she gave him and that he brought back with her to his fort on the Hill of Howth to the east of Dublin were a gilt chariot, a multicoloured cloak embroidered in gold, a golden chessboard inlaid with gems, a silver shield and a sword decorated with serpents. None of these, nor his magical wife, was enough to save his life when he fell from his horse a short time later.

## Cróchan
*Irish*

A handmaiden of ÉDÁIN. She accompanied Édáin and MIDHIR to BRÍ LEITH.

## Crom Cruach
*Irish*
See CENN CRÚIACH.

## Cronnchu
*Irish*
See CRUNDCHU.

## Cruithne
*Irish*

1 According to some sources, the wife of FIONN MAC CUMHAILL; elsewhere, however, his wife is named as SAAR or Sabia.
2 The name given by the IRISH to the PICTS.

## Crundchu
*Irish*
Also CRONNCHU

A wealthy peasant, the son of AGNOMAN[2], who boasted at a feast held by the men of ULSTER that his second wife, MACHA, who had appeared at his house soon after his first wife had died and remained there ever since as his wife, could easily outrun any of their horses. He was ordered to bring her before them by CONCHOBAR MAC NESSA to prove this boast. Macha, however, was heavily pregnant at the time, and begged to be let off until after she had given birth. The men of Ulster

refused, but she easily won the race. Just then she went into labour and, giving birth to twins, cursed the men of Ulster that they too, for the next nine generations, should feel the pangs of labour whenever they were called upon to go into battle. Macha died shortly afterwards.

## Cú
*Irish*

The brother of CIAN and CEITHIN, and thus an uncle of LUGH.

## Cú Chulain(n)
*Irish*
Also CUCHULAINN

The best known and greatest of all the Irish heroes and the guardian of the sacred land of ULSTER. The son of DEICHTINE (the sister or daughter of CONCHOBAR MAC NESSA), some say that his father was the god LUGH, others that it was none other than Conchobar mac Nessa himself, although the husband of Deichtine is usually named as SUALTAM. The inclusion of the possibility that his father was the god Lugh enables him to fulfil the role of the archetypal hero whose parents bridge the two worlds, their offspring being at once human and divine. Twin foals born at precisely the same time as Cú Chulainn were later to become his famous steeds; Black of SAINGLIU and Grey of MACHA.

Cú Chulainn was not the original name of this hero. His mother gave him the name SÉDANTA. It was while still known by this name that he undertook his first heroic deed, the defeat of the fifty youths in the service of Conchobar mac Nessa at EMHAIN MHACHA. Later, though still a youth, he was attacked by the fierce hound of CULANN the smith. Sédanta threw his ball down the animal's gaping throat and seized the animal before it had regained its senses, dashing out its brains on a rock. Culann complained about the loss of his hound, which elicited a promise from Sédanta that he would act as Culann's guard dog for as long as he required one. It was this act that earned him his popular name, Cú Chulainn, which means 'Culann's Hound'. Now known as Cú Chulainn, the hero was offered the chance of either a long life or fame. He chose the latter. Having assumed his new name he made a magical obligation, or *geis*, which was never to eat the flesh of a dog or hound, for that animal became his totem beast and to taste such meat would bring about his downfall. As he made the promise to Culann he underwent a magical transformation, during which a fountain of terrible power erupted from his head and he went through a frenzy of shape-changing.

As Cú Chulainn regained his human form, he took up arms and went out to do battle with the three monstrous sons of NECHTA SCÉNE. He leapt into his scythed chariot, when was equipped with iron points having thin edges and hooks, and hard spit-spikes, with sharp nails that studded over the axles and straps and the tackle that harnessed his two steeds, Black of saingliu and Grey of macha. Setting forth, he drove the chariot with such force that its iron shod wheels sank into the earth and made ruts that were of an equal depth to the wheels themselves. Having killed the three sons of Nechta Scéne with relative ease, he decapitated them and hung their heads from his chariot. On his way home again, he captured a stag and tethered a whole flight of swans which flew overhead as he approached Emhain Mhacha, his body still seething with the indiscriminate fury of battle.

Seeing him approach, and in order to calm his frenzy, MUGHAIN, Queen of Ulster, led her women out to meet him, every one of them completely naked. Overcome with embarrassment, Cú Chulainn cast his eyes aside allowing the king's warriors to capture him and dip him into three tubs of icy cold water they had ready. The first immediately burst, the second boiled, but the water in the third merely became warm. Now calm, and having been clothed by Mughain herself, Cú Chulainn entered the royal household.

Cú Chulainn wanted to take EMER, the daughter of FORGALL, to be his wife. To prove his worth he travelled from IRELAND to a land that is described as having been far to the east beyond the country of ALBA, or SCOTLAND. In this country, which remains nameless, Cú Chulainn became the pupil of the prophetess SCÁTHACH. While there he fought and overcame AÍFE, the great rival of Scáthach, and took her as his mistress. She later bore him a son named CONALL or CONLAÍ. He also failed to capture two magic birds for his wife-to-be, a failure that was punished by two dream-women, LI BAN and FAND, who lashed him with whips, a lashing that was so severe that it disabled him for a year.

After Cú Chulainn had returned to Ireland, his son CONALL came under the tutorage of Scáthach, tutorage that enabled him to grow into a mighty, magical warrior of almost equal power to his father. As a young man Conall was sent to Ireland to seek out his father, though Scáthach made him promise never to reveal his identity to any who challenged him. Approaching the Irish coast in his bronze boat, Conall so amazed the people there that they sent out their champion, CONALL CERNACH, to challenge him. Conall quickly overcame the champion, and whereas news of this was taken to Cú Chulainn he himself came to challenge the youth, even though his wife EMER warned him that the youth could only be his own son.

When challenged by Cú Chulainn, and having refused to give his name, Conall and his father fought long and hard before Cú Chulainn succeeded in inflicting a mortal wound. As Conall lay dying he revealed his true identity to his father, who, grieving at the sad loss of the son he had never known, took his corpse and showed the body of his son to the men of Ulster.

In sharp contrast to the tragic story of Cú Chulainn and Conall is the tale of *Fledd Bricrenn*. Based on a much earlier ribald tale *Scéla Mucce Maic Dá Thó*, this tells of the occasion on which Cú Chulainn was twice adjudged the champion of all Ireland, although chronologically this story must fall before that of Cú Chulainn and Conall, for in it Conall Cernach is still very much alive. The malicious BRICRIU organized a feast for all the men of Ulster and CONNACHT, the two great traditional rival provinces. At this feast the privilege of carving the roast, as was the custom, would fall to the greatest warrior there present. Bricriu had bribed three great warriors all to claim the honour for themselves, these three being Cu Chulainn, LOEGHAIRE BUADHACH and Conall Cernach. As each claimed the honour a brawl broke out, and it was eventually decided that all three must seek the judgement of MEDHBHA of Connacht. She decreed that the most worthy recipient of the honour was Cú Chulainn, but the other two refused to accept the decision, saying that Cú Chulainn must have bribed the queen. All three were then sent to CÚ ROÍ MAC DÁIRI, King of MUNSTER. He, too, chose Cú Chulainn, and once again the two others refused to accept the verdict, leaving the feud unsettled.

At Emhain Mhacha, when all the men of Ulster were assembled in the great hall, a rough giant entered and challenged Loeghaire Buadhach, Conall Cernach and Cú Chulainn first to cut off his head, and then, the following evening, to allow him to return and retaliate in kind. Loeghaire Buadhach agreed the challenge and swiftly beheaded the giant with an axe. The giant calmly picked up his head and left the hall, returning the next evening to fulfil the pact he had made. Loeghaire Buadhach, who had obviously thought that the giant would have been dead after he had cut its head off, welched on their agreement. Now Conall Cernach took his turn, but he, too, reneged on the bargain when the restored giant returned the following evening. Cú Chulainn then took his turn and, when the giant returned to fulfil their pact, Cú Chulainn knelt down and calmly awaited the blow. The giant lifted his axe, but only touched Cú Chulainn gently on the nape of his neck with the blade. Lifting Cú Chulainn to his feet, he proclaimed him champion of all Ireland.

The giant then revealed himself to the three he had challenged. He was none other than CÚ ROÍ MAC DÁIRI who had chosen this method to reaffirm the judgement he had previously made, and which the two cowards had refused to accept.

Cú Roí mac Dáiri appears in another episode in the life of Cú Chulainn. On this occasion the hero had taken his men to raid the OTHERWORLD, here depicted as Scotland, when Cú Roí mac Dáiri appeared in disguise and offered to help them. With his aid they managed to capture a magical cauldron, three magic cows, and the beautiful Otherworldly maiden BLÁTHNAD. However, when Cú Chulainn and his men failed to keep their promise to share the spoils with Cú Roí mac Dáiri, he simply seized the lot, and, when Cú Chulainn attempted to prevent him from leaving, Cú Roí mac Dáiri buried the hero up to his armpits and shaved off all his hair. After this Cú Chulainn had to go into hiding for a year to hide his shame.

On the feast of SAMHAIN, Cú Chulainn planned to take his revenge and conspired with Bláthnad, whom Cú Roí mac Dáiri had married. Cú Chulainn killed Cú Roí mac Dáiri and took Bláthnad to be his mistress. However, FERCHERDNE, the FILI of the dead king, avenged the death of his master when he noticed Bláthnad standing near the edge of a cliff. Launching himself at her, he caught her around the waist and plummeted with her to their deaths on the rocks below.

Cú Chulainn, having chosen fame to a long life, was foredoomed to an early death. In the *Taín Bó Cuailngè*, Cú Chulainn single handedly protected Ulster from the armies of AILILL and Medhbha but came into conflict with the powers of the MÓRRÍGHAN, whom he failed to recognize. He was forced into a situation whereby he ate the flesh of a dog, an act that broke his *geis* and immediately weakened his previously invincible skills and energy. Overcome by the magic powers of his enemies, he tied himself to a pillar so that he might die honourably while still erect. When his enemies saw three hooded crows land on Cú Chulainn's shoulders, they recognized the presence of the Mórríghan in her three aspects and calmly walked up to Cú Chulainn and cut off his head.

### Cú Roí mac Dáir-i, -e
*Irish*

A King of MUNSTER and a great sorcerer. He appears in two episodes of the life of the hero CÚ CHULAINN. The first occasion is when he is called upon to settle the dispute between LOEGHAIRE BUADHACH, CONALL CERNACH and Cú Chulainn, each of whom have, in the *Fledd Bricrenn*,

claimed the honour of carving the roast, and after MEDHBHA of CONNACHT's judgement in favour of Cú Chulainn has been refused by the two losers. Cú Roí mac Dáiri makes the same judgement which is again refused by the losers.

During a feast at EMHAIN MHACHA, to which all the men of ULSTER had come, a rough giant entered and challenged Loeghaire Buadhach, Conall Cernach and Cú Chulainn first to cut off his head, and then to allow him to return the following evening to retaliate in kind. Both Loeghaire Buadhach and Conall Cernach cut off the giant's head, but welch on their bargain when the giant, fully restored, returns to complete their bargain. Only Cú Chulainn kneels to accept the blow that will decapitate him. The giant, however, simply touches the blade against Cú Chulainn's neck and, helping the hero to his feet, proclaims him champion of all IRELAND. That giant was none other than Cú Roí mac Dáiri, the challenge being his way of reaffirming the judgement he had earlier made in favour of Cú Chulainn.

The second appearance of Cú Roí mac Dáiri in the life of Cú Chulainn occurs when that hero is, with his men, raiding the OTHERWORLD, which is in this instance portrayed as SCOTLAND. The king appears to Cú Chulainn and his men in disguise and offers to help them. They accept and agree to share any plunder equally with the stranger. However, having captured a marvellous cauldron, three magical cows and the beautiful maiden BLÁTHNAD, the heroes break their promise and refuse to share the booty. Cú Roí mac Dáiri simply retaliates by making off with the lot. When Cú Chulainn attempted to stop him, he buried the great hero up to his armpits and shaved off all his hair, an act that forced Cú Chulainn into hiding for a year to hide his shame.

Cú Chulainn plotted his revenge at the feast of SAMHAIN with the aid of Bláthnad whom Cú Roí mac Dáiri had married. Cú Chulainn killed the king and took the Otherworldly maiden as his mistress. The death of Cú Roí mac Dáiri was avenged by his FILI, FERCHERDNE, who saw Bláthnad standing close to the edge of a cliff. Rushing at her he caught her around the waist and together they plunged headlong to their deaths on the rocks below.

## Cua(i)lngè
*Irish*

1 The owner of the bull known as the DONN CUAILNGÈ that is the subject of the *Taín Bó Cuailngè*; the owner of this beast is also known as DARA.
2 A variant of CULANN, the divine smith of the TUATHA DÉ DANANN.

## Cuare
*Irish*

A son of SCÁTHACH.

## Cuchulain(n)
*Irish*

A simple variant of CÚ CHULAINN.

## Cuculatti
*Romano-British*

'Hooded Ones', protective spirits who appear in carvings near Hadrian's Wall as well as in the Cotswolds. They appear to be male, and usually appear in groups of three. They wear hoods and cloaks that reach to either their knees or their ankles. They are possibly a Roman interpretation of the triad deities common among the Celtic peoples, but Romanized to suit their own beliefs.

## Cu(a)l(l)ann
*Irish*
Also CUAILNGÈ

The divine smith of ULSTER whose hound attacked the youth SÉDANTA. Unperturbed, the youth threw his ball down the animal's gaping throat and killed it before it could regain its senses by dashing out its brains. When Culann complained at the loss, Sédanta promised to act as a guard dog for Culann for as long as the divine smith had need of him. This promise led to the youth being known as CÚ CHULAINN, which means 'Culann's Hound'.

Culann had two daughters, AINÉ[3] and MILUCHRADH, both of whom loved FIONN MAC CUMHAILL, but neither of whom had their love requited.

## Cúldub
*Irish*

A mischievous supernatural being who, on three successive nights, stole the food of the FIAN and took back to his SÍDH. FIONN MAC CUMHAILL followed him one night, but got his thumb caught in a doorway. Removing it with difficulty he sucked it and on doing so found that he knew all that had passed and all that would occur. This is not the usual account of how Fionn mac Cumhaill gained the thumb that could be sucked to give wisdom, and appears to have been a local story.

## Culhwch
*Welsh*
Also KILHWCH, KULHWCH

The hero of the *Mabinogion* story of *Culhwch and Olwen*, although this story undoubtedly owes its origins to a much earlier legend.

Culhwch was the son of KILYDD and

GOLEUDDYDD and the sister of EIGYR. During the course of her pregnancy Goleuddydd went insane and wandered aimlessly around the countryside. The pains of labour restored her sanity just as she was in the middle of a herd of swine, the shock of her returning senses causing her to give birth immediately. She named the child Culhwch to reflect the fact that he had been born in a pig run, for *hwch* means 'pig'.

After Goleuddydd died, Kilydd remarried, although the name of his second wife remains unknown. She told Culhwch that he would only love OLWEN, the daughter of the chief giant YSPADDADEN. Culhwch set out on his quest to locate the girl and formed a party, each chosen for a particular skill, to help him. The members of this party were CEI, BEDWYR, CYNDDYLIG the Guide, GWRHYR the Interpreter, GWALCHMAI FAB GWYAR and MENW FAB TEIRGAWAEDD. At length the party came to a shepherd whose wife proved to be the aunt of Culhwch. Although she had lost twenty-three of her twenty-four sons to Yspaddaden, she vowed to help Culhwch meet Olwen, who came to wash her hair at the women's cottage every Saturday.

Olwen came as the woman had said that Saturday, and when she met Culhwch she agreed to become his wife on condition that he ask her father for her hand, warning him not to flinch from any condition he might set. On three successive days Culhwch and his companions went to Yspaddaden's castle. On each occasion the giant told them to come back the following morning and, as they turned their backs on the castle, hurled a poisoned stone at them. Culhwch and his friends were always too quick and caught the stone and threw it back. On the fourth day, as the poisoned stones had taken effect on the giant, Yspaddaden agreed to Culhwch's suit, provided he complete three tasks. The first of these involved the felling and burning of a thicket, ploughing its ashes into a field, and sowing that new field with flax. The second involved the collection of a variety of provisions for the wedding feast, while the third was to obtain various preparations and pieces of equipment, among them a razor and comb from between the ears of the great boar TWRCH TRWYTH, with which to barber Yspaddaden.

The giant imposed innumerable conditions, and, as Yspaddaden mentioned each, he added that it would be impossible to fulfil. Culhwch, remembering the advice of Olwen, simply replied that he could accomplish any task with ease. Finally, unable to stand the continual opposition of the giant, even though he had completed all the tasks set him, Culhwch gathered together all of the giant's enemies, returned to his castle, and killed Yspaddaden. Culhwch married Olwen, and the two remained faithful to each other throughout their lives.

Later versions of this story are slightly elaborated to include King ARTHUR, saying that Culhwch was his cousin, and it was he who helped Culhwch to form the party that helped him in his quest and later to obtain the comb and razor from between the ears of the great boar Twrch Trywth.

## Culhwch and Olwen
*Welsh*

A complex, and possibly incomplete, pre-eleventh-century Welsh romance that forms a part of the *Mabinogion*. It tells of the attempts of CULHWCH to locate the maiden OLWEN whom he is to marry, and then to carry out the numerous tasks set him by her father YSPADDADEN. This story undoubtedly owes its origins to a much earlier legend, and it was subsequently embroidered to include King ARTHUR of whom Culhwch was said to be a cousin.

## Cumha(i)l(l)
*Irish*

The father of the great hero of the FIAN, FIONN MAC CUMHAILL, by MUIRNE, daughter of TADG. Fionn mac Cumhaill was born posthumously after Cumhaill had been killed by AODH[2].

## Cunedagius
*British*

The brother of MARGANUS, their mother being either GONERIL or REGAN, the elder daughters of LEIR. Five years after the death of Leir, the two brothers usurped CORDELIA's throne and took her prisoner. Cordelia, in despair, took her own life.

## Cunedda
*British*

His pedigree suggests that Cunedda originated from a Roman family. He was a ruler of the Votadini of North BRITAIN[1] who emigrated to WALES and rid a large part of that country of Irish invaders sometime around 430. It has been suggested that he took Gwawl, the daughter of COEL, as his wife. Cunedda was later incorporated into the Arthurian cycle as it was said that he was the great-grandfather of ARTHUR through his daughter GWERT whose own daughter was Arthur's mother IGRAINE, or EIGYR as she was known in Welsh tradition. This, however, is a confusion, for Eigyr was usually regarded as the sister of CULHWCH, whose parents were KILYDD and GOLEUDDYDD.

## Cunobelinus
*British*

'The Hound of Belinus', the son of TENUANTIUS and ruler of the CATU-VELLAUNI who, some time during the first century, made himself the king over a considerable part of southern BRITAIN[1] and ruled for thirty years in peace.

## Cunomorus
*British and Gaulish*

An historical ancient ruler of CORNWALL and BRITTANY. Warned that one of his sons would kill him, Cunomorus had each of his wives killed as soon as they announced they were pregnant. One wife, TREPHINA, escaped this fate and managed to avoid Cunomorus until after she had given birth to Judwal or TREMEUR. Her son was exposed and left to die while Cunomorus had her decapitated, but she was restored to life. Trephina picked up her head, which she tucked under her arm. She then went back to Cunomorus' castle, the battlements of which fell in and killed Cunomorus.

## Cur
*Irish*

A warrior of CONNACHT, the son of DALY. He went out to fight CÚ CHULAINN, obviously unaware of the prowess of the youth he was to be pitted against. Cú Chulainn was eating an apple as Cur approached and, turning to face his attacker, he threw it with such force that it smashed straight through Cur's head.

## Curcog
*Irish*

The daughter of MANANNÁN MAC LIR. Her handmaiden was EITHNE[4] who had been born at the exact same moment as she had.

## Cuscrid
*Irish*

The son of CONCHOBAR MAC NESSA. He appears in the story of MAC DÁ THÓ's pig as one of those warriors who challenges CET and is ridiculed by him.

## Custennin
*Welsh*

According to the pedigree of Anlawdd that has been postulated by T.W. Rolleston, Custennin was the son of Anlawdd and brother of YSPADDADEN and GOLEUDDYDD.

## Cyledyr the Wild
*Welsh*

One of those involved in the quest to locate OLWEN and the one who managed to snatch the shears required to barber YSPADDADEN from between the ears of the boar TWRCH TRWYTH.

## Cyllel Llawfrodedd
*Welsh*

A DRUID sacrificial knife, said to have numbered among the THIRTEEN TREASURES of BRITAIN[1].

## Cynan
*Welsh*

The son of EUDAF and brother of GADEON and ELEN. He and his brother later came to the help of MACSEN, whom Elen had married, and brought an army of Britons to help Macsen retake Rome. In return, Cynan was given the province of ARMORICA, where his men killed all the men but kept the women for themselves, cutting out their tongues so that they could not speak their native, alien language.

## Cynddylig the Guide
*Welsh*

One of the party who were to help CULHWCH locate and win the hand of the maiden OLWEN, daughter of the chief giant YSPADDADEN. The other members of the party were CEI, BEDWYR[2], GWRHYR, GWALCHMAI FAB GWYAR and MENW FAB TEIRGWAEDD. Each member of the party was chosen for a particular skill, that of Cynddylig being obvious from his epithet.

## Cyn-farch, -varch
*Welsh*

The father of URIEN.

## Cyngen (fab Cadell)
*Welsh*

Also CONCENN

A legendary King of POWYS, who was said to have reigned some time between the fifth and sixth centuries, although the Pillar of ELISEG puts his death in Rome somewhat later – 854.

## Cynon
*Welsh*

The lover of MORFUDD.

## Dá Chich nAnann
*Irish*

'The Paps of Anu', two hills in Kerry that resemble breasts and are named after DANU, although here under her variant ANU. The naming of these hills after that goddess reflects her chthonic nature as an earth and fertility deity.

## Da Derga
*Irish*

A lord of LEINSTER, whose home is described as a hostel, a place where travellers were always welcome. This home is the subject of the lengthy *Da Derga's Hostel*, which tells of the arrival of CONAIRE MÓR at the hostel, his death there after he had broken all the bonds placed on him at his birth and the destruction of the home of Da Derga.

## Dá Thó
*Irish*

A wealthy lord of LEINSTER and the father of MESRODA. His son owned a magnificent pig, or boar, the ownership of which became the subject of the ribald *Scéla Mucce Maic Dá Thó*. Because of this story, his son is better known simply as MAC DÁ THÓ.

## Dag(h)d(h)a
*Irish*

The son of ELADU, the Daghdha was an earth and father god and one of the two greatest kings of the TUATHA DÉ DANANN, although he was, on one occasion, forced to build the tyrant BRES[1] a fort. He originally lived at BRUGH NA BÓINNE, County MEATH. A hugely successful military leader of superhuman capacity, he owned a harp that played by itself and that could invoke the seasons, a wondrous cauldron of plenty called UNDRY, and a massive club, one end of which brought death to the recipient of the blow, while the other would restore a dead person to life. His wife had three names: BRENG meaning 'lie', MENG meaning 'guile' and MEABEL meaning 'disgrace'. She bore him three daughters, all of whom were named BRIGHID. His wife and daughters are yet further examples of the triad goddess that is common among Celtic and other pagan cultures, the most famous Celtic example being the MÓRRÍGHAN. The Daghdha is known as DUGAL the Brown in a traditional genealogy of St BRIDE.

With a name meaning 'Great God', the Daghdha was destined, if only by name, to become the greatest of all the Irish gods, although the description is principally meant to signify that he was not simply the master of one trade, but more a godly 'Jack of all trades' and master of all of them. He was also known as EOCHAIDH OLLATHAIR ('Eochaidh the Great Father') and RUADH ROFHESSA ('red one of great knowledge' or 'Mighty and Most Learned One'). His principal association appears to have been with the DRUIDS as the god of wisdom, a primal father deity of enormous power, combining elements of the sky father, war god and a chthonic fertility deity with those of a powerful sorcerer. His attributes of a club and a cauldron are potent spiritual and magical icons to the Celts, both of which appear to resurface in later Arthurian tradition as the Lance of Longinus and the Holy GRAIL.

His cauldron gave a perpetual supply of food, much of which he gave away to the needy, and had the power, just as one end of his club did, to restore the dead to life, although it could also heal those who had been merely wounded. It appears to have provided not simply physical nourishment but also nourishment of a spiritual nature. The dual polarity of the club signifies power, and the control of such a wonderful cauldron rightly asserts the position of the Daghdha as a god of fertility and abundance. His club was so massive that eight men could not lift it, and it had to be mounted on wheels for ease of transport, and yet the Daghdha had no trouble in wielding it. If he simply dragged it along the ground behind him it would leave a furrow that was as deep as a frontier ditch.

The Daghdha is usually, although not always, described as a giant wearing short peasant's clothing that revealed his buttocks. This mode of dress may have been an attempt to portray the sexuality of the god, for his sexual prowess was, even among the Celtic gods, outstanding. On one notable occasion he was said to have mated with the Mórríghan on the eve of SAMHAIN, this feat being accomplished while the goddess was straddling the river UNIUS, in which she continued to wash the armour of those who would die in the forthcoming Second Battle of MAGH TUIREDH. This theme of a god of life mating with a goddess of death is found in many pagan cultures, although not all of them adopt such an uncomfortable position.

The Daghdha was also said to have been the father of OENGHUS MAC IN OG through an illicit union with BOANN, this time in a position that is not specified, although usually this coupling is said to have taken place on the same day as he had straddled the River Unius with the Mórríghan. The Daghdha is also said to have been the father of, among others, OGHMA, MIDHIR and BODB.

His presence at the Second Battle of Magh Tuiredh led to an attempt by the FOMHOIRÉ to disable him. The Daghdha had an insatiable appetite, an appetite that resulted in his having an ugly and portly figure, quite often the butt of derisive remarks, his waddling walk causing much amusement. Before the battle that was to finally establish the Tuatha Dé Danann as the rulers of IRELAND, the Fomhoiré, boiled a huge cauldron of porridge, which they encouraged the Daghdha to eat. The cauldron they used was nothing more than a gaping hole in the ground, but the Daghdha easily finished the porridge, which consisted of eighty normal cauldrons full of oats, milk and fat that had been stuffed with whole sheep, pigs and goats. His spoon on this occasion was big enough to hold both a man and a woman. Having scooped out all he could with his spoon, he ran his finger around the gravel lining of the hole to make sure he had not missed a single drop. His physical appetite then satisfied, he sought to satisfy his sexual one with one of the Fomhoiré women, who was so impressed by his prowess that she agreed to use her magical powers against her own people during the forthcoming battle.

Following the victory of the Tuatha Dé Danann over the Fomhoiré, brought about when LUGH killed BALAR with a slingshot, he, Lugh and OGHMA recovered the stolen harp, thus restoring the seasons to their rightful order. Later, after the Tuatha Dé Danann had been conquered by the invading Sons of MÍL ÉSPÁINE, he gave each of the Tuatha Dé Danann a sídh in which to live after they had been awarded the underground half of Ireland by their conquerors. His own sídh contained a magical pig that could be eaten one day, but which would reappear the following day, whole again, and ready and willing to be eaten again.

Although the Daghdha is normally treated as a grotesquely comic figure, just as the god Thórr is in Norse-Teutonic tradition, there is little doubt about his ultimate authority, and the manner in which the Daghdha is portrayed seems to be little more than light-hearted ribaldry. See also AINGE.

## Dahut
*Gaulish*

A variant of AHES and the name by which she is known as the daughter of GRADLON, who threw her into the sea after she had caused the sea to engulf YS, a domain she is still said to inhabit, luring sailors to their death in the drowned city.

## Daire
*Irish*

A son of FIONN MAC CUMHAILL. He was swallowed by a monster but hacked his way out from inside the creature, thus setting free the other inhabitants of the monster's stomach.

## Daire mac Fiachna
*Irish*

A son of FIACHNA and one of the guardians of the DONN CUAILNGÈ, whom he led, in the company of the MÓRRÍGHAN, past CÚ CHULAINN, although that hero failed to recognize the Mórríghan, a mistake that was to cost him his life.

## Dál nAraidi
*Irish*

The Irish kingdom from which a group emigrated to found the kingdom of DÁL RIADA on the west coast of SCOTLAND. Close links remained between the two kingdoms, FIACHNA LURGAN, King of Dál nAraidi, remaining a close ally of AEDÁN MAC GADRÁIN, king of Dál Riada.

## Dál Ria-da, -ta
*Irish*

An ancient Hiberno-Scottish kingdom on the west coast of SCOTLAND, which today covers Argyllshire, although it also included a small region in the north of that country. It was founded by a group of emigrants from the kingdom of DÁL NARAIDI, and it is the alleged homeland of the Scottish people. The king of the newly founded domain, AEDÁN MAC GABRÁIN, maintained close links with the parent kingdom and was a close ally of FIACHNA LURGAN.

## Dalan
*Irish*

A DRUID who was employed by EOCHAIDH AIREMH to discover the whereabouts of his wife ÉDÁIN ECHRAIDHE after she had been abducted by MIDHIR. After a year Dalan reported to Eochaidh that he had located his wife at the sídh of BRÍ LEITH.

## Dall
*Irish*

The father of PHELIM MAC DALL, the court story-teller of CONCHOBAR MAC NESSA. The son is better known as FEDLIMID.

## Dalny
*Irish*

An anglicization of DEALGNAID, the wife of PARTHOLÁN.

## Daly
*Irish*

An inhabitant of CONNACHT and the father of CUR.

## Daman
*Irish*

One of the FIR BHOLG and the father of FERDIA.

## Damona
*Gaulish*

'Divine Cow', the goddess of a cow cult with whom the god BORMO is paired, a pairing that represents a plentiful supply of nourishment.

## Danand
*Irish*

A variant of DANU in which form she is mentioned in connection with BÉCHUILLE and was made a foster mother to the gods.

## Danann
*Irish*

A mistaken variant of DANU. It comes about from a misunderstanding of the TUATHA DÉ DANANN, which, as this variant illustrates, was once thought to mean the 'People of Danann'. However, the correct translation is the 'People of the Goddess Danu'.

## Dan-u, -a
*Irish*

A mother goddess, the daughter of the DAGHDHA and mother of a brood of gods who were collectively known as the TUATHA DÉ DANANN, or literally the 'People of the Goddess Danu'. A shadowy figure, about whom little is known, and possibly having OTHERWORLDLY connections, she also appears to have been known as BRIGHID, for her remembrance survives in the Christian calendar as St Brighid. The mother of BRIAN, IUCHAR and IUCHARBA, she is usually conceived of as a benevolent goddess, though she is sometimes, perversely, under her variant name of ANU, included within the malevolent triad that is the MÓRRÍGHAN, her partners in this association being BADHBH and MACHA. She also has connections with the moon goddess AINÉ, patroness of crops and cattle.

Some authorities have suggested that the Tuatha Dé Danann are a relatively late idea, their original name having been Danu, and it was only the later concept of a single MOTHER GODDESS that led to their subsequent naming.

## Danu, The People of the Goddess
*Irish*

The literal translation of TUATHA DÉ DANANN.

## Dara
*Irish*

1 The son of FACHTNA and the owner of the DONN CUAILNGÈ, the great Brown Bull that is the subject of the *Taín Bó*

*Cuailngè*. The owner of the beast is also known as Cuailngè.

2 The DRUID of CORMAC MAC AIRT. During the wedding feast of GRÁINNE and FIONN MAC CUMHAILL, it was Dara who told Gráinne about DIARMAID UA DUIBHNE, and about his BALL-SEIRC, which made him irresistible to women.

## Darerca
*Irish*

According to Jocelyn's *Life of Saint Patrick* Darerca was that saint's sister and had no fewer than seventeen sons. Her sister Tigridia was said to have married Grallo.

## Dathi
*Irish*

An historical ruler of IRELAND, one of the last Celtic kings to rule at TARA before the arrival of St PATRICK. He led a military campaign into BRITAIN[1], and from there into the continent, that was said to have been ordained by his DRUIDS. The campaign foundered when Dathi was struck by lightning while storming a tower in the Rhine Valley. His body was carried back to Ireland and he was buried in the royal cemetary of RELIGH NA RIGHT at RÁTH CRUACHAN. There, a 7-foot high stone pillar still marks his grave among the numerous earthworks.

## De Excidio et Conquestu Britanniae
*British*

This famous text, probably written between 516 and 547, by the British writer GILDAS is the only extant history of the Celts and the only contemporary version of events from the Roman invasion to his own time. An invaluable source to the Celtic researcher, the text mentions many of the events and places later to become associated with King ARTHUR, but does not actually mention him by name. It can therefore be considered a far truer account than those of writers such as NENNIUS[1] or GEOFFREY OF MONMOUTH.

## De Gabail int Sída
*Irish*

*The Conquest of the Fairy Mound*, one of the eight manuscripts that together form the *Book of Leinster*. This tells how the DAGHDHA apportioned the SÍDH among the TUATHA DÉ DANANN, although his son, OENGHUS MAC IN OG, was omitted as he was with his foster father MIDHIR. Returning, he claimed the sídh of BRUGH NA BÓINNE from his father, but his request was refused. Oenghus Mac in Og then asked to be allowed to stay the night, which he was, along with the following day. However, when the Daghdha asked him to leave, he refused as he had stayed in the sídh for a night and a day, and thus the sídh was rightfully his. The Daghdha had to agree and was thus dispossessed.

## Dea Caelistis
*Romano-British*

A Roman high goddess whose name appears in an inscription found on Hadrian's Wall that associates BRIGANTIA with Dea Caelistis, thus raising the status of the local deity to the highest ranking and ensuring her worship by both the native population and the Roman invaders.

## Dealgnaid
*Irish*

The wife of PARTHOLÁN, whom she accompanied to IRELAND, and the mother of RURY, although the true father of Rury may have been TOPA, manservant to

Partholán, rather than Partholán himself, for Dealgnaid is said to have seduced Topa and thus instigated the first legal proceedings ever. She, her husband and her son all died in the pestilence that ended the occupation of Ireland by the people of Partholán, the sole survivor being Partholán's nephew TUAN MAC STERN.

## Deca(i)r
*Irish*

An inhabitant of TÍR TAIRNGIRI, who brought a magical steed from that land to FIONN MAC CUMHAILL and the FIAN. This miserable looking animal reacted wildly when it was placed among the horses of the fian and bit them. CONAN MAC MORNA was ordered to ride the horse to its death, but it refused to move. Thirteen other members of the fian leapt on the animal's back, whereupon it fled, with another member of the fian swinging from its tail, back to Tír Tairngiri whence Decair returned by running under the sea. The members of the fian were later rescued by Fionn mac Cumhaill.

## Decies
*Irish*

A mysterious people, who only appear briefly in the story of the death of FIONN MAC CUMHAILL and the end of the FIAN. A son of the king asked for the hand of SGEIMH SOLAIS in marriage, which led the fian to ask for a customary tribute. Sgeimh Solais' father, CAIRPRE, was having none of this and went to war against the fian.

## Decter-a, -e
*Irish*
See DEICHTINE.

## Deerhurst
*British*

A small village 7 miles north of Gloucester and the ancient capital of the Celtic kingdom of HWICCE. Traces of a Roman settlement and a Celtic monastery have been discovered here. Various pagan and Christian kings ruled from Deerhurst until the seventh century, when Deerhurst was claimed for the Roman church.

## Deichtine
*Irish*

The sister or daughter of CONCHOBAR MAC NESSA, wife of SUALTAM, and the mother of the hero CÚ CHULAINN whose father was said to have been the god LUGH, although others say that it was none other than her father, Conchobar mac Nessa. Other sources call her Dectera and make her the daughter of CATHBHADH.

## De(i)mn-e, -a
*Irish*

The name by which FIONN MAC CUMHAILL was first known. He received the name by which he is better known at the age of ten when he was described as 'fair', both in looks and in play, after which it was ordered that he should be known as Fionn, for *fionn* means 'fair'. See also MUIRNE.

## Deirdre
*Irish*

An alternative, modern spelling of DERDRIU.

## Delbaeth
*Irish*

The brother of the DAGHDHA and, according to some, the father of the goddess DANU, although this relationship seems highly improbable, as it would be impossible for Danu to be the mother of the gods if she were not born until after the gods themselves. Another story makes Delbaeth a FOMHOIRÉ and the father of LUGH by ÉRI. See also ANU.

## Delbchaem
*Irish*

The mysterious female being whom BÉCUMA sent ART to fetch to TARA while she bewitched Art's father CONN CÉTCHATHLACH. Very little is said about Delbchaem other than that she lived in one of the Irish OTHERWORLDS. By sending Art to fetch her to Tara, Bécuma thought that she would be killing the youth, but he returned triumphant and Bécuma left in disgust.

## Delgnat
*Irish*
See DEALGNAID.

## Demetia
*Welsh*

The ancient name for the kingdom of DYFED in the south of WALES. According to GEOFFREY OF MONMOUTH the kingdom was ruled by STATER during the fifth or sixth century, but history knows nothing of a king of this name.

## Demetrus
*Welsh*

The maternal grandfather of MYRDDIN, whose name appears to be a simple variant of DEMETIA, the kingdom in southern WALES that was the home of MYRDDIN's mother.

## Deoca
*Irish*

A princess of MUNSTER who became betrothed to a CONNACHT chief called LAIRGNEN. She begged him to bring her the four marvellous singing swans she had heard of, these swans being the four children of LIR who had been condemned to take that form for 900 years by their step-mother AOIFE. Lairgnen duly trapped the four swans and brought them to his intended, but as soon as they arrived a dreadful transformation began, the sight of which made Lairgnen flee from the palace, never to be seen again. Their 900 years had come to an end and they began to revert back to their original form, though now they were old and withered. They were quickly baptized into the Christian faith, for death was near. FIONUALA, the only one of them to speak, asked that upon their death they should be buried in one grave with CONN[2] at her right, FIACHTRA at her left, and HUGH in front of her. Moments later they died and were buried as requested.

## Derbrenn
*Irish*

The first love of OENGHUS MAC IN OG, and the foster mother to the six children whose natural mother turned them into swine, after which Oenghus Mac in Og sent them to be cared for by BUICHET.

## Derdriu
*Irish*

The daughter of FEDLIMID, the FILI of CONCHOBAR MAC NESSA. The DRUID CATHBHADH prophesied that she would be exceptionally beautiful but that she would cause much suffering in ULSTER. At her birth, and remembering the prophecy, many wanted to have her killed, but

Conchobar mac Nessa decreed that she should live and that he would marry her when she came of age.

Derdriu was raised in the strictest seclusion by the wise woman LEBHORCHAM. One day, while she watched her foster father flay a newly killed calf in the snow, she saw a raven land and drink the blood. Remarking that she would love a man whose hair was a black as the raven, whose blood was as red as that of the calf and whose skin was as white as the snow, she learnt from Lebhorcham that just such a man was NAOISE, one of three brothers who were known as the sons of UISNECH. Immediately she contrived a plan that would allow her to meet him, which she did as he rode through the woods.

Naoise was everything Derdriu had hoped for, but he, remembering the prophecy of Cathbhadh and knowing of her betrothal, was reluctant to respond, even though he found Derdriu exceptionally beautiful. She countered by saying that if he did not become her lover she would make him a laughing stock. Caught in a hopeless trap, Naoise fled to SCOTLAND with Derdriu and his two brothers, ARDÁN and AINNLE. Conchobar mac Nessa was furious, and it was some time before the men of Ulster managed to persuade him to call a truce and ask the fugitives to return home. Finally, Conchobar mac Nessa sent FERGHUS MAC ROICH, DUBTHACH and Dubthach's son, CORMAC MAC DUBTHACH, to ask them to return and to guarantee their safety. However, when Derdriu and her companions returned, Conchobar mac Nessa reneged and had the young men killed by EOGHAN MAC DURTHACHT and his men. Furious at this deceit, Ferghus mac Roich, Dubthach and Cormac mac Dubthach stormed and razed EMHAIN MHACHA, killed 300 of the men of Ulster, and defected to AILILL and MEDHBHA

of CONNACHT, the great enemies of Conchobar mac Nessa.

For a whole year Derdriu pined, never once lifting her head. Finally, Conchobar mac Nessa asked her what she disliked most in the world. She replied that it was Conchobar mac Nessa himself, with Eoghan mac Durthacht a close second. Conchobar mac Nessa decreed that, since she had spent a year with him, she would spend the next with Eoghan mac Durthacht. The very next day, as she was travelling to Eoghan mac Durthacht, Derdriu threw herself from the chariot and dashed her brains out against a rock.

### Dermot (O'Dyna)
*Irish*

The latinized form of DIARMAID (UA DUIBHNE).

### Desa
*Irish*

The father of the monstrous sons who laid seige to the hostel of DA DERGA while CONAIRE MÓR was staying there.

### Devorgilla
*Irish*

The princess who was to be given to the FOMHOIRÉ as tribute by her father but was rescued by CÚ CHULAINN who was returning to IRELAND from his time with SCÁTHACH. Devorgilla was awarded to Cú Chulainn, but he gave her to LUGAID[2] as he was to be married to EMER. Devorgilla and her handmaiden changed themselves into birds to seek out Cú Chulainn, who fired a slingshot at them and wounded them, whereon they resumed their true form. Cú Chulainn sucked out the shot with which he had wounded them, but this made it impossible for Devorgilla even to entertain the thought of marriage to Cú Chulainn as he had swallowed her blood, which made him her brother.

## Dewrarth Wledig
*Welsh*

An alternative for GWYDDNO GARANHIR.

## Dian (Cécht)
*Irish*

The god of healing, depicted as a huge leech, and the mythical author of *The Judgements of Dian Cécht*, a tract concerning the legal responsibilities of one who has caused another injury or illness. The aggressor is held responsible for paying the bills incurred for the cure of the person hurt, with wounds being measured in grains of corn, so that even the smallest wound has its price.

Dian Cécht has, in later Romano-Celtic tradition, been assimilated with the Roman god Apollo, for he, like that god, slew a giant serpent that threatened the land. This serpent came from MEICHE, the son of the MÓRRÍGHAN, whom Dian Cécht killed. Cutting open the body, he discovered three hearts, one for each aspect of his triad mother, each being a snake's head. He immediately burned two hearts, but the third escaped and grew into the serpent he later killed. Dian Cécht threw the ashes of the burned hearts into the River Barrow, whose waters became corrosive.

With the serpent comes the undeniable iconography of the healer, for to this day a staff entwined by a serpent, the staff or *caduceus* of Asclepios, the Graeco-Roman god of medicine, remains in use as a symbol employed by numerous medical bodies. Again this further links Dian Cécht and Apollo, for Apollo was also considered a god of healing.

Dian Cécht was most notably active during the two battles of MAGH TUIREDH.

After the first, and with the help of the divine smith CREIDHNE, he fashioned and fitted an arm made out of silver to replace the one that NUADHA had lost in that battle. The Second Battle of Magh Tuiredh kept Dian Cécht particularly busy, for he revived the fallen and wounded TUATHA DÉ DANANN by plunging them into a magic well or bath. He had three sons, all of whom were healers and who helped him in this enormous task. Following the battle, he killed one of them, MIDACH, for he was becoming too skilful and thus represented a threat to his father's reputation and position.

Dian Cécht could also replace lost eyes or cure blindness by using the eyes of cats. This operation, however, had one distinct disadvantage in that the replacement eye would sleep during the day and be wide awake during the night, alert to every movement or sound and responsive to the slightest noise.

## Diarmaid ua Duibhne
*Irish*

The foster son of OENGHUS MAC IN OG, Diarmaid ua Duibhne received a spot on his forehead from a mysterious maiden, who informed him that any woman who saw that spot would instantly fall in love with him. It was this spot, his BALL-SEIRC, that made GRÁINNE become besotted with him, even though she was betrothed to the ageing FIONN MAC CUMHAILL, of whom Diarmaid ua Duibhne was a loyal subject. On the night of her wedding feast, Gráinne drugged Fionn mac Cumhaill and all those present and then, casting a GESSA spell on Diarmaid ua Duibhne, forced him to elope with her to a wood in CONNACHT where they were besieged by Fionn mac Cumhaill.

Gráinne was rescued from the wood by Oenghus Mac in Og, and Diarmaid ua

Duibhne escaped by jumping, in a single tremendous bound, straight over the heads of the attackers. Safe from attack, Diarmaid ua Duibhne still refused to break his oath to Fionn mac Cumhaill and to take the maiden as his mistress, and it was only after she had derided him wickedly that he was driven to be disloyal.

Gráinne bore Diarmaid ua Duibhne four sons and finally, with the help of Oenghus Mac in Og, they were reconciled with Fionn mac Cumhaill. With their quarrel patched up, Diarmaid ua Duibhne accompanied Fionn mac Cumhaill when he went to hunt the magical boar of BEANN GHULBAN, even though it had been prophesied that the boar, Diarmaid ua Duibhne's foster brother, would kill him. During the hunt, Diarmaid ua Duibhne was mortally gored, seconds before he struck the killing blow to the boar. His life could be saved only if Fionn mac Cumhaill, who had the gift of healing, would give him water out of his own hands. Fionn mac Cumhaill fetched some water but, remembering Diarmaid ua Duibhne's treachery, allowed it to trickle away through his fingers. Again he fetched some water, and again allowed it to seep away. By the time he returned the third time Diarmaid ua Duibhne had died.

### Diarmuid mac Cearbhaill
*Irish*

An historic sixth-century king of IRELAND whose latinized name is Dermot MacKerval. His reign marked the progress of the Irish towards true national unity. Diarmuid mac Cearbhaill upheld all the laws of the land, but this led him into trouble with the clergy, who had sought to shelter a chief by the name of Hugh Guairy who had murdered one of the king's officers. The king sought him

out and dragged him from the sanctuary he had been offered in order to stand trial at TARA. This offended the clergy who gathered at Tara and, through their prayers, cursed the royal court, which was thenceforth abandoned by subsequent kings of Ireland.

### Dil
*Irish*

The daughter of LUGMANNAIR who was loved by TULCHAINDE, DRUID to CONAIRE MÓR. Tulchainde wanted Dil to elope with him from the Isle of FALGA (Isle of MAN). Dil loved two magically conceived oxen, FEA and FERNEA, and begged Tulchainde to take them with her. He managed this with the help of the MÓRRÍGHAN who magically conveyed them from Falga to MAGH MBREG.

### Dillus
*Welsh*

In *Culhwch and Olwen* Dillus' beard was required by the giant YSPADDADEN as one of the conditions he set CULHWCH if he were to marry OLWEN. The task was completed by CEI, who cast Dillus into a hole in the ground and pulled out the hairs of his beard with a pair of tweezers.

### Dinabutius
*Welsh*

The name of a young boy who taunted the youthful MYRDDIN for not knowing his father's name. This taunting brought Myrddin to the attention of VORTIGERN's counsellors, for Vortigern was looking for a fatherless child to sacrifice in an attempt to cure the problem he was having with building his tower at DINAS EMRYS which, every time he built it, promptly fell down again.

## Dinas Dinnllev
*Welsh*

The home of GWYDION FAB DÔN in which he raised LLEU LLAW GYFFES from his birth until the second curse of ARIANRHOD.

## Dinas Emrys
*Welsh*

Situated 2 miles northeast of Beddgelert, GWYNEDD, is a wooded hill known as Dinas Emrys. Here VORTIGERN repeatedly attempted to build a tower, but every night the stones fell down again. His counsellors advised him that he needed to sacrifice a fatherless child, for which MYRDDIN was considered ideal, for he was supposed to have been born without a father, the offspring of an *incubus*. However, Myrddin advised Vortigern that the real problem was the fact that two DRAGONS, one white and one red, were confined beneath the site in a subterranean lake. Myrddin subsequently dealt with the dragons and built his own fortress on the hilltop.

Details of how the dragons came to be imprisoned beneath the hill can be found in the story *Lludd and Llefelys*. During LLUDD's reign a scream, whose origin could not be found, was heard on every eve of May Day LLEFELYS, the King of France and Lludd's brother, told him that it was caused by fighting dragons, which were subsequently captured and buried at Dinas Emrys.

Some earthworks of the ancient for may still be seen on this site, with the main entrance on the northern side of the hill. Traces of a ruined tower, some 36 feet by 24 feet, have been found on the summit, although whether these are the ruins of Vortigern's tower or Myrddin's fort remains open to speculation. Nearby lies a circle of tumbled stones, roughly 30 feet in diameter, which is said to be a mystic ring in which the battling dragons were contained. At one time the fort was known as *Dinas Fforan*, 'The Fort with High Powers'.

Myrddin's treasure is apparently hidden in a cave at Dinas Emrys. It was placed in a golden vessel in the cave along with his golden chair, and Myrddin then rolled a huge stone over the entrance of the cave and covered it with earth and grass. Tradition states that the discoverer of the treasure will be 'golden-haired and blue-eyed'. When that person comes near, a bell will be heard, inviting him, or her, into the cave, which will open of its own accord the instant that person's foot touches the stone covering the entrance. A youth living near Beddgelert once searched for the treasure. Taking a pickaxe with him he climbed to the top of the hill and started to dig on the site of the tower. As soon as he did, unearthly noises began to rumble beneath his feet and the whole of Dinas Emrys began to rock like a cradle. The sun clouded over and day became as night. Thunder roared over his head and lightning flashed all around him. Dropping his pick-axe, he ran for home and, when he arrived, everything was calm, but he never returned to retrieve the pick-axe.

Not far from Dinas Emrys is CELL-Y-DEWINIAID where Vortigern's counsellors were said to meet to discuss the events of their times. They were buried in an adjacent field, at one time each grave being marked by a stone, a white thorn tree annually decorating each with falling white blossoms.

## *Dinnshenchas*
*Irish*

*The Lore of the Prominent Places*, a twelfth-century Christian collection of Irish legends concerning the origins of local place-names, which has been described as 'mythological geography'. In places it echoes the stories of the *Taín Bó Cuailngè*, and mentions sacred trees that were alleged to have been planted by the gods as they passed.

## Dinsul
*British*

'Mount of the Sun', the pre-Christian Celtic name for ST MICHAEL'S MOUNT.

## 'Dis Pater'
*Romano-Gaulish*

Originally an unnamed deity who was given his name by the Romans to equate him with their own god Dis Pater, the god of death. JULIUS CAESAR wrote that the Celts of GAUL regarded this deity as the divine ancestor of mankind and not a god of death at all. It has been suggested that the association was made so that the indigenous Gauls would come to believe that even their divine ancestor could not save them from the Romans. Some authorities state that the original of 'Dis Pater' was the god SUCELLOS.

## Dithorba
*Irish*

The brother of MACHA and CIMBAOTH. When his sister Macha refused to give up the throne after the death of their father, Dithorba was fought and killed, and Cimbaoth was forced to marry his sister, who ruled all IRELAND as queen. The five sons of Dithorba fled to the west of Ireland and plotted their revenge. They were caught and forced to build the ramparts of EMHAIN MHACHA.

## Diuran
*Irish*

One of the companions of MAÍL DÚIN.

## Diwrnach
*Welsh*

The Irish owner of a wondrous cauldron, which he refused to hand over to CULHWCH. An expedition was mounted to IRELAND, Diwrnach slain and the cauldron seized. Subsequently this cauldron became one of the THIRTEEN TREASURES of BRITAIN[1]. The appearance of a wondrous Irish cauldron in this tale leads to a possible identification between Diwrnach and the DAGHDHA and, latterly, with the Holy GRAIL.

## Doel
*Irish*

The father of ACTHLAND and COIRPRE, as well as several other unnamed sons. The story of the disappearance of his sons from IRELAND, and their subsequent rescue by CÚ CHULAINN, is told in the *Longes mac nDuil Dermait*.

## Domnal
*Irish*

A warlike inhabitant of SCOTLAND whom FORGALL urged CÚ CHULAINN to seek out in the hope that he would be killed and thus not return to claim the hand of EMER. Domnal, however, recognized the power of Cú Chulainn and taught him all manner of wonderful feats before despatching him to learn even more from SCÁTHACH. During his time with Domnal, Cú Chulainn had rebuffed the amorous advances of DORNOLLA. In revenge she caused Cú Chulainn's companions to feel so homesick that Cú Chulainn was left alone in Scotland.

## Dôn
*Welsh*

MOTHER GODDESS, daughter of MATHONWY,

sister of MATH FAB MATHONWY and wife of BELI. She is the Welsh equivalent of the Irish DANU. Her children, known collectively as the Children of Dôn, included gods of the sky, sea and poetry, all of whom were locked in eternal battle with the children of LLYR, their opposites, the powers of darkness. Traditionally she was the mother of GILFAETHWY, ARIANRHOD and GWYDION FAB DÔN, as well as several others as illustrated in her traditional genealogy.

## Donn
*Romano-Gaulish*

A form of 'DIS PATER'.

## Dôn(n)
*Irish*

1 The discourteous leader of the Sons of MÍL ÉSPÁINE. He was drowned shortly after they arrived and, after he was buried on the island of TECH DUINN where he was shipwrecked, became god of the dead. He still welcomes dead warriors to the island. His name means 'Dark' or 'Brown One', and some authorities have sought to identify him with the DAGHDHA, but the two are clearly different characters. Modern Irish folklore sees Dônn not only as the god of the dead, but also as the ambivalent god of storms and shipwrecks, and a patron of crops and cattle.
2 Sometimes identified with DÔNN[1], this Dônn first appears in the form of a swineherd in the *Taín Bó Cuailngè* who, after a multitude of animal reincarnations, was reborn as the DONN CUAILNGÈ. Dônn is possibly to be identified with the Gaulish TARVOS TRIGARANS.
3 The father of DIARMAID UA DUIBHNE. He killed the boy born to his wife after she had an affair with ROC. This child

was reincarnated as the monstrous BEANN GHULBAN.

## Donn Bo
*Irish*

A famous story-teller and minstrel at the court of King FERGAL. Although he was killed in battle, he continued to sing the praises of his king, who had also been killed in the battle. His head was cut off and taken back to a feasting hall, where it continued to sing with such sweetness that it moved those attending to tears and caused many of them to renounce their pagan faith and accept Christianity.

## Donn Cuailngè
*Irish*

To be identified with DÔNN[2]. Donn Cuailngè was the name of the brown bull that belonged to CUAILNGÈ[1] or DARA[1]. This bull was the centre of attraction to MEDHBHA, who swore to own it whatever the cost. The epic story of her quest to locate and then take the bull is contained in the *Taín Bó Cuailngè*, a remarkable early text that tells of the heroic stance adopted by CÚ CHULAINN, who defended ULSTER single-handedly against the armies of Medhbha and AILILL but was eventually killed after he had failed to recognize the presence of the MÓRRÍGHAN. The Donn Cuailngè was finally captured, but it destroyed FINNBHENNACH before returning to Ulster to die.

## Donn Tetscorach
*Irish*

The brother or son of MIDHIR. He entertained FIONN MAC CUMHAILL and the FIAN in the SÍDH of his father.

## Dornolla
*Irish*

The ugly daughter of DOMNAL. Her love for CÚ CHULAINN was unrequited while that hero was in SCOTLAND, and revenge she caused his companions to feel so homesick that they left him to travel on to SCÁTHACH alone.

## Dragon
*General*

The usual form of dragon that appears in Celtic legend is that represented on the modern Welsh flag, a scaly lizard-like animal, with wings, that can breath fire. It is the symbolic image of the Celtic chief. Although the appearance of a dragon in Celtic myth is somewhat rarer than in other pagan cultures, particularly Chinese and Slavonic, those that do appear are all OTHERWORLDLY creatures, and all are usually dealt with in an heroic manner. Welsh myth is the most common place to find a dragon, but even here they do not leap out from every nook and cranny, being more usually confined to later folklore. See also DINAS EMRYS.

## Draidecht
*Irish*

The title used to refer to the DAGHDHA as the god of magic and Druidism.

## Druid(s)
*General*

The name given to the common priesthood of the Celtic peoples, although Druids were much more than simple priests – they were also teachers, seers, poets, judges, doctors, diviners and magicians. Their name is thought to come from *drus*, the ancient name for an oak tree, which was sacred to them. The Druids were the unifying force between different Celtic tribes, their efforts preserving common culture, religion, history, laws, scholarship and science. Because Druids represented the most powerful force within the Celtic society and because their office was sacred, they had freedom to move as they wanted, being instrumental in stopping battles and forcing opposing factions to settle their disputes by arbitration. The Druids managed the higher legal systems and established colleges where pupils would receive up to twenty years' oral instruction before being admitted to their order. They were also responsible for the education of minstrels and bards, who received a similarly lengthy tuition.

Knowledge of the ancient Druids comes directly from contemporary writers, although little can be gleaned from these sources of their rituals and customs, which remain shrouded in mystery. JULIUS CAESAR wrote that they had an intimate knowledge of the stars and their motions and of the universe and its size. They knew about the powers and authority of the gods, and taught the doctrine of the immortality of the soul. It appears that they also accepted the principles of reincarnation, for it was recorded that they allowed debts incurred in this lifetime to be repaid in the next.

Caesar significantly remarks that the first Druids came from BRITAIN[1], and it is quite possible that this is a factual comment, for Druidism retains the appearance of an insular religion. It seems increasingly likely that the first Celts to arrive in Britain found there a religion controlled by a priesthood. They simply adopted that religion and its priests, a supposition possibly supported by the religious importance placed by the Druids on ancient megalithic monuments such as STONEHENGE. Yet there is a fundamental difference between the Celtic Druids and the megalithic priesthood. The Druids abandoned the great stones and reverted to natural shrines, a change that implies religious reformation, a reformation that may have come about with the first influx of Celtic peoples and a realization by the priesthood that, if it were to retain its position of importance, it had to adapt its religion to match the beliefs of the new population.

It is almost impossible to put a date to this reformation, but it seems likely that the megalithic priests were in existence prior to 2000 BC. They appear to have enjoyed almost 1400 years of independence before the accepted date for the arrival of the first Celtic people in Britain, 600 BC. They then enjoyed a further 700 or 800 years of this independence before the first Christians arrived in Britain, and it was not until several centuries later that the pagan rituals of the Druids were finally eradicated from the Celtic Church when that was taken over by the church of Rome.

The regularization of the Celtic pantheon by the Druids was brought to an abrupt end by the Roman invasion, during which the priesthood and holy places were destroyed with systematic savagery. It was obvious to the Romans that the Druids represented the driving force behind Celtic power, and they thought that the only answer to such power was the sword. The nemeton, or holy groves, were put to the axe, and the Druids and their families slaughtered. Evidence of this massacre is to be found in the writings of Tacitus, although he refers to the slaughter of innocent women and children as 'heroism'. Having annihilated the religious order of the Celts, the Romans turned to the pen and assigned foreign and inappropriate names to the Celtic gods. This single act destroyed the Celtic way of life, but, more importantly for the student of Celtic times, made it impossible to determine the characteristics of many of the Celtic deities and their position within any pantheon that the Druids had devised.

If the Druids are indeed a priesthood that underwent a reformation with the arrival of the Celts in Britain, they must surely represent one of the oldest religions to have survived to the present, for there is today a great resurgence of the Druidic culture worldwide.

### Drynog
*Welsh*

The owner of a cauldron, known as PAIR DRYNOG, that numbered among the THIRTEEN TREASURES of BRITAIN[1] and was said to boil no meat save that of a brave man.

### Du
*Welsh*

The horse of GWYN AP NUDD, although some sources say that this horse was rather the one given by Gwyn ap Nudd to CULHWCH to enable the latter to catch the great boar TWRCH TRWYTH.

### Dub
*Irish*

The husband of ENNA. He once caused the seas to swell and drown AIDE, the wife of AED[3], and her family.

### Dubsaingl-u, -end
*Irish*

The true name of Black of SAINGLIU, one of the two horses that were born at the same time as CÚ CHULAINN and that were later to become his famous steeds. The other horse was known as Grey of MACHA.

## Dubthach
*Irish*

The father of CORMAC MAC DUBTHACH (literally 'Cormac son of Dubthach') and the owner of a spear that had to be kept in a brew of soporific herbs if it were not to fly forth on its own, eager for massacre. Dubthach was sent with his son and FERGHUS MAC ROICH to SCOTLAND by CONCHOBAR MAC NESSA to bring the fugitive DERDRIU, along with ARDÁN, AINNLE and NAOISE, back to IRELAND. When Conchobar mac Nessa reneged on his truce and had the three young men killed, Dubthach, Ferghus mac Roich and Cormac mac Dubthach attacked and burned EMHAIN MHACHA, killed 300 of the men of ULSTER and then defected to AILILL and MEDHBHA of CONNACHT, the great enemies of Conchobar mac Nessa.

## Dugal
*Irish*

A variant name for the DAGHDHA. A chanted protective hymn giving the genealogy of St BRIDE names the Daghdha as 'Dugal the Brown', making him the son of AODH[1], son of ART, son of CONN[1], son of CREAR, son of CIS, son of CARMAC, son of CARRUIN.

## Dumnonia
*British*

A considerable ancient Celtic kingdom, which survived the Roman invasion. It was said to have covered Devon, CORNWALL, and other areas of southwest ENGLAND, its most westerly portion being known as CORNUBIA to the Romans. Its name undoubtedly comes from the DUMNONII.

## Dumnonii
*British*

An ancient Celtic tribe that probably gave their name to the large kingdom of DUMNONIA. They were possibly related to the Irish FIR DHOMHNANN.

## Dunadd
*Irish*

The capital of DÁL RIADA in the Kintyre peninsula near Crinan.

## Dunatis
*Gaulish*

A generic name given to the deities of strongholds.

## Dusius
*General*

The Celtic name for an *incubus*, a demon believed to have intercourse with sleeping women, who thereby conceive demonic children. The mother of MYRDDIN was alleged by VORTIGERN's counsellors to have been visited by just such a being.

## Dwyfach
*Welsh*

One of the two survivors, named in the *Trioedd Ynys Prydein*, of a flood that wiped out the entire population of WALES. The other survivor is named as DWYFAN. They escaped in a boat, and later repopulated Wales. This story would appear to be a Welsh version of NOAH and the biblical Flood.

## Dwyfan
*Welsh*

One of the two survivors, named in the *Trioedd Ynys Prydein*, of a flood, perhaps even the biblical Flood, that wiped out the entire population of WALES. The other survivor is named as DWYFACH. They escaped in a boat, here echoing the biblical Ark, and following the flood the pair repopulated Wales.

## Dyfed
*Welsh*

The modern name for DEMETIA, a kingdom in the south of WALES.

## Dylan (Eil Ton)
*Welsh*

The first baby to be born to ARIANRHOD as she undertook the rite to attest her virginity after she had been put up for a maiden's post at the court of MATH FAB MATHONWY. A golden-haired boy, he was immediately named Dylan. Growing to maturity in an instant he set out for the sea whose nature he assumed, thereafter being known as Dylan Eil Ton, or 'Dylan, Son of the Wave'. Some have sought to explain this curious tale by saying that the boy was drowned in the sea, and that is how he came to adopt the sea's nature. However, this is pure supposition, as no evidence, legendary or otherwise, exists to support the theory. His grave is said to be MAEN DYLAN, a stone that stands on a gravel bank approximately 2 miles south of CAER ARIANRHOD, about three-quarters of a mile off shore, and thus visible at low tide only.

## Dylan, Son of the Wave
*Welsh*

The literal translation of DYLAN EIL TON.

## Dyrnwyn
*Welsh*

The sword of RHYDDERCH HAEL, which would burst into flame from the point to the cross if any man, save the true owner, drew it. It numbered among the THIRTEEN TREASURES of BRITAIN[1].

## Dysgyfdawd
*Welsh*

The father of GALL.

## Dysgyl a gren Rhydderch
*Welsh*

The platter of RHYDDERCH HAEL upon which any meat desired would appear. It numbered among the THIRTEEN TREASURES of BRITAIN[1].

## Eachtach
*Irish*

One of the two daughters of DIARMAID UA DUIBHNE and GRÁINNE. She attacked FIONN MAC CUMHAILL and wounded him so severely that it took four years for him to be fully healed.

## Eagle of Gwernabwy
*Welsh*

The oldest living creature in the world. The Eagle of Gwernabwy is said to have helped CULHWCH and his companions by introducing them to the SALMON OF LLYN LLW, although some sources make the Salmon of Llyn Llw older than the eagle.

## Eanna
*Irish*

The husband of one of MANANNÁN MAC LIR's daughters and the father of the maiden SGÁTHACH whom FIONN MAC CUMHAILL, having been lured to Eanna's SÍDH, said he would marry for a year. The following morning, however, Fionn mac Cumhaill woke up to find himself far away from the sídh with no way back.

## Eber (Donn)
*Irish*

One of the Sons of MÍL ÉSPÁINE to whom the TUATHA DÉ DANANN king MAC CUILL fell in battle. His surname, which is not usually used in the source texts, seems to link him with the character of DÔNN[1], the churlish king of the Míl Éspáine who was drowned shortly after they arrived in IRELAND, his death possibly being a punishment for killing Mac Cuill. His brother was EBER FINN.

## Eber Finn
*Irish*

One of the leaders of the Sons of MÍL ÉSPÁINE and the brother of EBER DONN. After the death of his brother he was involved in a struggle with EREMON, another of the leaders of the invasion, over who should rule IRELAND. AMHAIRGHIN decreed that Eremon should rule first, and that upon his death Eber Finn should rule. However, Eber Finn refused to accept this, and Ireland was split into two realms, Eber Finn taking the southern half, and Eremon the northern. Peace did not last long before war broke out. Eber Finn was killed and Eremon became the sole King of Ireland, which he ruled from TARA.

## Ebrauc(us)
*British*

A legendary king of BRITAIN[1] and the sixth king after BRUTUS. His rule was said to have started in 944 BC when he founded the city of YORK. The Romans called this city Eboracum when they captured it from the BRIGANTES in AD 71 and made it their northern headquarters. Ebrauc was also alleged to have founded Edinburgh and to have had twenty wives, twenty sons and thirty daughters.

## Echid
*Irish*

The father of NESSA, by whom he became the grandfather of CONCHOBAR MAC NESSA through Nessa's mariage to the giant FACHTNA.

## Echtra Condla chaim maic Cuind Chetchathaig
*Irish*

The section of the *Leabhar na hUidhre* (*The Book of The Dun Cow*) that tells the story of CONNLA[2] and his elopement with a supernatural maiden. It was certainly written prior to 1106, for that is the recorded date of the murder of its scribe Maelmori ('Servant of Mary').

## Echtra Nerai
*Irish*

The *Adventures of Nera*, an introductory tale to the *Táin Bó Cuailngè* in which the gods are regarded as demons that appear on the eve of SAMHAIN. NERA was the only one of AILILL's warriors brave enough to tie a withe around the leg of a hanged corpse, but the corpse came to life and asked Nera for a drink. He carried the corpse to a house and gave it some water, but it squirted that water in the faces of those sleeping there, and then died. Nera returned the corpse to the gallows. He then discovered the fort of Ailill burnt to the ground and a heap of human ashes nearby. Travelling to the SÍDH of Cruachan Nera was told that what he had seen was a premonition that would come true unless he could persuade Ailill to destroy the sídh. This

he did, and Ailill's forces proceeded to flatten the sídh.

## Echtrai
*Irish*

One of the two classifications of ancient Irish literature, the other being the IMMRAM. The *echtrai* are accounts of visits made by humans to supernatural lands, either by crossing endless tracts of water, or by entering one of the many SÍDH. The *immram* on the other hand is an account of a fantastic voyage to an island realm, either human or supernatural.

## Ecne
*Irish*

The name of the three sons, or of the grandsons, of DANU who is, in this instance, the daughter of the DAGHDHA. Ecne means 'knowledge' or 'poetry'. Some sources further complicate what is already a confused picture by saying that the three sons of Danu, all called Ecne, each had a single son, whom they also called Ecne. However, as Danu is often considered the goddess of light and knowledge, it may be that Ecne was simply an aspect of the goddess, and the story of the three or six young men carrying the same name was a later invention.

## Edaein
*Irish*

The sister of CLIODNA and AEIFE. She and her sisters eloped from TÍR TAIRNGIRI with CIABHAN, LODAN[1] and EOLUS, but MANANNÁN MAC LIR sent a huge wave after them, which engulfed the boat in which they had been travelling seconds after it had landed in IRELAND and either drowned the three sisters or carried them back to Tír Tairngiri.

## Édáin
*Irish*

The daughter of EOCHAIDH AIREMH and ÉDÁIN ECHRAIDHE. She was mistakenly chosen by Eochaidh Airemh when the king was presented with fifty identical women, all of whom were the exact likeness of Édáin Echraidhe. She subsequently bore her father a son, the hero CONAIRE MÓR, long before the king realized his mistake.

## Édáin (Echraidhe)
*Irish*

The daughter of King AILILL and described as the most beautiful woman in all IRELAND. Her name means 'Horse-riding Édáin', and she is possibly the Irish equivalent of the Welsh RHIANNON and the Gaulish EPONA. Her hand was sought by OENGHUS MAC IN OG on behalf of his foster father MIDHIR, a god who lived in TÍR TAIRNGIRI. Although he lived in the SÍDH of BRÍ LEITH in County Longford, Midhir was a god associated with rebirth, rather than with the OTHERWORLD.

FUAMHNACH, the first wife of Midhir, was so jealous of the beauty of Édáin Echraidhe that she turned the girl into a pool of water. That pool changed into a worm, and the worm into an enormous and incredibly beautiful fly whose music filled the air. Although no longer the maiden he had longed to make his wife, Midhir was more than content to have Édáin Echraidhe remain in this unusual, but equally beautiful form. Seething with resentment, Fuamhnach conjured up a huge wind, which blew Édáin Echraidhe away to the rocky coastline where she lay, buffeted by the waves, for seven years. At last Oenghus Mac in Og found the beautiful fly that was Édáin Echraidhe and placed her carefully in a crystal bower. Once again Midhir and Édáin Echraidhe had to endure the wrath of Fuamhnach, who thought she had seen the last of the girl. This time the wind that carried the unfortunate girl away deposited her in a wine glass and she was swallowed. However, being swallowed was not the end of Édáin Echraidhe, for the woman who swallowed her became pregnant, and, so some accounts say, 10, 12 years after her first birth, she was once more reborn, this time as Édáin, daughter of the daughter of the ULSTER hero ÉDAR.

At about the time Édáin came of age this second time around EOCHAIDH AIREMH became the King of Ireland, but, as he was unmarried his warriors would not follow him. Learning of the uncompromising beauty of Édáin, he set out to claim her to be his wife. News of the girl's beauty reached Midhir, and he set out to TARA to reclaim the girl who could only be the reincarnation of his long lost wife. When Midhir claimed her, Édáin refused to leave Eochaidh Airemh without his permission. He at first refused, but swore to give up the girl if Midhir could beat him in a chess contest. The god allowed Eochaidh Airemh to win the early round and accepted any forfeits the king might impose, one of which was to build a great causeway across the bogs of MEATH.

Having completed the causeway, Midhir returned to TARA to fight the deciding match. This he won and chose as his prize a kiss from Édáin. A month later, when Midhir returned to claim his fairly won prize he found all the doors of Tara barred against him, while inside the king sat feasting with all his warriors. Unperturbed, the god simply appeared in their midst, seized Édáin and the pair flew out of the great hall, in the shape of swans, through the central smoke hole.

Eochaidh Airemh and his company set out in hot pursuit, and, when they reached the sídh of Brí Leith, they began to dig it up. Midhir appeared to them and promised to return Édáin to the king, upon which he produced fifty women, all of whom were the exact likeness of Édáin. Although Eochaidh Airemh chose carefully, the Édáin he chose was actually his own daughter, also called Édáin, although some call her ESS. It was quite a considerable time before the king realized his mistake, and by that time Édáin had born the king a son, the hero CONAIRE MÓR.

## Édar
*Irish*

The hero of ULSTER whose daughter swallowed ÉDÁIN ECHRAIDHE (in the shape of a fly) when she was blown into the glass of wine she was drinking on a wind conjured up by the jealous FUAMHNACH. The girl subsequently gave birth to ÉDÁIN ECHRAIDHE for the second time.

## Efnisien
*Welsh*

The son of PENARDUN and EUROSSWYD, brother to NISIEN and half-brother of BENDIGEID VRAN. While MATHOLWCH, King of IRELAND, was in WALES seeking the hand of BRANWEN, daughter of LLYR and sister to Bendigeid Vran, Efnisien cruelly disfigured the hundreds of horses Matholwch had brought with him, an insult so bad that Matholwch took his revenge on Branwen by treating her cruelly after they had returned to Ireland. When Bendigeid Vran learnt of the suffering of his sister, he set out with his host to rescue her.

The Irish at first attempted to placate Bendigeid Vran by housing him in a splendid palace, but they had hidden one hundred warriors inside bags of provisions. Efnisien suspected the trick and circumvented it by crushing the heads of each of the hidden warriors while they were still in hiding. Matholwch and Bendigeid Vran met and decided that the best way to settle their argument was to bestow the kingship of Ireland on GWERN, the boy who had been born to Branwen and Matholwch. On hearing this, Efnisien cast the unfortunate boy into the fire and war broke out.

Because of the cauldron Bendigeid Vran had given Matholwch as a wedding gift, the Irish at first had the upper hand, for they could restore their dead to life. Efnisien changed the fortunes of the Welsh when he managed to destroy the cauldron, but he was killed in the attempt. So absolute was the carnage that only five pregnant Irish women remained hidden in a cave, and only seven of the invaders returned across the Irish Sea.

## Efrawg
*Welsh*
Also EVRAWG

According to the *Mabinogion*, the father of PEREDUR. Because the name means 'York' it would seem that this was not his true name, but simply a title indicating the city he ruled.

## Efrddf
*Welsh*

The twin sister of URIEN, ruler of RHEGED.

## Eigyr
*Welsh*

The Welsh form of IGRAINE. Her parentage in Welsh tradition is somewhat confused, although all the various pedigrees that exist tend to agree that she married GORLOIS, the Duke of CORNWALL. She then passed into the realm of Arthurian legend as the mother of King ARTHUR by UTHER.

## Einion
*Welsh*

The hero of the Welsh folktale *Einion and Olwen*, in which he travels to the OTHERWORLD to marry OLWEN, the daughter of the chief giant YSPADDADEN. They had child whom they named TALIESIN. Einion would appear to be a localized direct replacement for CULHWCH, the hero of the *Mabinogion* story of *Culhwch and Olwen*, who is usually connected with the quest to marry Olwen. However, as *Culhwch and Olwen* is generally considered an Arthurian story, the reverse may be true, with Culhwch replacing Einion whose story would then be the earlier.

## Einion and Olwen
*Welsh*

A Welsh folktale in which the hero, EINION, undertakes to travel to the OTHERWORLD to marry OLWEN, the daughter of YSPADDADEN. It seems without doubt that Einion was a local hero, either a direct replacement in the region of Wales (where the tale originated) for CULHWCH, the hero normally associated with the quest to locate and marry Olwen, or that the reverse is true, and Einion was replaced by Culhwch in a later Arthurian rendition of the story.

## Eire
*General*

The correct Gaelic name for IRELAND. It is derived from ÉRIU, one of the triad of goddesses who met the invading Sons of MÍL ÉSPÁINE. She promised that Ireland would forever be theirs, and they replied that the country would be named in her honour.

## Eisirt
*Irish*

The FILI of IUBDAN, the King of FAYLINN. He told his king about a race of giants who lived in ULSTER (humans) and was clapped in irons for his audacity at challenging the power of the people of Faylinn, whose warriors were said to be able to fell a thistle with a single stroke, for Faylinn was the realm of elfin beings. Eisirt said that he would gather proof for the king, and was sent on his way. He later returned from the court of FERGHUS MAC LEDA with AEDA1, a dwarf at the court of that king, and placed Iubdan and his wife, BEBO, under a bond to visit Ferghus mac Leda. They did so but were taken captive, only to be released after Eisirt had led the people of Faylinn against the men of Ulster and plagued their land.

## E(i)thne
*Irish*

1 The daughter of BALAR and, by CIAN, mother of LUGH, whom she conceived while imprisoned by her father who had been told of a prophecy that any child of Eithne's would lead to his death and the end of the FOMHOIRÉ. She conceived triplets, but all but one of them was drowned on the instructions of Balar, the surviving child being conveyed to Cian, who raised the boy.

2 The wife of ELCMAR. She was coveted by the DAGHDHA, who sent Elcmar on a diplomatic mission and then caused the sun to remain in the sky for nine months and Elcmar not to feel hungry for the same period. During his absence Eithne was seduced by the Daghdha and conceived a son, OENGHUS MAC IN OG, who was sent to be fostered by MIDHIR hours before Elcmar returned.

Midhir subsequently sent the boy back to be fostered by Elcmar, who obviously believed that Oenghus Mac in Og was the son of Midhir.

This story is possibly later than the better known story of Oenghus Mac in Og's conception and birth. In that version no mention is made of a maiden by the name of Eithne, for Oenghus Mac in Og's mother is BOANN, the sister of Elcmar, with whom she goes to stay, and it is while she is staying there that the Daghdha disposes of Elcmar for the nine months while Oenghus Mac in Og gestates and is subsequently born.

3 The mistress of CÚ CHULAINN, whom he offended by omitting her when he distributed a flock of beautiful birds he had captured to the maidens of ULSTER. To appease her, he went in search of two more beautiful birds he had heard of, but fell foul of LI BAN and FAND, daughters of AED ABRAT, at whom he aimed his slingshot while they were in the form of birds. He lay almost dead for a year until Li Ban and Fand healed him. The story does not say whether he ever managed to appease Eithne.

4 The daughter of the steward of ELCMAR, who remained in service after OENGHUS MAC IN OG had taken the SÍDH of BRUGH NA BÓINNE. At the same time as she was born, CURCOG was born to MANANNÁN MAC LIR who sent his daughter to be fostered by Oenghus Mac in Og. Eithne later became her attendant. Eithne grew up into a beautiful young lady, but one day it was discovered that she neither ate nor drank as she had been insulted by one of the TUATHA DÉ DANANN, and was instead sustained by an angel of God.

However, Manannán mac Lir and Oenghus Mac in Og brought two sacred cows to the sídh from a foreign land, and, since they had nothing to do with the Tuatha Dé Danann, Eithne was thenceforth sustained by their milk. She continued to thrive in this manner for 1,500 years until she was christened by St PATRICK, and subsequently died in that saint's arms after he had administered the last rites to her.

This story plainly owes its origins to a Christianization of the earlier pagan tales, a process that often leaves the pagan myths in a confused state.

## Eladu
*Irish*

The Father of the DAGHDHA, and possibly the husband of DANU, although this is by no means certain.

## Elatha(n)
*Irish*

A FOMHOIRÉ chieftain, who had a relationship with ÉRI, a TUATHA DÉ DANANN woman. This led to the subsequent birth of BRES[1], who later become a tyrannical king of the Tuatha Dé Danann.

## Elcm(h)a(i)r(e) or Elkmar
*Irish*

The foster father of OENGHUS MAC IN OG, who was the son of Elcmar's wife by the DAGHDHA, although other, possibly earlier stories, make Oenghus Mac in Og the son of Elcmar's sister, BOANN. The boy had originally been fostered by MIDHIR, but he subsequently returned the youth to his natural mother, with Elcmar still unaware of the child's true parentage. Oenghus Mac in Og subsequently succeeded in expelling Elcmar from his SÍDH, BRUGH NA BÓINNE, which then passed into his ownership. The earlier version of this story says that Brugh na Bóinne was originally the sídh of the Daghdha, and it was from him that Oenghus Mac in Og took possession.

## Elen
*Welsh*

The daughter of EUDAF and sister to CYNAN and GADEON. She accepted the marriage proposal of MACSEN, but said that she would not leave BRITAIN[1], and that if he wanted to marry her he must come to her. This he did and stayed, thus neglecting Rome. A popular queen, she embarked on a road-building plan that earnt her the name Elen Luyddogg ('Elen-of-the-Hosts'), which referred to the numbers of workmen she employed.

Seven years after their marriage, her husband received notice from Rome that, as he had been absent for so long, a new emperor had been chosen. She marched with her husband and her brothers to Rome at the head of a large British army, which succeeded in sacking Rome and reinstating Macsen as emperor, with Elen as empress. Cynan returned to Britain where he became king, while Gadeon settled in ARMORICA.

## Eliseg
*Welsh*

The son of GUAILLAUC and father of BROCHMAIL. A pillar, known as the Pillar of Eliseg, was erected in his honour by CONCENN, the last king of POWYS who died in Rome in 854. The pillar is located near the ruins of Valle Crucis Abbey in CLWYD, and was examined in 1696 by Edward Llwyd, who made an invaluable record of the inscription that was just visible at that time, although the crosshead had disappeared and the shaft of the pillar was broken in two. The inscription consisted of thirty-one lines divided into paragraphs, each of which

was marked with a cross. The translation made by Llwyd of this inscription reads as follows:

+ Concenn son of CADELL, Cadell son of BROCHMAIL, Brochmail son of Eliseg, Eliseg son of Guaillauc.
+ And so Concenn, great-grandson of Eliseg, erected this stone for his great-grandfather Eliseg.
+ This is that Eliseg, who joined together the inheritance of Powys ... out of the power of the ANGLES with his sword of fire.
+ Whosoever repeats the writing, let him give a blessing on the soul of Eliseg.
+ This is that Concenn who captured with his hand eleven hundred acres which used to belong to his kingdom of Powys . . .
+ [Illegible]
+ [Illegible]
+ BRITU son of VORTIGERN, whom GERMANUS blessed, and whom SEVIRA bore to him, daughter of MAXIMUS the king, who killed the king of the Romans.
+ CONMARCH painted this writing at the request of King Concenn.
+ The blessing of the Lord upon Concenn and upon his entire household and upon all the region of Powys until the day of doom.

Although it is quite obvious that the pillar was erected after the Welsh had been converted to Christianity, the inscription gives a valuable genealogy of the kings of Powys and confirms the historicity of the likes of Vortigern, his wife, father-in-law and son.

## Eliwlod
*Welsh*

The son of MADOG who was, in turn, a son of UTHER. This connection was later used to make Eliwlod the nephew of King ARTHUR.

## Ellyll
*Welsh*

The name given to an elf in Welsh tradition, elves being one class of the Plant (or 'children of') ANNWFN.

## Elmet
*British*

An ancient Celtic kingdom, centred on Leeds, that certainly existed prior to the fifth century but whose exact extent remains undetermined.

## Elphin
*Welsh*

The son of GWYDDNO GARANHIR. He rescued from the leather bag the child whom Cerridwen had thrown into the sea, naming the radiant child TALIESIN. In return, he was rescued by the bard when he was held captive by MAELGWYN.

## Eluned
*Welsh*

The owner of a ring that was numbered among the THIRTEEN TREASURES of BRITAIN[1], and that made the wearer invisible.

## Emer
*Irish*

The daughter of FORGALL and sister of FIALL. She was wooed by CÚ CHULAINN, who travelled beyond ALBA to become a pupil of the prophetess SCÁTHACH to prove his worth. Having conceived a son with AÍFE, Cú Chulainn returned to IRELAND and, having killed Forgall, married Emer. Many years later a mysterious, magical youth appeared off the Irish coast in a bronze boat. This youth quickly disposed of CONALL CERNACH, so Cú Chulainn himself went to challenge him, even though Emer warned him that the youth could only be his own son. Cú Chulainn mortally wounded the boy whereupon he revealed his name, CONALL, his son by Aífe.

## Emhain Abhlach
*Irish*

'Emhain of the Apple Trees', a paradisal land that is usually identified as the Isle of ARRAN. It also has associations with MANANNÁN MAC LIR, god of the sea, whose home was said to have been the Isle of MAN. Both islands have equal claim to be Emhain Abhlach, and, as is usual, no evidence exists to support the claim of one over the other.

## Emhain Mhacha
*Irish*

The chief court of ULSTER, or ULAIDH, situated approximately 2 miles west of Antrim. Legend says that it was built by the five sons of DITHORBA, the brother of MACHA and CIMBAOTH. After the death of their father at the hands of Macha, who compelled her other brother, Cimbaoth, to marry her so that she became sole ruler of IRELAND, the five sons of Dithorba attacked Macha. She easily captured them and, tracing the outline of a great fort on the ground with the pin of her brooch, made the brothers build Emhain Mhacha, which means 'Brooch of Macha'.

It is most famous as the court of the treacherous CONCHOBAR MAC NESSA. As his first heroic act, CÚ CHULAINN defeated all fifty of the youths in the king's service while he was still a boy and known as SÉDANTA. The court was attacked and razed by FERGHUS MAC ROICH, DUBTHACH and CORMAC MAC DUBTHACH in response to the treachery of Conchobar mac Nessa, who had had the three emissaries travel to SCOTLAND to elicit the return of DERDRIU and the sons of UISNECH, promising them safety, but instead having the three young men, NAOISE, ARDÁN and AINNLE, killed by EOGHAN MAC DURTHACHT and his men.

## En mac Ethomain
*Irish*

The poet and *senchaid* (historian, genealogist and folklorist) at TARA when LUGH came to the court.

## Enbarr
*Irish*
See AONBARR.

## Eneuavc
*Welsh*

The daughter of BEDWYR[2] and sister of AMREN.

## Eneyd
*Welsh*

According to some translations of the *Mabinogion*, Eneyd is one of the sons of DÔN, and thus a brother to the likes of ARIANRHOD, GWYDION FAB DÔN and GILFAETHWY.

## England
*General*

The largest division of BRITAIN[1], lying off the north coast of FRANCE from which it is separated by the English Channel. The first Celts to land in England are traditionally thought to have arrived *c*.600 BC. England remained a Celtic stronghold until the Roman invasion, although even then the English Celts retained a fair degree of autonomy. Following the departure of the Romans the country was laid open for invasion by the ANGLO-SAXONS, who pushed the Celts further and further west until they were confined to CORNWALL in the south west or in WALES. Very little of the Celtic way of life in England has survived, except in these small areas.

## Enna
*Irish*

The wife of DUB who caused the seas to swell and drown AIDE, wife of AED[3], and her family, although usually the casting of the spell is attributed to her husband.

## Eochaid(h)
*Irish*

1 'Beautiful', the name originally given to BRES[1], although this may have simply been a title, for he is also given the title GORMAC, 'dutiful son', to which he certainly did not live up.
2 An alternative name, sometimes used for EREMON.
3 The son of ERC[1]. Eochaidh became King of the FIR BHOLG and was killed during the First Battle of MAGH TUIREDH.

## Eochaidh Airemh
*Irish*

The King of IRELAND who married the reincarnated ÉDÁIN ECHRAIDHE. When news of this reached MIDHIR, the god travelled to TARA to reclaim the woman who could only be his former, and long lost, second wife. Édáin Echraidhe accepted Midhir's account, but would not leave without the consent of Eochaidh Airemh. The king refused, but accepted the challenge of Midhir to a chess match, the winner being granted a boon. Midhir lost the early game, his forfeit being to build a huge causeway for the king across the bogs of MEATH, but he won the final match and claimed his former wife, returning one month later to collect her. However, Eochaidh Airemh had barred all the doors of Tara against Midhir, so the god simply appeared among the company, took hold of Édáin Echraidhe and flew up with her through the smoke hole of the great hall in the guise of a pair of swans.

Eochaidh Airemh set out in hot pursuit, and, when he reached the SÍDH of BRÍ LEITH, began to dig it up. Midhir appeared to the king and said that he would return Édáin Echraidhe, although he then produced fifty identical women, all of whom were the exact likeness of Édáin Echraidhe. Eochaidh Airemh chose carefully, but he chose his own daughter, ÉDAIN, and did not realize his mistake until well after that girl had borne him the son CONAIRE MÓR.

Other accounts of this story say that the child born to Eochaidh Airemh and his daughter, here named as ESS to save confusion, was a girl by the name of MESS BUACHALLA. She then became the mother of Conaire Mór through her union with ETERSCEL, when that king flew into the house in which she was living in the guise of a bird and left again afterwards in the same manner.

## Eochaidh Bres
*Irish*

'Beautiful Bres', the name by which BRES[1] was originally called by his parents, although his later actions caused the 'Eochaidh' to be dropped so that he became simply known as Bres.

## Eochaidh Ollathair
*Irish*

'Eochaidh, the Great Father', one of the terms of reverence given to the DAGHDHA, another being RUADH ROFHESSA ('Mighty and Most Learned One').

## Eocho Glas
*Irish*

Possibly the brother of EOCHO ROND, Eocho Glas was responsible for the imprisonment of the sons of DOEL whom CÚ CHULAINN was cursed to find by Eocho Rond in the *Longes mac nDuil Dermait*. When CÚ CHULAINN, and his companions, arrived at the SÍDH of Eocho Glas, he succeeded in fending off Cú Chulainn several times before he was killed and the sons of Doel were freed.

## Eocho Mumho
*Irish*

Possibly an historical character, the alleged tenth king in succession from EREMON. The county of MUNSTER is said to have derived its name from this king, for Munster in Irish is Mumhan.

## Eocho Rond
*Irish*

The father of FINDCHOÉM. Eocho Rond is a mysterious character who appears in the *Longes Mac nDuil Dermait* in which he curses CÚ CHULAINN, a curse that will remain on him until he has discovered the whereabouts of the missing sons of DOEL. His brother appears to have been EOCHO GLAS, whom CÚ CHULAINN kills and then returns to EMHAIN MHACHA, where it becomes apparent that Eocho Rond had cursed Cú Chulainn because the hero loved his daughter Findchoém, whom he was now compelled to hand over as Cú Chulainn had completed the set task.

## Eochu Mugmedón
*Irish*

The husband of the SAXON CAIRENN and, by her, the father of NÍAL NOÍGIALLACH.

## Eogabal
*Irish*

The father of AINÉ[2] and AILLÉN. He was killed by FERCHESS.

## Eog(h)an
*Irish*

Mentioned in the *Leabhar Gabhála* as being hostile to the TUATHA DÉ DANANN. Later tradition makes him the son of OILILL. He killed LUGAID MAC CON, which led to the Battle of MAGH MUCRIME, in which Oilill's seven sons, Eoghan among them, perished.

## Eoghan mac Durthacht
*Irish*

A vassal of CONCHOBAR MAC NESSA, who, on that king's orders, killed the sons of UISNECH – ARDÁN, AINNLE and NAOISE – when they returned from exile in SCOTLAND.

## Eol
*Irish*

A supernatural being who appears in a fragmentary text as an ally of MANANNÁN MAC LIR who, on one occasion, fought CÚ CHULAINN. The outcome, regrettably, is not known, but it seems likely that Eol perished.

## Eolus
*Irish*

One of the two companions of CIABHAN, the other being LODAN[1], who travelled to TÍR TAIRNGIRI and eloped from there with the sisters CLIODNA, AEIFE and EDAEIN. One account of the story says that all six, along with some men from the LAND OF PROMISE, were drowned by a huge wave sent after them by MANANNÁN MAC LIR. Another says that only the three sisters drowned, while a third says that the three maidens were carried back to Tír Tairngiri by the wave.

## Epona
*Gaulish*

'The Great Mare', the goddess of a horse cult who is most likely to be identified with the Irish ÉDÁIN ECHRAIDHE or MACHA and the Welsh RHIANNON. As goddess of horses, she was of great importance within a horse-based culture such as that of the Celts. Her image appears on over 300 stones in GAUL, although rarely in BRITAIN[1], and she is usually depicted riding side-saddle. In Romano-Celtic imagery she is constantly associated with corn, fruit and, strangely, serpents – strangely because serpents are natural enemies of horses. These associations led to her also being considered a goddess of fertility and nourishment.

## Érainn
*Irish*

The eponymous ancient rulers of IRELAND. Their name undoubtedly comes from the goddess ÉRIU, the eponym of EIRE or Ireland.

## Erc

*Irish*

1 The father of EOCHAIDH[3] and thus one of the FIR BHOLG.

2 The son of CAIRPRE, who appears in the *Taín Bó Cuailngè*. He joined forces with the three monstrous sons of CALATIN and LUGAID[2], the son of CÚ ROÍ MAC DÁIRI, and marched against CÚ CHULAINN. During the fight that was to result in the death of Cú Chulainn, Erc used that hero's infallible spear, the GAE BOLGA, to kill Grey of MACHA.

## Ercol

*Irish*

The husband of GARMNA. According to one account of the *Fledd Bricrenn*, CÚ CHULAINN and his competitors for the right of champion were sent to Ercol to be judged. He challenged them to attack him and his steed. LOEGHAIRE BUADHACH's horse was killed by Ercol's horse and he fled to EMHAIN MHACHA and said that the others had been killed. CONALL CERNACH also fled, but Cú Chulainn fought on until Grey of MACHA killed Ercol's horse, and Cú Chulainn carried Ercol back to Emhain Mhacha, where he found the entire company lamenting his death. The judgement of champion was awarded to Cú Chulainn, but the others refused to accept it, so CONCHOBAR MAC NESSA sent them to CÚ ROÍ MAC DÁIRI.

## Erem

*Irish*

A son of MÍL. His trapper, COBA, was said to have been the first to set a trap and pitfall in IRELAND.

## Eremon

*Irish*

One of the Sons of MÍL ÉSPÁINE, he became the first king of all IRELAND after the death of EBER DONN and EBER FINN, his joint leaders in the expedition from Spain to Ireland. Eber Donn died before landing, although according to some he may have died shortly afterwards. AMHAIRGHIN then decreed that Eremon should rule until he died, when the kingship would pass to Eber Finn. Eber Finn refused, and so the country was divided into two, Eremon ruling over the northern half, and Eber Finn over the southern portion. Peace did not last long, and the two sides went to war. Eber Finn was killed, and Eremon ruled as sole king of Ireland from his court at TARA. Sometimes known as EOCHAID[2].

## Erfddf

*Welsh*

The daughter of CYNFARCH by NEFYN and twin sister of URIEN, according to the Welsh *Trioedd Ynys Prydein*.

## Éri

*Irish*

Possibly a variant of ÉRIU, Éri is recorded as the TUATHA DÉ DANANN mother of LUGH by DELBAETH, one of the monstrous FOMHOIRÉ. However, there appears to be a confusion here, as Éri is also recorded as one of the Fomhoiré, the sister of ELATHA by whom she became the mother of BRES[1].

## Erin

*Irish*

A mythical Irish queen whose name is also the ancient Gaelic name for IRELAND, a name still in use poetically.

## Ériu
*Irish*

One of the three aspects of the SOVER-EIGNTY OF IRELAND, the other two being BANBHA and FÓDLA. The wife of MAC GRÉINE, she was wooed by AMHAIRGHIN, who promised her that the land would bear her name for all time. In turn, she promised that IRELAND would belong to the invading Sons of MÍL ÉSPÁINE until the end of time. However, she also warned DONN[1], the discourteous king of the Sons of Míl Éspáine, that neither he nor his heirs would enjoy the land. He drowned soon after this encounter and was buried on the island of TECH DUINN, to which he still welcomes dead warriors.

It is quite possible that Ériu is the same as the earlier ÉRI.

## Esias
*Irish*

A wizard who lived in GORIAS. He is one of the four wizards said to have taught the TUATHA DÉ DANANN their magical arts. He is also said to have presented them with the invincible spear of LUGH. His three co-teachers were MORFESSA of FALIA, USCIAS of FINDAIS and SIMIAS of MURIAS.

## Ess
*Irish*

According to some sources, the daughter of EOCHAIDH AIREMH by the mortal ÉDÁIN was called Ess, although this name seems to have been derived as an attempt to avoid confusion between mother and daughter. Under this name she is said to have born MESS BUACHALLA to her father, and it was Mess Buachalla, rather than Ess herself, who became the mother of CONAIRE MÓR. The more usual version of this story makes Conaire Mór the son of Eochaidh Airemh and Édáin.

In the variant where Ess is the mother of Mess Buachalla, it is recorded that, after Eochaidh Airemh realized his mistake, he attacked MIDHIR who restored the true Édáin Echraidhe to him. Later Midhir's loss was avenged by his son SIUGMALL who killed Eochaidh Airemh.

## Estrildis
*British*

A beautiful German maiden who was taken captive by LOCRINUS who wanted to make her his wife. However, Locrinus was already betrothed to GWENDOLEN, the daughter of CORINEUS, who made Locrinus honour his promise by force. After his marriage, Locrinus installed Estrildis in a house in TROIA NOVA and made her his mistress. During the seven years Estrildis was kept in hiding, she bore him a daughter, HABREN, while Gwendolen bore him a son, MADDAN.

Following the death of Corineus, Locrinus deserted Gwendolen and made Estrildis his queen. Gwendolen raised an army in CORNWALL and marched against her estranged husband, killing him in a battle near the River Stour. Gwendolen then commanded that Estrildis and Habren be drowned in a river, which she also decreed would thenceforth be named Habren in honour of Locrinus' daughter. Habren became SABRINA in Latin, the river today being known as the River SEVERN.

## Esus
*Gaulish*

A mysterious deity who appears to be connected to a lost myth involving the ritual felling of trees, and whose totem animals appear to be three cranes and a bull. A Romano-Celtic altar to Esus depicts a man cutting down a tree. He seems to have connections with TARANIS and TEUTATES to form a triad of powerful deities. Human sacrifices are said to have been made to all three gods. See also AESUS.

## Étain
*Irish*

See ÉDÁIN ECHRAIDHE.

## Étain (Oig)
*Irish*

A variant of ÉDÁIN. The epithet 'Oig' means 'the younger', and is applied as a means of identifying this Édáin from ÉDÁIN ECHRAIDHE.

## Etan
*Irish*

The sister of LOEG with whom CÚ CHULAINN spent one night, giving her a ring as a token, *en route* to discover the whereabouts of the sons of DOEL, this story appearing in the *Longes mac nDuil Dermait*.

## Étar
*Irish*

The father of the mortal ÉDÁIN, his wife becoming pregnant after she had swallowed the fly into which ÉDÁIN ECHRAIDHE had been transformed. Étar also appears in a story about two kings who had incredibly beautiful daughters, the other king being CAIBELL. The hands of the kings' daughters were sought in marriage, and the two kings offered battle to test the worthiness of the suitors. The battle raged long and hard, but finally Caibell and the two suitors were killed, Étar alone surviving.

## Eter-scel, -skel
*Irish*

One of the possible fathers of CONAIRE MÓR, the more usual father being EOCHAIDH AIREMH. In the version where Eterscel is the father, he is married to MESS BUACHALLA, the daughter of Eochaidh Airemh and the reincarnated ÉDÁIN, although a further version makes Mess Buachalla the daughter of Eterscel and ESS and thus introduces the incestuous conception of Conaire Mór in a different form.

## Ethal Anubal
*Irish*

A prince of CONNACHT, father of CAER[2], and thus the father-in-law of OENGHUS MAC IN OG. When Oenghus Mac in Og came to him to ask for his daughter's hand, he replied that his daughter was more powerful than he was and that Oenghus Mac in Og would have to persuade her without his help. He did, however, explain to Oenghus Mac in Og how he might win his daughter, who spent alternate years in the form of a beautiful maiden and a magnificent swan.

## Ethlinn
*Irish*

One of the names given to the daughter of BALAR who became the mother of LUGH. She is better known as EITHNE[1].

## Ethnea
*Irish*

A variant of EITHNE[1], the mother of LUGH.

## Eudaf
*Welsh*

The father of CYNAN, GADEON and ELÉN. He became king of BRITAIN[1] after MACSEN, Elen's husband, removed BELI, son of MANOGAN, and placed Eudaf on the throne.

## Eurosswyd
*Welsh*

The father of EFNISIEN and NISIEN by PENARDUN, which makes his children the half-brothers of MANAWYDAN FAB LLYR, and the step-brothers of BRANWEN and BENDIGEID VRAN.

## Excalibur
*British*

The romanticized magical sword of ARTHUR, which was given to him by the Lady of the Lake. Sir Thomas Malory (d.1471) does not name the sword in his *Le Morte d'Arthur*. In the early Welsh story of *Culhwch and Olwen*, the sword is called CALADVWLCH, which can be linguistically linked with the magical sword CALADBOLG (derived from *calad*, 'hard', and *bolg*, 'lightning'), a sword borne by Irish heroes, and in particular CÚ CHULAINN. GEOFFREY OF MONMOUTH calls the sword Caliburnus, and so derives the Excalibur of the Arthurian cycle.

## Fachtna (Fathach)
*Irish*

The giant king of ULSTER, the husband or lover of NESSA, and, according to some, the father by Nessa of CONCHOBAR MAC NESSA. His son, DARA[1], was the owner of the DONN CUAILNGÈ, the huge brown bull, to gain possession of which MEDHBHA and AILILL attacked Ulster. The mother of Dara is not named, but it seems reasonable to assume that it was not Nessa.

## Faebor beg-beoil cuimdiuir folt scenbgairit sceo uath
*Irish*

The second ridiculous name that the MÓRRÍGHAN used when her identity was asked by CÚ CHULAINN in his defence of ULSTER against the forces of MEDHBHA and AILILL. The first name she gave was UAR-GAETH-SCEO LUACHAIR-SCEO.

## Fál
*Irish*

One of the four great treasures that were brought with the TUATHA DÉ DANANN when they returned from exile in the north to IRELAND. This stone, which came from the mythical city of FALIA, was said to cry out when a true king sat upon it. The stone was later sent to SCOTLAND and is today said to be the Stone of SCONE, which is housed within Westminster Abbey, although whether this is the original mythical stone is a matter of debate. The remaining three treasures were the invincible spear of LUGH, the inescapable sword of NUADHA and the inexhaustible cauldron of the DAGHDHA.

## Falga
*Irish*

An ancient name for the Isle of MAN.

## Falia(s)
*Irish*

A mythical city that was the home of MORFESSA, one of the four wizards who taught the TUATHA DÉ DANANN their magical arts. From this city came the LIA FÁIL or Stone of FÁL.

## Fan-d, -n
*Irish*

1  A daughter of FLIDHAIS.
2  A daughter of AED ABRAT and sister of LI BAN. The consort of MANANNÁN MAC LIR, she and her sister once so soundly thrashed CÚ CHULAINN that he lay immobile for a year until they relented and healed him. It seems that this thrashing was in revenge for Cú Chulainn having refused the love of Fand, although one version states that Fand and Li Ban were 'dream-women' who punished Cú Chulainn for failing to capture two magical birds for his

intended wife EMER. Some sources, however, say that Cú Chulainn spent a month with Fand, whereupon his wife Emer came to hunt him out. He left Fand for his wife, while she returned to her husband. Cú Chulainn pined for the love of Fand, and it was this that laid him low for a year until Manannán mac Lir caused him to fall asleep, and when he awoke he no longer remembered Fand.

## Faustus
*British*

A son of VORTIGERN.

## Faylinn
*Irish*

The mythical land inhabited by elfin people, whose king was IUBDAN and their queen BEBO.

## Fea
*Irish*

The red ox that was loved by DIL and whose companion, FERNEA, was a black ox.

## Feb(h)al
*Irish*

The father of BRÂN[1].

## Fedelm(a)
*Irish*

The prophetess wife of LOEGHAIRE BUADHACH who came to MEDHBHA while she was on the way to ULSTER in search of the DONN CUAILNGÈ, and foretold of the disaster that awaited her and her forces at the hands of CÚ CHULAINN.

## Fedlimid
*Irish*

The father of the beautiful DERDRIU and FILI to CONCHOBAR MAC NESSA.

## Féinn
*Irish*

An alternative name for the FIAN.

## Feis Temhrach
*Irish*

A ritual marriage feast held at TARA at which the king mated with a beautiful virgin who was considered the personification of a goddess, the SPIRIT OF IRELAND, their union symbolically binding sovereign to realm and sanctifying his reign.

## Fer Fídail
*Irish*

The son of EOGABAL, a divine DRUID in the service of MANANNÁN MAC LIR who sent him in the form of a woman to gain access to TUAG whom the god desired. Fer Fídail spent three nights with Tuag before conveying her by boat back towards TÍR TAIRNGIRI. On the way their boat was swamped by MANANNÁN MAC LIR, who could not stand the treacherous behaviour of Fer Fídail. Tuag drowned and Fer Fídail was killed by the angry god after he had landed in Tír Tairngiri.

## Feramorc
*Irish*

A mythical kingdom within MUNSTER. It appears in the story of MAON, at which time SCORIATH was said to be king.

## Fercherdne
*Irish*

The FILI of CÚ ROÍ MAC DÁIRI who avenged the death of his master at the hands of CÚ CHULAINN and BLÁTHNAD. Fercherdne saw BLÁTHNAD standing alone near the edge of a cliff. Flinging himself at her, he caught her around the waist and plummeted with her to their deaths on the rocks below.

## Ferchess
*Irish*

An ally of OILILL and the killer of EOGADAL.

## Ferdia(d(d))
*Irish*

The son of DAMAN, a FIR BHOLG, a member of the RED BRANCH and the foster brother of CÚ CHULAINN, Ferdiadd was a terrible, yellow-haired, monstrous hero who did battle with Cú Chulainn. His magical armour is well described. First, there was a kilt of striped silk with a border of spangled gold. Over this went an apron of brown leather to protect the lower, more delicate, parts of his body. For added protection he also hung a large stone over the apron. Finally, his lower half was protected by a further apron, this time made of purified iron. Ferdiadd thought this would protect him from the GAE BOLGA, the terrible, inescapable spear of Cú Chulainn.

On his head he wore a huge, crested battle helmet, each quarter embellished with a flashing gem, its entire surface encrusted with crystals and rubies. He hung his curved battle sword, with a golden hilt and red pommel of pure gold, on his left side, and slung a huge shield upon his back, this shield consisting of fifty bosses, each of which would bear the weight of a full grown boar, with a central boss of red gold. Finally, he took his sharp pointed spear in his right hand.

The preparations completed, he stepped out to meet Cú Chulainn. The battle raged long and hard. The first day neither could inflict even a single wound. The second day each fared a bit better, but not much. The third day both warriors received horrible wounds, cutting away huge chunks of each other's flesh. The fourth day saw Cú Chulainn call for his invincible spear, the Gae Bolga, and, although he had been terribly wounded himself, he let fly with the Gae Bolga, which easily penetrated the armour of Ferdiadd who died in his arms.

## Fergal
*Irish*

Possibly the historical king of ULSTER who was killed in a battle along with DONN BO. The head of Fergal was cut off and taken to the hall of the king whose army had defeated Fergal's. There it was treated with great respect. The king combed its hair and washed the face, before setting it on a velvet cloth and positioning it in the place of honour at a feast to commemorate the battle. Afterwards the head was taken away for burial. *The Yellow Book of Lucan* records that the eyes opened and the head gave thanks to God for the respect with which the head had been treated.

## Fergar
*Irish*

One of the three great-grandsons of DESA, the foster father of CONAIRE MÓR, with whom that hero grew up. The names of the other great-grandsons of Desa are recorded as FERLEE and FERROGAN.

## Ferg(h)us
*Irish*

1 One of the people of NEMHEDH who, during the uprising against the FOMHOIRÉ, managed to kill CONANN, one of the Fomhoiré kings, but was himself killed by MORC, another Fomhoiré ruler.

2 One of the three sons of ERC[2], he left IRELAND to establish a kingdom in SCOTLAND, this settlement being the nucleus of DÁL RIADA, the kingdom that was ruled over from DUNADD and is considered the realm from which present day Scots are descended. He borrowed the LIA FÁIL, or Stone of FÁL, from his brother MURTAGH MAC ERC, King of Ireland, and apparently forgot to return it, for this is now the Stone of SCONE to be found in Westminster Abbey.

## Ferg(h)us mac Leda
*Irish*

A King of ULSTER and a contemporary of CONCHOBAR MAC NESSA, and possibly a vassal king. He features in a story which brings him into contact with the elfin inhabitants of FAYLINN. The king of Faylinn, IUBDAN, had always thought his warriors to be the strongest of all living beings, but his bard, EISIRT, told him of a giant race living in Ulster of which but a single man could destroy an entire battalion of the people of Faylinn. Iubdan refused to believe this, so Eisirt said he would bring him evidence, which he did in the form of AEDA[1], a dwarf at the court of Ferghus mac Leda, although, as Eisirt explained, he was not a true representation of the men of Ulster, for those men could carry Aeda as if he were a child.

Eisirt now placed Iubdan under a bond to travel to Ulster and see for himself.

Iubdan took his wife BEBO with him and sneaked into the palace of Ferghus mac Leda at night. However, they were captured, and Ferghus mac Leda refused to let them go. Led by Eisirt, the people of Faylinn attacked Ulster, ruined crops and dried up the milk of cows. Still Ferghus mac Leda would not release his tiny captives, but agreed to ransom them against some of the finest of the treasures of Faylinn. Iubdan and Bebo were released after Ferghus mac Leda had been presented with a cauldron that could never be emptied, a harp that played itself and shoes with which a man could walk on water.

This story seems to represent an early incarnation of the LEPRECHAUN of popular Irish folk belief.

## Ferg(h)us mac Roi-ch, -gh
*Irish*

A son of ROSS AND ROICH, and the tutor of CÚ CHULAINN, Ferghus mac Roich is perhaps best known as the leader of the RED BRANCH, and one of the three heroes despatched by CONCHOBAR MAC NESSA to SCOTLAND to offer a truce to NAOISE, ARDÁN, AINNLE and DERDRIU who had fled there after DERDRIU, the betrothed of Conchobar mac Nessa, forced Naoise to elope with her. The other two heroes who went were DUBTHACH and his son CORMAC MAC DUBTHACH.

However, when the three returned with the exiles. Ferchus mac Roich was placed under bond to feast with BARUCH, another member of the Red Branch. Without the protection of Ferghus mac Roich, the exiles travelled on to EMHAIN MHACHA where Conchobar mac Nessa broke his word, and had EOGHAN MAC DURTHACHT and his company kill the three young men. Outraged by this deceit, Ferghus mac Roich, Dubthach and Cormac mac Dubthach attacked and razed Emhain Mhacha, killing 300 of the men of ULSTER in the process, before defecting to AILILL and MEDHBHA of CONNACHT, the traditional enemies of Conchobar mac Nessa.

## Fergn-a, -e
*Irish*

1 An ally of BODB.
2 A cunning leech (physician) who diagnosed the love-sickness that plagued OENGHUS MAC IN OG for a year after he had dreamt of, but been unable to locate, a beautiful maiden. Fergna then had BOANN search for a second year, but still she could not be found. Finally, Fergna suggested the intervention of the DAGHDHA, who advised his son to ask the advice of Bodb.

## Ferlee
*Irish*

One of the three great-grandsons of DESA, the foster father of CONAIRE MÓR, with whom that hero grew up. FERGAR and FERROGAN are recorded as the names of the other great-grandsons of Desa.

## Fernea
*Irish*

The black ox of DIL whose companion, FEA, was a red ox.

## Ferrex
*British*

A son of GORBODUC and JUDON, and brother of PORREX. As the two brothers came of age, Porrex plotted to ambush Ferrex. Ferrex got wind of this and fled to GAUL where he raised an army for his return. Porrex succeeded in killing his brother shortly after he had returned. However, as Ferrex had been his mother's

favourite, his death unhinged her, and she hacked the sleeping Porrex to pieces. As neither Ferrex or Porrex left an heir, the line of descent from BRUTUS died out with the death of Gorboduc.

## Ferrogan
*Irish*

One of the three great-grandsons of DESA, the foster father of CONNAIRE MÓR, with whom that hero grew up. The names of the other great-grandsons of Desa are recorded as FERLEE and FERGAR.

## Féth Fiada
*Irish*

The mantle of invisibility that was worn by the gods so that they might remain unseen by mortals. Some sources say that the Féth Fiada was a spell that might be cast to cover a whole group of beings and thus make them invisible. In this form it was said to be a power used by the DRUIDS and later by the Christian saints, who could use it not only to make themselves invisible but also to change their form.

## Fiachna
*Irish*

1 The son of FIRABA. He joined MEDHBHA and AILILL after the treacherous murder of the sons of UISNECH by CONCHOBAR MAC NESSA. Later he came to the aid of CÚ CHULAINN when that hero had been outnumbered by the sons of CALATIN and killed all twenty-eight of them, although some sources say he simply cut off their hands, and then Cú Chulainn finished them off.
2 An inhabitant of MAGH MELL who came to seek the help of LOEGHAIRE[2] to release his wife who was the prisoner of GOLL. Loeghaire and fifty of his men followed Fiachna to the underwater

realm of Magh Mell, and there released Fiachna's wife. In return, Fiachna gave each of the men of CONNACHT a wife, giving his own daughter SUN TEAR to Loeghaire. Loeghaire and his men stayed a year in Magh Mell before briefly returning to Connacht. However, none of them could forget the wonders they had beheld, and soon returned, Loeghaire becoming the joint ruler of Magh Mell beside Fiachna.

## Fiachna Lurgan
*Irish*

The King of DÁL NARAIDI who went to SCOTLAND to join his ally AÉDAN MAC GABRÁIN, the king of DÁL RIADA, in his fight against invading SAXONS. While in ALBA, a stranger arrived at Fiachna Lurgan's court and informed his wife that, unless she would bear him a son, her husband would die the very next day. Convinced that the stranger had prophesied truthfully, the queen consented to lie with the man that night. The following morning he had disappeared, and was seen that day on the battlefield in Alba, where his prowess enabled Fiachna Lurgan and Aédan mac Gábrain to rout the Saxon forces.

When Fiachna Lurgan returned home, his wife immediately told him all that had happened in his absence, for she had, by that time, determined that the stranger she had lain with and who had subsequently protected her husband and his ally, was none other than MANANNÁN MAC LIR, for the god had left the queen a poem that enabled her to determine whose son she was to bear. Legend says that the child born of this union was MONGÁN.

## Fiachtra
*Irish*

A daughter of LIR and AOBH, and sister to FIONUALA, HUGH and CONN[2]. She was one of the four children of Lir who were condemned to spend 900 years as swans by their jealous step-mother AOIFE. They regained their human form during the time of St PATRICK and died shortly afterwards.

## Fial(1)
*Irish*

A daughter of FORGALL and elder sister of EMER.

## fian
*Irish*

(pl. *fiana*) A generic name for a roving band, or bands, of warriors. This name is said, by some, to be the root of the name of FIONN MAC CUMHAILL. The *Annals of Tigernach*, which date from the eleventh century, say that the fian was a hireling militia defending IRELAND, this militia being made up of seven legions each of 3,000 men under a single commander. It is worth noting that, during the time of Fionn mac Cumhaill and the fian, Ireland was not invaded once.

## Fiannuigeacht
*Irish*

The title adopted by the leader of the FIAN, although it was also used to describe the leading battalion, or clan, within the fian.

## fidchell
*Irish*

A symbolic board game, often called 'chess' in the translations of the Irish myths and legends. Fidchell has its Welsh equivalent in GWYDDBWYLL.

## Figol
*Irish*

A DRUID at TARA during the preparations for the Second Battle of MAGH TUIREDH. He is recorded as having promised to rain showers of fire on the FOMHOIRÉ during the battle and to reduce their strength by two-thirds, their loss of strength being transferred to the TUATHA DÉ DANANN, whose strength would increase proportionately.

## fili
*Irish*

(pl. *filidh* or *file*) The Gaelic for a bard or poet. They were normally found, in this position, within a royal court, examples of royal filidh being AMHAIRGHIN, FERCHERDNE and FEDLIMID.

## Finchory
*Irish*

The sunken island to which the sons of TUIRENN were sent by LUGH to retrieve a magical cooking spit as part of their punishment for having killed CIAN.

## Find
*Irish*

'The Fairhaired One', a title that was most likely applied to LUGH. His continental equivalent was VINDONNUS.

## Findaba(i)r
*Irish*

The daughter of MEDHBHA and AILILL who loved FRAOCH. Ailill, fearing Fraoch's divine parentage, attempted to kill him, but he overcame the obstacles placed in his path, and Ailill could no longer refuse the betrothal of his daughter. In return, Fraoch agreed to fight on the side of Medhbha and Ailill in the forthcoming attack on ULSTER to secure the DONN CUAILNGÈ. During the course of this battle Medhbha offered Findabair to FERDIA as his wife, even though by this time she was married to Fraoch, although she may have been widowed, for the *Taín Bó Cuailngè* does not record what happened to Fraoch.

## Fin(d)ch-oém, -oom
*Irish*

The daughter of CATHBHADH and MAGA, sister of DEICTHINE and Elva, mother of CONALL CERNACH by AMORGHIN, and aunt of CÚ CHULAINN, whom she helped to raise while he was still known as SÉDANTA. Some sources call Findchoém the daughter of EOCHO ROND, which leads to the supposition that Eocho Rond and Cathbhadh are one and the same.

## Fin(d)ias
*Irish*

A mythical city that was the home of USCIAS, one of the four wizards who taught the TUATHA DÉ DANANN their magical arts. From this city came the invincible sword of NUADHA. The other three mythical cities and their associated wizards are: FALIA (MORFESSA), GORIAS (ESIAS) and MURIAS (SIMIAS).

## Finegas
*Irish*
See FINNÉCES.

## Fingal
*British*

The name given by the Irish living in

SCOTLAND to FIONN MAC CUMHAILL. Under this name he is supposed to have constructed the Giant's Causeway in Northern IRELAND, the legend saying that he built it to walk across to Scotland. Fingal's Cave on Staffa is so called because the hero was alleged to have used that island as his base for the defence of the Hebrides against Norse invaders.

## Fingen
*Irish*

The physician to CONCHOBAR MAC NESSA. He told that king that the 'brain ball' that had become lodged in his forehead could not be removed, otherwise he would die. Instead he simply sewed it into place with golden thread and told Conchobar mac Nessa that he had nothing to worry about provided he did not become agitated. Conchobar mac Nessa died when he could not control his emotions and the 'brain ball' burst from his head.

## Finn mac -Cool, -Cumhal
*Irish*

Popular versions of FIONN MAC CUMHAILL.

## Finnabair
*Irish*

The wife of RIANGABAIR and mother of LOEG and of three beautiful daughters. She and her husband were visited twice by CÚ CHULAINN, Loeg and LUGAID[1] on their quest to discover the whereabouts of the sons of DOEL, once on their way from EMHAIN MHACHA and once on the way back again. On the first occasion ETAN, one of the daughters, spent the night with Cú Chulainn, who gave her a ring as a token.

## Fin(n)éces
*Irish*
Also FINEGAS

A DRUID to whom FIONN MAC CUMHAILL was sent to learn science and poetry. Finnéces lived on the banks of the river BOYNE. Near his home a hazel tree dropped its Nuts of Knowledge into a stream, where there were eaten by a salmon. This salmon, known as the SALMON OF WISDOM, had long been sought by Finnéces, but he could never catch it. Fionn mac Cumhaill caught it at the first attempt and took it to Finnéces, who told him to cook it. As it was cooking, Fionn mac Cumhaill accidentally touched it with his thumb, which he sucked to soothe it, and he was immediately filled with the potency of the fish, when he reported this to Finnéces, the Druid said that it had been prophesied and that he should eat the fish. In this way Fionn mac Cumhaill was able to chew his thumb and know of all events, past and future. Finnéces then sent the youth on his way, for he already knew more than he could possibly be taught. See also BLACK ARCAN.

## Finnb(h)ennach
*Irish*

'The White-horned', a bull owned by AILILL, although it had been calved among the herds of MEDHBHA. It was the adversary of the DONN CUAILNGÈ, the brown bull of Cuailngè in the final conflict of the saga *Taín Bó Cuailngè*. The two bulls fought for a day and a night, a fight that was so fierce that it shook the mountains. The following morning the Donn Cuailngè trotted back into the camp of Medhbha and Ailill with all that remained of Finnbhennach hanging from his horns.

## Finnen
*Irish*

A sixth-century abbot who is reputed to have sought the hospitality of TUAN MAC CARELL, who dwelt not far from his monastery in Country Donegal. Tuan mac Carell at first refused him entry, but, after Finnen had fasted for a day and a night on his doorstep, he relented and admitted him.

Some time later, Tuan mac Carell visited Finnen, and it was then that he revealed that, although he was now known as Tuan mac Carell, he had first been incarnated as TUAN MAC STARN, one of the people of PARTHOLÁN who had been the first humans to set foot on IRELAND. Tuan mac Carell told Finnen the history of Ireland, and lived with Finnen and his monks until his death during which time Finnen and his company wrote down all Tuan mac Carell told them.

## Finnilene
*British*

One of the four ALAISIAGAE, war goddesses who originated in the Teutonic heartland but whose worship was possibly brought to BRITAIN[1] by the Romans. The names of all four of the Alaisiagae – the other three being BEDE[1], BAUDIHILLIE and FRIAGABI – appear on three stones at Housesteads on Hadrian's Wall, where they are connected with Mars, the Roman god of war.

## Fintan
*Irish*

1 The only survivor of the early settlers of IRELAND were led to the island by CESAIR, although some name the leader of the expedition as BANBHA. Of this expedition, only three were men – Fintan, BITH and LADRA – the other

fifty members all being women who were shared out among the three, Fintan obtaining Cesair. After Ladra died, the women were reapportioned, and Fintan and Bith received twenty-five each. Shortly after the death of Bith, all his surviving compatriots were killed during the biblical Flood. Fintan survived and lived on, first as a falcon, then an eagle and then a hawk, and he saw all that came to pass in later days. Later tradition says it was this Fintan who became the SALMON OF WISDOM, cooked and eaten by FIONN MAC CUMHAILL.

2 The father of CETHERN.

3 The name of the SALMON OF WISDOM according to a late tradition. This magical fish, which was cooked and eaten by FIONN MAC CUMHAILL, is thought by some to have been the final form taken by FINTAN[1], the sole survivor of the first people to land in IRELAND under the leadership of CESAIR. If this is the case it would certainly explain why Fionn mac Cumhaill instantly knew all that had passed before, because Fintan would have been the oldest living thing in Ireland and a veritable historical encyclopedia.

## Fi(o)nn mac Cumhaill
*Irish*

The legendary Irish hero who has been identified with a general or chieftain who organized the first regular Irish army in the middle of the third century. He was called FINGAL by James Macpherson (1736–96) in his popular epics (1762–63), which were supposedly translations of the writings of a third-century bard named OSSIAN, although Ossian is actually a variant of OISÎN, the son of Fionn mac Cumhaill. Fionn mac Cumhaill is most popularly known as FINN MAC COOL, and is, from his possession of a shield that had belonged to LUGH, which was given to that god by MANANNÁN MAC LIR, possibly a degenerate version of the god Lugh himself.

The son of CUMHAILL and MUIRNE, Fionn mac Cumhaill was born posthumously at the home of BODHMHALL, Muirne's sister, and was originally called DEIMNE. At a very early age he was judged to be 'fair' in looks as well as in play, and from this judgement he received his name Fionn, for 'fionn' means fair. A poet (FILI) and seer, Fionn mac Cumhaill became the leader of a famous warrior troop, or FIAN, at the age of just eight (ten according to some sources) by defeating the monstrous AILLÉN MAC MIDHNA, who, every year on the feast of SAMHAIN, came to TARA and having first bewitched the entire company with beautiful music, burned down the court. Fionn mac Cumhaill remained immune to the magical music of Aillén mac Midhna by pressing the point of his spear into his forehead. As Aillén mac Midhna drew near to Tara, belching smoke and fire, Fionn mac Cumhaill calmly stepped out and beheaded the monster. He later killed whole hordes of monstrous serpents throughout IRELAND, each of which had various attributes of fire and water.

Fionn mac Cumhaill was blessed with a supernatural wisdom, some saying that this came from his drinking an OTHERWORLDLY brew. However, most accounts say that it came about after he accidentally touched the SALMON OF WISDOM with his thumb while staying with his mentor FINNÉCES. Thenceforth, all he had to do was bite his thumb to learn what the future held. This ritual biting of the thumb was known as IMBAS FOROSNAI, and appears it to have carried across the Irish Sea to WALES were it resurfaces in the story of CERRIDWEN and GWION BACH.

Fionn mac Cumhaill had many wives and mistresses. One wife was CRUITHNE[1], while another was SAAR or SABIA, the daughter of BODB DEARG and the mother, by Fionn mac Cumhaill, of Oisîn.

His two famous hounds, BRAN[2] and SGEOLAN, were in fact his nephews, for their father ILLAN married TUIREANN, the sister of Fionn mac Cumhaill's wife, but Illan's supernatural mistress changed Tuireann into a wolf-hound, in which form she bore the two famous dogs.

As an ageing widower, Fionn mac Cumhaill became betrothed to the beautiful, and much, much younger GRÁINNE. Unfortunately for Fionn mac Cumhaill, she loved DIARMAID UA DUIBHNE so deeply that, on the night of their wedding feast, she drugged all the guests and her new husband, and casting a GESSA spell on Diarmaid ua Duibhne, eloped with him to a wood in CONNACHT. When they had recovered from the effects of the drug, Fionn mac Cumhaill and his men went after the lovers and surrounded the wood in which they were hiding. Diarmaid ua Duibhne's fosterfather, OENGHUS MAC IN OG, carried Gráinne to safety, while Diarmaid ua Duibhne made good his escape by bounding over the heads of the beseiging horde in a single leap. However, Diarmaid ua Duibhne remained loyal to his former master and would not take Gráinne as his lover. It was only after he had endured her intolerable derision that he eventually broke his oath to Fionn mac Cumhaill.

Fionn mac Cumhaill, Gráinne and Diarmaid ua Duibhne were finally reconciled through the efforts of Oenghus Mac in Og. So complete was the reconciliation that Fionn mac Cumhaill invited Diarmaid ua Duibhne to accompany him in the hunt for the great boar BEANN GHULBAN. Diarmaid ua Duibhne accepted, even though it had been foretold that Beann Ghulban, his foster brother, would bring about his end. Sure enough, seconds before he delivered the killing blow, Diarmaid ua Duibhne was mortally gored by the boar. Only Fionn mac Cumhaill, who had the divine gift of healing, could save the dying man if he would give him water from his own hands. Fionn mac Cumhaill went to fetch water, but on the way back he remembered the treachery of Diarmaid ua Duibhne and allowed the water to trickle away. By the time he had done this for the third time, Diarmaid ua Duibhne was dead.

Fionn mac Cumhaill was said to have died at the age of 230, his death causing the decline and eventual disbanding of the fian. He was later alleged to have been reincarnated as the seventh-century Irish chieftain MONGÁN, whose death is recorded as AD 625. See also AINÉ[3], MILUCHRADH.

## Fion(ngh)uala
*Irish*

The eldest daughter of LIR, and one of his four children who were transformed into swans by Lir's second wife AOIFE, a form they were condemned to retain for 900 years. At the end of the allotted time, in the time of St PATRICK, Fionuala, her sister, and her brothers regained their human form, but now as ancient, white-haired beings on the verge of death. They were accepted into the Christian faith and baptized moments before they died. Fionguala was the only one to speak, and she gave precise details of how they were to be buried, saying that CONN[2] should be laid at her right, FIACHTRA at her left and HUGH at her face.

## Fir Bholg
*Irish*

The leaders of the fourth invasion of

IRELAND, which consisted of three parties, the Fir Bholg, the GAILIÓIN and the FIR DHOMHNANN. The Fir Bholg were said to have been descended from SEMION, son of STARIAT. All three were made up of the survivors of an earlier Irish people known as the people of NEMHEDH, who had been forced to flee to Greece. Having successfully landed and taken Ireland, the Fir Bholg divided the country into the five CÓIGEDH, or provinces, of ULSTER, LEINSTER, MUNSTER, CONNACHT and MEATH. The Gailióin became known as the LAIGHIN after they settled in Leinster, while the Fir Dhomghnann settled in Connacht. The other three provinces were occupied by the Fir Bholg, who ruled Ireland until they were beaten by the TUATHA DÉ DANANN at the First Battle of MAGH TUIREDH, when their king FOCHAIDH MAC ERC was killed, and they were forced into exile among the FOMHOIRÉ.

## Fir Dea
*Irish*

'Men of the god' or 'the divine tribe'. This was possibly the original name of the TUATHA DÉ DANANN, although this is open to speculation.

## Fir Dhomhnann
*Irish*

One of the two parties, survivors of the people of NEMHEDH, who came from Greece to IRELAND under the leadership of the FIR BHOLG. The other company to invade Ireland on this occasion, the fourth such invasion in the early history of the island, was the GAILIÓIN. The Fir Dhomhnann settled in CONNACHT, the Gailióin in LEINSTER, whereafter they became known as the LAIGHIN, while the Fir Bholg occupied the remaining three CÓIGEDH, ULSTER, MUNSTER and MEATH. Some authorities believe that the Fir

Dhomhnann may have moved across the Irish Sea to become the origins of the DUMNONII.

## Fir Sídh
*Irish*

The name by which the inhabitants of the SÍDH were sometimes referred. Meaning 'men of the sídh', the expression was used when there was no better way to refer to supernatural beings that lived within the boundaries of IRELAND, rather than in the OTHERWORLDLY realms, which usually lay overseas. It is possibly a relatively late term, coming into use after the power of the TUATHA DÉ DANANN had started to decline.

## Firaba
*Irish*

The father of FIACHNA[1].

## Fledd Bricrenn
*Irish*

*Bricriu's Feast*, a quasi-tragic, even comedic tale, which was based on the much earlier ribald tale, *Scéla Mucce Maic Dá Thó*. The story tells of the maliciousness of BRICRIU, who, during a feast, bribed three great heroes to claim the honour of carving the roast, which led to an unseemly brawl. The matter was first judged by MEDHBHA and subsequently by CÚ ROÍ MAC DÁIRI. Both judges came out in favour of CÚ CHULAINN. See also BUDA.

## Flidhais
*Irish*

The goddess of forest animals to whom the deer was sacred, roaming herds being seen as her 'cattle'. Some sources name her as the mother of FAND[2] and LI BAN. In the *Taín Bó Cuailngè*, Flidhais is named as the wife of AILILL, although his wife is usually named as MEDHBHA, and she is here called the owner of a magnificent cow that could feed a whole army for seven days on the results of one milking.

## Flower Face
*Welsh*

The literal translation of BLODEUWEDD, the magically made wife of LLEU LLAW GYFFES.

## Fódla
*Irish*

The wife of MAC CÉCHT and one of the triad of goddesses known as the SOVEREIGNTY OF IRELAND. She and her other aspects, ÉRIU and BANBHA, were encountered by the Sons of MÍL ÉSPÁINE while they were on their way to TARA.

## Foill
*Irish*

A son of NECHTA SCÉNE. He was killed by CÚ CHULAINN, along with his two brothers, while Cú Chulainn was travelling to EMHAIN MHACHA. He cut off the brothers' heads and tied them to his chariot, along with a stag and sixteen wild swans he had caught and tethered.

## Follaman
*Irish*

The son of CONCHOBAR MAC NESSA. He led the youth of EMHAIN MHACHA to the aid of CÚ CHULAINN, who stood alone protecting ULSTER against the forces of MEDHBHA and AILILL. He and his companions were all killed.

## Fom(h)oiré
*Irish*

One of the great tribes of Celtic IRELAND and the sworn enemies of the TUATHA DÉ DANANN. Coming to Ireland after the time of the biblical Flood, their name means, literally, 'sea giants'. They were a race of half-human monsters, each of whom had a single leg, a single hand, one eye in the centre of the forehead and three rows of razor-sharp teeth. Having enjoyed free reign of Ireland for a considerable time, they were eventually defeated by PARTHOLÁN and forced into exile on the Hebrides and the Isle of MAN. They returned many years later, after Parthplán had himself been conquered by NEMHEDH, and set about reclaiming the island. Quickly reducing the people of Nemhedh to subserviency, compelling them to pay a tribute of two-thirds of their wine, corn and children, it was not too long before the people of Nemhedh rebelled. Only one boat-load of the people of Nemhedh survived the rebellion, and they fled to Greece from whence they were later to return as the FIR BHOLG, GAILIÓIN and FIR DHOMHNANN.

When the Fir Bholg, Gailióin and Fir Dhomhnann returned and invaded Ireland they quickly established the five CÓIGEDH and settled down. However, the Tuatha Dé Danann then arrived and shattered their peace. They met the forces of the Tuatha Dé Danann at the First Battle of MAGH TUIREDH, when they were soundly beaten and forced into exile among the Fomhoire, their earlier enemies.

The Fomhoiré and Tuatha Dé Danann settled into an uncomfortable peace, each keeping to their own territory, although that of the Fomhoiré was but a small corner of the country. A strange relationship between the two enemies occurs with the birth of BRES[1] whose parents were the Fomhoiré ELATHA and a Tuatha Dé Danann woman. When Bres was forced to abdicate as the leader of the Tuatha Dé Danann, he carried off the magic harp of the DAGHDHA, an act that shattered the fragile truce and led to the Second Battle of Magh Tuiredh.

*Bres* had mustered an army against the Tuatha Dé Danann when LUGH sent the Daghdha to attempt to reclaim the harp and call a truce. The Fomhoiré, well aware of the power of the Daghdha, attempted to incapacitate him by feeding him an enormous meal, finished off by a bout of love-making with a Fomhoiré maiden. The plan backfired, for the Daghdha had an insatiable appetite, and his sexual prowess so impressed the Fomhoiré maiden that she agreed to use her magical powers against her own people.

The Second Battle of Magh Tuiredh, during which the sea god TETHRA was said to have fought alongside the Fomhoiré, was brought to an abrupt end when Lugh aimed a slingshot into the single monstrous eye of BALAR with such force and accuracy that it exploded Balar's brains to the four winds, and carried on to decimate the Fomhoiré army. The remnants of the monstrous race were then driven from the country. See also AIDED CHLAINNE TUIRENN.

## Fomoiri
*Irish*

A variant sometimes used to refer to the FOMHOIRÉ in the plural form, although Fomhoiré is both singular and plural.

## Fomorian(s)
*Irish*

A semi-latinized variant of FOMHOIRÉ.

## Forbay
*Irish*

The son of CONCHOBAR MAC NESSA. He is said to have killed MEDHBHA with a slingshot as she bathed in a lake on the island to which she had retired after the death of AILILL.

## Forgall
*Irish*

The father of FIALL and the maiden EMER, who was later to marry the hero CÚ CHULAINN after he had proved his worth by becoming a pupil of the prophetess SCÁTHACH. Forgall did not welcome the union between his daughter and Cú Chulainn, and his sending the hero beyond ALBA was his attempt to ensure that he never returned. Cú Chulainn did, of course, return, and Forgall was killed in his attempt to protect his home.

## Fort of Glass
*Welsh*

CAER WYDYR, an OTHERWORLDY city that has become associated with both GLASTONBURY and AVALON. Some sources have identified the Fort of Glass with CAER FEDDWIDD or CAER SIDDI, another Otherworldly realm, but this mysterious fort is better known as the Fort of CAROUSAL.

## Fothad (Airglech)
*Irish*

A king slain in the third century by FIONN MAC CUMHAILL, although it was later revealed that Fothad was actually killed by KEELTA.

## Fragarach
*Irish*

'The Answerer', the invincible sword owned by LUGH.

## France
*General*

A large European country usually referred to by its older name of GAUL. During the late Celtic period France was a Frankish kingdom, that race having established themselves there about AD 457. Indeed, the present name of France derives from their name.

## Franks
*General*

A Germanic people who were influential in Europe between the third and eighth centuries. Believed to have originated in Pomerania on the Black Sea, they had settled on the Rhine by the third century, spread into the Roman Empire by the fourth, and gradually conquered most of GAUL and Germany under the Merovingian (481–751) and Carolingian (768–987) dynasties. The kingdom of the western Franks became FRANCE, to which they gave their name, while that of the eastern Franks became Germany.

## Fraoch
*Irish*

The subject of the *Táin Bó Fráich*, the son of BÉBIND which makes him the nephew of BOANN. He was loved by FINDABAIR, the daughter of AILILL and MEDHBHA, whom Fraoch travelled to see with a vast hoard of treasure for her parents. Fraoch was entertained regally until he asked Ailill and Medhbha to allow him to marry their daughter. They refused and thought of a way to kill Fraoch so that he did not seek to bring divine retribution upon them.

While Fraoch was swimming in a lake, Ailill had him fetch a branch from a rowan tree that hung over the water. On the second trip to the tree the guardian monster of the tree attacked Fraoch, but, although he was horribly wounded, he managed to behead the beast with the sword his beloved Findabair threw him. Fraoch was carried back to the SÍDH of his mother, from whence he appeared the following day fully healed. Ailill and Medhbha could not refuse him now, and agreed to the betrothal on the condition that Fraoch helped them in the coming battles with ULSTER to secure the DONN CUAILNGÈ.

### Friagabi
*British*

One of the four Teutonic ALAISIAGAE, the others being BEDE[1], BAUDIHILLIE and FINNILENE, to whom an altar was dedicated at Housesteads on Hadrian's Wall. Her name may mean 'Ruler of Battle'. It seems quite likely that the four goddesses were brought to BRITAIN[1] by the invading Romans, who introduced their worship to the warlike Celts.

### Friuch
*Irish*

A swineherd of MUNSTER, in the employ of BODB. He appears in the COPHUR IN DÁ MUCCIDA along with RUCHT, a swineherd in CONNACHT, in the employ of OCHALL OICHNI. The two are on the best of terms, leading their respective herds of swine to feed with each other depending on where the pasture was best. However, the people of Munster and Connacht conspired to make the two fall out, which they did, each casting spells on the other's herd. Briuch and Rucht turned themselves into ravens and fought for a year in Munster and a year in Connacht. Next, they became water-beasts, then demons and finally worms. These worms were subsequently swallowed by cows and reborn as FINNBHENNACH and the DONN CUAILNGÈ, although which great bull represented which swineherd is not known.

### Fuamhnach
*Irish*

The first wife of MIDHIR. Her jealousy at the beauty of Midhir's second wife, ÉDÁIN ECHRAIDHE, knew no bounds, and her first act was to turn the beautiful young woman into a pool of water. That became a worm, and that worm became a huge and astoundingly beautiful fly, whose perfume filled the air. Midhir was quite contented to have Édáin Echraidhe around him, even in this unusual form. This once more enraged Fuamhnach, so she conjured up a strong wind that blew the fly over a cliff to lie helpless on the rocky coast for a total of seven years before OENGHUS MAC IN OG found her, placed her in a crystal bower and brought her back to Midhir. Fuamhnach finally, in her lifetime, managed to dispose of Édáin Echraidhe when she once again called up a strong wind, which this time blew the fly into a goblet of wine which was subsequently swallowed.

## Gabhra
*Irish*

A mythical battle, known popularly as the Battle of GOWRA, was fought between two opposing factions within the FIAN and was ultimately to lead to the end of the supremacy of the fian within IRELAND. See also CAIRBRE, DECIES, SGEIMH SOLAIS.

## Gadelius
*Irish*

An ancestor of the Sons of MÍL ÉSPÁINE. He was said to have been bitten by a venomous snake and then to have been cured by Moses.

## Gadeon
*Welsh*

The son of EUDAF and brother of CYNAN and ELEN. After Elen had married MACSEN, he and Cynan mustered an army and marched with Macsen against Rome, which had chosen a new emperor to replace Macsen. Triumphant after having reinstated Macsen as emperor, Cynan and Madaon conquered ARMORICA. Cynan returned to BRITAIN[1], while Gadeon and a large number of the British troops settled in Armorica, where they killed all the men and cut out the tongues of the women so that they could not talk a foreign language.

## Gae Bolga
*Irish*

The invincible spear of CÚ CHULAINN. It was launched, as Cú Chulainn had been taught by SCÁTHACH, from between his toes. The hero used the spear on two memorable instances, when he used it to kill his son CONALL and his foster brother FERDIA.

## Gaels
*Irish*

The name by which the human inhabitants of IRELAND, and latterly SCOTLAND, are properly known, their name giving rise to the Gaelic language. The definition was first used to describe the Sons of MÍL ÉSPÁINE, the first human inhabitants of Ireland.

## Gaí Dearg
*Irish*

The magical, red-shafted spear owned by DIARMAID UA DUIBHNE. GRÁINNE advised him to take it on the hunt for BEANN GHULBAN, but he thought that this gave him an unfair advantage. His refusal to take his magical weapon, once owned according to some by MANANNÁN MAC LIR, cost him his life.

## Gaibhde
*Irish*

A variant of GOIBHNIU that is commonly used in Irish folklore.

## Gaible
*Irish*

The son of NUADHA. He once stole a bundle of twigs that AINGE, a daughter of the DAGHDHA, had gathered to build herself a tub that did not leak. Gaible threw away the twigs, and where they landed a mature wood sprang out of the ground.

## Gailióin
*Irish*

One of the three companies made up of the descendants of the survivors of the people of NEMHEDH, who came from Greece and invaded IRELAND, settling in LEINSTER where they became known as the LAIGHIN. The other two companies were the FIR BHOLG, the leaders of the invasion, and the FIR DHOMHNANN. It has been suggested that the FIAN were descended from the Gailióin.

## Gall
*Welsh*

The son of DYSGYFDAWD. He was said to have killed the birds of GWENDDOLAU.

## Ganieda
*Welsh*

The twin sister of MYRDDIN who appears in Welsh poetry as GWENDYDD and, under this name, in the *Vita Merlini*, which says she was the adulterous wife of RHYDDERCH whose philandering was spotted by her brother. In origin, Ganieda would appear to be LANGUORETH, in Jocelyn's *Life of*

*Saint Kentigern* the wife of RHYDDERCH, who became enamoured with a soldier.

## Garanwyn
*Welsh*

The son of CEI.

## Garman
*Irish*

The son of GLAS. From his grave a lake was said to have formed.

## Garmangabi
*British*

A goddess whose name is known only from an inscription found at Lanchester near Durham. Her name appears to mean 'Giving' or 'Generous', thus connecting her with the later goddess GEFION as a bestower of gifts. It is thought that her name may be Teutonic in origin and that she was introduced to BRITAIN[1] during the Roman invasion.

## Garmna
*Irish*

The consort of ERCOL to whom MEDHBHA and AILILL sent CÚ CHULAINN, LOEGHAIRE BUADHACH and CONALL CERNACH to be judged during the aftermath of the feast thrown by the malicious BRICRIU.

## Gartnán
*Irish*

A King of SCOTLAND and the father of CANO who, after a period in exile, succeeded him. His historicity is slightly doubtful, although if he did live it was certainly prior to AD 688, as this is the recorded date for the death of his son.

## Gaul
*General*

A Roman province in western Europe, which stretched from what is now northern Italy to the southern part of the Netherlands. The name is most commonly used nowadays to refer to FRANCE, but this is not strictly accurate. The Gauls themselves were divided into several distinct groups, but united under a common religion that was controlled by the DRUIDS. One group of Gauls invaded Italy *c*.400 BC, sacked Rome and settled between the Alps and the Apennines. This region, known as Cisalpine Gaul, was conquered by Rome *c*.225 BC. The Romans conquered southern Gaul between the Mediterranean and the Cevennes *c*.125 BC, the remaining Gauls as far as the Rhine being conquered by JULIUS CAESAR between 58 and 51 BC.

## Gavida
*Irish*

An alternative name applied to Giobhniu in his role as foster father to his nephew LUGH.

## Gef(io)n
*British*

A chthonic goddess of giving whose name is thought to have derived from GARMANGABI and is possibly the ANGLO-SAXON form of that name.

## Geis
*Irish*

A variant of GESSA.

## Geniti Glinne
*Irish*

'Damsels of the Glen'. Although it is not clear what, or who, these beings were, it is thought that they may be a resemblance of a pre-Celtic nature spirit. They appear in the Celtic literature as being associated with the TUATHA DÉ DANANN. In the *Taín Bó Cuailngè* the Geniti Glinne are associated with NEMHAIN or BODB, and they wreak confusion on the forces of MEDHBHA, but they appear to have been afraid of the DONN CUAILNGÈ, for they would not go near him.

## Gen-vissa, -uissa
*British*

According to GEOFFREY OF MONMOUTH the daughter of the Roman emperor CLAUDIUS. She married ARVIRAGUS and, when her husband revolted against her father, restored the peace.

## Geoffrey of Monmouth
*General*

The twelfth-century chronicler (*c*.1100–*c*.1154) who wrote two important Latin works. Thought to be the son of Breton parents, he studied at Oxford and was archdeacon of Llandarff or Monmouth (*c*.1140), being appointed bishop of St Asaph in 1152. His totally fictitious *Historia Regum Britanniae* deals with a pseudo-mythical history of BRITAIN[1]. Although worthless as history, it is notable for its substantial section on King ARTHUR. According to Geoffrey on Monmouth, this work was based on an earlier British work that he alone had seen and was the first to contain a coherent narrative account of King Arthur. The second, *Vita Merlini*, is wholly Arthurian and, in verse, tells of the madness and adventures of MERLIN.

## Germân
*Irish*

A companion of MAÍL DÚIN.

## Germanus
*British and Gaulish*

A Gallic bishop who came to BRITAIN[1] in AD 429 to regulate the church, which had been divided by Pelasgian heresy. News reached him of a combined SAXON and PICT raid, which he met with a British force that lay in ambush until Germanus rose and shouted 'Hallelujah!' three times, a cry that was, apparently, sufficient to cause the Saxons and the Picts to turn tail and flee.

The name Germanus appears on the Pillar of ELISEG in the eighth paragraph of the inscription on that pillar. This states that Germanus blessed BRITU, son of VORTIGERN, but, seeing that Germanus was sided against the *Saxons*, this would seem to indicate that his blessing was not of a kindly nature but one that would today be called a curse.

## gessa
*Irish*
Also GEIS

A form of magical spell, or enchantment. It was famously used during the wedding feast of GRÁINNE and FIONN MAC CUMHAILL, when Gráinne used it to induce DIARMAID UA DUIBHNE to elope with her.

The gessa appears to have originated as a form of bond that, if broken, would lead to dishonour or even death. The Celtic people were a very honourable people and lived by the motto that a 'man's word is his bond'. CONCHOBAR MAC NESSA used the gessa of FERGHUS MAC ROICH that he may not refuse the hospitality of another to good effect when he wanted to dispose of

the sons of UISNECH, who were being escorted back to EMHAIN MHACHA under Ferghus mac Roich's protection. Conchobar mac Nessa simply had a member of the RED BRANCH, BARUCH, invite Ferghus mac Roich to feast with him, knowing that Ferghus mac Roich dare not refuse. This left the sons of Uisnech without their guardian, and they were easily disposed of.

Tradition embroidered the gessa into a magical spell that embodied the life forces of the individual. The death of CÚ CHULAINN was attributed to his breaking the gessa (here plural) that governed his very existence. To break the gessa was to break a promise, and to the Celts this would mean dishonour and death, either at their own hand or by the hand of another. It has even been suggested that a Celt so dishonoured would commit suicide rather than live, but this has never been proved or disproved.

## Gewissei
*Welsh*

An ancient people who inhabited the southeast of WALES and who were at one time ruled by Octavius, who made himself king of BRITAIN[1] and chose MACSEN as his successor.

## G(h)ulban
*Irish*

The owner or, more correctly, the foster father of the monstrous BEANN GHULBAN.

## giant
*General*

Many giants are to be found in Celtic mythology and legend. BRITAIN[1] was said to have been ruled by a race of giants before the arrival of BRUTUS, who defeated them, though even he was accompanied by a 'giant', CORINEUS. Later giants tended to be portrayed as clumsy, greedy cannibals who dominated whole districts. Traditionally, a giant could not be overcome by sheer strength but could be defeated by trickery and cunning. One of the best known of all children's fairy tales is 'Jack and the Beanstalk', in which a giant is defeated by JACK THE GIANT-KILLER. This giant is none other than the Cornish giant CORMORAN.

## Giants' -Ring, -Round, -Dance
*British*

(Latin *Chorea Gigantum*) The legendary name given to STONEHENGE in Wiltshire. According to legend it was a memorial commissioned by AMBROSIUS AURELIUS to honour the British warriors slain by the SAXONS. The ring of stones was transported from Mount KILLARAUS in County Kildare, IRELAND, to be re-erected on Salisbury Plain by MYRDDIN and 15,000 men. Each of the stones of the ring was said to have medicinal qualities and was alleged to have been originally carried to Ireland by giants who originated in Africa, giants whom some say where the first inhabitants of the earth and who were the forefathers of ALBION. This is, of course, pure fantasy as Stonehenge predates the time of the Saxons by several thousand years.

## Gidolin
*Welsh*

A dwarf who was said to keep flasks of hag's blood warm on the 'hearth of hell'. CULHWCH was set the task of fetching these flasks as one of the conditions imposed on him by YSPADDADEN in his quest to marry OLWEN.

## Gildas
*British*

A Romano-British historian working in the fifth or sixth century. Born in Strathclyde, he fled the strife that raged in his neighbourhood and went to WALES where he married. He became a monk only after his wife had died. His famous work, *De Excidio Et Conquestu Britanniae*, was probably written between 516 and 547, most likely while he was still quite a young man. It is the only extant history of the Celts and the only contemporary British version of events from the invasion of the Romans to his own time. It is, however, only a pseudo-history, for it mixes both mythology and history with free abandon. Later tradition said that Gildas himself was a friend of King ARTHUR.

## Gildas Junior
*British*

An alternative name for TREMEUR.

## Gilfaethwy
*Welsh*

The son of DÔN and brother of GWYDION FAB DÔN. Gilfaethwy fell for the beautiful GOEWIN, who held the post of footholder at the court of MATH FAB MATHONWY, a post that could be held only by a virgin. Learning of his brother's desire, Gwydion fab Dôn used his magic arts to conjure up a quarrel between Math fab Mathonwy and PRYDERI. While Math fab Mathonwy was away fighting Pryderi, Gilfaethwy and Gwydion fab Dôn abducted Goewin, whom they took turns in ravishing. When Math fab Mathonwy returned and discovered what had happened, he punished the brothers by condemning them to spend three years in animal forms, the first as male and female deer, the second as swine and the third as wolves. At the end of each year, having produced an offspring, Math fab Mathonwy changed them into their next form. At the end of the three years, each having been male and female, he considered their punishment to be complete and changed them back into human form.

## Gillomanius
*Irish*

A King of IRELAND who was allied to PASCHENT when the latter invaded BRITAIN.

## Giraldus Cambrensis
*Welsh*

The Norman-Welsh chronicler and ecclesiastic (c.1146–c.1223). Of noble birth, he was born in Manorbier Castle, DYFED, his father being Gerald de Barri, Lord of Manorbier, and his mother being Angharad, daughter of Gerald of Windsor by the Welsh Princess Nest. He was educated at the abbey of St Peter, Gloucester, and later studied in Paris. He became archdeacon of St David's, but when his uncle the bishop died (1176), he was overlooked for the position because he was a Welshman. He was again overlooked for the same vacancy in 1198, and after that time concentrated on his studies and writing, although his important *Itinerarium Cambriae* was written after he had travelled the length and breadth of WALES in 1188 in the company of Baldwin, then archbishop of CANTERBURY.

## Glas
*Irish*

The father of Garman.

## Glastonbury
*British*

A small town in Somerset, ENGLAND, arguably the most magical town in BRITAIN[1], around which there are many legends, particularly concerning its famous tor and ruined abbey. It is the home of countless legends, Celtic, ANGLO-SAXON and Christian, and even today it is a magical, mystical place with an air of mystery about it. Even the noise and fumes of modern day traffic cannot detract from the unique atmosphere of Glastonbury. According to tradition the abbey was founded by missionaries from Rome about AD 166. Others say it was founded by St PATRICK prior to his mission to the Irish, or, most popularly, by JOSEPH OF ARIMATHEA. However, there is no real evidence to support the existence of an abbey on this site before the seventh century, but there is evidence of a much smaller and older church on the site, and it is perhaps this that has become elevated to the status of abbey before the true date for the foundation of the abbey church itself.

According to medieval traditions, Glastonbury was visited by Jesus when a boy, in the company of his uncle, Joseph of Arimathea, a tin trader, who came to the west country for Mendip lead and Cornish tin. This particular trip is said to have been the inspiration for William Blake's hymn 'Jerusalem', which begins:

And did those feet in ancient time
Walk upon England's mountains green?

Joseph of Arimathea, who took Jesus' body down from the cross and placed it in the sepulchre, is said to have returned to Britain some years later – 37 or 63 – bringing the Christian message with him. With eleven followers he made his way to Glastonbury, wishing to be among the friendly and influential DRUIDS he had met during his earlier visits. On his arrival he stuck his staff into the ground, and it immediately took root and blossomed as a young tree. He took this as a divine sign that he had reached his journey's end. This tree is now immortalized as the GLASTONBURY THORN, which had the special attribute of blossoming twice a year, in the spring and at Christmas.

Joseph of Arimathea was alleged to have brought the Chalice Cup of the Last Supper with him, as well as two cruets containing the blood and sweat of Christ. While the latter two were said to have been buried with him in his Glastonbury grave, the whereabouts of the Chalice Cup were, and still remain, unknown, although some commentators have said that it too was buried with Joseph of Arimathea. It has become entangled in myth, and is identified with the Holy GRAIL of Arthurian fame.

The local king, ARVIRAGUS, gave Joseph of Arimathea and his disciples twelve hides of land (a hide being a medieval measure of land equal to the area that could be tilled with one plough in a year). On this land they built their wattle and daub church, dedicated to the Virgin Mary, and which has its traditional site as the location of the Lady Chapel within the abbey. It had the name *Vetusta Ecclesia*, or Old Church, and, although dilapidated in later years, did not disappear until a fire swept through the Abbey on the night of 25 May 1184.

The legends continued in the century following Joseph of Arimathea's arrival. At the request of King LUCIUS, Arviragus' grandson, the Pope sent two emissaries to revitalize the work at Glastonbury. These two are credited with the foundation of the Abbey, although other accounts say that it was founded in the fifth century by St Patrick, who was the abbot at Glastonbury before leaving to convert the Irish people to Christianity.

The patron saint of WALES, St David, is said to have travelled to Glastonbury at a later date accompanied by seven bishops to dedicate the Old Church, but was warned in a dream that Christ had already done so. Instead, David added another church and dedicated that.

The town remains most famous for its Arthurian connections, which started to appear during the seventh century but which did not really gain ground until 1191, when the monks of the abbey claimed to have unearthed the bodies of both ARTHUR and GUINEVERE. From that day to this the abbey has become a place of especial mystery, for, if the monks were indeed correct, that would make Glastonbury the AVALON of legend.

## Glastonbury Thorn
*British*

A thorn tree situated within the grounds of GLASTONBURY Abbey. It was said to have grown from the staff of JOSEPH OF ARIMATHEA, although some sources state that the original tree grew on Weryall Hill. The thorn had the special attribute of flowering twice a year, in the spring and at Christmas. The tree is first mentioned in the *Lyfe of Joseph of Arimathea*, which dates from c.1500, but only its descendants remain alive today, for the original thorn was cut down in 1643 by a Puritan zealot. The best known surviving tree is that in front of the Church of St John the Baptist in Glastonbury, from which a sprig is sent every Christmas to the reigning monarch.

Various other legends exist about this Holy Tree. Some accounts say that the original tree, from which Joseph of Arimathea's staff had been cut, grew from a thorn from the Crown of Thorns worn by Christ. Local Somerset legends also tell of those who wished the tree harm. Usually the Puritans were blamed in these stories, but the tree always seemed to get the better of them. One particular assailant attacked the thorn with an axe, but it slipped from the trunk and embedded itself in the man's leg, while wood chips flew into his eyes.

An alternative legend says that the Glastonbury Thorn was not a thorn tree at all but a walnut tree. Early writers described this tree, again said to have sprung into life from the staff of Joseph of Arimathea, saying that it budded on St Barnabas' Day (11 June) and never before. It seems that, until this tree was cut down, it was held with the same degree of reverence as the Glastonbury Thorn, for both trees, walnut and thorn, were thought, by some, to have once existed in the town.

## Glastonbury Tor
*British*

The hill at GLASTONBURY, Somerset, around which various legends have arisen. The Tor is said to be the home of GWYNN AP NUDD, Lord of the Dead, and is thus regarded as a portal between the world of the living and the OTHERWORLD. The summit of the Tor is reached by a man-made, labyrinthine spiral path that winds its way around the side of the hill, which, according to some, was also man-made and should thus be considered alongside such places as SILBURY Hill. The tower that stands at the summit is all that remains of the Church of St Michael, a fourteenth-century church that replaced a much earlier building.

Celtic hermits occupied cells on the summit and slopes of the hill, and traces of a prehistoric settlement have also been found. It seems natural for the Celts, and later the Christians, to have maintained the sanctity of the Tor, for the survival of a few ancient stones around the Tor indicates that the hill also had a religious significance to the megalithic peoples. See also COLLEN.

## Glenvissig
*Welsh*

The realm of ATHRWYS, which has been identified by some with GWENT.

## Glewlwyd (Gafaelfawr)
*Welsh*

The gatekeeper who appears in the poem PA GUR and in the *Mabinogion* story of *Culhwch and Olwen*. In both tales he resides at the court to which CULHWCH came to seek help at the start of his quest to locate OLWEN, and in later tradition he became the gatekeeper or porter to King ARTHUR. When Culhwch arrived at the court Glewlwyd exclaimed that never, in all his long and varied career, had he seen so handsome a youth as Culhwch. Glewlwyd's epithet 'Gafaelfawr' means 'great grasp', a logical epithet for a porter.

## Glifieu
*Welsh*

One of the seven survivors of the expedition to IRELAND mounted by BENDIGEID VRAN to avenge the cruelty being dealt out to his sister BRANWEN by the Irish king MATHOLWCH. He and his six compatriots carried the severed head of Bendigeid Vran back from Ireland and, following Bendigeid Vran's instructions, after a lengthy journey, buried it under the WHITE MOUNT in LONDON. Glifieu's companions are named as PRYDERI, MANAWYDAN FAB LLYR, TALIESIN, YNAWAG, GRUDDIEU and HEILYN, Glifieu himself sometimes being called GLUNEU EIL TARAN. They brought the unfortunate Branwen home with them, but, when she sat down and thought of the destruction wreaked on her behalf, she died of a broken heart.

## Gliten
*Welsh*

The name of one of the nine sisters of MORGEN.

## Glitonea
*Welsh*

The name of one of the nine sisters of MORGEN, and thus co-ruler of an OTHERWORLD kingdom that is usually identified with AVALON.

## Gluneu eil Taran
*Welsh*

Named in some sources as one of the seven survivors of the expedition to IRELAND mounted by BENDIGEID VRAN. He is more usually referred to as GLIFIEU.

## Goban
*Irish*

See GOIBHNIU.

## Gobbán (Saer)
*Irish*

'Gobban the Wright', a miraculous builder and marvellous mason who is an aspect of the divine smith GOIBHNIU, although some authorities simply give Gobbán Saer as a more modern variant of Goibhniu.

## Goemagot
*British*

A variant of GOGMAGOG, although it is possible that this is the original name of that particular giant, and that Gogmagog is a later Christianization taken from the Gog and Magog who appear in the Bible (Revelation 20: 8).

## Goewin
*Welsh*

The beautiful daughter of PEBIN. She held the post of footholder, a post that could be only held by a certified virgin, at the court of MATH FAB MATHONWY. There she came to the attention of GILFAETHWY, the brother of GWYDION FAB DÔN. Gwydion fab Dôn magically contrived a quarrel between Math fab Mathonwy and PRYDERI, and while Math fab Mathonwy was away fighting Pryderi, Gilfaethwy abducted Goewin. The two brothers ravished the maiden, but were made to suffer a humiliating punishment for this crime on the return of Math fab Mathonwy, who made them spend three years in animal form and have three offspring as a result.

## Gofannon
*Welsh*
Also GOVANNON

The divine smith whose honour it was, according to ancient Welsh law, to have the first drink or toast at any feast held in a chieftain's court. Gofannon was said to have struck the blow that killed DYLAN EIL TON. Gofannon is undoubtedly the Welsh version of GOIBHNIU.

## Gog
*British*

A legendary giant whose companion was MAGOG, although this pairing are perhaps none other than the giants of the same name that appear in the Bible (Ezekiel 38, *passim*; Revelation 20: 8). The pair are usually combined into one giant named GOGMAGOG, but in this form they were said to have been defeated by BRUTUS and chained to a palace that once stood on the site of the Guildhall in LONDON, the palace possibly being the one established by BRUTUS in his capital of TROIA NOVA.

Legends from the Middle Ages said that Gog and Magog led similarly named nations that had been confined behind an immense range of mountains by Alexander the Great after he had conquered BRITAIN[1]. This is, of course, a complete fabrication, for Alexander the Great never landed anywhere on the British Isles.

## Gogmagog
*British*

A legendary giant, one of the original inhabitants of BRITAIN[1], he led twenty others against BRUTUS when he landed at TOTNES, Devon. Gogmagog, who also appears as the two giants GOG and MAGOG, was engaged in single combat by CORINEUS who overcame him and hurled him from Plymouth Hoe to his death. His name possibly derives from the Bible (Ezekiel 38, *passim*; Revelation 20: 8).

## Gogvran
*Welsh*

One of the names, along with OCVRAN, given to the father of GUINEVERE in Welsh tradition.

## Go(i)b(h)niu
*Irish*
Also GOBAN

The divine smith and leader of the triad TRÍ DÉ DÁNA. He was accompanied by two other deities, or aspects, sometimes referred to as his brothers, these aspects being CREIDHNE, the god of metalworking, and LUCHTAINE, the divine wheelwright. His name is thought to come from the Old Irish *goba*, 'smith'. All three were particularly active during the Second Battle of MAGH TUIREDH when they worked at lightning speed to make and repair the weapons of the TUATHA DÉ DANANN, these weapons being magically empowered and thus causing wounds from which none could recover.

In the OTHERWORLD Goibhniu once hosted a feast at which his guests, through a magical, highly intoxicating drink, were rendered immortal. See also AN GHLAS GHAIBHLEANN, COLUM CUALLEINECH.

## Goleuddydd
*Welsh*

The wife of KILYDD. During her pregnancy, she lost all reason and aimlessly wandered the countryside. As the first labour pains started, her sanity returned, although this happened while she was standing in the middle of a herd of swine. So frightened was Goleuddydd that she immediately delivered the child, a boy, who was named CULHWCH to commemorate the place of his birth, for in Welsh *hwch* means 'pigs'. Later Arthurian legend additionally made Goleuddydd the sister of IGRAINE and the aunt of King ARTHUR.

## Goll
*Irish*

The son of the King of MAGH MELL, and the nephew of FIACHNA[2]. Goll abducted the wife of Fiachna and staved off all attempts made to release his captive. Fiachna travelled from the OTHERWORLD and secured the help of LOEGHAIRE[2], who accompanied him back to Magh Mell and released Fiachna's wife.

## Goll mac Morna
*Irish*
Also AODH[2]

The son of MORNA, leader of the FIAN before the arrival of FIONN MAC CUMHAILL, and a friend of DIARMAID UA

DUIBHNE. He was out hunting with Darmaid ua Duibhne and two other members of the fian when, as night fell, they came to a small hut where they were welcomed and entertained by an old man and his beautiful young daughter. That night each of the four men propositioned the girl, but she turned each of them down, saying that she was the personification of Youth, and that, though once she had belonged to them, they might never have her again.

Goll mac Morna was also present at the wedding feast of Fionn mac Cumhaill and GRÁINNE and was one of those not drugged by Gráinne when she sought to make off with Diarmaid ua Duibhne, for she needed witnesses to the bond under which she placed Diarmaid ua Duibhne. The other witnesses were OISÍN, OSCAR and CAOILTE MAC RONAN.

## Goneril(la)
*British*

One of the two older daughters of the mythical King LEIR, her sister of comparable age, some say her twin, being REGAN. The two played upon the vanity of their father to give them a quarter of his kingdom each as their dowries. Their younger sister CORDELIA refused to be a part of this deceit, and so received nothing. Subsequently Goneril and Regan, along with their respective husbands, MAGLAURUS, Duke of ALBANY, and HENWINUS, Duke of CORNWALL, seized the rest of Leir's kingdom. Maglaurus intially allowed Leir to keep a retinue of 140 men, but Goneril reduced that to eighty, then Regan reduced it to five, before Goneril once more reduced it to a single man.

## Gorboduc
*British*

A King of BRITAIN[1], the husband of JUDON and the father of FERREX and PORREX. Because neither of his sons left an heir, Porrex killing Ferrex, and Porrex being killed by Judon, the line of descent from BRUTUS died out when Gorboduc himself died.

## Gorddu
*Welsh*

The 'Hag of Hell', the collection of whose blood was one of the tasks set CULHWCH by YSPADDADEN.

## Gorias
*Irish*

A mythical city, the home of ESIAS, one of the four wizards who taught the TUATHA DÉ DANANN their magical arts. The city was the origin of the invincible sword of LUGH.

## Gorlois
*British*

The husband of EIGYR, the beautiful woman who became the subject of the infatuation of UTHER. Helped by MYRDDIN, who magically altered Uther's appearance so that he resembled Gorlois, Uther was able to enter Gorlois' castle at Tintagel, CORNWALL, and lie with Eigyr. That very same night the real Gorlois was killed in battle with Uther's troops, so Eigyr later married Uther. Later legend has extended what was obviously a local legend to the point where this story relates the magical conception of King ARTHUR. See also IGRAINE.

## Gormac
*Irish*

'Dutiful son', one of the names of BRES[1] and one to which he certainly did not live up.

## Gorsedd
*General*

The name given to a meeting place of bards, augurs and DRUIDS.

## Gourmaillon
*British*

An alternative name that has been applied to both CORMORAN and GOGMA-GOG. This has led to a possible identification between these gigantic figures, making the giant disposed of by CORINEUS, Gogmagog, the same as the one disposed of by JACK THE GIANT-KILLER and commonly known through nursery rhyme, Cormoran. Further, the application of this variant to both giants leads to the supposition that Jack the Giant-killer is a memory of the gigantic Corineus.

## Govannon
*Welsh*

See GOFANNON.

## Gowra
*Irish*

The popular name for GABHRA, the site of the mythical battle between opposing factions within the FIAN.

## Gradlon
*Gaulish*

An historical sixth-century king of BRITTANY, whose statue today stands between the towers of the medieval cathedral at Quimper. His daughter was DAHUT, also called AHES, who was said to have been responsible for the inundation of the legendary city of YS.

## Grail
*British*

Possibly the most widely known of all the Arthurian legends is the Quest for the Holy Grail. The Grail itself was thought to be the Chalice used by Christ at the Last Supper or, according to some sources, the cup used to catch the blood of Christ from the wound inflicted upon him by the centurion Longinus while Christ hung upon the cross.

When JOSEPH OF ARIMATHEA came to GLASTONBURY in either AD 37 or 63, he was said to have brought with him two cruets containing the blood and sweat of Christ as well as the Chalice. It is this Chalice that has become embroiled in the legends concerning the Holy Grail. However, the Grail may have had other, older origins. The basis of the quest appears to come from Celtic traditions. The word Grail is derived from the Old French *graal*, meaning a type of dish, but the magical qualities of the Grail stories suggest a much older, OTHERWORLDLY connection.

The expedition to the Otherworld to obtain a magical cauldron, as recorded in the *Preiddeu Annwfn*, seems to reflect the ability of the Grail to provide unending sustenance. This story has a direct parallel in the story of *Culhwch and Olwen*. Both have aspects that relate directly to the Grail quest as we know it today, so either or both may have been used as the originals, thus the magical cauldron of Celtic tradition becomes transformed into the symbolic cup of the eucharist. The romanticized events surrounding the quest itself are, however, without doubt, purely the inventions of the various authors who have related the tale.

## Gráinne
*Irish*

The beautiful daughter of CORMAC MAC AIRT. The ageing FIONN MAC CUHMAILL became betrothed to her, some accounts saying that he first saw Gráinne in the form of a deer into which she had been transformed, although this deer is usually called SAAR. Gráinne, however, loved DIARMAID UA DUIBHNE. During the wedding feast Gráinne drugged the entire company and then cast a GESSA spell on Diarmaid ua Duibhne and induced him to elope with her to a wood in CONNACHT, where they were beseiged by Fionn mac Cumhaill.

Gráinne was rescued by OENGHUS MAC IN OG, the foster father of Diarmaid ua Duibhne, who escaped himself by leaping over the heads of Fionn mac Cumhaill and the FIAN in a single, tremendous bound. Even at this stage Diarmaid ua Duibhne did not break his oath to Fionn mac Cumhaill and take Gráinne as his mistress. It was only after suffering the considerable derision of Gráinne that he finally committed this disloyal act.

Gráinne bore Diarmaid ua Duibhne four sons, and, at length, having been forced to live the life of fugitives, they were reconciled with Fionn mac Cumhaill through the good offices of Oenghus Mac in Og. However, the reconciliation was not perfect, for after Diarmaid ua Duibhne had been mortally gored by his foster brother, the boar BEANN GHULBAN, his only hope was to be given water out of the hand of Fionn mac Cumhaill. Three times Fionn mac Cumhaill let the life-giving water spill from his hands as he remembered the treachery of Diarmaid ua Duibhne and Gráinne. By the time the third lot of water had spilled away Diarmaid ua Duibhne was dead.

## Grallo
*Irish*

The husband of Tigridia.

## Grannus
*Gaulish*

A healing deity who was possibly assimilated with the Graeco-Roman Apollo and who appears to have associations with the Irish GRIANAINECH, a title applied to the god OGHMA which means 'Sun-face'. His consort appears to have been the goddess SIRONA, whose name means 'star', a connection that is reminiscent of the major concept that underpins Celtic mythology, the Three Worlds of star, sun and moon. Historical records show that Grannus was invoked by the Emperor Caracalla in AD 215 in association with the Roman deities Aesculapius and Serapis, both healing deities, a record that confirms the medical attributes of Grannus.

## Greidawl
*Welsh*

The father of GWYTHR.

## Grian(ainech)
*Irish*

A title, applied to the god OGHMA, that means 'sun-face'. It is this title that has led to the association between Oghma and the Gaulish GRANNUS.

## Gronw -Bebyr, -Pebyr
*Welsh*

The hunter whom BLODEUWEDD took as her lover. Together the lovers plotted the death of Blodeuwedd's husband LLEU LLAW GYFFES. At Gronw Bebyr's suggestion, Blodeuwedd set about discovering how

Lleu Llaw Gyffes might be killed, and at length managed to persuade him to reveal that he could be killed only by a spear that had been worked for a year and a day at Mass time on Sundays, and then only if he were standing with one foot in a bathtub and the other on the back of a billy goat.

At length Blodeuwedd persuaded Lleu Llaw Gyffes to demonstrate the position to her. Gronw Bebyr, furnished with the necessary spear, hid in some nearby bushes and, when Lleu Llaw Gyffes adopted the ridiculous position, stood and hurled the spear at him but managed only to inflict a wound. Lleu Llaw Gyffes changed into an eagle and flew away to die from his wound, but was sought out and healed by GWYDION FAB DÔN. Lleu Llaw Gyffes returned to kill Gronw Bebyr, while Gwydion fab Dôn dealt with the infidelity of Blodeuwedd by changing her into an owl.

## Grud-dieu, -yen
*Welsh*

One of the seven survivors of the expedition to IRELAND mounted by BENDIGEID VRAN to avenge the treatment of his sister BRANWEN by MATHOLWCH. He and his six compatriots carried the severed head of Bendigeid Vran back from Ireland and buried it, after a lengthy journey, under the WHITE MOUNT in LONDON. Gruddieu's companions are named as PRYDERI, MANAWYDAN, TALIIE-SIN, YNAWAG, GLIFIEU and HEILYN. They brought the unfortunate Branwen home with them, but she died of a broken heart when she sat down and thought of the destruction wreaked on her behalf.

## Guaillauc
*Welsh*

According to an inscription found on the Pillar of ELISEG, Guaillauc was the father

of Eliseg, and the founder of the line of descent of the kings of POWYS.

## Guaire
*Irish*

A king of CONNACHT and the father of the beautiful CRÉD, who became the wife of the elderly MARCÁN, and the ill-fated lover of CANO.

## Guendoloena
*Welsh*

A flower-maiden who, in the medieval *Vita Merlini*, is married to MYRDDIN. It is possible that she is to be identified with CHWIMLEIAN who is mentioned in *Afollonau*, although she may also be identified with that other famous Welsh flower-maiden, BLODEUWEDD. She is said to have been divorced by Myrddin. It seems quite likely that this Guendoloena is an immediate forerunner of GUINEVERE of the later Arthurian cycle.

## Guiderius
*British*

According to GEOFFREY OF MONMOUTH, this King of BRITAIN[1] was killed during the Roman invasion that was led by CLAUDIUS. He was succeeded by his brother ARVIRAGUS.

## Guinevere
*Arthurian*

The wife of King ARTHUR, whose roots appear to lie with the Welsh flower-maidens BLODEUWEDD and GUENDOLOENA, the latter seeming the more likely as in the medieval *Vita Merlini* she is said to have been married to, and subsequently divorced by, MYRDDIN who was, himself, later to resurface as the magician MERLIN at King Arthur's court.

## Gündestrup Cauldron
*General*

One of the most beautiful of all extant Celtic relics. The Gündestrup Cauldron, a ceremonial vessel, dates from the first or second century BC. It was found in 1891 by a man cutting peat in Vesthimmerland in North Jutland, Denmark. The cauldron had been beaten out of a single sheet of silver and decorated, both inside and out, with a series of panels. A round medallion fitted the centre, and there were seven outer and five inner panels on which traces of gilding were found. Before the cauldron was buried, however, these panels had been torn off with some considerable force and placed inside. Sadly, even though a careful search of the area was made, several portions of the rim, perhaps originally made of gold, were never found.

The decoration of the cauldron is remarkable. The outside plates show the busts of four male and three female figures. It is thought that one plate is missing because the seven found within the cauldron do not extend the full way around it, although the gaps may have been filled with gold sections that were thought, even in those days, too valuable to leave, even as a votive offering. The inner plates of the cauldron are far more varied in content, and it is these that have led to the most conjecture.

One of these plates contains what is the most widely published Celtic scene ever – being that of an antlered figure sitting cross-legged in the company of a stag and a boar. This is thought to be a representation of CERNUNNOS. Another shows the bust of a goddess, who closely resembles one of the three goddesses depicted on the outside plates. Below her are two small wheels, and she is accompanied by two elephants, two griffins and what appears to be a lion. A third plate shows a bearded deity in the company of a figure in a horned helmet holding part of a wheel, several griffins and lions, as well as a serpent.

The fourth plate shows three animals, thought to be bulls, which are about to be killed by the three men carrying swords shown with them. The final plate also shows another famous Celtic scene in which one large, upright figure is accompanied by two rows of smaller warriors, those at the top on horseback and those below on foot. They are accompanied by three small figures playing the *carnyx*, a Celtic war trumpet, which ends in a boar's head. The dominant figure in the scene is holding a smaller man, whom he is either plunging into a barrel or lifting out of it, and beside him is a leaping dog. The central medallion has an altogether different scene and depicts a majestic bull that is apparently being attacked by the man and his dogs who surround it.

The Gündestrup Cauldron measures 27 inches in diameter and is 16½ inches high. It is one of the most important of all Celtic relics, providing an invaluable insight into Celtic art and culture. Its artistic representations have caused endless discussion and argument, for there is no true indication as to which deities are represented within its complex artistry, if indeed any of the figures are of a godly status.

## Gurguntius
*British*

The son of BELINUS according to GIRALDUS CAMBRENSIS.

## Gurgustius
*British*

The son of RIVALLO, whom he succeeded. He was himself succeeded by a relative named SISILLIUS. It is likely that Gurgustius is the GURGUNTIUS named in the works of GIRALDUS CAMBRENSIS.

## Gwadyn Odyeith
*Welsh*

A seldom mentioned companion of CULHWCH in his quest to locate OLWEN. Gwadyn Odyeith's particular skill was to be able to strike as many sparks from the soles of his feet as would fly from a hammer striking white hot metal. He, like GWADYN OSSOL and several others, appears to have been dropped from later traditions, which altered the story to give it an Arthurian content.

## Gwadyn Ossol
*Welsh*

A seldom mentioned member of the party formed to help CULHWCH in his quest to locate OLWEN. Each member was chosen for a particular skill, that of Gwadyn Ossol being that under his feet even the highest mountain would become a plain.

## Gwaelod
*Welsh*

A legendary drowned kingdom, better known as CANTRE'R GWAELOD, said to lie beneath the waters of Cardigan Bay.

## Gwal-chafed, -chaved
*Welsh*

'Falcon of Summer'. Suggested by some sources as originally being identifiable with GWALCHMAI, this character is thought, by a few, to have been the original of the Arthurian Sir Galahad.

## Gwalchmai (fab Gwyar)
*Welsh*

Son of GWYAR and one of the party formed to help CULHWCH locate the maiden OLWEN. His companions were CEI, BEDWYR[2], CYNDDYLIG the Guide, GWRHYR the Interpreter and MENW FAB TEIRGWAEDD. Gwalchmai fab Gwyar later resurfaced in the Arthurian cycle as the knight Gawain.

## Gwales
*Welsh*

A stopping place in Pembroke of the seven survivors of the expedition to IRELAND mounted by BENDIGEID VRAN to avenge the ill-treatment of BRANWEN at the hand of the Irish King MATHOLWCH. They remained in a great hall at Gwales for a total of eighty years, the severed and uncorrupted head of Bendigeid Vran keeping them company, until one member of the seven opened a door facing towards CORNWALL. At once, all seven were filled with memories of what had passed and left to continue their journey to LONDON where they fulfilled the last orders of Bendigeid Vran and buried his head, face towards FRANCE, under the WHITE MOUNT. The seven survivors are named as PRYDERI, MANAWYDAN FAB LLYR, GLIFIEU, TALIESIN, YNAWAG, GRUDDIEU and HEILYN.

## Gwalhafed
*Welsh*

Mentioned in the *Mabinogion* story of *Culhwch and Olwen*, Gwalhafed was the brother of GWALCHMAI FAB GWYAR and thus one of the sons of GWYAR. His name should, perhaps, more correctly be Gwalhafed fab Gwyar. Later tradition seems to suggest that he is the original of the Arthurian knight Sir Galahad.

## Gwawl fab Clud
*Welsh*

The rejected suitor of RHIANNON who, disguised as a handsome, richly dressed youth, came to HEFEYDD's house and asked a boon of PWYLL, a boon that was unthinkingly granted. Gwawl fab Clud asked for Rhiannon. Although horrified by the boon, both Pwyll and Rhiannon were honour-bound to comply, Rhiannon suggesting that they should postpone her meeting with Gwawl fab Clud for a year, a suggestion that was accepted by both parties.

Rhiannon advised Pwyll that he should, on the night in question, have ready one hundred of his men hiding in the orchard. He himself was to enter her wedding feast in the guise of a shabbily dressed beggar carrying a sack. He should then ask for enough food to fill the sack, a request to which she would accede. They would trick Gwawl fab Clud into treading the food down into the sack, and thus capture him. Everything went as planned, and, as the sack was tied around Gwawl fab Clud, Pwyll blew his horn and summoned his men, who began to kick the sack around the hall until Gwawl fab Clud was forced to beg for mercy and to withdraw his claim to Rhiannon. Only when he had also promised never to seek vengeance was Gwawl fab Clud released and sent on his way.

## Gwenddol-au, -eu
*Welsh*

A British prince who fought the Battle of ARFDERYDD against his cousins GWRGI and PEREDUR. He was killed during the battle. The Welsh MYRDDIN poems say that he was Myrddin's lord at the battle, his retinue being described as one of the six faithful companies of BRITAIN[1], for it continued to fight on for six weeks after the death of Gwenddolau. One of the *Trioedd Ynys Prydein* elaborates the story, saying that he had birds which were tethered by a yoke of gold and which ate two corpses for dinner and supper. The *Vita Merlini* contradicts all the earlier sources by saying that Gwenddolau was on the side opposing Myrddin at the battle.

## Gwendolen
*British*

The daughter of CORINEUS whom LOCRINUS married, although he had to be forced to do this by her father after Locrinus had captured the beautiful German maiden ESTRILDIS, whom he would rather have married. For seven years Locrinus kept Estrildis as his mistress, and during that time she bore him a daughter, HABREN, while Gwendolen gave him a son and heir, MADDAN.

After the death of Corineus, Locrinus deserted Gwendolen and installed Estrildis as his new queen. Gwendolen went to CORNWALL and raised an army. During a battle near the River Stour, Locrinus was killed by an archer. Gwendolen then commanded that Estrildis and Habren be drowned in a river, but in honour of the fact that Habren was Locrinus' daughter she ordered that the river should thenceforth carry her name. That river became known as the SABRINA to the Romans, and is today known as the River SEVERN.

Gwendolen reigned as queen for fifteen years before she abdicated in favour of her son Maddan and retired to Cornwall.

## Gwendydd
*Welsh*

The name under which GANIEDA appears in Welsh poetry as well as in the *Vita Merlini* by GEOFFREY OF MONMOUTH, in which she appears as the philandering wife of RHYDDERCH, whose infidelities were spotted and reported to her husband by her twin brother, MYRDDIN.

## Gwenhwy-far, -var
*Welsh*

The Welsh name for GUINEVERE. It is a late name that does not appear to have been in use prior to the establishment of the Arthurian cycle. In one version of the story of *Culhwch and Olwen*, however, a character named as Gwenhwyfar, who may be the same, is said to have had two servants named YSKYRDAW and YSEUDYDD, who could run as rapidly as their thoughts, both of whom joined the expedition mounted by CULHWCH to locate OLWEN.

## Gwen(n)
*Welsh*

1 The name given to a mantle that made its wearer invisible. In other sources it is simply referred to as MANTELL, or as the Mantle of Invisibility, and was said to number among the THIRTEEN TREASURES of BRITAIN[1]. Later tradition made King ARTHUR the owner of this treasure.
2 In Welsh tradition, the daughter of CUNEDDA and maternal grandmother of ARTHUR. See also EIGYR.

## Gwent
*Welsh*

The kingdom of southern WALES that is thought to be identifiable with GLENVISSIG, the realm of MEURIG, father of ATHRWYS.

## Gwern
*Welsh*

The son of BRANWEN and MATHOLWCH.

After BENDIGEID VRAN had mounted his expedition to IRELAND to avenge the cruelty being shown to Branwen, his sister, by Matholwch, the two sides entered into discussions, and they decided that the best way to solve the dispute was to make the infant Gwern king of Ireland. All seemed to be agreed until EFNISIEN picked up the infant and threw him onto the fire. Fighting broke out, which eventually left only five pregnant women alive in Ireland and all but seven of Bendigeid Vran's forces dead.

## Gwevyl
*Welsh*

A seldom listed member of the expeditionary force led by CULHWCH on his quest to locate the maiden OLWEN. Gwevyl was chosen as he was able, when sad, to let one of his lips fall to his stomach, and raise the other as a hood over his head.

## Gwiawn
*Welsh*

One of the many seldom mentioned members of the party formed to help CULHWCH find OLWEN. Gwiawn became a member as he was skilled enough to remove a speck of dirt from the eye of a gnat without injuring it.

## Gwion (Bach)
*Welsh*

The tiny son of GWREANG. He was given the job of tending the cauldron in which CERRIDWEN was brewing a divine potion of inspiration and knowledge for her son AFAGDDU. At the end of the allotted time, a year and a day, three drops of the magical brew splashed out of the cauldron onto Gwion's thumb. He sucked the thumb to cool it and immediately knew all that had passed and all that was to happen in the future. This knowledge filled him with dread, for it told him that, having ingested the potency of the brew, Cerridwen would kill him. Gwion Bach thus took to his heels.

When Cerridwen found the potency of her potion had been stolen, she set off in hot pursuit of the fleeing Gwion Bach. He first changed into a hare in order to be able to run faster, but Cerridwen countered by becoming a greyhound. Gwion Bach leapt into a river and became a salmon, but the hag followed assuming the form of an otter. Gwion Bach rose out of the river as a bird, but Cerridwen followed as a hawk. Finally, Gwion Bach settled on a threshing floor and became one of the thousands of grains lying there, but even there he was not safe, for Cerridwen became a hen and swallowed him. Nine months later he was reborn as a beautiful boy, whom Cerridwen set adrift in a leather bag. This boy was rescued by ELPHIN and named TALIESIN.

Certain similarities may been seen between this story and that of FIONN MAC CUMHAILL who, in Irish legend, accidentally touched the SALMON OF WISDOM, and gained knowledge and inspiration by simply biting the thumb that had touched that wonderful fish. It has even been suggested that Gwion Bach was an historical character who studied the Druidic arts and, filled with inspiration by what he had learned, began to compose poetry under the name of Taliesin.

## Gwragedd Annw(f)n
*Welsh*

The name sometimes used to refer to supernatural women who lived in lakes. It means 'Dames of the Lower Regions' or 'Dames of Annwfn'.

## Gwreang
*Welsh*

The father of GWION BACH.

## Gwrgi
*Welsh*

One of the two cousins of GWENDDOLAU, whom they fought at the Battle of ARFDERYDD; the other was PEREDUR.

## Gwrgi Gwastra
*Welsh*

A vassal of PRYDERI who was, along with twenty-three others, at one stage offered as a hostage to MATH FAB MATHONWY if he would put an end to the war between them that had been caused when GWYDION FAB DÔN tricked Pryderi out of the swine his father had been given by ARAWN.

## Gwrhyr (Gwalstawd Ieitheodd)
*Welsh*

Usually known with the epithet 'the Interpreter', Gwrhyr was one of the party formed to help CULHWCH in his quest to locate OLWEN. Each of the party, which consisted of CEI, BEDWYR[2], CYNDDYLIG the Guide, GWALCHMAI FAB GWYAR and MENW FAB TEIRGWAEDD, was chosen for their particular skills. Gwrhyr was chosen because he could interpret the language of animals. During the quest to locate Olwen, Gwrhyr first asked for directions from the BLACKBIRD OF CILGWRI. That bird sent them to the STAG OF RHEDYNFRC who in turn passed them on to the OWL OF CWN CAWLWYD, who passed them on to the EAGLE OF GWERNABWY who finally sent them to the SALMON OF LLYN LLW.

## Gwri
*Welsh*

The name given to the child born to PWYLL and RHIANNON after it had mysteriously disappeared one night from its crib. TEYRNON TWRYF LIANT took the child in and treated him as his own. A year later, learning of the loss of the child and because of the child's uncanny likeness to Pwyll, Teyrnon Twryf Liant concluded that the boy must be none other than the lost child of Pwyll and Rhiannon. He took the child back to his parents who subsequently named him Pryderi.

## Gwrvan Gwallt-avwy
*Welsh*

A character who appears in the *Mabinogion*, and is thought, by some, to be the origin of the Arthurian knight Sir Gawain.

## Gwyar
*Welsh*

The father of GWALCHMAI FAB GWYAR and GWALCHAFED. Later tradition made him the father of Gawain in the Arthurian cycle.

## gwyddbwyll
*Welsh*

An early Celtic board game that is, in essence, the same as the Irish FIDCHELL, meaning 'wood sense'. The board was seen as the world in miniature, and games played, particularly in the legends, may have been a ritualistic combat with the sole purpose of deciding an argument or quarrel without having to resort to bloodshed. The Gwyddbwyll board of GWENDDOLAU numbers among the THIRTEEN TREASURES of BRITAIN[1].

## Gwyddno Garanhir
*Welsh*

The father of ELPHIN who possessed a fish-weir that yielded many salmon. He also owned a *mwys*, or basket, which could feed one hundred people at a time. In origin, Gwyddno Garanhir may have been a god whose purpose appears to be either agricultural, as the *mwys* signifies, or with a more watery association, as reflected in the fish-weir. His basket or hamper was said to have been one of the THIRTEEN TREASURES of BRITAIN[1].

Under the name of DEWRARTH WLEDIG, Gwyddno Garanhir was said to have been, during the fifth century, the king of the lost realm of CANTRE'R GWAELOD or the Lowland Hundred, which is said to lie under the waters of Cardigan Bay. *See also* MAES GWYDDNO.

## Gwydion (fab Dôn)
*Welsh*

An all-powerful British father god, magician and poet, a son of DÔN and brother of GILFAETHWY and ARIANRHOD. While he was in the service of MATH FAB MATHONWY, Lord of GWYNEDD, Gwydion fab Dôn learned of a herd of magic swine in the possession of PRYDERI whose father had received them as a gift from ARAWN. Gwydion fab Dôn told his master of the swine and promised to obtain them for him. He disguised himself as a bard and, in the company of eleven others all similarly disguised, travelled to DYFED, where they were hospitably received by Pryderi.

Gwydion fab Dôn told Pryderi of his errand and promised to show him a fair exchange for the swine the very next morning. That night Gwydion fab Dôn secretly created, by magic, twelve magnificent stallions, twelve greyhounds with golden collars and twelve golden shields. Pryderi was shown the magically created animals and shields and, after consulting his lords, agreed to the exchange. Gwydion fab Dôn made off quickly with the herd of swine, for he knew that after two days his spell would fail. When the enchantment wore off and Pryderi was left with nothing, he set off in hot pursuit of Gwydion fab Dôn. Math fab Mathonwy mustered an army against Pryderi and after two bloody battles agreed that Gwydion fab Dôn should meet Pryderi in single combat to settle the issue. However, the whole issue of the herd of swine was nothing more than a smoke screen, invented by Gwydion fab Dôn to help his brother, GILFAETHWY, who had fallen for Math fab Mathonwy's footholder, the virgin GOEWIN. While Math fab Mathonwy was absent fighting Pryderi, the two brothers abducted Goewin and took turns in ravishing her. Gwydion fab Dôn then met with Pryderi at MAEN TYRIAWG, where he used his magic to overcome and kill Pryderi.

Although the acquisition of the swine should have placed Gwydion fab Dôn in high favour with Math fab Mathonwy, his behaviour towards Goewin led to him and his brother being humiliated by a punishment in which they were, for three years, forced to live in the shape of animals, each carrying out the role of male and female, and each year mating and producing an offspring. At the end of the three year period Math fab Mathonwy considered they had been humiliated enough and restored them to their human form.

The position of footholder, which had to be filled by a virgin, was still vacant, so Gwydion fab Dôn put forward his sister ARIANRHOD. However, during the rite to attest her virginity, two bundles dropped from her, for Arianrhod had been pregnant, and her time came during the test, which is referred to as stepping over the wand. The first was a golden-haired baby, who was named DYLAN. Immediately reaching maturity, Dylan set off for the sea whose attributes and nature he adopted, whereafter he was known as Dylan Eil Ton, or 'Dylan Son of the Wave'. Some have suggested that this story was concocted to cover the drowning of the first baby in the sea.

Gwydion fab Dôn quickly snatched up and concealed the second baby in a chest. He subsequently adopted the boy, but four years later could not resist showing him to his mother. Embarrassed by the reminder of her shame, Arianrhod cursed the boy, saying that he should bear no name until she herself gave him one. Gwydion fab Dôn circumvented this curse by disguising himself and the boy and tricking Arianrhod into calling the boy LLEU LLAW GYFFES. Gwydion fab Dôn could not resist boasting to his sister on how he had tricked her. Furious she cursed the boy for the second time, this time saying that he would not bear arms until she herself armed him. Again Gwydion fab Dôn found a way around the curse. Finally Arianrhod cursed Lleu Llaw Gyffes for a third time, saying that he would never have a mortal wife.

Gwydion fab Dôn and Math fab Mathonwy worked together to evade this third curse by making Lleu Llaw Gyffes a wife from the flowers of oak, broom and meadowsweet, whom they named BLODEUWEDD ('Flower Face'). However, she was unfaithful to Lleu Llaw Gyffes with the hunter GRONW BEBYR, the lovers unsuccessfully trying to kill Lleu Llaw Gyffes. Gwydion fab Dôn found the wounded Lleu Llaw Gyffes and healed him before changing Blodeuwedd into an owl. Lleu Llaw Gyffes himself dealt with Gronw Bebyr.

Later tradition says that Gwydion fab Dôn was responsible for the magical creation of TALIESIN, although in the

*Mabinogion* he simply appears as a shape-shifter, an obvious reference to his magical abilities.

## Gwyn Gloyw
*Welsh*
See GWYN GOHOYW.

## Gwynedd
*Welsh*

A medieval kingdom in North WALES. It was called VENDOTIA in Latin.

## Gwyn(n) (ap Nudd)
*Welsh*

The son of NUDD, Lord of the Dead of the UNDERWORLD (rather than of the OTHERWORLD) and Master of the WILD HUNT. Some sources name his father as LLUDD LLAW EREINT, in which case he is to be considered as the Welsh equivalent of the Irish FIONN MAC CUMHAILL. In later tradition he was said to have resided beneath GLASTONBURY TOR, which acted as a portal to his realm. He was also said to have fought GWYTHR, son of GREIDAWL, for the maiden CREIDDYLED, a contest that was ruled should take place every May Day until Doomsday, when the winner would claim the hand of the maiden. The Arthurian cycle adds to the stories of Gwynn ap Nudd, saying that it was ARTHUR who made the judgement

regarding the contest over Creiddyled and that it was also Arthur who made Gwynn ap Nudd Lord of the Dead, ruler over the demons of ANNWFN, though this combines the Otherworld and the Underworld in an entirely non-Celtic union. Yet another story says that he was deafeated by St TOLLEN on GLASTONBURY TOR, though this fabrication undoubtedly owes its origins to the thought that Glastonbury Tor was a supernatural portal to the Underworld.

## Gwyn(n) Gohoyw
*Welsh*
Also GWYN GLOYW

Euphemistically referred to as the 'Great', the father of CIGFA who became the wife of the heroic PRYDERI.

## Gwynn (Hen)
*Welsh*

The father of HEILYN.

## Gwythr
*Welsh*

The son of GREIDAWL who, with his followers, entered into a battle against GWYNN AP NUDD and the latter's followers over the maiden CREIDDYLED. To end the senseless bloodshed, it was arranged that each leader should fight until Doomsday on each May Day, the eventual winner gaining the hand of Creiddyled.

## Habren
*British*

The daughter of LOCRINUS by his mistress ESTRILDIS. After Locrinus had been killed in a battle against his estranged wife GWENDOLEN, Habren and her mother were drowned by Gwendolen in a river. Gwendolen, however, decreed that the river should, thenceforth, carry Habren's name in honour of the fact that she was Locrinus' daughter. The river Habren became known as the River SABRINA to the Romans, and is today known as the River SEVERN.

## Ha-fgan, -vgan
*Welsh*

The enemy of ARAWN who was disposed of by PWYLL while he spent a year in ANNWFN in the form of Arawn, Arawn having adopted Pwyll's form to rule over DYFED for the year. Pwyll was instructed by Arawn that Hafgan could only be killed by a single blow, for he had the ability to recover instantly upon receiving a second blow. When Pwyll met Hafgan he struck a mortal blow. As Hafgan lay dying he beseeched Pwyll to finish him off, but Pwyll refused and Hafgan died.

## Hag of Hell
*Welsh*

A mysterious, supernatural woman whose blood had to be obtained by CULHWCH as one of the tasks set him by YSPADDADEN if he were to be allowed to marry OLWEN.

## Halstatt
*General*

An Austrian town, near Salzburg, in whose salt-mines the first examples of Celtic art were unearthed in 1846. These, coupled with the discoveries at LA TÈNE, Switzerland, a few years later, were the first indicators of the richness of the Celtic culture. The site at Halstatt revealed a number of rich burials that were subsequently dated at between 700 and 400 BC. The term 'Halstatt' was then employed to refer to any artefacts discovered that fell within this broad date range. The Halstatt findings proved that the early continental Celts had traded with Etruria and Greece and were also capable of producing their own 'works of art' that were impressive in their individuality.

## Ham
*Irish*

The son of NOAH from whom the FOMHOIRÉ were alleged to have been descended.

## Hanlon
*Irish*
See ANLUAN.

## Haydn

*Welsh*

See HYDWN.

## Hefeydd (Hên)

*Welsh*

With his epithet *Hên*, meaning 'the Old', Hefeydd was the ageing father of the beautiful RHIANNON who became the wife of PWYLL.

## Heidyn

*Welsh*

According to some sources, the name of TALIESIN's murderer.

## Heil

*British*

One of the later names applied to the obscure sun-god HELITH, who was apparently only worshipped in a small region of Dorset. See also CERNE ABBAS.

## Heilyn

*Welsh*

The son of GWYNN HÊN and one of the seven survivors of the expedition led to IRELAND by BENDIGEID VRAN to avenge the cruelty of MATHOLWCH against BRANWEN. The other survivors are named as PRYDERI, MANAWYDAN FAB LLYR, GLIFIEU, TALIESIN, YNAWAG and GRUDDIEU. Heilyn is named as the member of the party who opened a door in the hall at GWALES in which they had feasted contently for eighty years, thus causing all their suppressed memories to come back and make them leave for LONDON to bury Bendigeid Vran's head.

## Heithiurun

*Irish*

A curious British idol mentioned in the *Dinnshenchas* that is possibly cognate with the continental TARANIS.

## Helena

*British*

The daughter of COEL. Legend says that she married the Roman emperor Constantius Chlorus after peace had been restored between her father and the emperor who had been besieging his city of Colchester for three years. Their son, born about AD c.265, was Constantine the Great. Helena is better known as St Helena, her dates being given as AD c.225–330. Tradition makes her the daughter of an innkeeper in Dreparnum, Bithynia. She was divorced, for political reasons, in 292, but, when Constantius Chlorus was declared emperor by his army in YORK, he made her the Empress Dowager. In 312, when toleration was extended to Christianity, she was baptized, and in 326, according to tradition, she visited Jerusalem, and founded the basilicas on the Mount of Olives and at Bethlehem. Her feast-day is 18 August.

## Heli

*British*

A little used variant of BELI, the variant occurring in the works of GEOFFREY OF MONMOUTH whose chronology was all wrong, and thus placed Beli well out of the normally accepted line of descent. To counter this he simply appears to have changed the first letter of Beli to make Heli.

## Helig (Vael) ap Glan(n)o(w)g
*Welsh*

A legendary sixth-century ruler of a lost kingdom, which is said to lie approximately 2 miles out to sea in Conwy Bay. Even today it is claimed that the sunken ruins of his palace may be seen at the lowest of tides. The first recorded sighting of the ruins was in 1864, and subsequent sightings estimated that the palace would have occupied no less than 5½ acres. Earlier, however, in 1816, Edward Pugh wrote that he had floated over the ruins of the palace and is said to have also identified a causeway beneath the water. See also TRWYN YR WYLFA.

## Hel-ith, -is
*British*

An ancient sun god who appears only to have been worshipped in Cerne, an ancient name for a district of modern Dorset. His name has been connected with the giant figure that lies on the hills overlooking CERNE ABBAS, although this is purely conjectural, and is not based on any evidence, historical or archaeological. The variant Helis appears to have been a later invention, for it is first reported in 1746 by William Stukeley, who says that the Cerne Abbas giant was known locally as Helis.

## Hên Wen
*Welsh*

A pig whose offspring were, according to tradition, going to cause untold trouble for BRITAIN[1]. Later she entered the Arthurian cycle which said that she was pursued, while heavily pregnant, by ARTHUR, and gave birth to various progeny. She was eventually forced to dive from a cliff into the sea at Penryn Awstin. It has been suggested that Hên Wen was

the mother of the CATH PALUG, but that particular animal is also said to have been a kitten raised by CERRIDWEN, the witch who was also known as Hên Wen.

## Henwinus
*British*

The Duke of CORNWALL and one of the husbands of REGAN, one of the elder daughters of the mythical King LEIR, the other being MAGLAURUS, who, along with another of Leir's daughters, GONERIL, seized the remainder of the ageing king's domain that had not already been seized by their scheming. Leir's youngest daughter CORDELIA, who married AGANIPPUS, had nothing to do with the underhand usurping of her father's kingdom and welcomed her father to FRANCE after he had been deposed.

## Hern(e) the Hunter
*British*

The leader of the WILD HUNT. He was a legendary antlered giant who is still said to live in the forests of Windsor Great Park and who probably owes his existence to the cult of CERNUNNOS, of whom he is undoubtedly a lingering memory. He has even been linked with Robin Hood, some making the link as that hero's father, although this is extremely tenuous, for Herne the Hunter is, without doubt, a far older figure.

## Heveydd (Hên)
*Welsh*
See HEFEYDD.

## Hir Atrym
*Welsh*

The brother of HIR ERWN. Mentioned in the story of *Culhwch and Olwen*, the two brothers were said to have gigantic, insatiable appetites, which meant they would eat all that was provided for them and then leave the land bare as well.

## Hir Erwn
*Welsh*
The brother of HIR ATRYM.

## Historia Britonum
*British*

This clumsily put together Latin work is ascribed to NENNIUS[1], and it dates from, perhaps, the ninth century. The work purports to give an account of British history from the time of JULIUS CAESAR to towards the end of the seventh century. It gives a mythical account of the origins of the British people and recounts the Roman occupation, the settlement of the SAXONS and King ARTHUR's twelve victories. Although it contains fanciful material of doubtful historical significance, its real value lies in its preservation of material needed for the study of early Celtic literature in general and the Arthurian legends in particular.

## Historia Regum Britanniae
*British*

*History of the Kings of Britain*, the eleventh-century Latin work by GEOFFREY OF MONMOUTH, which gives a legendary account of the early kings of BRITAIN[1]. It is notable as it contains the first coherent narrative of the legends of King ARTHUR.

## Hogalen Tudno
*Welsh*

The whetstone of TUDNO. It numbered amongst the THIRTEEN TREASURES of BRITAIN[1], being said to sharpen none but the weapon of a brave man.

## Hok-Braz
*Gaulish*

A Celtic giant who inhabited the coastline of BRITTANY, where he was said to swallow three-masted ships for his breakfast. What he had for his dinner and his supper remains unrecorded.

## Holy Grail
*British*
See GRAIL.

## Holy Thorn
*British*
See GLASTONBURY THORN.

## Horn of Brangaled
*Welsh*

One of the THIRTEEN TREASURES of BRITAIN[1], which MYRDDIN had to acquire before he could be given any of the others. It had originally belonged to a centaur, which was slain by Hercules, its particular property being that it was capable of containing any drink one wished it to.

## Hudibras
*British*

According to GEOFFREY OF MONMOUTH, an early king of BRITAIN[1] (ninth century BC), the ninth ruler after BRUTUS, the legendary founder of WINCHESTER and the father of the magical BLADUD. He sent his son to Athens to study philosophy, but while he was there his father died, and he returned to claim the throne.

## Hugh
*Irish*

A son of LIR and AOBH and one of the four children of Lir who were transformed into swans by AOIFE, a shape in which they were condemned to stay for 900 years. The other three are named as FIONUALA, FIACHTRA and CONN[2]. They regained their human form in the time of St PATRICK and died shortly afterwards.

## Humber
*British*

The leader of a mythical invasion of Huns who killed ALBANACTUS but were routed by KAMBER and LOCRINUS. Humber drowned in the river that still carries his name.

## Hunting Causeway
*British*

The route between Cadbury Castle and GLASTONBURY that, local Somerset legend says, King ARTHUR rides each Christmas Eve in the company of his knights. Usually he remains invisible except for the glint of silver horse shoes, but the sounds made have reputedly been heard by many people. This legend is obviously a variant of the much older legends of the WILD HUNT that occur throughout the ancient Celtic lands.

A local variant of this story says that, rather than Christmas Eve, the spectral ride occurs on 24 June, St John the Baptist's Day, when Arthur and his knights ride to Glastonbury to do homage to the abbot there.

## Hwicce
*British*

An ancient Celtic kingdom that had its capital at DEERHURST, and once covered the modern counties of Gloucestershire and Worcestershire.

## H(w)ychdwn
*Welsh*

The name of the second boy born to GWYDION FAB DÔN and GILFAETHWY during the year they spent as wild pigs, part of their three-year punishment by MATH FAB MATHONWY for the rape of his footholder GOEWIN. His brothers, also conceived as animals but turned into human boys by Math fab Mathonwy, were BLEDDYN and HYDWN.

## Hy-Br(e)asil
*Irish*

An enchanted OTHERWORLDLY island that, according to legend, is visible off the west coast of IRELAND once every seven years and that, if once touched by fire, would remain above the surface of the sea as an accessible paradise. MANANNÁN MAC LIR was thought to have condemned this once earthly realm to its watery grave, although he gave its inhabitants the right to breathe fresh air once every seven years.

## Hydwn
*Welsh*

The name given to the boy who was born to GWYDION FAB DÔN and GILFAETHWY during their year as deer, the first of three years they spent in animal form as punishment for the rape of the maiden GOEWIN. MATH FAB MATHONWY named the boy after he had turned him into a human child from the fawn he had been born as. His brothers, HWYCHDWN and BLEDDYN, were also originally born as young animals, Hwychdwn as a wild pig, and Bleddyn as a wolf-cub.

## Ialonus
*Gaulish*

An agricultural deity with special responsibility for cultivated fields.

## Iath n'Anann
*Irish*

An ancient name for IRELAND. It appears to be derived from ANA, one of the variants of DANU.

## Ibhell
*Irish*

The beautiful wife of AED[1]. The King of LEINSTER fell in love with her, at which point MONGÁN changed himself to take the form of Aed, and a hag into the beautiful IBHELL, a ruse intended to restore Mongán's wife to him after she had been abducted by the King of Leinster. The ploy worked, for Mongán in the form of Aed agreed to exchange the hag in the form of Ibhell for his wife. Mongán and his wife disappeared, and the hag returned to her original hideous form.

## Iceni
*British*

An ancient British tribe that lived in Norfolk. Their most famous rulers were BOUDICCA and her husband PRASUTAGUS. After the death of Prasutagus, the Iceni and the TRI-NOVANTES, allied under the leadership of Boudicca, attacked the Roman invaders but, after three notable successes, were routed, when Boudicca took her own life.

## Idris
*Welsh*

A giant, said to have his home on the appropriately named mountain of CADAIR IDRIS in GWYNEDD. He is said to have been a poet, astronomer and philosopher, which leads to the conjecture that his description as a giant related to his intellect rather than his physical size.

## Igern-a, -e
*British*
See IGRAINE.

## Ignoge
*Graeco-British*

The daughter of the Greek king PANDRASUS. She became the reluctant bride of BRUTUS after he had fought and defeated her father. She travelled to BRITAIN[1] with Brutus and the Trojan slaves whom he compelled Pandrasus to release, in the ships furnished by her father, and subsequently became known as IMOGEN.

## Igraine
*British*
Also IGERNA

Having her roots in the Welsh character

EIGYR, Igraine was the name given in the Arthurian cycle to the daughter of AMLAWDD, wife of GORLOIS and mother of ARTHUR by UTHER. See also GOLEUDDYDD.

## ildánach
*Irish*

A little used variant of SAMILDÁNACH.

## Ildáthach
*Irish*

An inhabitant of the realm of TÍR TAIRNGIRI who was, along with his sons, drowned by the wave sent by MANANNÁN MAC LIR after the sisters CLIODNA, AEIFE and EDAEIN. Ildáthach and his sons were in love with Cliodna.

## Illan
*Irish*
Also ULLAN

A traditional king of LEINSTER, who was thought to have led raids into BRITAIN[1], and who traditionally reigned between 495 and 511 AD. The history of Leinster at this time is obscure, and Illan may have reigned on either side of these dates, or not at all. Legend makes him the husband of TUIREANN, the sister-in-law of FIONN MAC CUMHAILL. Shortly before the birth of his two sons, Illan's supernatural mistress changed Tuireann into a wolf-hound, and it was in that form that she gave birth to BRAN and SGEOLAN, the two famous hounds of Fionn mac Cumhaill. After Illan had promised to desert Tuireann, Illan's mistress restored her human form.

## Imbas forosnai
*Irish*

A pagan rite that implied that chewing the raw flesh of the thumb imparted sagacity. FIONN MAC CUMHAILL was said to have been blessed with this ability after he accidentally touched the SALMON OF WISDOM, which he was cooking for FINNÉCES. The rite appears to have crossed the Irish Sea to reappear in the story of GWION BACH and the witch CERRIDWEN.

## Imbol-c, -g
*General*

The spring festival celebrated on 1 February, it later became the feast-day of St BRIGHID, the Christian feast of Candlemas. Imbolc was one of the four main festivals of the Celtic calendar, the others being SAMHAIN, BELTANE and LUGHNASADH.

## immram
*Irish*

(pl. *immrama*) The name given to a 'voyage tale', one of the two main branches of early Irish literature, the other being the ECHTRAI. The earliest of these was the *Immram Curaig Maíle Dúin*.

## Immram Curaig Maíle Dúin
*Irish*

The earliest of the *immrama*, or 'voyage tales', which was later to inspire the famous story of St Brendan. It concerns the travels of one MAÍL DÚIN, who is bent on revenge after the murder of his father, but discovers that it is better to forgive those who have transgressed. The account of this voyage names numerous island realms, which may be found under the heading ISLANDS OF MAÍL DÚIN.

## Imogen
*British*

The wife of BRUTUS according to some

sources. The name is a simple variant of
IGNOGE, the daughter of PANDRASUS,
whom Brutus brought to BRITAIN[1] with
him from Greece.

## In Daghdha
*Irish*

The full title of the Irish father god, who
is more usually known simply as the
DAGHDHA.

## Indech
*Irish*

The co-ruler of the FOMHOIRÉ, along
with ELATHA and TETHRA, and father
of the Fomhoiré maiden with whom the
DAGHDHA had intercourse before the
Second Battle of MAGH TUIREDH.

## Ingcel
*Irish*

A monstrous being, described as the son
of the King of BRITAIN[1], whose single eye
was said to have three pupils. He appears
in the legend of CONAIRE MÓR and the
hostel of DA DERGA, in which, together
with a band of outlaws, he storms the
hostel and razes it to the ground.

## Inis Manann
*Irish*

A name for the Isle of MAN as the home
of MANANNÁN MAC LIR. It literally means
'Isle of Manann(án)'.

## Innis Ealga
*Irish*

'The Noble Isle', one of the first names given
to IRELAND by the Sons of MÍL ÉSPÁINE.

## Innis Fail
*Irish*

'The Isle of Destiny', the name allegedly
given to IRELAND as the Sons of MIL
ÉSPÁINE first spotted the island, which
they also called INNIS EALGA.

## Iona
*British*

A tiny island, 3½ miles long by 1½ miles
wide, which was a pagan stronghold for
centuries before the Christians arrived
and claimed it as their own. COLUMBA
landed there on 12 May 563 and quickly
set about establishing his famous monastery. The island's Gaelic name is *Innis-
nam Druidbneach*, which translates as
'Island of the Druids', reflecting its long
Celtic history. However, within a century
of the landing of St COLUMBA, Iona was
pre-eminently Christian.

## Ireland
*General*

A large island lying to the west of Great
BRITAIN[1] from which it is separated by
the Irish Sea. It consists of the provinces
of ULSTER, LEINSTER, MUNSTER and
CONNACHT and is, today, divided between
the Republic of Ireland, or EIRE, which
occupies the south, central and northwest of the island, and Northern Ireland
which occupies the northeast corner and
forms a part of the United Kingdom.

## Irnan
*Irish*

One of the three sorceress daughters of
CONARAN. She and her two sisters took a
large number of the fian captive on the
order of their father because the fian had
trespassed onto his land. Her two sister
were slaughtered by GOLL MAC MORNA,

but Irnan was spared on condition that she released the members of the fian who were held by her enchantment. As the last of the men was released she vanished, but later reappeared and demanded single combat to avenge the death of her sisters. FIONN MAC CUMHAILL was about to go into battle when Goll mac Morna stepped forward and took his place. After a long battle Goll mac Morna ran Irnan through, after which the fian sacked the home of Conaran.

## Is Elfydd
*Welsh*

'Beneath the World', a name sometimes used to refer to ANNWFN.

## Island of the Mighty
*Irish and Welsh*

A term commonly used in both Irish and Welsh stories to refer to BRITAIN[1], although the term could quite equally apply to WALES, ENGLAND or SCOTLAND in the Irish tales. The Welsh used the term more correctly to refer to England.

## Islands of Maíl Dúin
*Irish*

The *Immram Curaig Maíle Dúin* tells the story of a voyage undertaken by MAÍL DÚIN and three companions to discover the identity and whereabouts of the murderers of Maíl Dúin's father. During their voyage, they visit a large number of mysterious island realms. These are briefly described below in the order in which they appear in the text.

- **The Island of the Slayer**  A day and a half into the voyage Maíl Dúin and his crew came across two small, bare islands, each having a fort on it. One of these islands was the home of the murderer of Maíl Dúin's father, AILILL, who was boasting of this to his neighbour in a loud voice. Maíl Dúin was about to land when GERMÂN and DIURAN cried out that God had guided them. A high wind then sprang up and blew the small boat out to sea again. Maíl Dúin chided them for speaking of God, but it was of little use, for the islands had disappeared from sight.

- **The Island of the Ants**  Having drifted for three days and three nights Maíl Dúin came to a small island where a swarm of ferocious ants, each the size of a new-born foal, swarmed down to the beach to meet him. Needless to say he hurriedly put back to sea.

- **The Island of the Birds**  This heavily wooded island was the first land on which Maíl Dúin set foot since departing from IRELAND. He and his companions killed and ate a large number of the birds inhabiting the island, and took many more on board to re-provision themselves.

- **Island of the Fierce Beast**  A large, sandy island, inhabited by a ferocious horse-like beast that had clawed feet. They quickly shoved off, but were pelted with pebbles thrown by the beast as they drew away.

- **The Island of the Giant Horse**  A large, flat island that Germân and Diuran set out to explore. They discovered a huge racecourse, which was pock-marked with hoof prints, each hoof being the size of the sail on their boat. They quickly turned tail and set out to sea again. As they sailed away they heard the roar of a crowd at a horserace and turned to see massive horses that ran like the wind competing against each other.

- **The Island of the Stone Door**  A week after leaving the Island of the Giant Horses, they came to a smaller island, where a single house stood on the shore. A stone door with an opening into the sea received hordes of salmon, which the rolling surf hurled into the house. Maíl Dúin and his crew entered the house, which they found unoccupied, although four massive beds stood ready for the giant owners. Maíl Dúin and his companions ate from the feast they found laid out on the vast table, and then sailed away.

- **The Island of the Apples** An island surrounded by unsurmountable cliffs, which the boat reached after all supplies had been exhausted. Over the edge of these cliffs hung the branch of a tree, which Maíl Dúin broke off. For three days and three nights they circled the island unable to find a place to land. However, by that time the branch of Maíl Dúin had grown three apples, each apple being sufficient to maintain the crew for forty days.

- **The Island of the Wondrous Beast** An island with a stone fence around it that retained a huge beast that ran round and round in a frenzy. Shortly it ran to the top of the hill and made its skin revolve around its body while it held that body quite still, and then caused its body to revolve within its stationary skin. Maíl Dúin and his companions hurriedly left that island, but were pelted with stones by the beast, one stone lodging itself in the keel of their boat.

- **The Island of the Biting Horses** An island that housed a herd of monstrous horse-like beasts, which continually gnawed huge chunks of flesh from each other so that the island ran with blood. Needless to say, Maíl Dúin and his crew did not bother to land.

- **The Island of the Fiery Swine** With all their provisions once again exhausted, Maíl Dúin arrived at an island inhabited by huge red beasts which kicked the trees that grew on the island and ate the apples they knocked down.

At night they retired into caverns beneath the island. Maíl Dúin and his crew came ashore at night and felt the ground hot with the heat of the fiery swine sleeping underground. They quickly replenished their stores with the apples that grew on the island and put back out to sea.

- **The Island of the Little Cat** An island that was like a tower of chalk that reached almost to the clouds. Atop were several great white houses. Maíl Dúin and his crew entered the largest of these and found a small cat leaping in play from pillar to pillar. The cat ignored them as they ate from the feast they found laid out. They then took as much food as they could carry and made ready to leave. As they did, one member of Maíl Dúin's crew sighted a wonderful necklace and picked it up. The small cat immediately changed into a ball of fire and reduced that member of the crew to ashes. Maíl Dúin spread those ashes on the water as they left the island.

- **The Island of the Black and White Sheep** An island containing two flocks of sheep, one black and the other white, which were divided by a bronze fence. They were tended by a huge shepherd, who periodically took one of the white sheep and placed it in with the black ones, whereupon it immediately changed colour, and vice versa. Maíl Dúin threw a white stick amongst the black sheep and when it, too, immediately changed colour, they changed course and did not attempt to land.

- **The Island of the Giant Swine** A wide island on which there lived a herd of huge swine. They killed a small one and roasted it on the spot because it was too large for them to carry. Later, Germán and Diuran explored the island and located a herd of cattle being tended by a huge man on the far side of a wide river. To test the depth of the water Germân dipped his spear into it and it was instantly dissolved. After that they set sail again.

- **The Island of the Mill** The location of a grim-looking mill, inside which they found a huge miller grinding, as he said, half the grain of Ireland. He also told them that he was sent to grind all that men begrudge each other. Maíl Dúin and his companions crossed themselves and sailed away.

- **The Island of the Black Mourners** An island full of black people who constantly mourned and wept. As soon as Maíl Dúin's companions set foot on shore they, too, turned black and started to mourn. Maíl Dúin rescued them by shrouding his head so that he could not look on the place, nor breathe its air, and they quickly left the island.

- **The Island of the Four Fences** An island divided into four by fences of gold, silver, brass and crystal, one region being occupied by kings, the second by queens, the third by warriors and the fourth by maidens. Maíl Dúin and his companions were welcomed by the maidens, who gave them cheese which tasted to each man exactly as he wanted it to. They were then given a drink, which made them sleep for three days and nights. When they woke they found themselves back at sea, with no trace of the island to be seen.

- **The Island of the Glass Bridge** An island on which there stood a fort with a brass door and a glass bridge leading to it. When they tried to cross the bridge, it threw them off. For four days they attempted to gain entrance to the fort, each day watching as a maiden came out and filled her pail from the moat that ran below the bridge. On the fourth day she crossed the bridge and bade them follow her into the fort. Inside, she fed

each man with what he most desired, each meal coming from her pail. For three days they were entertained in this manner. However, when they woke on the fourth morning there was no trace of the maiden, the fort or the island, as they found themselves far out at sea again.

- **The Island of the Shouting Birds** An island full of black birds and speckled brown ones that spoke to and shouted at each other. They sailed past without landing.

- **The Island of the Anchorite** An island covered in trees, full of birds and inhabited by a man whose only clothing was his own hair. This man told them that he had sailed from Ireland on a sod of turf that God had turned into the island. Each year God added a foot's breadth and one tree to the island where he and the birds were to remain until Doomsday, being nourished by the angels. The hermit entertained them for three days before they set sail again.

- **The Island of the Miraculous Fountain** An island crowned by a golden castle, within which they found another hermit clothed only in his hair. The castle housed a fountain that gave water on Fridays and Wednesdays, milk on Sundays and the feast-days of martyrs, and ale and wine on the feast-days of the Apostles, Mary, John the Baptist, and the high tides of the year.

- **The Island of the Smithy** An island they did not land on, for they heard a giant smith talking about their approach. As they sailed away he emerged from his forge and cast a huge lump of red-hot metal after them, which made the sea boil.

- **The Sea of Clear Glass** Not an island, but one of the events of the voyage that is best left in its correct order. The sea was so clear that it was said to resemble 'green glass'. For a whole day they sailed across its surface, marvelling at the clarity of the water and the formation of the seabed, which was clearly visible.

- **The Undersea Island** An island viewed through a sea whose waters seemed to be only just capable of supporting their boat. Through the water they saw roofed fortresses and a monstrous beast lodged in a tree, with droves of cattle around it and an armed warrior beneath it. Despite the warrior, the beast continued to stretch down and devour the cattle. Sorely afraid that they might sink in the thin waters, they hurriedly sailed away.

- **The Island of the Prophecy** An island around which the sea built up into a wall so that Maíl Dúin and his crew looked down on the people, who seemed to be expecting them but were afraid of them. One woman pelted them, from below, with large nuts, which they collected to replenish their stores. Then they sailed away, sure that they would not be received warmly if they landed.

- **The Island of the Spouting Water** A stream on this island spouted its water in a great arc from one side to the other. Maíl Dúin had only to thrust his spear through the water to catch great numbers of salmon. Having filled their boat with the fish, they sailed on.

- **The Island of the Silver Column** Not so much an island, but rather a huge, square, silver pillar that rose from the sea. Each side was as wide as two oarstrokes of the boat. It rose straight from the seabed, with its top lost in the clouds. As they looked on, a huge silver net was cast down into the sea, through which Maíl Dúin steered the boat, and from which Diuran cut away a section said to have weighed 2½ ounces. They sailed away, as they were unable to find any way of landing or ascending the pillar.

- **The Island of the Pedestal** This island was suspended above the sea on a huge pedestal in which there was a locked door. Unable to gain entry, Maíl Dúin sailed away.

- **The Island of the Women** On this island was a mansion housing seventeen maidens. They watched those maidens prepare a bath. At length, a rider approached. One of the maidens took the horse and led the rider, a woman, into the mansion where she entered the bath. After a while one of the maidens came out to Maíl Dúin and his comrades and bade them enter. Inside they were bathed and sat down to eat, each man having a maiden in close attendance. After the meal, Maíl Dúin was married to the queen of the island, and each of his comrades to the most comely of the maidens. For three contented months during the winter they lived on the island where no one ever knew old age or sickness.

At the end of the three months Maíl Dúin and his companions sailed away in their boat while the queen was away on business. However, they had not gone far when the queen appeared on the shore and threw Maíl Dúin a ball of thread that stuck to his hand. Thus, the queen pulled Maíl Dúin and the boat back to the shore. For a further three months Maíl Dúin and his crew lived with the maidens.

Twice more they attempted to make their escape, and twice more they were hauled back by the queen and her clew of thread. Diuran suspected that Maíl Dúin loved the queen so much that he caught and held onto the thread on purpose. Therefore, the next time the queen threw the ball of thread at them, Diuran leapt in front of Maíl Dúin and caught it instead. The clew stuck to his hand, so he cut it off with his sword, and it fell into the sea. It was only because Diuran had severed his head that they were finally able to make their escape.

- **The Island of the Red Berries** This island contained trees upon which grew red berries which yielded a highly intoxicating juice. They mixed it with water to moderate its power and sailed on.

- **The Island of the Eagle** An island on which there lived an ageing anchorite, clad only in his hair. While they were there, a monstrous eagle alighted near a lake and started to preen itself. It was joined by two others, and all three bathed in the lake for three days before flying away again, their flight stronger than it had been when they had arrived. Seeing this, Diuran, against the advice of Maíl Dúin, plunged into the lake, and from that day until he died he never had a day's illness.

- **The Island of the Laughing Folk** On this island they discovered a great company of men who laughed and played incessantly. They drew lots as to who should set foot on the island, but as soon as one foot touched the beach, that man also began to laugh and had to be quickly hauled back onto the boat. Some accounts say that the man could not be rescued and was left on the island as Maíl Dúin sailed away.

- **The Island of the Flaming Rampart** A flaming wall of fire circled this island. Through an opening in the fire they could see the wonders of the island, but could not land.

- **The Island of the Monk of Tory** A rock in the sea on which lived a monk who had come from the monastery on TORY Island off the coast of Donegal. Dressed only in white, the monk told Maíl Dúin of his adventures in reaching the island. He had gathered together a vast treasure and set sail, meaning to keep the plunder for himself. However, his boat was becalmed, and an angel told him to throw all his booty over the side and then to dwell wherever his boat took him. This he did, and he came to the rock on which he had been living, nourished by otters who brought him salmon and even flaming firewood, for seven years. Maíl Dúin and his men were fed in the same manner and then prepared to leave. The monk advised Maíl Dúin where he would find the killer of his father, and told him to forgive him his crime.

- **The Island of the Falcon** The last island on the epic voyage of Maíl Dúin. This was inhabited by no humans, only herds of sheep and oxen. They landed and ate their fill when one of the sailors saw a large falcon. Commenting that the falcon was like those seen in Ireland they vowed to follow it.

At the end of the epic voyage, Maíl Dúin ran his boat ashore on a small island off the coast of Ireland where he discovered the man who had killed his father. Remembering the words of the monk he forgave him his crime and then made his way back to his own home.

## Isle of Honey
*Welsh*

An early name for BRITAIN[1], according to the *White Book of Rhydderch*.

## Ith
*Irish*

One of the Sons of MÍL ÉSPÁINE who were to become the first human inhabitants of IRELAND. A descendant of BREGON, Ith is alleged to have spied the far-off land of Ireland from the top of the tower his ancestor had built in Spain. Ith set off with ninety followers and landed in Ireland, where he was warmly welcomed by the TUATHA DÉ DANANN who had just lost their king, NEIT, in a battle with the FOMHOIRÉ. The Tuatha Dé Danann asked Ith to judge the rights of MAC CUILL, MAC CÉCHT and MAC GRÉINE to rule, but, as Ith spoke so favourably about the island, the Tuatha Dé Danann began to suspect that he had designs on their homeland and killed him. His body was recovered and carried back to Spain, from where a second, better prepared expedition set out, this second expedition conquering the Tuatha Dé Danann and thus making Ireland a home of mortal men for the first time.

## Itinerarium Cambriae
*Welsh*

*Itinerary of Wales*, an important source text by GIRALDUS CAMBRENSIS. It was written after he had travelled through WALES in the company of Baldwin, archbishop of CANTERBURY, in 1188 preaching the Third Crusade. He recorded everything he saw or heard and appeared to believe even the most outrageous stories that the people of Wales told him. This text is fascinating because it records details of saints, sunken forests and kingdoms, miracles, strange lakes and mountains, and a host of other mythological and quasi-historical or legendary material.

## Iubdan
*Irish*

The elfin King of the realm of FAYLINN and husband of BEBO. He and his wife were taken captive by FERGHUS MAC LEDA, but released after they had been ransomed by EISIRT.

## Iuchar
*Irish*

A son of TUIRENN and brother of BRIAN and IUCHARBA, some accounts naming BRIGHID as their mother. The three brothers were responsible for the murder of CIAN, the father of LUGH, who made them pay for their crime by obtaining magical implements the TUATHA DÉ DANANN needed for the Second Battle of MAGH TUIREDH against the FOMHOIRÉ. The three brothers succeeded in all the tasks set them, but died from the wounds they received in accomplishing the final one.

## Iucharba
*Irish*

A son of TUIRENN and brother of BRIAN and IUCHAR.

## Iuchna
*Irish*

In some versions of the legend of CLIODNA, Iuchna is named as the mortal who persuades Cliodna to elope with him from TÍR TAIRNGIRI, this time, however, as the emissary for OENGHUS MAC IN OG, who was apparently in love with her.

## Iweriadd
*Welsh*

According to a traditional genealogy of BENDIGEID VRAN, Iweriadd was the mother of both Bendigeid Vran and BRANWEN by LLYR, although her attributes and characteristics remain unknown. It has been suggested that she personifies IRELAND and thus explains the connection between Llyr and LIR, but this theory is somewhat suspect.

## Jack the Giant-killer
*British*

The famous giant-killer from nursery stories, who is perhaps best known for his exploits with a beanstalk and a goose that laid the golden egg. Jack started his career by killing the giant CORMORAN, whom he trapped in a large pit and then hacked to pieces. He was then himself captured by the giant BLUNDERBOAR; however, he managed to escape and kill Blunderboar and his brothers. He was also said to have tricked a Welsh giant into killing himself. There is no evidence that Jack was a hero of early tales, possibly being a composite of several and invented sometime around the end of the eighteenth or beginning of the nineteenth century. Classical influences may have played some part in his creation, for there are marked similarities between his character and that of Perseus who killed the Gorgon Medusa and married Andromeda. Even his attributes are similar.

## Japheth
*British*

According to a few early English chroniclers, the first inhabitants of BRITAIN[1] were descendants of Japheth, one of the sons of NOAH. However, all trace of these people vanished by the time the country came to be inhabited by the giants whose king was ALBION.

## Jonas
*British*

According to the traditional genealogy of CUNOMORUS, Jonas was the husband of TREPHINA and the father by her of Judwal or TREMEUR.

## Joseph of Arimathea
*British*

A biblical character. He may have been the uncle of Jesus and a tin trader who regularly visited the West Country for Mendip lead and Cornish tin, on one occasion allegedly accompanied by Jesus. Alternatively, he was a soldier of Pilate who gave him the Chalice Cup used at the Last Supper. The former version is possibly the better known of the two.

Tradition says that he was the uncle of Jesus and that following the crucifixion Joseph travelled to BRITAIN[1] in either AD 37 or 63, bringing the Christian gospel with him and accompanied by eleven or twelve disciples. Arriving at GLASTONBURY, he pushed his staff into the ground, and it immediately rooted, a divine sign that his journey had come to an end. The local king gave him and his followers twelve hides of land, and on that land they founded the Old Church, later to be incorporated into Glastonbury Abbey. The sprouting staff grew into a thorn tree, the GLASTONBURY THORN, that had the special distinction of flowering twice a year, once in the spring and again at

Christmas. Tradition also says that Joseph brought three holy relics with him, the first two being cruets containing the blood and sweat of Jesus, while the third, and the most famous, was the Chalice Cup used by Christ at the Last Supper, and also, according to some sources, used to catch the blood of Christ while on the cross from the wound in his side made by the Lance of Longinus. This vessel has become known as the Holy GRAIL, the subject of the quest by ARTHUR's knights.

Alternative tradition makes Joseph a soldier of Pontius Pilate. Following the resurrection, and having been thrown into a dungeon, Jesus appeared to him and returned to him the Chalice Cup of the Last Supper, which Pilate had originally given him but which had become lost. He was set free when Jerusalem fell to the armies of Vespasian and he went into exile with a group of companions. When they were suffering from famine, those among their number who had not sinned were sustained by the Chalice Cup, the Grail. Joseph travelled to Britain, and most sources say that he brought the Grail with him. His journey to Britain is variously described, and in one version he crosses the sea on a miraculous shirt (sic).

There are various other legends concerning Joseph of Arimathea, although these are all Arthurian. John of Glastonbury provides us with some information about Joseph's arrival in Britain. He mentions the cruets of blood and sweat, but does not mention the Grail. He also says that Joseph was despatched to Britain by St Philip who was preaching in GAUL. Gallic tradition states that he was placed in an oarless boat in the company of Lazarus, Martha, Mary Magdalene and others, which was then guided by the divine hand to Marseilles. Another tale, Spanish in origin, says that this party went to Aquitaine, while an Aquitanian story says that Joseph and his party landed at Limoges. All these seem to be an attempt to claim Joseph for Gaul, but most are no longer seriously regarded by hagiologists.

Coptic tradition claims that he had a daughter, St Josa. Attempts have even been made to connect Joseph with Joachim, the father of the Virgin Mary, or with Joseph, the father of Jesus. These attempts have found no following, for biblical information alone is sufficient to prove their invalidity.

## Judon
*British*

The wife of GORBODUC who, following the murder of her favourite son FERREX by his brother PORREX, became insane. In her insanity she hacked Porrex to pieces in his sleep. Because neither son had left an heir and because she and Gorboduc were too old to have further children, the line of descent from BRUTUS died along with Gorboduc.

## Judwal
*British*
See TREMEUR.

## Julius Caesar
*General*

A famous Roman statesman, born 100 or 102 BC, made ruler of Rome in 49 BC, and assassinated in the Forum in 44 BC. He led three expeditions to BRITAIN[1], the first two of which were unsuccessful. The third invasion laid the foundations for the later invasion of CLAUDIUS.

**Jupiter Optimus Maximus Tanarus**
*Romano-British*

A celticized form of the Roman sky god Jupiter. The only evidence that remains of this deity is a worn altar dedicated to him, which was found at Chester. The last part of the name comes from the Celtic thunder god known from GAUL and further afield.

**Jutes**
*General*

A germanic people who originated in Jutland but later settled in Frankish territory. They occupied KENT about AD 450 and conquered the Isle of Wight and the opposite coast of Hampshire in the early sixth century.

**K**

**Kaerbadus**
*British*

The original name of BATH.

**Kaerleir**
*British*

'Leir's Fort', the original name of the city of Leicester, which was founded by King LEIR.

**Kai**
*Welsh*

A variant of CEI. Kai was later to resurface in the Arthurian cycle, his name only slightly altered, as the knight Sir Kay.

**Kamber**
*British*

The son of BRUTUS and brother of LOCRINUS and ALBANACTUS. After the death of his father, Kamber became the king of WALES, while Locrinus ruled over ENGLAND and Albanactus over SCOTLAND. Kamber later helped his brother Locrinus to defeat the Huns after the invaders had killed Albanactus. The leader of the Huns, HUMBER, was drowned in a river that has ever since carried his name.

**Keelta (mac Ronan)**
*Irish*

A leading member of the FIAN, one of the house-stewards of FIONN MAC CUMHAILL, a strong warrior and an unrivalled story-teller. He was said to have lived for a long time after the fian had died out and to have been christened by St PATRICK, to whom he told the stories of the fian. In one notable instance, King MONGÁN called upon the spirit of Keelta to prove a wager, and it was during the course of this that it was revealed that Keelta was the killer of FOTHAD, rather than Fionn mac Cumhaill who had, until that time, been held responsible.

**Keevan**
*Irish*

A latinized variant of CIABHAN.

**Keltchar**
*Irish*
See CELTCHAR.

**Keltoi**
*General*

The term used by both the Greeks and the Romans to refer to the northern barbarians who at times posed a considerable threat to the Mediterranean countries from their western and central European heartland. This name is possibly the origin of the word Celt.

18

**Kent**
*British*

The kingdom of Gwyrangon during VORTIGERN's time, which the latter gave to the SAXONS. BEDE[2] says that Kent was originally settled by the JUTES.

**Kesair**
*Irish*
See CESAIR.

**Ket**
*Irish*
See CET.

**Keva**
*Irish*

The daughter of FIONN MAC CUMHAILL. He gave her to GOLL MAC MORNA after Goll mac Morna had taken the place of Fionn mac Cumhaill and killed IRNAN, the third of the sorceress daughters of CONARAN, having earlier killed her two sisters.

**Kian**
*Irish*
See CIAN.

**Kicva**
*Welsh*
See CIGFA.

**Kilhwch**
*Welsh*

A little used variant of CULHWCH.

**Killaraus, Mount**
*Irish*

The mount in IRELAND from where MYRDDIN was said to have transported the GIANTS' RING that was re-erected on Salisbury Plain as STONEHENGE.

**Kil(w)ydd**
*Welsh*

The father of CULHWCH and GOLEUDDYDD.

**Kimbay**
*Irish*

A latinization of CIMBAOTH.

**Klust**
*Welsh*

One of the seldom mentioned members of the party formed to help CULHWCH locate OLWEN. His special skill, for which he was chosen, was the acuteness of his hearing, for, even if he were buried deep underground, he could hear an ant leave its nest 50 miles away.

**Korriganed**
*Gaulish*

The Breton name for a supernatural woman. It is thought that these beings gave rise to the CORANIEID, who were said to have invaded and plagued BRITAIN[1] during the reign of LLUDD, although one of the *Trioedd Ynys Prydein* specifically states that the Coranieid came from Arabia.

**Kulhwch**
*Welsh*

A little used variant of CULHWCH.

**Kymbelin**
*British*

The seventy-first British king after the time of BRUTUS. His reign was said to have lasted just one year, 22 BC. William Shakespeare later calls this character Cymbeline, in his play of the same name.

## Kymideu Kymeinvoll
*Welsh*

The giantess wife of the giant LLASSAR LLAESGYVNEWID, both of whom hailed from IRELAND but were expelled. They crossed the Irish Sea and were received hospitably by BENDIGEID VRAN. In return for his kindness, the two giants gave him an inexhaustible cauldron that had the power to rejuvenate anyone placed into it. This cauldron later found its way back to Ireland when Bendigeid Vran gave it to MATHOLWCH as part of the peace offering to appease the insult of EFNISIEN.

## Kyn-farch, -varch
*Welsh*

According to Welsh tradition, the father of URIEN of RHEGED by NEFYN, the daughter of BRYCHAN.

## La Tène
*General*

A settlement at the northeastern end of Lake Neuchâtel, Switzerland, that revealed a large number of metal Celtic relics when the site was excavated in 1858. These are thought to have been votive offerings that date from 400 BC. They represent the next stage of the development of the Celtic art form after the artefacts found at HALSTATT, and as a result the name La Tène has come to be used as a term to describe the post-400 BC Celtic period.

## Labhraidh
*Irish*

The brother of LI BAN and FAND.

## Labhraidh Lamfhada
*Irish*

A Druidic sorcerer who appears in the *Cath Finntrága*, delivering the magical weapons forged by Tadg to FIONN MAC CUMHAILL and the FIAN.

## Labhraidh Loingsech
*Irish*

A King of LEINSTER, the son of AILILL AINE. He was originally named MAON, and is traditionally said to have reigned c.268 BC. Driven into exile by COBTHACH COEL, who made him eat a portion of his father's and his grandfather's hearts, along with a mouse and all her young, he lost his voice and travelled to GAUL where he mustered his forces and returned. With the additional help of the men of MUNSTER, he later reclaimed his kingdom and made a false peace with Cobthach Coel. Unsuspecting, Cobthach Coel accepted the invitation proferred and visited Labhraidh Loingsech at his court with his thirty vassal kings. There Labhraidh Loingsech had an iron chamber readied for his visitors and, after they had retired for the night, had the door closed and a huge fire lit underneath it, thus roasting Cobthach Coel and his supporters to death. He then sought out and married MORIATH, the daughter of SCORIATH, whom he had loved before his enforced exile.

Labhraidh Loingsech had a secret that none but his barber knew, and that was that he had horse's ears. Each year he would have his hair cropped, and each year he made his barber swear to keep the secret. Eventually the strain of keeping the secret made the barber unwell, and he sought the advice of a DRUID who told him to tell the secret to a tree. This he did and soon became well again. However, CRAFTINY cut down that very tree to make a new harp and, to his amazement, the first time he played it at the royal court it sang out about Labraidh Loingsech's ears. Labhraidh Loingsech stood up and revealed his ears, and never tried to conceal them again. This story has a parallel in the story of the classical Greek king Midas.

## Ladra
*Irish*

The pilot who led CESAIR and her party to the shores of IRELAND. Ladra was one of just three men among the expedition, the other men being BITH and FINTAN[1]. They were accompanied by fifty women whom they shared among themselves, but Ladra died from excessive sexual activity, leaving Bith and Fintan with twenty-five women each.

## Laeg(h)
*Irish*
See LOEG.

## Laery
*Irish*

A latinized form of LOEGHAIRE.

## Laighin
*Irish*

The name that the GAILIÓIN adopted after they settled in LEINSTER, although some say that this name was used only by their descendants. The Gailióin were one of the three companies that invaded IRELAND from Greece, the other two being the FIR DHOMHNANN and the FIR BHOLG.

## Lailoken
*Welsh*

A wild man in Welsh tradition whose career resembles to some degree that of MYRDDIN. He spent some time at the court of RHYDDERCH HAEL, revealed that the wife of King MELDRED was adulterous, and made several prophecies regarding his own death. It is possible that Lailoken was simply a nickname applied to Myrddin, for the word is similar to that for 'twin', and Myrddin was believed to have had a twin sister, GANIEDA.

## Lairgnen
*Irish*

The chief of CONNACHT who became betrothed to DEOCA. She begged him to obtain four marvellous singing and talking swans whose fame had spread far and wide. This he did, but as he brought them before her they began a hideous transformation, for these swans were the four children of LIR whom AOIFE had condemned to remain as swans for 900 years. That time was now up and they changed from beautiful swans into decrepit old people on the verge of death. Lairgnen fled, and nothing more was heard of him.

## Land of Promise
*Irish*

The literal translation of TÍR TAIRNGIRI.

## Land of the Living
*Irish*

The literal translation of TÍR INNA MBEO.

## Land of -the Young, -Youth
*Irish*

The literal translation of TÍR NA NOC.

## Land of Women
*Irish*
See WOMEN, LAND OF.

## Languoreth
*Welsh*

In Jocelyn's *Life of Saint Kentigern*, the wife of RHYDDERCH who became enamoured with a soldier. It seems that she may be identifiable with GANIEDA, MYRDDIN's twin sister.

## Laoghaire
*Irish*

An historical King of IRELAND, who was reigning at the time of the arrival of St PATRICK. It was not long before St Patrick thought it necessary to attack the pagan religion practised by Laoghaire and his subjects. On the eve of May Day the DRUIDS were assembled at TARA, awaiting the lighting of the royal fire, when they were amazed to see smoke rising from the nearby hill of Slane, the smoke coming from a fire lit by St Patrick. The DRUIDS brought him before King Loeghaire whom he challenged to a magic contest to see whose God was the more powerful.

The official Christian account of this event says that two huts were set alight. Inside one was a Christian youth, wearing the robe of a royal magician, while in the other was a DRUID wearing St Patrick's own cloak. From the ashes of one hut the boy emerged unscathed although the magician's cloak had been burnt to a cinder, while from the ashes of the second hut St Patrick's cloak was retrieved unharmed, but the Druid had been incinerated.

From that day Christianity became popular throughout Ireland, although Loeghaire remained a pagan until he died, appropriately enough from a bolt of lightning. He was buried standing up, sword in hand, facing LEINSTER, the county from which his enemies had come.

## Laufrodedd
*Welsh*

The owner of a knife that was considered one of the THIRTEEN TREASURES of BRITAIN[1].

## Lavarcham
*Irish*
See LEBHORCHAM.

## Leabhar Gabhála Éireann
*Irish*

*The Book of the Conquest of Ireland,* popularly known as *The Book of Invasions,* is a twelfth-century pseudo-history that embodies and embroiders earlier tradition. It places emphasis on the prestige of the late Gaelic ruling classes and remains one of the essential sources concerning early Irish legend. It lists six successive invasions, as briefly detailed below.

- **The First Invasion – The people of Cesair** In a time before the biblical Flood a company of people came to IRELAND under the leadership of CESAIR, daughter of BITH, a son of NOAH, or by BANBHA, the SPIRIT OF IRELAND. Of these people, all but one, FINTAN, perished in the Flood, but he lived on in various forms to oversee all that later befell the country.
- **The Second Invasion – Partholán** Between the death of the people of Cesair and the coming of this second group, Ireland had become inhabited by the monstrous FOMHOIRÉ, a race of half-human monsters that each had a single leg, hand and eye and three rows of razor sharp teeth. The Fomhoiré were defeated by PARTHOLÁN and his people and forced into exile to the Hebrides and the Isle of MAN. Ireland itself was nothing like an recognizable country at this time, so Partholán had his people clear four plains and create seven lakes, thus starting to create a recognizable landscape. Partholán also built the first guest house, brewed the first beer and established laws and crafts. Partholán's people were wiped out by a plague, leaving Ireland open once more.
- **The Third Invasion – Nemhedh** Arriving from an unknown place, NEMHEDH and his people quickly settled in Ireland as there was no one to resist them. They cleared twelve plains

and created four more lakes. Following the death of Nemhedh, the Fomhoiré returned from their exile and quickly suppressed the people. Every SAMHAIN they compelled the people to pay them a tribute of two-thirds of their corn, wine and children. Finally the people rebelled and attacked the Fomhoiré. The rebellion failed, and only one boatload of people survived, some of them settling in Greece, others in unnamed northern lands.

- **The Fourth Invasion – the Fir Bholg** The remnants of the people of Nemhedh who had settled in Greece multiplied sufficiently so that they could return to Ireland and reclaim it from the Fomhoiré. During their exile they had split into three tribes, the FIR BHOLG, who led the return expedition, the GAILIÓIN and the FIR DHOMHNANN. Their invasion was successful, and the FIR BHOLG divided the land into five CÓIGEDH, or provinces, ULSTER, LEINSTER, MUNSTER and CONNACHT with MEATH in the centre. The GAILIÓIN settled in Leinster, whence they became known as the LAIGHIN, and the Fir Dhomhnann in Connacht. The Fir Bholg inhabited the remaining three provinces.
- **The Fifth Invasion – the Tuatha Dé Danann** The remnants of the people of Nemhedh who had fled to the north now returned. During their time in exile they had learned much magical lore and now called themselves the TUATHA DÉ DANANN. Led by the DAGHDHA, they brought four great treasures with them; the stone of FÁL, the invincible spear of LUGH, the inescapable sword of NUADHA and the inexhaustible cauldron of the Daghdha. There followed the two battles of MAGH TUIREDH, the first against the Fir Bholg, whom they utterly routed, and the second against the Fomhoiré, whom they also defeated.

- **The Sixth Invasion – the Sons of Míl Éspáine** The last invasion came from Spain, as the name of the invaders would suggest. They landed on the feast of BELTANE (1 May), their leader being AMHAIRGHIN, the FILI. They defeated a massive Tuatha Dé Danann army and marched towards TARA, the capital. On the way they encountered three goddesses, BANBHA, FÓDLA and ÉRIU, the wives of the Tuatha Dé Danann kings MAC CUILL, MAC CÉCHT and MAC GRÉINE respectively. These goddesses disputed the right of the Sons of MÍL ÉSPÁINE to Ireland, but they proved their right by overcoming the Tuatha Dé Danann at the Battle of TAILTIU, having completed a magical test. The Tuatha Dé Danann still refused to accept their defeat and used their magic to deprive the invaders of milk and corn. Finally, they two companies agreed to divide the land, the Tuatha Dé Danann receiving the underground half.

The *Leabhar Gabhála Éireann* demonstrates that, like the mythology of early BRITAIN[1], the island was originally inhabited by a race of giants, but those of Irish origin are far more mysterious and terrible than those that were said to have been the mythical inhabitants of Britain. The landscape of Ireland was successively shaped by human invaders, until it resembled something akin to the geography of Ireland that would have existed in Celtic times. Finally, the gods were suppressed by human inhabitants who did not seek to annihilate them, but rather to subjugate them and have them near at hand should their help ever be needed. It is, however, worth mentioning that as this work dates from the twelfth century, a long time after Christianity had arrived in Ireland, it cannot be taken as a true representation of the early mythology of Ireland, but a more romanticized version that has its grounding in the Celtic oral tradition.

### Leabhar na hUidhre
*Irish*

*The Book of the Dun Cow*, an eleventh- or twelfth-century text that is, without doubt, based on material of a much earlier date. It was certainly written before 1106, because this is the recorded date for the murder of its scribe Maelmori. It is one of the main sources for the study of Irish mythology along with *The Book of Leinster*. One of the most famous stories contained in the *Leabhar na hUidhre* is that of ÉDÁIN ECHRAIDHE and the god MIDHIR, although it is also notable for its version of the battle in which CUMHAILL, the father of FIONN MAC CUMHAILL, was killed, and for the story of CONNLA², which is told in a section of the book known as the *Echtra Condla chaim maic Cuind Chetchathaig*.

### Leapacha Dhiarmada agus Ghráinne
*Irish*

'Beds of Diarmaid and Gráinne', a popular name throughout IRELAND for dolmens, which are believed to have once sheltered the fugitives DIARMAID UA DUIBHNE and GRÁINNE.

### Lebhorcham
*Irish*
Also LAVARCHAM

The wise woman who raised the infant DERDRIU in the strictest seclusion. She told Derdriu that NAOISE, son of UISNECH, had the attributes that Derdriu desired most in a man, even though, from birth, Derdriu had been betrothed to CONCHOBAR MAC NESSA. She is also said to have been at EMHAIN MHACHA on the

occasion when CÚ CHULAINN approached, still seething with the frenzy of battle, and is alleged to have devised the plan by which he was cooled down sufficiently to be allowed entry to the court. A woman of extraordinary powers, considered by some a prophetess, Lebhorcham was said to cross all of IRELAND every day, though whether she physically did this or let her mind travel is open to speculation.

### Leinster
*Irish*

One of the five original provinces into which IRELAND was divided by the FIR BHOLG and still one of the provinces of that country. Situated in the southeast of Ireland, Leinster today covers the counties of Carlow, Dublin, Kildare, Kilkenny, Laoighis, Longford, Louth, MEATH, Offaly, Westmeath, Wexford and Wicklow.

### Leinster, Book of
*Irish*

One of the major sources of Irish mythology, the *Book of Leinster* was written before 1160 and is now one of the most prized possessions of Trinity College Library, Dublin. This book contains an ancient list of saga titles that refer to mythological tales that, sadly, no longer exist.

### Leir
*British*

A legendary early British king who was the prototype of William Shakespeare's tragic King Lear. The son of King BLADUD, Leir ruled for sixty years and founded the town of KAERLEIR or Leicester. He had three daughters – CORDELIA, REGAN and GONERIL. The two eldest, Regan and Goneril, played on his vanity and persuaded him to give them each one-quarter of his kingdom as their dowries. Cordelia refused to have any part of this and remained faithful to her father until his death. Goneril and Regan, along with Regan's two husbands, MAGLAURUS, Duke of ALBANY, and HENWINUS, Duke of CORNWALL, then seized the remainder of Leir's kingdom. MAGLAURUS allowed Leir to keep a retinue of 140 men, but Goneril reduced this to eighty. Regan then had her turn and reduced it to just five, before Goneril finally reduced it to just one man. Leir exiled himself to FRANCE where he was greeted and treated as an honoured guest by Cordelia and her husband AGANIPPUS, who equipped an army and sailed back to BRITAIN[1] and restored Leir to the throne. Three years later Leir died. Cordelia buried him in a vault dedicated to the Roman god Janus, which lay beneath the River Soar, downstream from Leicester, the town her father had founded.

## Lén Linfiaclach
*Irish*

The brazier of BODB. He lived in Loch Léin, which was named after him, where he made wonderful vessels for FAND[1], the daughter of FLIDHAIS. Every evening he threw his anvil far eastwards to the grave-mound at Indeóin na nDése. He then threw a shower of water, then one of fire and finally one of purple gems at the grave-mound.

## Lena
*Irish*

The grandson of MAC DÁ THÓ who had been responsible for the raising of the huge boar owned by his grandfather and then for slaughtering it for the feast, the goings-on at which are described in the ribald *Scéla Mucce Maic Dá Thó*.

## Lendar
*Irish*

The wife of CONALL CERNACH. During the feast thrown by BRICRIU she was persuaded to challenge the right of EMER, wife of CÚ CHULAINN, and Fidelma, wife of LOEGHAIRE BUADHACH, to be regarded as the premier woman of ULSTER.

## Lenus Ocelus Vallaunus
*Romano-British*

The name by which the Roman god Mars was known in south WALES, where he was perhaps worshipped as a healing deity rather than as a god of war.

## leprechaun
*Irish*

A small, roguish elf, often thought of as a cobbler, who possesses a huge buried treasure, although this treasure is popularly thought to be hidden at the end of a rainbow. If caught, a leprechaun can be made to tell his secrets and grant wishes, but if his captor stops looking at him, even for a split second, he will vanish. Leprechauns were said to guard the gold mines of County Wicklow, which, to this day, have not been found, and yet golden ornaments of ancient Irish design, and dating back to at least 1500 BC, have been discovered throughout Europe.

## Ler
*Irish*
See LIR.

## Li Ban
*Irish*

The daughter of AED ABRAT. A dream-woman who, with her sister, FAND[2], whipped CÚ CHULAINN and disabled him for a year after he had failed to capture two magical birds for his wife.

## Lia
*Irish*

A lord of LUACHAR in CONNACHT and the treasurer of the FIAN. He kept the hereditary treasures of the fian, said to have been passed down to them directly from the TUATHA DÉ DANANN, in a bag made of crane's skin. Lia was killed by DEIMNE.

## Lia Fáil
*Irish*

The Stone of Destiny, otherwise known as the stone of FÁL and today as the Stone of SCONE. It was allegedly brought to IRELAND by the TUATHA DÉ DANANN to whom it had been given, in FALIA, by the wizard MORFESSA.

## Liagan
*Irish*

A member of an unnamed band of warriors who chose to pick a fight with the FIAN. He faced the cowardly CONAN MAC MORNA in single combat, laughing heartily at the poor champion the fian had put forth. Conan mac Morna nervously replied that Liagan was in more danger from the man behind him than he was from the man in front of him. As Liagan turned, Conan mac Morna cut off his head and rushed back to the security of the fian, where he was met with derision.

## Liath
*Irish*

The young prince of the TUATHA DÉ DANANN who loved BRÍ, the daughter of MIDHIR, a love she welcomed. Her father did not approve, however, and so, when Liath came to meet Brí, MIDHIR had his servants fire their slingshots at Liath. So heavy was the bombardment that Liath had to turn away, and Brí died of a broken heart.

## Linné
*Irish*

A friend of OSCAR, by whom he was mistakenly killed.

## Lir
*Irish*
Also LER

An ancient god of the sea who has his Welsh equivalent in LLYR. Not much is said about Lir himself, other than he was the father of MANANNÁN MAC LIR, as well as four other children, by his first wife AOBH, who were condemned to spend 900 years in the form of swans by his second wife AOIFE.

## Llallawc
*Welsh*

A variant name for MYRDDIN.

## Llallogan Vrydin
*Welsh*

A variant name for MYRDDIN.

## Llasar Llaesgywydd
*Welsh*

Possibly a variant of LLASSAR LLAES-GYVNEWID, this character is said to have taught MANAWYDAN FAB LLYR the arts of saddle-making, which he was later able to employ to provide a living for himself and PRYDERI, along with their respective wives, RHIANNNON and CIGFA.

## Llassar Llaesgyvnewid
*Welsh*

A giant, the husband of KYMIDEU KYMEINVOLL and the father of countless riotous children, who were apparently born once every six weeks as fully grown and clad warriors. These children wreaked havoc in their native IRELAND, so MATHOLWCH devised a plan to rid his kingdom of them. He had an iron house made and enticed the entire giant family into it. He then slammed the door and lit huge fires around the house in an attempt to roast them alive. However, as soon as the walls became pliable, the giant and his wife burst through and escaped, although all their children perished.

They travelled from Ireland to WALES where they were hospitably greeted by BENDIGEID VRAN. They brought with them a wonderful cauldron that had the power to heal the wounded or to bring the dead back to life. With the aid of this cauldron the realm of Bendigeid Vran became a wonderfully prosperous place.

Some years later the cauldron returned to Ireland. Matholwch married BRANWEN and was given the cauldron as recompense for EFNISIEN's insult. It was subsequently destroyed by Efnisien during the expedition mounted by Bendigeid Vran to Ireland to avenge the cruelty shown by Matholwch towards Branwen, even though the effort killed Efnisien. What happened to Llassar Llaesgyvnewid and his wife is not recorded, but some suggest that they accompanied Bendigeid Vran to Ireland and were killed there.

## Llawfrodedd
*Welsh*

According to some sources, the owner of CYLLEL LLAWFRODEDD, a DRUIDIC sacrificial knife, numbered among the THIRTEEN TREASURES OF BRITAIN[1].

## Llefelys
*Welsh*
Also LLEVELYS

A King of FRANCE, son of BELI and brother of LLUDD, CASWALLAWN and NYNNIAW[2], who, in the story of *Lludd and Llefelys*, told Lludd that a scream heard on the eve of every May Day, and whose source could not be found, was actually caused by fighting DRAGONS. These were subsequently caught and interred at DINAS EMRYS.

## Lleu Llaw Gyffes
*Welsh*

A Welsh hero god who is, perhaps, a degenerative version of the Irish LUGH, and who is, curiously, depicted as being a skilled cobbler. He was the second son born to ARIANRHOD, much to her shame, as she was being put through a rite that would attest her virginity. This rite was being carried out because her brother, GWYDION FAB DÔN, had put Arianrhod forward for the post of footholder, a post that could be held only by an accredited virgin, at the court of MATH FAB MATHONWY. Her first-born son was immediately named DYLAN.

Gwydion fab Dôn snatched up Arianrhod's second child and hid him in a chest, later adopting the boy as his own. Four years later, and still without a name, the child was shown by Gwydion fab Dôn to his sister Arianrhod. Reminded of her shame, she cursed the child, saying that he would never bear a name until she herself gave him one. Some time later Gwydion fab Dôn managed to circumvent this curse by disguising himself and the young boy and travelling to Arianrhod's castle, where she was tricked into calling the boy Lleu Llaw Gyffes, which means 'Bright One with the Nimble Hand'. Gwydion fab Dôn could not resist revealing their true identity to his sister, and in her fury she cursed the boy a second time, this time saying that he would never bear arms until she herself armed him.

Later Gwydion fab Dôn and the now maturing Lleu Llaw Gyffes travelled to Arianrhod's castle, placed in these legends on the isle of ANGLESEY, and by use of magic made it seem as if the castle was under attack. In her fright, Arianrhod armed Lleu Llaw Gyffes, but again Gwydion fab Dôn could not resist boasting of the deception, and Arianrhod cursed the youth for a third time, saying that he would never marry a mortal woman.

Enlisting the help of Math fab Mathonwy, Gwydion fab Dôn also by-passed this final curse, for together the two magically created a woman of the flowers of oak, broom and meadowsweet whom they named BLODEUWEDD. Lleu Llaw Gyffes married Blodeuwedd, and this time at least Gwydion fab Dôn appears to have resisted the temptation of boasting to his sister.

All did not go well with Lleu Llaw Gyffes' marriage, however, for after a short time Blodeuwedd started an affair with the hunter GRONW BEBYR. Together, the lovers plotted to kill Lleu Llaw Gyffes, but they knew that this could not be accomplished before their victim had revealed the exact manner in which he could be dealt a mortal blow. Finally, Blodeuwedd managed to persuade her husband to reveal that he could be killed only by a spear that had been worked for a year and a day at Mass time on Sundays, and then only if he had one foot in a bathtub and the other on the back of a billy goat. Gronw Bebyr immediately set about forging the required weapon. A year and a day later, with the spear ready, Blodeuwedd managed to convince Lleu Llaw Gyffes to demonstrate to her the ridiculous position he would need to adopt to be killed. As he took up the stance, Gronw Bebyr rose from his hiding place, but managed only to wound Lleu Llaw Gyffes, who changed into an eagle and flew away to die from his injury.

Gwydion fab Dôn tracked down Lleu Llaw Gyffes by following a sow that fed on the maggots that dropped from the eagle's festering wound. He found the dying hero perched in the branches of a tree and cured his wound before changing Blodeuwedd into an owl for her infidelity. Lleu Llaw Gyffes resumed his human form and killed Gronw Bebyr.

## Llevelys
*Welsh*
See LLEFELYS.

## Llew
*Welsh*

An anglicized and shortened variant of LLEU LLAW GYFFES.

## Lloeg(y)r
*Welsh*

The ancient Welsh name for ENGLAND. It was later thought to have given rise to the naming of England as LOGRES in the Arthurian legends.

## Llongad Grwrm Fargod Eidyn
*Welsh*

The killer of ADDAON, son of TALIESIN.

## Lluagor
*Welsh*

The horse belonging to CARADOC VREICHVRAS.

## Lludd
*Welsh*

The father of GWYNN AP NUDD and brother of LLEFELYS and NYNNIAW[2], he is the equivalent of the Irish LUGH. He is of great mythical importance for, along with his brother, he appears in a legend concerning three 'plagues' that infected ENGLAND. One of these was a scream, heard every May Day eve, whose source could not be located. Llefelys told Lludd that the scream came from two DRAGONS battling for supremacy. These dragons were finally captured in an underground chamber, a plan devised by Llefelys, and subsequently imprisoned beneath DINAS EMRYS in WALES. A direct comparison can be made between this tale and that concerning the dragons found in an underground lake, as foretold by MYRDDIN, on the site where VORTIGERN was attempting, without success, to erect his tower. It seems safe to assume that these were the same dragons.

## Llud and Llefelys
*Welsh*

A part of the *Mabinogion*. It tells how on the eve of every May Day a scream was heard, the source of which could not be located. LLEFELYS, the King of FRANCE, told his brother LLUDD that the scream was caused by fighting DRAGONS. These were eventually caught and interred at DINAS EMRYS.

## Llud(d) Llaw Ereint
*Welsh*

'Lludd of the Silver Hand', the Welsh equivalent of NUADHA AIRGEDLÁMH, and the British NUDD[2] or NODENS. His daughter was CREIDDYLED, the original of CORDELIA, while his son was GWYNN AP NUDD, the Welsh equivalent of the Irish hero FIONN MAC CUMHAILL.

## Llwyd fab -Cil Coed, -Kilcoed
*Welsh*

The magician who cast a spell on CIGFA, RHIANNON, MANAWYDAN and PRYDERY to avenge PWYLL's treatment of his friend GWAWL FAB CLUD.

## Llychlyn
*Welsh*

The Welsh legendary name for Scandinavia, which has its Irish equivalent in LOCHLANN. It may originally have been used to refer to an OTHERWORLDLY kingdom.

## Llyfr Du Caertyddin
*Welsh*

*The Black Book of Carmarthen*, written prior to 1105. This work was written by the black-robed monks of CARMARTHEN, hence its name, and it is today housed in the National Library of WALES at Aberystwyth. Along with the *Red Book of Hergest*, it is one of the most important sources of Welsh mythological and legendary beliefs.

## Llyn Cau
*Welsh*

A small lake situated on the south side of CADAIR IDRIS in GWYNEDD. Legend claims that it is bottomless and the home to a monster. This legend was embellished some time during the eighteenth century when it is said a young man attempted to swim across Llyn Cau when suddenly, as the man reached the mid-point, the monster appeared, took him in its mouth and disappeared. See also IDRIS.

## Llyn Eiddwen
*Welsh*

A lake in DYFED that, according to legend must never be allowed to dry up. MYRDDIN prophesied that, if it did, CARMARTHEN would suffer a catastrophic disaster.

## Llyn Tegid
*Welsh*

The largest natural lake in WALES and the legendary home of TEGID VOEL and his wife CERRIDWEN. A familiar legend surrounds its creation, the same form of legend that is associated with many other lakes, including Loch Ness in SCOTLAND. Local people used to draw their water from a well that had to be capped after use. One night, however, the well-keeper neglected his duties, and the well gushed out its water while the local people slept. By morning, having had to flee their houses in the night, the local people looked down from the surrounding hills to see a lake some 3 miles long and 1 mile wide. Today Llyn Tegid is 5 miles long, and local belief holds that it will continue to grow.

## Llyn-y-Fan Fach
*Welsh*

A small lake at the foot of Bannau Sir Gaer near Llanddeusant in DYFED. It is the site of a fascinating legend, thought to have been one of the inspirations for the later Arthurian character of the Lady of the Lake. Regrettably, the lake was dammed to form a reservoir early in the twentieth century. A maiden left the allegedly bottomless lake to marry a local farmer's son, bringing with her herds of sheep, goats, cattle and horses. However, after several years of marriage, the lady's husband broke the condition that he must refrain from giving her three blows, and she returned to the lake with all the animals she had brought with her. The farmer followed but was drowned as he attempted to find her.

## Llyr
*Welsh*

The Welsh sea god (*llyr* means 'sea') is the equivalent of the Irish LIR and, like that character, is highly important, but little recorded. The father of BRANWEN, BENDIGEID VRAN and MANAWYDAN FAB LLYR, he would appear to have been the original of the mythical King LEIR.

## Llyr Marini
*Welsh*

The father of CARADOC VREICHVRAS.

## Llys Helig
*Welsh*

The lost realm of HELIG AP GLANNOWG, which is alleged to lie beneath the waters of Conwy Bay, approximately 2 miles out. It is still claimed that the sunken ruins of his palace can be seen at the lowest of tides. Llys Helig joins CENTRE'R GWAELOD and CAER ARIANRHOD to form a triad of legendary lost kingdoms off the coast of WALES.

## Llywarch Hên
*Welsh*

A celebrated Welsh poet, who is thought to have flourished about AD 600. Said to have been the cousin of URIEN of RHEGED, he is sometimes, incorrectly, identified with TALIESIN. Various traditions place him in POWYS or among the North Briton tribesmen. He is later listed as one of the knights of King ARTHUR but appears to have been a reasonably late addition to the Arthurian tales.

## Loch
*Irish*

The son of MOFEBIS, Loch was a warrior of CONNACHT who refused the order of MEDHBHA to fight CÚ CHULAINN, saying that he would not fight a beardless youth. Cú Chulainn stuck some dried grass to his chin to resemble a beard and then disposed of Loch when he eventually came to fight him, even though he also had to battle against the magical powers of the MÓRRÍGHAN at the same time.

## Lochlann
*Irish*

An ancient realm, whose king was killed by FIONN MAC CUMHAILL, although the hero spared his son, MIDAC, who later took his revenge of the members of the FIAN.

## Locrinus
*British*

A son of BRUTUS and brother of ALBANACTUS and KAMBER. After the death of his father, Locrinus became the ruler of ENGLAND, Kamber the ruler of WALES and Albanactus the ruler of SCOTLAND. After Albanactus had been killed by invading Huns, Locrinus and Kamber joined forces and routed the Huns. Among the captives taken was a beautiful maiden by the name of ESTRILDIS. Locrinus wanted to marry her, but he was already betrothed to GWENDOLEN, the daughter of CORINEUS. Forced to honour his commitment to Gwendolen, Locrinus took Estrildis as his mistress and hid her in LONDON. For seven years he visited her in secret, during which time Estrildis bore him a daughter, HABREN, while Gwendolen bore him a son, MADDAN.

After the death of Corineus, Locrinus deserted Gwendolen and made Estrildis his queen. Gwendolen went to CORNWALL and mustered an army, which she led into battle against Locrinus near the River Stour. Locrinus was killed, and Gwendolen had Estrildis and Habren drowned in a river that she decreed would thenceforth carry the name of Locrinus' daughter. This river became the SABRINA to the Romans, and is today known as the River SEVERN.

## Locris
*British*

According to GEOFFREY OF MONMOUTH, this early name for ENGLAND derived from LOCRINUS. This is false etymology, for the name Locris is actually an anglicization of the Welsh LLOEGR. See also LOGRES.

## Lodan
*Irish*

1   The son of the King of India, India here being used to signify a foreign land. He, along with EOLUS, son of the King of Greece (used in the same manner), accompanied CIABHAN on his journey to TÍR TAIRNGIRI, where they met the sisters CLIODNA, AEIFE and EDAEIN whom they persuaded to elope with them. However, MANANNÁN MAC LIR sent a huge wave after them, which engulfed the three sisters, as well as ILDÁTHACH and his sons who were pursuing them, and either drowned them or carried them back to the LAND OF PROMISE.

2   The son of LIR, brother of MANANNÁN MAC LIR and father of Sinend. Some have sought to equate this Lodan with LODAN[1], but if this were the case Lodan[1] would not have needed to persuade Cliodna and her sisters to elope with him and his companions, for inhabitants of the same OTHERWORLDLY kingdom could come and go as they pleased.

## Loeg
*Irish*
Also LAEG

The charioteer of CÚ CHULAINN. He was killed by LUGAID[2] who used the GAE BOLGA, the invincible short spear of Cú Chulainn.

## Loeghaire
*Irish*

1 A son of UGAINY and KESAIR and the brother of COVAC. After the death of Ugainy the kingdom passed to Loeghaire, which consumed Covac with jealousy. He sought the advice of a DRUID, who told him to feign death and have word sent to his brother. This he did, and, when Loeghaire bent over the supposed corpse, Covac thrust his knife into Loeghaire's heart and killed him. He also had to kill Loeghaire's son AILILL, who had accompanied his father. In this way Covac ascended to the throne he so desired. See also COBTHACH COEL, LOEGHAIRE LORC.

2 The son of the King of CONNACHT who went to the aid of FIACHNA[2] whose wife had been taken captive by GOLL, the son of the King of MAGH MELL. Loeghaire and fifty of his men followed Fiachna to his OTHERWORLDLY land and there succeeded in freeing Fiachna's wife. Fiachna gave Loeghaire his daughter, SUN TEAR, in thanks. After a year Loeghaire and his men briefly revisited their families in Connacht, but they then returned to Magh Mell and were never seen again.

## Loeghaire Buadhach
*Irish*

One of the three champions who were persuaded by the mischievous BRICRIU to claim the honour of carving the roast at a feast he had thrown, the other claimants being CONALL CERNACH and CÚ CHULAINN. The decision went in favour of Cú Chulainn on two occasions, the first at the judgement of MEDHBHA of CONNACHT, and the second by decree of CÚ ROÍ MAC DÁIRI. On both occasions the two losers refused to accept the judgement, but they were later forced to concede after Cú Roí mac Dáiri proved his judgement to be correct.

## Loeghaire Lorc
*Irish*

A King of IRELAND and father of AILLIL AINE, King of LEINSTER. He and his son were killed by Loeghaire Lorc's brother COBTHACH COEL when he usurped the throne. See also COVAC, LOEGHAIRE[1].

## Loeghaire mac Neill
*Irish*

A pagan king of IRELAND who appears in a late Christian legend found in the twelfth-century *Book of the Dun Cow*. St PATRICK summoned CÚ CHULAINN from Hell to prove the truths of Christianity and the horrors of damnation. Sure enough, Cú Chulainn rode up from Hell on his chariot, converted Loeghaire mac Neill, and then prayed for admittance to heaven, a prayer that was apparently answered, thus allowing Christianity to claim the conversion of one of the most powerful and popular figures of the pagan Irish tradition.

## Logres
*British*

The archaic name for ENGLAND that is thought to have derived from the Welsh LLOEGR. The name Logres was used throughout the Arthurian legends to refer not just to England, but to the entire British realm of King ARTHUR.

## London
*General*

The capital city of Great BRITAIN[1]. It was allegedly founded by BRUTUS, who named the city TROIA NOVA, which means 'New Troy'. The city subsequently became the capital of LLUDD, the sixty-eighth ruler after Brutus, who fortified the walls, at which time it was known as CAER LLUDD, 'Lludd's Fort', or CAER LUNDEIN. Some time later the 'Caer' was dropped, and the city simply became known as LUNDEIN, of which the modern name is a simple derivation.

## Long Meg
*British*

A semi-mythical giantess who was, according to the historian John Hale (c. 1640), said to be buried on the south side of the cloisters of Westminster Abbey, LONDON, a site that had held a sacred status long before the arrival of Christianity. Long Meg is immortalized in a megalithic stone circle at Little Salkeld, northeast of Penrith in Cumbria.

## Longes mac nDuil Dermait
*Irish*

The Exile of the Sons of Doel the Forgotten, a text that tells the story of EOCHO ROND's bonding of CÚ CHULAINN to discover the whereabouts of the sons of DOEL and of Cú Chulainn's adventures and his ultimate success.

## Lothar
*Irish*

A brother of BRES[2], NÁR, MEDHBHA, CLOTHRU and ETHNE, the latter two both being said to have been the wife of CONCHOBAR MAC NESSA after MEDHBHA had left him for AILILL. Clothru once bewailed her childlessness to her three brothers, and as a result had a child by each of them, each child being given the name LUGAID[1].

## Lough Neagh
*Irish*

The lake in which MOYLINNY is situated, and from where MONGÁN ruled in the early seventh century.

## Luachar
*Irish*

A kingdom within CONNACHT over which LIA, the keeper of the treasure of the FIAN, ruled.

## luchorpáin
*Irish*

A form of LEPRECHAUN that lives under the sea. They are said to be able to guide humans beneath the sea either by placing a cloak over their head or by stuffing herbs into the human's ears.

## Luchta(ine)
*Irish*

One of the TRÍ DÉ DÁNA, the three divine smiths, the others being COIBHNIU and CREIDHNE, although Luchtaine is sometimes described as a carpenter rather than a smith. The three are most famous for their efforts during the Second Battle of MAGH TUIREDH, when they worked at lightning speed to make and repair the weapons of the TUATHA DÉ DANANN, weapons magically empowered so that none wounded by them would ever recover. See also COLUM CUALLEINECH.

## Lud
*British*

A mythical early British king, who is an

anglicized version of the Welsh LLUDD, and thus also of the Irish LUGH. His mythical exploits are the same as those of Lludd in connection with the city of LONDON.

## Lug
*Gaulish*

The Gaulish variant of the Irish LUGH.

## Lugaid
*Irish*

1 Three sons of CLOTHRU were given this name, their fathers being Clothru's brothers BRES[2], NÁR and LOTHAR. That Lugaid born to Nár also bore Clothru a son who was named CRIMTHANN NIA NÁIR.

2 The son of CÚ ROÍ MAC DÁIRI, who marched with ERC[2] and the monstrous sons of CALATIN against CÚ CHULAINN. Lugaid took possession of the GAE BOLGA and with it wounded both Grey of MACHA and Cú Chulainn, who tied himself to a pillar so that he might die standing up. Realizing that Cú Chulainn was beaten, Lugaid strode boldly up to him and cut off his head, but as he did so Cú Chulainn's sword fell from his hand and cut off Lugaid's own hand. CONALL CERNACH and Grey of Macha pursued Lugaid and caught him up whereupon Grey of Macha took great bites of his flesh before Conall Cernach cut off his head.

## Lugaid mac Con
*Irish*

The companion of EOGAN, the son of OILILL, with whom he discovered a tiny magical harper concealed within a yew tree that had been conceived as part of the vengeance planned by AINÉ[2] after she had been outraged by Oilill. The harper caused a quarrel between Eogan and Lugaid mac Con, which resulted in the death of Lugaid mac Con. His death led to the Battle of MAGH MUCRIME, in which all seven of Oilill's sons were killed.

## Lugh
*Irish*

The Irish god of light, the patron of the festival of LUGHNASADH and often associated with the Roman god Mercury. His cult spread as far as Spain and Switzerland. His Gaulish name was LUG or LUGUS, while in WALES he was LLUDD. His name means 'shining one', and JULIUS CAESAR referred to him as the Gaulish 'MERCURY'. Reputedly coming to IRELAND from across the sea, he is said to have spoken with a 'stammer', meaning that he did not speak native Erse. One story says that his mother was the wife of one of the TUATHA DÉ DANANN, and it was she who trained him to bear arms, most notably the slingshot. Another source says that he was born in the OTHERWORLD, the sole survivor of divine triplets, and raised by MANANNÁN MAC LIR who acted as his foster father and armed him with four wonderful weapons – an inescapable spear, a great sling (his favourite weapon), a helmet of invisibility and the wondrous shield that was later owned by the hero FIONN MAC CUMHAILL. Lugh's most unlikely relation was the FOMHOIRÉ giant BALAR, although this relationship may explain Lugh's ownership of his inescapable spear. This spear appears in the story of the DAGHDHA, who is said to have brought it to Ireland when the Tuatha Dé Danann first arrived. The spear was carried by the Daghdha in the First Battle of MAGH TUIREDH where it was, so it would seem, lost to the Fomhoiré. As Balar is said to be the grandfather of Lugh it would appear that he passed the spear, which had come into his possession, on to his grandson.

Lugh arrived at the gates of the royal palace of NUADHA, King of the Tuatha Dé Danann, and asked for a job, claiming that he was a carpenter. However, when he learned that there was already a carpenter at the court, he said that he was a harpist, then a FILI, an historian, a hero, a magician, an astrologer, a cook and a great many other things. It was his ability to turn his hand to anything that rightfully earned him the honorific SAMILDÁNACH, which means 'of many skills', skills that are said to have become his on the death of his two divine siblings. It was his multitude of abilities that led to his being admitted to the court of the Tuatha Dé Danann, and to Nuadha, who immediately recognized his superiority, resigning in his favour.

With Lugh enthroned as their king, the Tuatha De Danann prepared for the coming Second Battle of Magh Tuiredh. They went into combat armed with the magical weapons forged for them by the TRÍ DÉ DÁNA, and reinforced by a battery of powerful charms obtained by Lugh. During the battle Lugh appeared, in characteristic sorcerer's form with a single leg and single eye, everywhere among the forces of the Tuatha Dé Danann, chanting words of magic and putting new strength into every man. Those who were wounded or killed were speedily restored to full vitality by DIAN CÉCHT and his three sons, who cast them into a magic bath, cauldron or well.

As a last, desperate measure the Fomhoiré called for a single combat between Balar and the Tuatha Dé Danann's champion. Lugh stepped forward and faced the hideous monster, his own grandfather. Like his compatriots, Balar had but a single eye in the middle of his forehead, an eye that was so powerful that a single glance could kill an entire army. It took four men to lift the eyelid, and as they did the Tuatha Dé

Danann took cover. Lugh, however, stood his ground and, once the eye was fully open, aimed his sligshot with such accuracy that the shot passed straight through Balar's eye and continued on through his head to force his brains out of the back. The slingshot had been fired with such power that it continued its path of destruction and decimated the Fomhoiré army. The few survivors of the Fomhoiré then fled the country and were never heard of again.

This myth described two very important events in early Irish mythology. The first was the establishment of a single deity whose skills were not singular, a concept that was revolutionary at the time. The second was the establishment of a new order of gods and goddesses who drove the primal beings from the land and brought skill and order to the sacred land.

## Lugh Laebach
*Irish*

A wizard, possibly an aspect of LUGH, who was sent out against the monstrous CARMAN and her sons by the TUATHA DÉ DANANN.

## Lugh Lamfhada
*Irish*

A name given to LUGH that means 'Lugh of the Long Arm'. It does not mean that Lugh possessed unusually long arms, but rather signified the magical power of his sling and spear as typical attributes of a god of light and victory.

## Lughnasadh
*General*

One of the four great Celtic festivals, the Celtic harvest festival. It was celebrated on 1 August and was later to become

Christianized as Lammas, the feast day of St BRIGHID. The other three major Celtic festivals were SAMHAIN, IMBOLC and BELTANE. The major sites for the observance of Lughnasadh were those that had associations with fertility goddesses, associations that are entirely appropriate for a festival that celebrates the fertility of the earth.

## Lugmannair
*Irish*

The father of DIL and an inhabitant of the Isle of FALGA (the Isle of MAN).

## Lugus
*Gaulish*

A variant of LUG, the Gaulish version of the Irish god of light LUGH. The continental Romans quickly identified Lugus with Mercury.

## Lundein
*British*

One of the ancient names of LONDON and one from which the modern name may be seen to be directly derived. Its origin is slightly confused. Some say that it comes from the Old English Lud-Dun, a name given to the capital after LUD, mythical king of BRITAIN[1], had fortified the walls, Lud-Dun meaning 'Lud's Fortress'. Others, however, say that it comes from CAER LLUDD, a name of obviously Welsh origin, and that it was this name that degenerated into Caer Lundein, the 'Caer' later being dropped and the spelling slightly altered, both changes being made to eliminate the Welsh influence.

## Lwndrys
*British*

Another obviously Welsh name that was, at some point, applied to the capital LONDON. The source of this name is uncertain, but some say that it is a derivative form of CAER LLUDD.

## Lyonesse
*British*

A mythical lost land that is said to have once occupied most of the area off of the south coast of CORNWALL as far out as the Scilly Isles. The land is most famous as becoming the home of the last remnants of the court of King ARTHUR after the death of that king, the sea flooding the land to stop the knights being followed. The only remaining traces of Lyonesse are said to be the Scilly Isles and ST MICHAEL'S MOUNT.

## Mabinogion
*Welsh*

One of the most important of all Welsh source texts, although it was not compiled until the mid-nineteenth century. The name comes from the Welsh word *mabinogi*, which means 'instruction for young poets'. Drawing on two much earlier manuscripts, *The White Book of Rhydderch* (1300–25) and *The Red Book of Hergest* (1375–1425), the *Mabinogion* proper consists of four branches or tales, three of which concern the hero PRYDERI. The four stories are those of PWYLL, BRANWEN, MANAWYDAN FAB LLYR and MATH FAB MATHONWY. Later editions of the *Mabinogion* have been extended to include much Arthurian material, although these undoubtedly draw on earlier and entirely relevant material. The extensions include the stories *Gereint and Enid*, *Culhwch and Olwen*, *Owain*, PEREDUR and the *Dream of Rhonabwy*. The most famous translation of the *Mabinogion*, that made by Lady Charlotte Guest, also includes the story of TALIESIN.

## Mabon
*Welsh*

A derivation of the god MAPONOS. Said to be the son of MODRON, herself a variant of the goddess MATRONA, Mabon was worshipped as the god of liberation, harmony, unity and music. It appears that his cult was extremely widespread, and he might possibly be one of the most universally worshipped Celtic deities. Welsh tradition said that he had been held captive since he was stolen from his mother at the age of just three days, his prison being at Caer Loyw (Gloucester), a location that is here taken to symbolize the OTHERWORLD. A Romano-Celtic inscription equates him with the Roman god Apollo Citharoedus, 'the lyre player'. His Irish equivalent appears to have been OENGUS MAC IN OG.

Mabon, as is the case with many other Celtic deities, later passed into the Arthurian cycle, his release from captivity in these stories being effected by CULHWCH whom he helped to hunt the boar TWRCH TRWYTH. Like Maponos, Mabon also appears in the Arthurian cycle with various other names, such as Mabuz and Mabonagrain.

## Mac an Daimh
*Irish*

A child born at the same time as MONGÁN to one of the attendants of FIACHNA LURGAN's wife. As Mongán is said to be the son of MANANNÁN MAC LIR, it is thought that Mac an Daimh is also one of the offspring of this amorous god.

## Mac Cécht
*Irish*

One of the three TUATHA DÉ DANANN

kings at the time of the invasion by the Sons of MÍL ÉSPÁINE by whom they were conquered. His co-rulers at TARA were MAC CUILL and MAC GRÉINE. Mac Cécht's wife was FÓDLA, while Mac Cuill's was BANBHA and Mac Gréine's was the goddess ÉRIU. He was killed by AIREM, one of the leaders of the Sons of Míl Éspáine.

## Mac Con
*Irish*

Possibly an historical predecessor of CORMAC MAC AIRT, who traditionally gained the throne in the year AD 227 by having Mac Con stabbed.

## Mac Cuill
*Irish*

One of the three TUATHA DÉ DANANN kings at the time of the invasion by the Sons of MÍL ÉSPÁINE by whom they were conquered. His co-rulers at TARA were MAC CÉCHT and MAC GRÉINE. Mac Cuill's wife was BANBHA, while Mac Cécht's was FÓDLA and Mac Gréine's was the goddess ÉRIU. Mac Cuill was killed by EBER, one of the leaders of the Sons of Míl Éspáine.

## Mac Dá Thó
*Irish*

A King of LEINSTER and the owner of the pig that is the central character in the ribald story *Scéla Mucce Maic Dá Thó*. This story later formed the basis of *Fledd Bricrenn*, which tells how the hero CÚ CHULAINN came to be regarded, after two judgements in his favour, as the champion of all IRELAND.

Mac Dá Thó owned not just the famous pig, but also a wondrous hunting dog, which was famed throughout the land, being able to run all around Leinster in a single day. This dog was sought both by MEDHBHA and AILILL of CONNACHT and by CONCHOBAR MAC NESSA of ULSTER. Mac Dá Thó promised it to both and invited both monarchs and their retinues to a feast, sincerely hoping that he would be able to escape the argument that was bound to arise. The chief dish at this feast was the pig that Mac Dá Thó's grandson LENA had raised, nurturing it for seven years on the flesh of fifty cows. After it had been killed by Lena, it took sixty oxen to drag its carcass, and its tail alone required sixty men to carry it.

Nothing more is said of this wonderful animal in the story, apart from the quarrel that arose over who should have the right to carve it. CET originally claimed the right, but he was eventually made to cede in favour of CONALL CERNACH. Mac Dá Thó did indeed escape the quarrel, but by promising his dog to both monarchs he lost not only that dog, which fled the scene, but also his marvellous pig.

## Mac Erc
*Irish*

The leader of the FIR BHOLG forces in their battle with the TUATHA DÉ DANANN at the First Battle of MAGH TUIREDH, during which he was killed.

## Mac Gré(i)ne
*Irish*

One of the three TUATHA DÉ DANANN kings at the time of the invasion by the Sons of MÍL ÉSPÁINE by whom they were conquered. His co-rulers at TARA were MAC CUILL and MAC CÉCHT. Mac Gréine's wife was the goddess ÉRIU, while Mac Cuill's was BANBHA and Mac Cécht's was FÓDLA. He was killed by AMHAIRGHIN, the FILI.

## Mac in(d) O-c, -g
*Irish*

A shortened variant of OENGHUS MAC IN OG.

## Mac Lugach
*Irish*

A prominent member of the FIAN, although he is mentioned only in passing.

## Mac Mhaol
*Irish*

A giant whom CÚ CHULAINN fought in single combat for the unlikely trophy of the two front teeth of the King of Greece, Greece in this instance being used as a name to suggest an OTHERWORLDLY kingdom. Mac Mhaol was easily overcome and led his vanquisher to where he might obtain the trophy he required.

## Mac Roth
*Irish*

The steward of MEDHBHA who told her of the existence of the DONN CUAILNGÈ and who may thus be considered responsible for the quest undertaken by that queen against ULSTER to secure that marvellous animal and thus also for the eventual death of CÚ CHULAINN.

## *Macgnímartha Finn*
*Irish*

*The Boyish Deeds of Finn*, a story copied from the tenth-century Psalter of Cashel. It tells of the boyhood of FIONN MAC CUMHAILL, from his posthumous birth to his becoming the head of the FIAN.

## Macha
*Irish*

A daughter of MIDHIR, an Irish fertility and mother goddess, and a formidable warrior, who built the fortress named after her, EMHAIN MHACHA, the ancient capital city of ULSTER, a prehistoric and probably ritual site, which is today known as Navan Fort. She is also associated with the city of Armagh, or Ard Macha, which was later to become the centre of Celtic Christianity. Legend says that Macha had two brothers, DITHORBA and CIMBAOTH. She fought and killed Dithorba for the right to become Queen of IRELAND and forced her other brother to marry her. The five sons of Dithorba attacked her, but she easily overcame them, and, having drawn the outline of a massive fort in the earth with the pin of her brooch, she made her five captives build her fort, which became known as Emhain Mhacha or 'Brooch of Macha'.

The wife of CRUNDCHU, she was, while pregnant, forced by the men of Ulster to run a race against the horses of CONCHODAR MAC NESSA. The race brought on her labour, and she gave birth to twins. Although she died as a result of childbirth, she remained alive long enough to curse the men of Ulster so that, at critical moments in any battle from that day forth, they would suffer the labour pains of women in childbirth. Her race against the horses of Conchobar mac Nessa led to Macha becoming regarded as the patroness of ritual games and festivals but, more importantly, as the horse goddess, who was also known as ÉDÁIN ECHRAIDHE in Ireland, RHIANNON in WALES and EPONA in GAUL.

Following her untimely death, Macha became connected with BADHBH and NEMHAIN in the triple aspect goddess the MÓRRÍGHAN, her guise now being that of a war goddess, who foretold war and fire slaughter. She, and her companions, were sometimes said to have been witnessed actually on the field of battle in the form of carrion birds.

## Macha, Grey of
*Irish*

One of twin foals, the other being Black of SAINGLIU, that were born at exactly the same time as the hero CÚ CHULAINN. The two horses later became the famous steeds of that warrior. Grey of Macha was killed by ERC[2], of the warriors who had taken part in the hunt for the DONN CUAILNGÈ.

## Macsen (Wledig)
*Welsh*

The name by which the Roman emperor MAXIMUS was known in Welsh tradition. In this guise he is said to have married ELEN, daughter of EUDAF, and to have been later restored as emperor with the help of Elen's brothers CYNAN and GADEON.

## Maddan
*British*

The son of LOCRINUS and GWENDOLEN, and thus grandson of CORINEUS. His right to the accession was upheld by his mother who, after Locrinus had abandoned her for his mistress ESTRILDIS, mustered an army in CORNWALL and, in a battle near the River Stour, killed her wayward husband. Gwendolen then reigned for fifteen years before abdicating in favour of her son.

## Madog Morfryn
*Welsh*

According to Welsh genealogies, the father of MYRDDIN, although some sources name MORGAN FRYCH as Myrddin's father.

## Maelgwyn
*Welsh*

A sixth-century ruler of GWYNEDD. The son of CLUTARIUS, he has been tenuously identified with MELKIN.

## Maen Dylan
*Welsh*

The Stone of Dylan, which stands on a stretch of gravel approximately 2 miles south of a reef of stones off the coast of GWYNEDD that is known as CAER ARIANRHOD. Maen Dylan is alleged to mark the grave of DYLAN EIL TON, the first of the two children mysteriously born to ARIANRHOD.

## Maen Tyriawg
*Welsh*

An ancient name for Maentwrog where GWYDION FAB DÔN used his magical powers to overcome and kill the good King PRYDERI.

## Maes Gwyddno
*Welsh*

An alternative name for CANTRE'R GWAELOD, the lost realm of GWYDDNO GARANHIR in Cardigan Bay. The name is also sometimes used to refer to the fish-weir of Gwyddno Garanhir, this weir appearing in the story of CERRIDWEN and the birth of TALIESIN.

## Maeve
*Irish*

An alternate name for MEDHBHA, Queen of CONNACHT.

## Maga
*Irish*

The daughter of OENGHUS MAC IN OG and the mother of FACHTNA by ROSS, and thus the grandmother of CONCHOBAR MAC NESSA. However, she married for a second time, to the DRUID CATHBHADH, and by him became the mother of FINDCHOÉM, Elva and DEICHTINE, and was therefore also the grandmother of CÚ CHULAINN, the sons of UISNECH and CONALL CERNACH. Maga is also said to have been the mother of CET and ANLUAN, but by whom is unrecorded.

## Mag(h) mBreg
*Irish*

A supernatural realm, mentioned in the story of DIL and TULCHAINDE as being the place to which the MÓRRÍGHAN, here benevolent rather than malevolent, arranged to have the oxen loved by Dil transported so that she and her lover might elope from the Isle of FALGA (Isle of MAN).

## Mag(h) Mel-l, -d
*Irish*

An OTHERWORLDLY realm, whose name means 'The Delightful Plain'. It is a paradisal land of the righteous dead, the home of FIACHNA[2], and the land to which LOEGHAIRE[2] travelled with fifty of the men of CONNACHT to release Fiachna's wife from the clutches of GOLL. It is also the realm in which CONNLA[2], the son of CONN CÉTCHATHLACH, was enticed to live by a beautiful maiden.

## Magh Mór
*Irish*

A supernatural kingdom, the 'Great Plain', a paradise where the gods were entertained with magical music. The inhabitants are described as graceful, and nothing belongs to any one person. There is a choice between wine and mead to drink. Conception is considered without crime or sin, and the people live on salted pork and new milk, such dishes being confined to the gods. In the *Leabhar na hUidre* it is the realm to which MIDHIR attempts to entice the reincarnated ÉDÁIN.

## Magh Mucrime
*Irish*

The scene of a battle ultimately caused by the outrage of AINÉ[2] by OILILL. Ainé swore revenge and caused LUGAID MAC CON and EOGAN (who was one of Oilill's sons) to fall out over a diminutive harper she had created. Lugaid mac Con was killed, and his family went to war against the family of Oilill, whose seven sons were killed in the resulting battle.

## Magh Tuiredh
*Irish*

Pronounced MOYTURA, Magh Tuiredh was the location of two major battles between the TUATHA DÉ DANANN and the then inhabitants of IRELAND. However, the name is slightly misleading, for the First Battle of Magh Tuiredh took place in County Mayo and the second in County Sligo. The First Battle of Magh Tuiredh was fought after the Tuatha Dé Danann demanded that the FIR BHOLG, the then rulers of Ireland, resign their kingship or fight for it. They chose to fight, but were utterly defeated and forced into exile among the terrible FOMHOIRÉ.

In the course of the battle, the king of the Tuatha Dé Danann, NUADHA, lost an arm and was forced to abdicate because no physically blemished king might rule. He passed the kingship to BRES[1], a slightly strange choice when it is considered that his mother was a Tuatha Dé Danann woman, but his father a Fomhoiré warrior. Bres was not the best of kings, proving tyrannical beyond belief and even forcing the DAGHDHA and OGHMA to be his slaves. Finally, COIRBRE satirized Bres so savagely that he broke out in boils and had to abdicate. He fled to the Fomhoiré and there mustered an army against the Tuatha Dé Danann.

Nuadha was restored to the kingship after the giant leech (physician) DIAN CÉCHT, with the help of the smith CREIDHNE, manufactured and fitted the king with an artificial arm made of silver. Thenceforth he was known as Nuadha Airgedláhm. He then prepared to lead the Tuatha Dé Danann against the Fomhoiré forces mustered by Bres at the Second Battle of Magh Tuiredh.

Shortly before the battle, however, LUGH arrived at the royal palace, and Nuadha abdicated in his favour. Under new leadership the Tuatha Dé Danann made their preparations for the forth-coming battle, which they entered armed with the magical weapons forged for them by the TRÍ DÉ DÁNA and the spells and charms of Lugh, who appeared instantaneously all over the battlefield to encourage and invigorate his men, appearing to them in typical sorcerer's guise with a single leg and a single eye. All those who were killed or wounded were restored to full vitality by Dian Cécht and his three children, who immersed them in a magic cauldron or well.

Sensing defeat, the Fomhoiré demanded that the outcome of the battle be decided in single combat between BALAR and the Tuatha Dé Danann's champion. They put forward Lugh, who stood his ground as the Fomhoiré raised the huge eyelid of the monstrous Balar to expose his single eye, an eye that had the power to kill an entire army at a glance. As the eyelid was opened

Lugh fired his slingshot with such accuracy and force that it smashed straight through Balar's eye and scattered his brains to the four winds as it continued out of the back of his head and decimated the Fomhoiré, the remnants of whom were forced to flee the land.

Bres was taken captive during the battle and pleaded for his life, promising that in return he would ensure four harvests a year and a continual supply of milk from the cows. The Tuatha Dé Danann rejected these offers, although they did spare his life in return for his advice on the best times for ploughing, sowing and reaping.

## Magh Tuiredh, The Battle of
*Irish*

An epic poem that tells the stories of the first and second Battles of MAGH TUIREDH. It is an important source text because it also records the names and attributes of numerous Irish Celtic deities.

## Maglaurus
*British*

The Duke of ALBANY, one of the husbands of REGAN, who was one of the elder daughters of King LEIR, her sister of a comparable age being GONERIL. Together with Regan's other husband, HENWINUS, Duke of CORNWALL, and Regan, he helped Goneril seize what remained of Leir's kingdom after he had given each of these daughters one-quarter as their dowry. Their younger sister CORDELIA, who had nothing to do with the deceit, remained faithful to her father, went to FRANCE and married AGANIPPUS. Maglaurus originally allowed Leir to retain a retinue of 140 men, but Goneril reduced this to eighty. Regan had her turn and reduced it to five, before Goneril finally reduced it to just one man. Leir left for France, where Cordelia and her husband raised an army and restored him to the throne for the last three years of his life.

## Magog
*British*

One of two giants said to be among the earliest inhabitants of BRITAIN[1], although they are usually combined into a single gigantic being known as GOGMAGOG. If the two were originally separate beings, their combination might have been a later Christian attempt to far remove them from the Biblical characters of GOG and Magog (Ezekiel 38, *passim*; Revelation 20:8).

## Maia
*Gaulish*

A little used alternative name for ROSMERTA.

## Maíl Dúin
*Irish*

The central character of the IMMRAM, or voyage tale, IMMRAM CURAIG MAÍLE DÚIN. The story, which possibly dates from the eighth century, although the text is from the tenth century, tells how Maíl Dúin, the son of a nun, set out on a voyage to find the murderer of his father, who was said to have come from the Isle of ARRAN. After a long time he came to a hermit who told him and his travelling companions that, even though they would eventually locate the murderer, they should spare his life as a token of the gratitude they felt to God for sparing them from so many dangers during their long voyage. Eventually, having found and forgiven his father's murderer, Maíl Dúin and his companions were guided by a falcon back to their home.

The many islands visited by Maíl Dúin

and his companions may be found under the heading ISLANDS OF MAÍL DÚIN.

## Maíl Fothartaig
*Irish*

The handsome son of RÓNÁN, whose step-mother fell in love with him and attempted to seduce him. He repulsed her advances, so she accused him of rape. At first Rónán refused to believe that his son could be possible of such an act, but finally, convinced of Maíl Fothartaig's guilt, he had the boy killed.

## Maine
*Irish*

A son of AILILL who fought, and was killed by, CÚ CHULAINN during the hunt for the DONN CUAILNGÈ.

## Mair
*Irish*

The wife of BERSA. She fell in love with FIONN MAC CUMHAILL and sent him nine enchanted nuts that, if he had eaten them, would have caused him to fall for her. Instead, he simply buried the nuts.

## Malmesbury, William of
*British*

An English chronicler (c.1090–c.1143) who became a monk in the monastery at Malmesbury and, in due course, became librarian and precentor. He took part in the council at WINCHESTER in 1141 against King Stephen. His *Gesta Regum Anglorum* provides a lively history of the kings of England from the SAXON invasion until 1126, and the *Historia Novella* brings down the narrative to 1142. His *Gesta Pontificum* is an ecclesiastical history of the bishops and chief monasteries of England to 1123. Other works are an account of the church at GLASTONBURY and lives of St Dunstan and St Wulfstan.

## Man, Isle of
*Irish and British*

A large island in the Irish Sea with a long Celtic history. Irish legend says that it was the island to which some of the FOMHOIRÉ were exiled after their defeat by the people of PARTHOLÁN, other exiles going to the Hebrides. Later tradition made it the home of MANANNÁN MAC LIR. CORMAC MAC CUILENNÁIN (*fl.*900) attempted to establish MANANNÁN MAC LIR as an historical person by declaring him a magnificent navigator and merchant who hailed from the island, and by saying that it was these skills that led both the Irish and British to regard him as a god. The island has, in more recent times, been linked with AVALON.

## Man-a, -u
*Irish*

The Irish name for the Isle of MAN, the equivalent of the Welsh MANAW.

## Manannán mac Lir
*Irish*

The son of LIR, god of the sea, who lived in TÍR NA NOC or TÍR TAIRNGIRI, both OTHERWORLDLY realms, although the Isle of MAN has also been named as his home. He is also associated with the paradisal EMHAIN ABHLACH, 'Emhain of the Apple Trees', a realm that is usually identified with the Isle of ARRAN. He is said to have raised LUGH in the Otherworld when he acted as that god's foster father. In WALES he became known as MANAWYDAN FAB LLYR, while later tradition has also connected him with the shadowy character of BARINTHUS. The Welsh connection between Manannán mac Lir

and Manawydan fab Llyr has always been a tenuous one, although the medieval chronicler CORMAC MAC CUILENNÁIN attempted to reconcile the connection by declaring that Manannán mac Lir was an historical navigator and merchant who traded on both sides of the Irish Sea, leading to his being regarded as a god by both Irish and Welsh. Manannán mac Lir is a primal god of the depths of the ocean, with associations with stellar navigation. He was clearly an important deity, because IRELAND had a long tradition of having been invaded from the sea. He remains the only Irish sea deity about whom much is recorded. There was another, named TETHRA, who fought on the side of the FOMHOIRÉ, but little more is known about him.

Manannán mac Lir is usually depicted dressed in a green cloak fastened with a sliver brooch, a satin shirt, a gold fillet and wearing golden sandals. He has the ability to adopt various forms and to calm the waters or to whip them into a frenzy. On one occasion, when BRÂN[1] set out for TIR INNA MBAN, he was encountered driving his chariot across the waters, which he had turned into a beautiful flowery plain. Singing a wondrous song, Manannán mac Lir was accompanied by salmon that appeared as calves and lambs, the waves as flowering shrubs and the seaweed as fruit trees. Once Manannán mac Lir had passed, the sea returned to its normal state.

In his attempt to lure CORMAC MAC AIRT to his real in order to reward that king, Manannán mac Lir assumed the guise of a warrior and appeared to the king on the ramparts of TARA at dawn. He told Cormac mac Airt that he came from a kingdom where decay, old age, death and falsehood were unknown, and, in exchange for the promise of three wishes, gave the king a branch that held three golden apples, which would heal when shaken. A year later, as had been agreed, Manannán mac Lir returned to claim his three wishes and made off with Cormac mac Airt's wife and children. The king set off in hot pursuit, but was enveloped in a thick mist. This cleared to reveal a beautiful plain in the middle of which stood a wondrous palace. Entering, the king and his company were entertained by a warrior and a beautiful maiden, whom he told of his quest. Lulled to sleep by the singing of the warrior, Cormac mac Airt awoke the following morning to find himself beside his wife and children. The warrior then revealed himself as Manannán mac Lir, and he presented the king with a beautiful golden cup. Intending to set off for Tara the following day, Cormac mac Airt, his wife and children awoke to find themselves on the grass outside their home, the cup and bough of golden apples beside them.

Manannán mac Lir used his shape-changing ability for a number of purposes. Some believed that he used this skill to control reincarnation. He also fathered mortal children, who thus became his personifications, and one such occasion was the fathering of a son on the wife of FIACHNA LURGAN, King of DÁL NARAIDI. Manannán mac Lir came to Fiachna Lurgan's queen in the guise of a nobleman and forced her to lie with him saying that if she did not her husband would die the very next day. The following morning she awoke to find the nobleman had gone, leaving only a poem behind by which she identified him as Manannán mac Lir. Later the same day he was seen on the battlefield in ALBA where he overcame all the SAXON forces and thus enabled Fiachna Lurgan and AEDÁN MAC GABRÁIN to win an outstanding victory.

When Fiachna Lurgan returned home, the queen told him all that had happened. Three days after her child MONGÁN had been born, Manannán mac Lir came and took him to Tír Tairngiri, where the boy remained until he was either twelve or sixteen when he was returned. The taking of the boy to an Otherworldly realm, and the boy's subsequent rebirth, is just one example of Manannán mac Lir's associations with reincarnation, an attribute he shares with MIDHIR.

## Manaw
*Welsh*

The Welsh name for the Isle of MAN, the equivalent of the Irish MANA.

## Manawydan (fab Llyr)
*Welsh*

A Welsh sea god, the son of LLYR, as his epithet shows, and perhaps the Welsh aspect of the Irish MANANNÁN MAC LIR. The MABINOGION makes him the brother and heir of BENDIGEID VRAN and a cousin of PRYDERI.

Following the destructive expedition led by Bendigeid Vran to IRELAND, PRYDERI found that his cousin Manawydan fab Llyr had been disinherited by CASWALLAWN, son of BELI. Pryderi compensated for the loss by giving Manawydan fab Llyr his mother RHIANNON to be his wife together with the seven *cantrefs* of DYFED.

The most famous story concerning Manawydan fab Llyr is that of the curse of LLWYD FAB CIL COED. One night, as Pryderi, Manawydan fab Llyr and their wives were feasting, they heard a loud clap of thunder. This was followed by a dark cloud from which there emanated a brilliant light that enveloped them all. When the light disappeared they found all their men, houses and beasts had disappeared, leaving only the four of them alone in the entire realm. For two years they lived quite happily, hunting the game that freely roamed the forests and catching the fish that filled the streams and rivers. At length, growing tired of their solitary life, Pryderi and Manawydan fab Llyr decided to go from town to town to earn a living.

A short time later, while they were out hunting in the forest, their dogs disappeared into a CAER. Against Manawydan fab Llyr's advice, Pryderi entered to bring them out, but he could not leave because he was bound fast by an enchantment. Manawydan fab Llyr waited until dusk for his cousin to reappear before returning to Rhiannon. She immediately went to the caer and seeing a door in it, a door that remained invisible to Manawydan fab Llyr, she too entered the caer and was trapped. That night the caer vanished, taking Rhiannon and Pryderi with it.

When CIGFA, Pryderi's wife, realized that they had been left alone, Manawydan fab Llyr promised to provide for her and, having neither dogs to hunt nor any other means of support, set himself up as a cobbler. So skilful was he that they soon prospered and were, within a year, able to return to establish three crofts. These Manawydan fab Llyr sowed with wheat. When the time came to reap the first he found that the entire crop had been eaten. The same happened when the second ripened, so he kept a watch on the third. As it ripened he saw a host of mice appear and start to devour every last ear. He caught one of the mice and took it home, vowing that he would solemnly hang it the following day for theft. Cigfa tried to dissuade him from carrying out such a ridiculous punishment, but Manawydan fab Llyr insisted.

The next day, as he was preparing the tiny gallows, a poor clerk came by, then a richly dressed priest and finally a bishop with all his retinue, the first people either Manawydan fab Llyr or Cigfa had seen in over a year. Each offered Manawydan fab Llyr a purse of money to save the life of the mouse. All their offers were refused, but the bishop raised his offer, saying that, in return for the life of the mouse, he would grant Manawydan fab Llyr whatever he wished. Manawydan fab Llyr demanded the return of Pryderi and Rhiannon and that the spell over their land be lifted. The bishop agreed, adding that the mouse was his wife and that he was Llwyd fab Cil Coed who had cast the spell to avenge PWYLL's treatment of his friend GWAWL FAB CLUD. The spell was immediately lifted the moment Manawydan fab Llyr handed the mouse to the bishop. Pryderi and Rhiannon reappeared and the lands of Dyfed were restored to their former prosperous state.

## Manés
*Irish*

The collective name for the seven sons of AILILL and MEDHBHA.

## Manogan
*Welsh*

The father of BELI.

## Mantell
*Welsh*

A robe that numbered among the THIRTEEN TREASURES of BRITAIN[1] and that had the ability to keep the wearer warm, no matter how severe the weather. Some sources say that, rather than keeping the wearer warm, the robe would render that person invisible. It was also known as GWENN[1].

## Maol
*Irish*

One of the FOMHOIRÉ. He and his companion, MULLOGUE, were sent by BALAR to the mainland from TORY Island every time one of Balar's tenants married to demand the right to spend the first night with the bride. On one such occasion GOIBHNIU was at the wedding feast, and he killed both Maol and Mullogue to put a stop to the evil custom.

## Maon
*Irish*

The son of AILILL. Maon was made to eat a portion of his father's and his grandfather's hearts, along with a mouse and all her young, by his uncle COVAC after Covac had killed Ailill. The disgust Maon felt struck him dumb. Maon travelled to MUNSTER and stayed for a while with SCORIATH, whose daughter MORIATH fell in love with him, before going to GAUL. CRAFTINY, the FILI to Scoriath, followed him at the behest of Moriath and serenaded him so wondrously that his voice returned.

Maon now gathered together an army and returned to IRELAND, where he killed Covac and all his retinue save one DRUID who questioned one of the Gauls as to the identity of their leader, for he had begun to suspect that this was Maon returned. The Gaul replied that their leader was the mariner ('Loingsech'). Now the Druid asked if he could speak. The Gaul replied that he could ('Labraidh'). From that day forth Maon became known as LABRAIDH LOINGSECH, and he married Moriath, whose love had restored his voice.

## Mapon-os, -us
*Gaulish and British*

The divine youth. An early Celtic deity, the son of MATRONA, he later became known as MABON the son of MODRON. In northern BRITAIN[1] he was especially revered as a hunter.

## Marcán
*Irish*

'Little Mark', the ageing husband of the young and beautiful CRÉD. He entertained CANO during his exile from SCOTLAND.

## Marganus
*British*

One of the nephews of CORDELIA, the other being CUNEDAGIUS. Following the death of LEIR, Cordelia reigned in peace for five years. However, her nephews, having by that time inherited their fathers' kingdoms, resented female rule, so rose up against her and took her prisoner. Cordelia took her own life. Marganus and his brother divided the kingdom between them, but the peace lasted only two years before Marganus tried to overturn his brother. His attempt was unsuccessful, because he was killed by his brother who went on to rule for thirty-three years as the sole monarch.

## Mari-Morgan(s)
*Gaulish*

A class of water-fairy of Breton origin. It has been suggested that they gave rise to Morgan Le Fay, because they are sometimes simply referred to as MORGANS. One in particular is of interest. Called either AHES or DAHUT, this fairy was held responsible for the destruction of the legendary city of YS.

## Marius
*British*

An early king of BRITAIN[1] who was, according to GEOFFREY OF MONMOUTH, the son of ARVIRAGUS. He soundly defeated the PICTS but bestowed Caithness on them under a treaty that confined them to that area.

## Mart(in)es
*Gaulish*

A peculiarly Breton class of fairy, akin to the MARI-MORGANS. Martes, or Martines, were huge women with masses of brown hair and huge breasts, who would rush after passers-by so that they could suckle them.

## Math (fab Mathonwy)
*Welsh*

The lord of GWYNEDD and the magical son of MATHONWY. GWYDION FAB DÔN brought to his attention the herd of magic swine owned by PRYDERI to his attention and sought his permission to bring them back for him. Math fab Mathonwy agreed, and Gwydion fab Dôn set off, returning with the swine, originally the property of ARAWN, which he had magically acquired. Two days later the enchantment wrought by Gwydion fab Dôn wore off, and Pryderi marched against Math fab Mathonwy, who mustered his army and went out to meet the attack.

This was exactly what Gwydion fab Dôn wanted, for he had caused the quarrel between Pryderi and his master solely for the purpose of getting Math fab Mathonwy out of the way, his intention being to help his brother, GILFAETHWY, ravish the maiden GOEWIN, who held the post of footholder. Gwydion fab Dôn and Gilfaethwy abducted Goewin and took turns in raping her.

The battle between Math fab Mathonwy and Pryderi was at stalemate, so it was agreed that Gwydion fab Dôn, who had caused the argument in the first place, should meet Pryderi in single combat. He did, and at MAEN TYRIAWG quickly overcame and killed Pryderi by using his magical powers. Returning triumphant to the court of Math fab Mathonwy, Gwydion fab Dôn and his brother were punished for their rape of Goewin. Math fab Mathonwy decreed that the two should spend the next three years as male and female animals, each year producing at least one offspring. The first year they spent as deer, the second as swine and the third as wolves. At the end of the third year Math fab Mathonwy restored the brothers to their human form and forgave them their crime.

The post of footholder had remained unfilled since Goewin had been raped, so Gwydion fab Dôn put forward his own sister, ARIANRHOD, for the position. She claimed to be a virgin, a necessary qualification for the post, but proved to be pregnant for she gave birth to two boys, DYLAN EIL TON and LLEU LLAW GYFFES, during the test to prove her virginity. Gwydion fab Dôn adopted Lleu Llaw Gyffes and overcame the first two curses placed on the boy by Arianrhod. Math fab Mathonwy helped him to overcome the third by helping Gwydion fab Dôn to create the flower maiden BLODEUWEDD out of the flowers of oak, broom and meadowsweet to become Lleu Llaw Gyffes' wife.

## Math Hên
*Welsh*

'The Ancient', an old Welsh high god who is remembered as the magician who taught his arts to the young GWYDION FAB DÔN. The winds were said to be under his command and would bring him the least whisper wherever it might be held. He showed unrivalled compassion to the suffering, and would hand down justice without vengeance.

## Mathgen
*Irish*

A wizard. One of the TUATHA DÉ DANANN during the Second Battle of

MAGH TUIREDH, he caused the mountains to crash down upon the FOMHOIRÉ.

## Mathol-wch, -och
*Welsh*

A King of IRELAND to whom BENDIGEID VRAN, in an attempt to cement good relations between the two countries, married his sister BRANWEN. At the wedding feast however Matholwch was so insulted by EFNISIEN, half-brother to Bendigeid Vran, that he returned to Ireland, along with the magic cauldron given to him as a wedding present by Bendigeid Vran, and took his revenge on Branwen by treating her cruelly.

Bendigeid Vran learned of the mistreatment of his sister and mounted an expedition to Ireland to save her. At first Matholwch's forces had the upper hand, thanks to the cauldron Bendigeid Vran had given him, for the dead and wounded of the Irish forces could be restored to full vitality simply by dipping them in it. However, the tide turned when Efnisien managed to destroy the cauldron. So complete was the destruction that Matholwch and his entire race were wiped out, except for five pregnant women who hid in a cave and subsequently gave birth to five boys whom they later married and set about repopulating Ireland.

The Welsh forces fared little better, for only seven of the expedition survived, Bendigeid Vran himself suffering a mortal wound. The seven survivors, named as PRYDERI, MANAWYDAN, GLIFIEU, TALIESIN, YNAWAG, GRUDDIEU and HEILYN, carried the severed head of Bendigeid Vran back to BRITAIN[1] and, after a somewhat delayed journey, buried it under the WHITE MOUNT in LONDON. Branwen, the cause of the expedition, was brought back to WALES, but died of a broken heart when she sat down to contemplate the destruction brought about on her behalf.

## Mathonwy
*Welsh*

The father of the magician MATH FAB MATHONWY. More than this remains unclear, as his role was never developed further.

## Matres
*Gaulish*

A triad of goddesses who are better known as the MOTHERS.

## Matrona
*Gaulish*

The divine mother and goddess of the River Marne, near the source of which she had her main sanctuary. Some sources say that she was the mother of the god MAPONOS. Welsh tradition names her MODRON and her son MABON.

## Maxim(ian)us
*British*

A Roman emperor who was known in Welsh tradition as MACSEN WLEDIG. Called Maximianus by GEOFFREY OF MONMOUTH, he was said by this writer to have made CONAN MERIADOC the ruler of BRITTANY. Welsh tradition says that he married ELEN, the daughter of EUDAF, and decided to stay in BRITAIN[1]. Seven years later he received word from Rome that he had been replaced as emperor. With the help of CYNAN and GADEON, his brothers-in-law, he took Rome and was restored as emperor.

## Mazoe
*Welsh*

One of the nine sisters of MORGEN.

## Meabel
*Irish*

'Disgrace', one of the three names given to the wife of the DAGHDHA. Her other names were BRENG and MENG.

## Meath
*Irish*

One of the five original provinces of IRELAND that were established by the FIR BHOLG. Today Meath is no longer a province, but rather a county within the province of LEINSTER.

## Medar
*Irish*

One of the many brothers of the DAGHDHA. He appears only in passing references.

## Med(h)bh(a)
*Irish*

The Queen of CONNACHT and, along with her consort AILILL, the enemy of CON-CHOBAR MAC NESSA. Her name means 'intoxication', and she appears originally to have been a personification of the SPIRIT OF IRELAND, the goddess whom any king must ritually marry before his office is recognized. She was said to have been the wife of nine Irish kings and that only her mate could be called the true King of IRELAND. In the *Fledd Bricrenn*, Medhbha awarded the title of champion of all Ireland to the hero CÚ CHULAINN rather than to CONALL CERNACH LOEGHAIRE BUADHACH.

Medhbha is possibly most famous for her desire to own the fabulous DONN CUAILNGÈ, the story of her quest being told in the *Taín Bó Cuailngè*. Because the bull was owned by a man of ULSTER, the county that was her traditional enemy, Medhbha had to go to war with that county in order to achieve her desire. At that time, however, the men of Ulster had been cursed by MACHA and were unfit for battle. The only Ulster warrior not afflicted was Cú Chulainn, still only a youth, and he held off the forces of Medhbha and Ailill with ruthless efficiency, although he was eventually killed and the Donn Cuailngè taken to Medhbha where it did battle with FINNBHENNACH, the bull owned by Ailill, which it totally annihilated.

## Medyr
*Welsh*

One of the less often mentioned members of the party formed to help CULHWCH. Medyr was chosen for his speed. It was said that in a single blink of an eye he could travel from CORNWALL TO IRELAND and be back again before an onlooker had the chance to blink again.

## Meiche
*Irish*

The son of the MÓRRÍGHAN. He was killed by DIAN CÉCHT, and when his body was cut open Dian Cécht discovered three hearts, one for each aspect of his mother, each heart being a vile serpent's head. Two of these were burnt, but the third escaped and grew into a huge serpent, which threatened the entire country. Dian Cécht later killed this serpent.

## Meldos
*Welsh*

Originally a Celtic god and possibly the father of MABON.

## Meldred
*Welsh*

A king who had the infidelities of his wife revealed to him by LAILOKEN.

## Melkin
*British*

A vaticinator (prophet) mentioned by John of Glastonbury, who says that he lived before MYRDDIN and uttered prophecies about GLASTONBURY so couched in obscure Latin phraseology that they are difficult to interpret. It has been suggested that they may refer to Glastonbury as a place of pagan burial and to the future discovery of the tomb of JOSEPH OF ARIMATHEA. Melkin may possibly be identifiable with MAELGWYN, a sixth-century ruler of GWYNEDD, although this seems tenuous. John Leland (c.1503–52), royal antiquary to King Henry VIII, claimed to have seen Melkin's book at Glastonbury Abbey.

## Meng
*Irish*

'Guile', one of the three names by which the wife of the DAGHDHA was known. Her other names were BRENG and MEABEL.

## Menw fab Teirgwaedd
*Welsh*

The son of TEIRGWAEDD and one of the party chosen to help CULHWCH locate the maiden OLWEN. Each member of the party was chosen for their particular skills, and Menw fab Teirgwaedd was chosen for his mastery of magic, which would preserve the party in foreign and heathen lands because he could render them invisible. The other members of the party were CEI, BEDWYR[2], GWALCHMAI FAB GWYAR, CYNDDYLIG and GWRHYR.

## Mercia
*British*

An ANGLO-SAXON kingdom that emerged in the sixth century and that, by the late eighth century, dominated all ENGLAND south of the River Humber. From c.825 Mercia came under the power of WESSEX. Mercia eventually came to denote an area bounded by the Welsh border, the River Humber, East Anglia and the River Thames.

## 'Mercury'
*Gaulish*

The name given by JULIUS CAESAR to the chief Gaulish deity, the inverted commas being used to distinguish the Celtic god from the Roman god of the same name. 'Mercury' was a war god, credited with the invention of all the art forms and honoured as the patron of commerce and travel. His consort is named as ROSMERTA. The evidence in Gaulish place-names and his similarity to the Irish god LUGH makes it almost a certainty that 'Mercury' was more commonly known as LUG or LUGUS.

## Merlin
*Welsh*

The most famous wizard of all times. He was ARTHUR's counsellor, who guided the young king at the start of his reign, although later the king did not always follow the advice given to him. We know Merlin by that name simply because the latinized form of his Welsh name, MYRDDIN, would be *Merdinus*, and that would unfortunately have connected it with the Latin word *merdus*, 'dung'. Merlin is not a personal name, but rather a place-name, the Welsh form of his name originating in the Celtic Maridunon, CARMARTHEN, Welsh Caerfyrddin. It seems that the wizard was so called because he originated from that city. At least, GEOFFREY OF MONMOUTH seems to think so, and other sources agree in principle, although saying that the city was founded by him and therefore named after him.

His career within the Arthurian cycle is a relatively late invention, for Myrddin was active in WALES long before he was incorporated into the Arthurian cycle.

## Merlin's Hill
*Welsh*

A hill, 3 miles east of CARMARTHEN, at the summit of which there is a rock resembling a chair. Legend says that this was where MYRDDIN sat to deliver his various prophecies. It is also the alleged site of the cave in which Myrddin was buried, but this cave has yet to be found.

## Merlin's Precinct
*Welsh*

An early name for BRITAIN[1], which appears in the Welsh *Trioedd Ynys Prydein* and has been taken by some to indicate that MYRDDIN was, in origin, a deity with territorial rights.

## Merlin's Tree
*Welsh*

Also called the PRIORY OAK, this tree in CARMARTHEN was believed to maintain the good fortune of Carmarthen, for it was believed that if it fell so would the city. The tree was removed by the Local Authority in 1978 because it constituted a traffic hazard, and, to date, MYRDDIN's prophecy of the destruction of Carmarthen has not been fulfilled.

## Mesca
*Irish*

The daughter of BODB who was abducted by GARMAN but died of shame at having allowed herself to be loved by a mere mortal.

## Mesge-dra, -gra
*Irish*

A king of LEINSTER. He was killed by CONALL CERNACH, who mashed the dead king's brain and mixed the remains with lime to make a sling-ball. This was one of the treasures of CONCHOBAR MAC NESSA at EMHAIN MHACHA from where it was stolen by CET. Cet later fired the sling-ball at Conchobar mac Nessa with such force that it lodged in his forehead. Conchobar mac Nessa's physician FINGEN told him that it could not be removed as he would die if it was, but added that, provided he did not become agitated, there was no reason why he could not lead a relatively normal life. Sometime later, when he was unable to quell his emotions, the sling-ball burst from his head and Conchobar mac Nessa died.

## Mesroda
*Irish*

The son of DÁ THÓ. He is best known simply as MAC DÁ THÓ.

## Mess Buachalla
*Irish*

The daughter of EOCHAIDH AIREMH by his own daughter, who is named as either ÉDAIN or ESS, the latter probably being introduced to save confusion between the two ÉDÁINS. Mess Buachalla married ETERSCEL and became the mother of CONAIRE MÓR, although other sources say that Conaire Mór was the son born of an incestuous relationship between Eochaidh Airemh and his daughter.

A later story says that Mess Buachalla was the daughter of Ess and Eterscel and was fostered by a cowherd of Eterscel's. She was visited by a curious bird man, NEMGLAN, King of the Birds, to whom she gave herself freely. He told her that she would bear a son, to name him Conaire Mór and to say that he was the natural son of Eterscel, whom Mess Buachalla later incestuously married.

## Meuric
*Welsh*

The son of CARADOC VREICHVRAS.

## Meurig
*Welsh*

A king of GLENVISSIG, whose son, ARTHRWYS, has been identified with ARTHUR.

## Midac
*Irish*

The son of the King of LOCHLANN. After his father had been killed by the FIAN, Midac sought revenge by inviting FIONN MAC CUMHAILL and his men to a feast. After they had arrived, Midac left the palace. Four of the fian had remained outside on guard, which was just as well, for Midac now led an army against the fian, whom he had magically adhered to their chairs. The four guards fought the army and at length repulsed it, before entering the palace to release their comrades using the blood of three kings. Unfortunately for one, CONAN MAC MORNA, the blood ran out before they came to him, whereupon DIARMAID UA DUIBHNE took a firm hold of him and wrenched him out of the chair, leaving a large section of his skin behind.

## Midach
*Irish*

A son of DIAN CÉCHT and brother of AIRMED. Like his father, he was an impressive physician, so good, in fact, that his father struck him four times. The first

three times, Midach managed to heal his wounds, but the fourth occasion the winds were fatal. From his grave a vast array of herbs grew, all of which had medicinal properties. These herbs were gathered together and sorted by his sister Airmed, but Dian Cécht muddled them up as he feared the power of his son even from beyond the grave.

## Midhir
*Irish*

A god of TÍR TAIRNGIRI. Although Midhir lived in the SÍDH of BRÍ LEITH, he was, like MANANNÁN MAC LIR, associated with rebirth. He took as his first wife FUAMHNACH, but later became besotted with ÉDÁIN ECHRAIDHE, the daughter of King AILILL. Her hand was sought on his behalf by OENGHUS MAC IN ÓG, his foster son. She consented to the union and they were married.

Theirs, was not to be a happy marriage, however, for Fuamhnach, who clearly regarded Midhir as her sole property, was extremely jealous of Midhir's new wife. She used magic to turn Édain Echraidhe into a pool of water. That turned into a worm, which in turn, became a huge and beautiful fly whose perfume and music filled the air. Fuamhnach need not have thought that this would be the end of Édain Echraidhe, for Midhir was quite content to have his new wife around him, even in this strange form. Driven to despair by her jealousy, Fuamhnach conjured up a huge gust of wind, which blew the beautiful fly far away, so that it fell on a rocky coastline. There Édain Echraidhe lay helpless for seven years until she was discovered by Oenghus Mac in Og, who placed her in a crystal bower and brought her back to Midhir. Fuamhnach once again magically created a huge gust of wind, which this time blew the fly into a glass of wine, which was swallowed. The woman who swallowed the fly became pregnant, and, 1,012 years after she had been first born, Édain Echraidhe was reborn, this time being simply known as ÉDAIN, the grand-daughter of ÉTAR.

As Édain reached maturity, EOCHAIDH AIREMH became the King of IRELAND. However, none would pay him due respect as he was unmarried, so he sent out messengers to search out the most beautiful woman in Ireland. Eventually Édain was chosen and became his wife. News of the marriage and of Édain's beauty reached Midhir, who set out to TARA to reclaim her, but she would not leave her husband without his express permission. Midhir thus challenged Eochaidh Airemh to a chess contest, but he let the king easily win the opening game and accepted the forfeit of building a great causeway across the bogs of MEATH.

Midhir then returned to Tara and duly won the final game, claiming as his boon a kiss from Édain. A month later Midhir came to Tara to claim his prize, but found all the doors barred to him, for Eochaidh Airemh had no intention of giving up his beautiful wife. As the king sat feasting with his company, Midhir appeared among them, seized Édain and together the pair flew out of the smoke hole of the great hall as a pair of white swans.

Eochaidh Airemh and his company pursued them to the sídh of Brí Leith and began to dig it up. Midhir appeared to the king and promised to return Édain to him, whereupon he produced fifty identical women, all of whom were the exact likeness of Édain. Even though Eochaidh Airemh chose carefully, he actually chose his own daughter, and realized the mistake only much later, after she had born him a son, CONAIRE MÓR.

The game of chess played between Midhir and Eochaidh Airemh is of special significance, for the playing of board games in Celtic mythology always signifies the interplay of great forces. It is at once both a magical and a cosmological game, which was to have later parallels in the interaction of the forces of good and evil, right and wrong.

## Míl(e)
*Irish*

The son or grandson of BREGON and the forefather of the first human rulers of IRELAND who were known as the Sons of MÍL ÉSPÁINE, or the Sons of Míl of Spain. His brother ITH led the first expedition to Ireland, but was killed by the TUATHA DÉ DANANN. After the body of Ith had been brought back to Spain, Míl organized the second expedition under the leadership of DÔNN[1], EBER FINN and AMHAIRGHIN, and, although he did not accompany them, himself, his son EREMON was among the invaders.

## Míl Éspáine, Sons of
*Irish*

'The Sons of Míl of Spain', the tribal name of the sixth and final force of invaders, who came to IRELAND according to the *Leabhar Gabhála Éireann*. As the name suggests, they were of Spanish origin, the sons or descendants of MÍL, and they landed in Ireland on the feast of BELTANE under the leadership of AMHAIRGHIN, the FILI. They were the first true GAELS to inhabit Ireland.

Having defeated the TUATHA DÉ DANANN army, the invaders set out for TARA. On the way they met the three goddesses BANBHA, FÓDLA and ÉRIU, the wives, respectively, of MAC CUILL, MAC CÉCHT and MAC GRÉINE. The invaders promised each goddess in turn that the land would forever carry her name if she helped them in their cause, but it was only Ériu who countered by saying that Ireland would forever belong to their descendants, although she warned their discourteous king, DÔNN[1], that neither he nor his heirs would enjoy the land. Dônn drowned shortly afterwards and was buried on the island of TECH DUINN, to which he now welcomes dead warriors. The help, advice and promise of Ériu led the Sons of Míl Éspáine to name the land EIRE.

At Tara the three Tuatha Dé Danann kings disputed the right of the invaders to the ownership of the land, and they asked Amhairghin to judge each claim. He ruled that the invaders should put out to sea again beyong a magical boundary referred to as the ninth wave. This they did, but as they turned and tried to return to land the Tuatha Dé Danann conjured up a great wind to hold them off shore. Amhairghin called upon the SPIRIT OF IRELAND for help, and the wind duly dropped. The invaders once more landed, and again defeated a Tuatha Dé Danann army at the Battle of TAILTIU.

Although they had lost the right to rule, the Tuatha Dé Danann were determined not to be exiled from the land that had been theirs, and so they used their magic to deprive the Sons of Míl Éspáine of milk and corn. At length the invaders agreed to divide the land between them, the Tuatha Dé Danann receiving the underground half, and their leader, the DAGHDHA, built a SÍDH for each of the Tuatha Dé Danann chiefs and kings.

The new rulers of Ireland now faced their first problem. They had two leaders, EBER FINN and EREMON, both of whom claimed the right to be sole monarch. To settle the dispute, Eber Finn took the southern half of the country, and Eremon the northern. A short time later, the two kingdoms went to war, Eber Finn was killed and Eremon became the first human king of all Ireland.

## Miled
*Irish*
See MÍL(E).

## Milesians
*Irish*

An alternative way of referring to the Sons of MÍL ÉSPÁINE.

## Miluc(h)ra(dh)
*Irish*

A daughter of CULANN, smith to the TUATHA DÉ DANANN, and sister of AINÉ[3]. Both sisters fell in love with FIONN MAC CUMHAILL, but Aine said that she could never marry a man with grey hair. On hearing this, Miluchradh contrived to turn Fionn mac Cumhaill's hair grey, which assured her that Ainé would have nothing more to do with him. It did her little good though, for Fionn mac Cumhaill found out who had turned his hair grey, and afterwards would have nothing to do with Miluchradh.

## 'Minerva'
*Gaulish*

An important Celtic goddess who was so called by JULIUS CAESAR, the inverted commas being used to distinguish her from the Roman goddess of the same name. It seems most likely that this goddess was none other than BRIGHID or BRIGANTIA.

## Minocan
*British*

The name given by NENNIUS[1] to the father of BELINUS.

## Miodhchaoin
*Irish*

The warrior friend of CIAN. He was under a bond never to allow anyone to shout from the summit of the hill he lived on. When the three sons of TUIRENN came to the hill as the last of the tasks set them by LUGH as a fine for their murder of Cian, they had to fight Miodhchaon, who would not allow them to complete their task. Miodhchaon was killed, but not until he had left each of the three sons of Tuirenn barely alive. They gave three feeble shouts from the top of the hill and so paid their fine to Lugh. When they beseeched Lugh to heal them, however, he refused, and they died on the hill.

## Mná sídh
*Irish*

A collective term, meaning 'women of the sídh', used to refer to goddesses. It was used to refer to any number of goddesses when they were being talked about generally rather than individually.

## Mocc-os, -us
*Gaulish*

The boar god; the deification of the pig as a totem animal. The word Moccos itself simply means 'pig'.

## Mochaen
*Irish*
See MIODHCHAOIN.

## Mod
*Irish*

A compatriot of MANANNÁN MAC LIR. He joined in the hunt for a massive boar that was laying waste vast tracts of IRELAND. They chased the boar across to MUIC INIS where their hounds cornered and killed the boar, although not until after Mod had been mortally gored.

## Modron
*Welsh*

The divine mother, whose name simply means 'mother'. Her divine child was the god MABON, a name that, in turn, simply means 'son'. Her name appears to be a form of the Gaulish MATRONA.

## Modrwy Eluned
*Welsh*

The ring of ELUNED, one of the THIRTEEN TREASURES of BRITAIN[1], which made the wearer invisible.

## Mofebis
*Irish*

The father of LOCH and a vassal of MEDHBHA and AILILL.

## Mog Ruith
*Irish*

A DRUID who appears in a legend that says he once dressed in a bird costume, which he wore over an inner garment made from bull's hide. Then, in a trance, he rose into the air and abruptly vanished. See also ROTH FÁIL.

## Molmutius
*British*

The son of CLOTEN whose kingdom, CORNWALL, he inherited and immediately set about enlarging. The rest of ENGLAND was, at that time, ruled by a king named PINNER. Molmutius defeated his army, and Pinner fell in battle. He then defeated the combined forces of RUDAUCUS, King of CAMBRIA, and STATER, King of ALBANY, so that he reigned supreme, the twenty-first in line from BRUTUS. Molmutius reigned for forty years and during that time formulated the Molmutine Laws, which laid down a code of ethics that has survived, in some extent, to the present day. Molmutius was allegedly buried on the WHITE MOUNT in LONDON where BENDIGEID VRAN's head had previously been buried, as had Brutus himself. He left two sons, BELINUS and BRENNIUS, both of whom laid claim to his throne, thus once again throwing BRITAIN[1] into turmoil.

## Mona
*Romano-Celtic*

The Ancient name for the Isle of ANGLESEY.

## Mongán
*Irish*

The son of FIACHNA LURGAN, although in truth the son of MANANNÁN MAC LIR, for Mongán was conceived when Manannán mac Lir appeared to Fiachna Lurgan's queen while her husband was in SCOTLAND and told her that unless she bore him a son her husband would die the very next day. She consented, for she had no other choice, and the next day the stranger had disappeared, only to reappear on the battlefield in Scotland, where he helped Fiachna Lurgan and AEDÁN MAC GABRÁIN win a great victory over the SAXONS. Three days after Mongán was born Manannán mac Lir came and took the child away to TÍR TAIRNGIRI, where he remained until he was either twelve or sixteen.

Mongán later used his magical skills to win back his wife, who had been abducted by a King of LEINSTER. He took the guise of AED[1], the son of the King of CONNACHT, and transformed a hag into the form of IBHELL, Aed's beautiful young wife. The King of Leinster fell in love with the pretend Ibhell, so Mongán agreed to exchange her for his own wife, although, of course, the King of Leinster did not find out about the trick until after Mongán and his wife were far away.

The historicity of Mongán is unquestionable for he ruled at MOYLINNY on Lough NEAGH early in the seventh century, his death being recorded as c.625. This would suggest that the strange tale of his conception and birth is possibly post-Christian. A contemporary legend says that Mongán was the reincarnation of FIONN MAC CUMHAILL, for he calls KEELTA back from the OTHERWORLD to settle a wager as to who actually killed FOTHAD. Keelta reveals that he himself had killed Fothad but adds that surely Mongán should have known that for he rode alongside him in his former life.

## Moonremur
*Irish*

A warrior of ULSTER who tentively challenged CET for the right to carve the boar of MAC DÁ THO, but was derided and quickly withdrew his challenge.

## Mor
*Welsh*

1 According to tradition, the great-grandfather of MYRDDIN.
2 An alternative, although little used, name for DYLAN EIL TON.

## Morann
*Irish*

A DRUID at the court of CONCHOBAR MAC NESSA who prophesied the arrival of SÉDANTA and the great deeds that that hero, better known as CÚ CHULAINN, would do.

## Morc
*Irish*

The co-ruler of the FOMHIORÉ, along with CONANN, at the time of the rebellion of the people of NEMHEDH. Conann was killed in the battle, but Morc routed the rebellious people and forced the thirty survivors into exile.

## Mord-a, -u
*Welsh*

The blind man placed by CERRIDWEN to kindle the fire under the cauldron stirred by GWION BACH in which she was brewing a magical potion. When Gwion Bach ran away after imbibing the potency of the brew, Cerridwen at first blamed Morda and beat him so hard over the head with a billet of wood that one eye fell out onto his cheek. When Morda protested his innocence, Cerridwen stopped and saw that he was telling the truth, for it had been Gwion Bach who had spoiled her work.

## Morfessa
*Irish*

A wizard of the mythical city of FALIA. He was one of the four wizards to teach the TUATHA DÉ DANANN their magical arts prior to their arrival in IRELAND. He is said to have given them the LIA FÁIL or Stone of FÁL. The other three wizards said to have taught the Tuatha Dé Danann were ESIAS from GORIAS, USCIAS from FINDAIS and SIMIAS from MURIAS.

## Morfran (ab Tegid)
*Welsh*
Also MORVRAN AB TEGID

The ugly son of CERRIDWEN and TEGID VOEL who, because of his hideousness, was nicknamed AFAGDDU, a name by which he is more commonly known.

## Morgan(s)
*Gaulish*

A type of Breton water-fairy, more usually known as MARI-MORGANS.

## Morgan Frych
*Welsh*

The father of MYRDDIN according to tradition. He was sometimes identified as MADOG MORFRYN and sometimes said to have been a prince of GWYNEDD.

## Morgan Mwynfawr
*Welsh*

The owner of a magical form of transport, described as either a chair or car, which could carry a person seated in it to wherever they wanted to go. This magical item was known as CADAIR, NEU CAR MORGAN MWYNFAWR, and it numbered among the THIRTEEN TREASURES of BRITAIN[1]. Some commentators have incorrectly sought to identify the ownership of this enchanted mode of travel with Morgan Le Fay.

## Morgen
*Welsh*

A DRUIDIC goddess, patroness of priestesses, who lived on an island usually identified as AVALON with her nine sisters who included MORONOE, MAZOE, GLITEN, GLITONEA, CLITON, TYRONOE and THITIS. There can be little doubt that Morgen is the original of the Arthurian Morgan Le Fay, although she herself seems to have her origins in MODRON, who, in turn, has her origins in MATRONA. One account says that she was an historical person who married URIEN of RHEGED and bore MORFUDD and OWAIN.

GIRALDUS CAMBRENSIS refers to her as a *dea phantastica* ('imaginary goddess'), although earlier sources say that she was the master of the healing arts, could fly on artificial wings and could change her shape. It was once believed that Morgen, and subsequently the Arthurian Morgan Le Fay, originated in the Irish MÓRRÍGHAN, but this has now been almost universally discounted. Her name change may have been effected in BRITTANY, where there was a belief in a class of water-fairies known as MORGANS, or more correctly MARI-MORGANS. They also believed in one particular Morgan, known as DAHUT or AHES, who, it was said, caused the destruction of the legendary city of YS.

With such a diverse origin it is not difficult to see why so many attributes were added to her character when later romancers made her the incestuous sister of King ARTHUR, a magician on a par with MERLIN, but malevolent rather than benevolent.

## Moriath
*Irish*

The daughter of SCORIATH, King of FERAMORC. She fell passionately in love with the youth MAON while he stayed within the royal court, even though he was a mute. Later he left for GAUL, but she found she could not forget him. She sent her father's harper CRAFTINY to Gaul to serenade Maon on her behalf. So beautiful was the music that Maon regained the use of his voice and, after he had returned to IRELAND (by which time he was known as LABRAIDH LOINGSECH) and disposed of his usurping uncle COVAC, he married Moriath.

## Morna
*Irish*

The leader of one of the clans that made up the FIAN, and the father of AODH[2],

who later became known as GOLL MAC MORNA. See also BASCNA.

## Moronoe
*Welsh*

One of the nine sisters of MORGEN.

## Mórríghan
*Irish*
Also BAV

The red-haired goddess of battle and procreation, whose name means 'Phantom Queen', she often appeared in triple form, one of the myriad of triad deities that clutter Celtic and other pagan cultures. Her other aspects were NEMHAIN which means 'Frenzy', and BADHBH, which means 'Crow' or 'Raven'. The Mórríghan combines the energies of life and death, sexuality and conflict in one all powerful and terrifying deity. She had a British counterpart in the goddess ANDRASTE, who was envoked by Queen BOUDICCA during her revolt against the Romans in the first century.

Although essentially a goddess of death, the Mórríghan was also a consummate fertility goddess, who is commemorated in a range of low hills known as the Paps of the Mórríghan. The combination of a goddess of death and one of fertility is illustrated in the story of the DAGHDHA, who met with the Mórríghan shortly before the Second Battle of MAGH TUIREDH. The Daghdha came across the terrible goddess on the eve of the feast of SAMHAIN as she stood astride the River UNIUS washing the bloody corpses and armour of those foredoomed to die in the coming battle. The two had intercourse in this uncomfortable position, such a ritual mating signifying that, although many were to die, many would ultimately be born to take their place.

## Morrigu
*Irish*

A little used variant of the MÓRRÍGHAN.

## Morvran (ab Tegid)
*Welsh*
See MORFRAN (AB TEGID).

## Morydd
*Welsh*

According to a traditional genealogy, the grandfather of MYRDDIN.

## Mother Goddess
*General*

A generic term used to denote the beneficent powers of the earth, which were normally personified in a powerful fertility goddess. The Mother Goddess, sometimes called the Earth Goddess, is common to most pagan cultures, and she was usually developed so that various aspects of her all-powerful nature manifested themselves in many different deities.

## Mothers, The
*Celtic and Teutonic*

A collective name given to goddesses of plenty who were worshipped during the Roman period by both the Celts and Teutonic tribes. The Mothers were usually a triad of goddesses, who represented a triple aspect of the MOTHER GODDESS. In WALES they are commemorated in the *Y Foel Famau*, the 'Hall of the Mothers', one of the Welsh mothers being the ill-fated BRANWEN.

## Moylinny
*Irish*

The capital on Lough Neagh where the historical MONGÁN ruled.

## Moytura
*Irish*

The literal pronunciation of MAGH TUIREDH, the location of the two famous battles of the TUATH DÉ DANANN, although the two battles were actually fought in different locations.

## Mucca Mhanannain
*Irish*

'Pigs of Manannán', the mythical food of the gods. These pigs crop up in a great many of the Irish myths and are described as varying in number from two to many hundreds. No matter how many there are, they always have the same attribute, for killed, cooked and eaten one day, they are alive and willing to go through the same process the next.

## Mughain
*Irish*

A Queen of ULSTER. When she saw the battle-crazed CÚ CHULAINN, who had just defeated the three terrible sons of NECHTA SCÉNE, approaching EMHAIN MHACHA, she led her women out to meet him, all of them stark naked. Overcome with embarrassment, Cú Chulainn averted his eyes and was seized by the king's warriors, who dunked him in three tubs of icy cold water to cool him down. The queen then dressed the hero herself before admitting him to the royal court.

## Mugna
*Irish*

A mythical oak tree upon which three fruits – acorn, apple and nut – grew, each fruit being instantly replaced by a fresh one when it fell. It is possibly a remembrance of a world-tree, similar to the tree Yggdrasil that is found in Norse mythology.

## Muic Inis
*Irish*

'Pig Island', the name given to the island to which MANANNÁN MAC LIR and MOD chased a huge boar where their hounds cornered it. The boar was killed, but not until after it had mortally gored Mod.

## Mu(i)rcheartach
*Irish*

An historical fifth-century Irish king, ruling at TARA, who is thought to have been the origin of the various characters in the Arthurian tales.

## Muirdris
*Irish*

A hideous monster, a sort of river-horse, said to inhabit Loch RURY. One day FERGHUS MAC LEDA came face to face with the monster and was so scared that his face was permanently disfigured. Since no blemished man could reign, his courtiers banished all mirrors from the palace so that Ferghus mac Leda would not find out what had happened and would thus be allowed to remain the monarch. He remained blissfully ignorant of the fact, until one day a maidservant, whom he had slapped for some misdemeanour, retaliated by telling him of his disfigurement. Ferghus mac Leda donned the magic water-shoes he had received as part of his ransom for IUBDAN and BEBO, and went out onto the waters of Loch Rury, where he beheaded the Muirdris before sinking below the waves, never to be seen again.

## Muireartach
*Irish*

A one-eyed, hideous hag whose husband was an ocean god, some say a smith. While she was the foster mother of the King of LOCHLANN she captured from the FIAN the ceremonial cup of victory, a clay vessel whose contents made them victorious. The fian attacked her, killed the King of Lochlann and regained the cup. Muireartach recovered and stormed the fian, killing a great many of them before FIONN MAC CUMHAILL cut out the ground from under her and then cut her to shreds.

## Mu(i)rn-e, -a
*Irish*

The daughter of TADG and thus a grand daughter of NUADHA AIRGEDLÀMH and sister to TUIREANN. Muirne's hand was sought by CUMHAILL, but Tadg refused, where upon Cumhaill abducted her. He was then killed in battle when he refused to return her to her father. Muirne had already conceived by the time Cumhaill was killed, and she called her son DEIMNE. He was raised in isolation and later became better known as FIONN MAC CUMHAILL.

## Mullo
*Gaulish*

The patron god of mules and asses, whose name simply means 'mule'.

## Mullogue
*Irish*

A FOMHOIRÉ warrior who, with his companion MAOL, was sent by BALAR to demand the right to spend the first night with any of the new brides of any of Balar's tenants. On one such occasion GOIBHNIU was at the wedding feast and, horrified by the idea, he killed both Maol and Mullogue and so put an end to the foul custom.

## Mumu
*Irish*

One of the four Irish provinces that are referred to in the *Taín Bó Cuailngè*. The capital of Mumu was in west Kerry, the province itself later becoming better known as MUNSTER.

## Munster
*Irish*

One of the original five provinces of IRELAND that were established by the FIR BHOLG. Munster remained an independent kingdom until the twelfth century. Today, it is still a province occupying the southern part of Ireland and consisting of the counties of Clare, Cork, Kerry, Limerick, North and South Tipperary, and Waterford.

## Murias
*Irish*

A mythical city that was the home of SIMIAS, one of the four wizards said to have taught the TUATHA DÉ DANANN their magic arts before their arrival in IRELAND. Murias was said to have given the DAGHDHA his inexhaustible cauldron. The other three wizards are named as MORFESSA of FALIA, ESIAS of GORIAS and USCIAS of FINDIAS.

## Murtagh mac Erc
*Irish*

The brother of FERGHUS MAC ERC to whom he lent the Stone of FÁL for his brother's coronation in DAL RIADA. The stone was never returned and was for many years housed at SCONE, where successive kings of SCOTLAND were crowned. It was removed in 1297 by Edward I, and it is now known as the Coronation Stone, being housed, in the chair which British monarchs are crowned.

## Mwys Gwyddno
*Welsh*

The hamper or basket that belonged to GWYDDNO, which was said to be one of the THIRTEEN TREASURES of BRITAIN[1]. It had the power to turn any meat placed in or on it into sufficient to feed a hundred people.

## Myrddin (Emrys)
*Welsh*

The original Welsh name for the wizard MERLIN. It has been suggested that Myrddin derives from a mistaken analysis of CAERFYRDDIN (CARMARTHEN). In other early Welsh poems he is called LLALLAWC and LLALLOGAN VRYDIN.

There are many stories about his birth, but he is usually said to have been the offspring of an incubus (evil spirit) and a nun, set on earth by the devils of hell who were determined to counterbalance the good introduced by Christ. Their plans went awry, however, when their intended evil being was promptly baptized. This is not by any means the only account of his birth, but it does appear to pre-date any of the others. In Welsh tradition his mother was called ALDAN, but whether or not she was a nun is not made clear. Welsh tradition further contradicts his supposed lack of a father by naming his father as MADOG MORFRYN although he was also said to have been MORGAN FRYCH, claimed by some to have been a prince of GWYNEDD, and thus making Myrddin of royal blood. GEOFFREY OF MONMOUTH made him the King of POWYS.

Myrddin's story and his connection with the Arthurian legends begin long before the birth of the king he was to advise and whose downfall he so rightly prophesied. While he was still a youth he became connected with VORTIGERN, the King of BRITAIN[1] some time after the end of the Roman occupation. Vortigern was attempting to erect a tower on DINAS EMRYS but with little success, for, every time he built it up, it promptly fell down again. His counsellors told him that it would be necessary to sacrifice a fatherless child in order to rectify the problem, and, as these were hardly thick on the ground, the supposedly fatherless son of the incubus, Myrddin, now a youth, was picked. When he was brought to the site of the tower, Myrddin told Vortigern that the problem lay beneath the ground in the form of two DRAGONS secreted in an underground lake. The excavation of the site proved this to be the case (subsequent archaeological excavation has revealed the underground pool), and two dragons, one red and one white, emerged, causing Myrddin to utter a series of prophecies.

There seems to be an unrecorded gap in Myrddin's life at this point, for he next appears when AMBROSIUS AURELIUS defeated Vortigern and wished to erect a monument both to his success and to commemorate the dead. Myrddin advised him to go to IRELAND and to bring back from there certain stones that formed the GIANTS' RING. This was done, and they were erected on Salisbury Plain as STONEHENGE. Following the death of Ambrosius Aurelius, UTHER ascended to the throne, but, during a war with GORLOIS, became infatuated with EIGYR, the wife of Gorlois, so one of Uther's men suggested that they consult Myrddin. When they did so, Myrddin consented to help and altered Uther's appearance so that he resembled Gorlois and, on the night Uther lay with Eigyr, her true husband was killed in battle. Uther married Eigyr, but two years later he died. The country was thrown into disarray, for there was no worthy successor to the throne, a situation that continued for thirteen years after Uther's death.

The kingdom was in disarray, and after the battle of ARFDERYDD Myrddin went mad and took to living as a wild man in the woods. GIRALDUS CAMBRENSIS gives the reason for Myrddin's loss of sanity: it followed his beholding some horrible sight in the sky, a bad omen, during the fighting, in which he had been on the side of RHYDDERCH HAEL, King of Cumbria and husband of Myrddin's sister, GANIEDA. Three of Myrddin's brothers were also reputed to have been killed during the battle. In his frenzy, he acquired the gift of prophecy. This story relates Myrddin to the Irish king SUIBNE GEILT, from whose legend the tale may be derived, although Myrddin is first referred to in the tenth-century poem Armes Prydein, while the BUILE SUIBNE, which recounts the Irish legend, is probably two centuries older. After a while Ganieda persuaded Myrddin to give up his wild life in the woods and return to civilization, but on his return he revealed to Ganieda's husband, Rhydderch Hael, that she had been unfaithful to him. Once again madness took hold of him, and he returned to the forest, urging his wife, the flower maiden GUENDOLOENA, to marry again and apparently divorcing her to free her. She agreed, but in his madness Myrddin arrived at the wedding riding a stag and leading a herd of deer (clearly a reworking of an earlier pagan tradition). Enraged and forgetting that it was he who had urged his wife to remarry, he tore the antlers off the stag and hurled them at the bridegroom, who remains unnamed, and killed him. He returned to the forest once more, and Ganieda built him an observatory from which he could study the stars.

Welsh poetic sources that are considerably earlier in date than the writings of Geoffrey of Monmouth largely agree with his account (they are obviously his sources), although they state that Myrddin fought against Rhydderch Hael, rather than for him. Similar tales are told in Welsh tradition about a character by the name of LAILOKEN, who was in the service of Rhydderch Hael, and it would appear as if this caused Geoffrey of Monmouth to change the allegiance of Myrddin. Lailoken is similar to the Welsh word meaning 'twin' and, as Myrddin and Ganieda were thought to be twins, this may have simply been a nickname for Myrddin himself, although, as has already been noted, Myrddin is not actually a personal name.

Geoffrey of Monmouth appears to draw still further on earlier Welsh sources when he connects Myrddin with TALIESIN, a character with whom he seems to be inexorably intertwined in the Welsh mind. One Welsh tradition says that Myrddin was not just one, but three incarnations of the same person, the first appearing in Vortigern's time, the second being as Taliesin himself, while the last was as Myrddin the wild man of the forests. This idea of a multiple Myrddin is again found in the writings of the twelfth-century Norman-Welsh chronicler Giraldus Cambrensis, who says there were two, wizard and wild man. This theory doubtless springs from the impractically long lifespan usually attributed to Myrddin. Modern thinking even had him reincarnated once more as Nostradamus

(the latinized form of Michel de Notre-dame), the sixteenth-century prophet.

His death is as clouded in legend and fable as his life. One Welsh tradition says that he was held captive by a scheming woman in a cave on Bryn Myrddin near CARMARTHEN, a location shown on Ordnance Survey maps as MERLIN'S HILL. Some say that if you listen in the twilight you can still hear his groans and the clanking of the iron chains that bind him, while others say that this is the noise of him still working away in his underground prison. His place of confinement is also said to be a cave in the park of Dynevor Castle, DYFED, in the vicinity of Llandeilo. It is also claimed that he died and was buried on BARDSEY Island, while Breton tradition has him spellbound in a bush of white thorn trees in the woods of Bresilien in BRITTANY. The Welsh *Trioedd Ynys Prydein* (TRIADS) say, however, that he put to sea in a house of glass and was never heard of again. On this voyage he took with him the THIRTEEN TREASURES of BRITAIN[1].

Myrddin's historicity is now thought to be without doubt, although not as the mythologized wizard of the Arthurian legends. There were, in fact, two Myrddin's alive during the time of Vortigern and ARTHUR. One was called MYRDDIN WYLLT, who lived in SCOTLAND, and one called Myrddin Emrys, who was born and raised in Carmarthen. It is the second Myrddin who has become the Arthurian Merlin. It is generally believed that he must have been a man of very high intelligence with extremely advanced knowledge for his time, when magic was simply another name for scientific expertise. He may have been, as has been suggested, a latter-day DRUID who took part in shamanistic rituals, but many attempts have also been made to link Myrddin with earlier Celtic deities.

One theory states that Myrddin represented the morning star, while his sister, Ganieda, was the evening star. His character may indeed have been that of a deity, for the Welsh Triads indicate that he may have had territorial rights as a god over Britain, because this work says that the earliest name for Britain was MERLIN'S PRECINCT. The truth behind this is, however, probably that the prophet became connected with an earlier deity and took on many of his attributes, such would have been the astonishing power of this character. To the peasants of his time, his wisdom and foresight must have seemed very godly indeed. Other attempts have been made to connect him with the god MABON or, through his association with stags, with CERNUNNOS. Many theories have been put forward, but the truth of the matter, as with so much, may never be known.

Countless prophecies are attributed to Myrddin, some of which appear to have been strangely fulfilled, while others may well be fulfilled in the future. In the Vale of Twy near Abergwili there stands a large stone in a field. Many years ago a young man was killed while digging for buried treasure under this stone, it being popular belief at the time that such stones marked the burial sites of riches beyond belief. Myrddin had once prophesied that one day a raven would drink the blood of a man from this stone. Whether or not a raven actually did so is not known, but the prophecy seems to have come true.

The most famous prophecies attributed to Myrddin were those relating to the town of Carmarthen, which still awaits some fearful catastrophe.

> Llanllwch a fu,
> Caerfyrddu a sud,
> Abergwili a saif.
>
> (Llanllwch has been,

> Carmarthen shall sink,
> Abergwili shall stand.)

and

> Caerfyrddin, cei oer fore,
> Daerr a'th lwnc, dwr i'th le.
>
> (Carmarthen, thou shalt have a cold morning,
> Earth shall swallow thee, water into thy place.)

There are still old folk living in Carmarthen who await the catastrophe that they believe will one day befall their town. At the end of one street there used to stand an ancient and withered old oak tree known as MERLIN'S TREE or the PRIORY OAK. Every care was taken over the centuries to protect it from falling, for Myrddin had prophesied that when it did Carmarthen would fall. In 1978 the Local Authority decided to risk the prophecy and remove the tree, which had become a hazard to the town's traffic and which consisted mainly of concrete and iron bars anyway.

Myrddin also prophesied that Carmarthen would sink when LLYN EIDDWEN, a lake in Dyfed (then Cardiganshire), dried up. He also foretold that one day a bull would go to the very top of the tower of St Peter's Church in Carmarthen. This strange prophesy was one day fulfilled by a calf.

## Myrddin Wyllt
*Welsh*

Living in SCOTLAND at the same time as MYRDDIN EMRYS, this character has sometimes been incorrectly identified as the historical person who became better known as MERLIN. The true wizard of the Arthurian legends was the Welsh Myrddin Emrys, who was born and raised in CARMARTHEN.

## Nantos-velta, -uelta
*Gaulish*

A water goddess, who is usually associated with SUCCELLOS.

## Na(o)is-e, -i
*Irish*

A son of UISNECH and brother of ARDÁN and AINNLE, the three boys being collectively referred to as the sons of Uisnech. DERDRIU was told, by LEBHORCHAM, that Naoise would have the exact attributes she most desired in a man, even though she had, from birth, been betrothed to CONCHOBAR MAC NESSA. Derdriu contrived a meeting between herself and Naoise and left him in no doubt that she found him attractive. Naoise, however, would not at first be drawn, for he knew of the prophecy of CATHBHADH that Derdriu would cause untold suffering. He also knew of her betrothal. DERDRIU finally got her way when she threatened to make Naoise a laughing stock. To preserve his honour he fled with Derdriu and his two brothers to SCOTLAND.

Some time later Conchobar mac Nessa was persuaded by the men of ULSTER to call a truce and to let the four fugitives return. Conchobar mac Nessa sent FERGHUS MAC ROICH, DUBTHACH and CORMAC MAC DUBTHACH to Scotland to guarantee them safety once they had returned. The four travelled back to IRELAND with the three messengers, but, once they had arrived at EMHAIN MHACHA, Conchobar mac Nessa reneged on the truce and had the sons of Uisnech killed by EOGHAN MAC DURTHACHT and his men. The three heroes, Ferghus mac Roich, Dubthach and Cormac mac Dubthach, were so appalled by the deceit that they attacked and burned Emhain Mhacha, killed a hundred of the men of Ulster and defected to AILILL and MEDHBHA OF CONNACHT.

## Ná(i)r
*Irish*

1 The brother of MEDHBHA, CLOTHRU, ETHNE, BRES[2] and LOTHAR. All three of his sisters: – Medhbha, Clothru and Ethne – were at one stage married to CONCHOBAR MAC NESSA, Clothru and Ethne filling the void the king felt after Medhbha had left him for AILILL. Clothru remained childless and so arranged a tryst with her three brothers by whom she conceived three boys, each of whom she named LUGAID. That Lugaid who was the son of Nár also fathered a son by Clothru, who was named CRIMTHANN NIA NÁIR, which means 'Nár's Man'.

2 A witch with whom CRIMTHANN NIA NÁIR, the son of NÁR[1] and CLOTHRU, had a brief affair. This story seems to have an historical equal, for King Crimthann, who reigned for a single year (*c*.74 AD), was said to have married a fairy named Náir whom he

met while on a military campaign. She gave him many wonderful gifts, but he died in a riding accident shortly after his return to IRELAND.

## Natchrantal
*Irish*

A champion of CONNACHT, whose epic battle with CÚ CHULAINN gave MEDHBHA the opportunity she had been seeking to penetrate deep into ULSTER and return with the DONN CUAILNGÈ.

## Nechta Scéne
*Irish*

A monstrous being who is mentioned in the legend of CÚ CHULAINN as having three terrible sons, one named FOILL, whom the hero conquered and beheaded. He then decorated his chariot with their severed heads.

## Nechta(i)n
*Irish*

1 The river god husband of the goddess BOANN.
2 A King of MUNSTER who can possibly be identified with NECHTAN[1], although in this instance he is a member of the TUATHA DÉ DANANN. On the advice of LUGH, he is able to poison BRES[1] and thus kill the tyrannical leader of the Tuatha Dé Danann. This version does not, however, lead on to the Second Battle of MAGH TUIREDH, which the author of this tale seems to neglect altogether.
3 One of the companions of BRÂN on his voyage to the paradisal TÍR NA MBAN. Having lived there for what seemed like just one year, Nechtan was overcome with homesickness and persuaded his comrades to travel back to IRELAND. However, when they arrived back in Ireland the people that came to meet them did not know of Brân or his fellow travellers, their only knowledge of Brân being one of their ancient stories. Nechtan leapt from the boat onto the beach, but as his foot touched the sand he disintegrated into a heap of dust. Brân then realized that they had been absent for many hundreds of years and, having shouted their story to the people on the beach, sailed away and was never heard of again.

## Nefyn
*Welsh*

The daughter of BRYCHAN. She married CYNFARCH and became the mother of URIEN.

## Neit
*Irish*

The king of the TUATHA DÉ DANANN who was killed by the FOMHOIRÉ shortly before the arrival of ITH in IRELAND. Ith was asked to judge who should be the next king, but he admired Ireland so much in reaching his conclusion that he was killed.

## Nemed
*Irish*

A simple variant of NEMHEDH.

## Nemedians
*Irish*

A name often used to refer to those followers of NEMHEDH whom he led to IRELAND.

## Nemedius
*Irish*

Irish tradition states that the son of Nemedius was the eponym of BRITAIN[1] because he was apparently called 'Britain' and settled on the island. This is, however, not the accepted manner by which Britain gained its name.

## Nemetona
*Romano-Celtic*

The goddess of the grove (*nemed* or *nemeton* means 'grove'). She held special significance to the Celts, who regarded woodlands as spiritual places. Her name, it is thought, might be a derivation of NEMHEDH.

## Nemglan
*Irish*

The King of the Birds is one of the possible fathers of CONAIRE MÓR, for it is said that he visited the maiden MESS BUACHALLA while she was hidden away. She conceived his son, who was to be passed off as the son of ETERSCEL.

## Nem(h)a(i)n
*Irish*

'Frenzy', one of the aspects or forms of the MÓRRÍGHAN.

## Nem(h)ed(h)
*Irish*

According to the *Leabhar Gabhála Éireann*, the leader of the third invasion of IRELAND. Nemhedh, son of AGNOMAN[1] and his company of just eight others, who were thenceforth known as the 'People of Nemhedh' or Nemedians, met no resistance when they arrived in Ireland, for the former inhabitants, those who came to the island under the leadership of PARTHOLÁN, had been wiped out by a plague. Nemhedh and his people cleared twelve plains and made four lakes, thus furthering the work already started by the previous inhabitants.

Following the death of Nemhedh, his people were conquered by the monstrous FOMHOIRÉ, who, every SAMHAIN, demanded a tribute of two-thirds of their corn, wine and children. Finally, unable to withstand any more, the people rebelled and attacked the Fomhoiré stronghold, an attack that left only one boat load of survivors. These survivors split into two groups, one fleeing to Greece and the other to unnamed northern lands. The former group later returned as the FIR BHOLG, GAILIÓIN and FIR DHOMHNANN, while the latter were to re-appear much later as the fifth invasionary force who were by this time known as the TUATHA DÉ DANANN.

## Nennius
*British*

1 Welsh writer (*fl.*769) who was reputedly the author of the clumsily put together Latin work *Historia Britonum*, which purports to give a history of BRITAIN[1] from the time of JULIUS CAESAR until towards the end of the seventh century. The book gives mythical accounts of the origins of the Britons, the settlement of the SAXONS and King ARTHUR's twelve victories.

2 The brother of LUD and CASSIVEL-LAUNUS. He was known as NYNNIAW[2] to the Welsh, who named his brothers as LLUDD, CASWALLAWN and LLEFELYS. Nennius is alleged to have fought JULIUS CAESAR in battle and, although mortally wounded, managed to take Caesar's sword from him. The sword was later buried beside him.

## Nera
*Irish*

A courtier at the court of AILLIL and MEDHBHA. During a feast held on SAMHAIN he left the proceedings and went outside.

There a corpse, hanging from the gallows, complained of thirst. Nera took it down and gave it a drink. When he re-entered the hall he found that all those at the feast, except Aillil and Medhbha, had been killed by a SÍDH host, which he pursued into the OTHERWORLD. There he was hospitably greeted by the king, who immediately gave him a wife and a home, a gift he was to repay by collecting the king's firewood. Almost a year had passed when his wife warned him that she had foreseen the SÍDH host attacking the court of Aillil and Medhbha on the coming feast of Samhain. Nera secretly left the Otherworld to warn Aillil and Medhbha, taking primroses, fern and wild garlic with him to prove his whereabouts for the last year. Aillil and Medhbha set out with a large company from the court and destroyed the sídh, but Nera had already returned to his wife and so was caught in the Otherworld, with no way of ever returning.

## Nessa
*Irish*

The daughter of ECHID, wife of FACHTNA and mother of CONCHOBAR MAC NESSA.

## Nét
*Irish*

The war god of the FOMHOIRÉ and grandfather of BALAR.

## New Grange
*Irish*

The common name for BRUGH NA BÓINNE, the home of the DAGHDHA and then of OENGHUS MAC IN OG. After TARA, New Grange is the most important Bronze Age monument in IRELAND.

## Nial Noígiallach
*Irish*

'Níal of the Nine Hostages', the founder of the fifth Irish province, which was formed by the division of the ancient ULAIDH. He established his capital at TARA. The UÍ NÉILL, his descendants, gained control over all of central and northern IRELAND. These descendants of Níal Noígiallach are believed to have been a new group of invading Celts, the sixth such invasion to land on the island. In the legendary tales they are referred to as the Sons of MÍL ÉSPÁINE.

Níal Noígiallach was considered by some to be an historical person, the foster son of the poet TORNA ÉICES, who came from MUNSTER. His father was named as EOCHU MUGMEDÓN, while his mother was a Saxon from Britain, sometimes named as CAIRENN.

## Niam(h)
*Irish*

1 The daughter of CELTCHAR and wife of CONALL CERNACH. Together with DEICHTINE, CONCHOBAR MAC NESSA and CATHBHADH, she begged CÚ CHULAINN not to be enticed into attacking the sons of CALATIN, for they knew that this would lead to his death, after one of Calatin's daughters, BAVE, had assumed the form of Niamh and implored him to protect ULSTER against its foes.

2 The exquisite daughter of the King of TÍR NA NOC whom OISÍN accompanied to her home. He remained there for 300 years, although to him it seemed that only a week had passed. Some versions of the story say that he became the king after he had outraced Niamh's father, who had said he would abdicate in favour of any son-in-law who could beat him in a foot race. Other accounts say that he also killed

a giant who had abducted the daughter of the King of TÍR NA MBEO.

At length, Oisîn began to miss his homeland and arranged to return, although Niamh did her best to dissuade him. When she saw that this was hopeless, she instructed him not to dismount from his horse, otherwise he would never be able to return. Back in IRELAND he found that the FIAN had been long forgotten and a new faith filled the land. On his way back to Niamh, he stopped to help some peasants, but as soon as he dismounted his horse disappeared and he became a blind and decrepit old man.

## Nis-ien, -syen
*Welsh*

The son of PENARDUN and EUROSWYDD, brother of EFNISIEN and half-brother to BENDIGEID VRAN, MANAWYDAN FAB LLYR and BRANWEN. Described as a gentle youth who would do no one any harm, he appears briefly in the story of Branwen and MATHOLWCH as a mediator, but after that nothing more is heard of him.

## Niwalen
*Welsh*

'White Track', the goddess of the road or spirit of the journey. She is also known as OLWEN, the name under which she appears as the daughter of the giant YSPADDADEN.

## Noah
*Biblical, Irish and British*

A biblical patriarch who was chosen by God to survive the Flood along with his family, and their families, and two of every living creature. Several of Noah's descendants are alleged to have found their way to IRELAND, among them CESAIR,

his granddaughter by way of BITH, and his son, who was said to have been among the first settlers of Ireland. The ancient Britons also laid claim to a biblical ancestry by saying that ALBION and his race of giants, the first inhabitants of BRITAIN[1], came from a race of giants living in Africa who were descended from HAM, another of Noah's sons, although the Irish also claimed a connection to Ham, saying that the FOMHOIRÉ were descended from him. See also DWYFACH, DWYFAN.

## Nod-ens, -ons
*British*

The tutelary deity of the healing sanctuary at Lydney, Gloucestershire, although by no means solely confined to that site. Nodens was a god with definite connections to both healing and water, his totem animal appearing to have been the dog. The Romans sometimes equated him with their own god Neptune, a connection that led Nodens to be regarded, by some, as a sea deity. His name is likely to be a derivative of his Irish counterpart NUADHA AIRGEDLÁMH, while his Welsh equivalent appears to have been LLUDD LAW EREINT, or perhaps NUDD[2] from whom his name might also have been derived.

## Noricum
*General*

An ancient Celtic kingdom in the eastern Alps, of which BOLENOS was the tutelary deity.

## Northumbria
*British*

The ANGLO-SAXON kingdom that covered northeast ENGLAND and southeast SCOTLAND, consisting of the sixth-century kingdoms of Bernicia (Forth-Tees) and

Deira (Tees-Humber), which were united in the seventh century. It accepted the supremacy of WESSEX AD 827 and was conquered by the Danes in the late ninth century.

## Nuadha (Airgedlámh)
*Irish*

The leader of the TUATHA DÉ DANANN, who was originally known without his epithet. However, even though he possessed an inescapable sword that he had brought with him when the Tuatha Dé Danann arrived in IRELAND, Nuadha lost an arm during the First Battle of MAGH TUIREDH. Since no physically imperfect king could retain the throne, he was forced to abdicate in favour of the tyrannical BRES[1]. Bres was himself forced to abdicate some time later. During the time Bres was king of the Tuatha Dé Danann, the giant leech (physical) DIAN CÉCHT, with the assistance of CREIDHNE, fitted Nuadha with an artificial arm made out of silver, this arm earning him his epithet, which simply means 'Silver Hand'. With the throne vacant after the abdication of Bres, Nuadha Airgedlámh was reinstated as the king, a position he held until just before the Second Battle of Magh Tuiredh, when LUGH arrived at the court. Recognizing the newcomer's superiority, Nuadna Airgedlámh abdicated in his favour.

## Nuadha of the Silver Hand
*Irish*

The literal translation of NUADHA AIRGEDLÁMH.

## Nudd
*Welsh*

1 The father of GWYNN AP NUDD.
2 A shortened and popularized version of GWYNN AP NUDD, Master of the WILD HUNT and Lord of the Dead. Some have equated Gwynn ap Nudd with the Irish NUADHA AIRGEDLÁMH, although this appears to be a fairly late theory that relies on the similarity of the shortened versions Nudd and Nuadha. The shortened version of Gwynn ap Nudd is also said, by some, to have later given rise to the Romano-Celtic deity NODENS, but this again appears to be false etymology.

## Nwyvre
*Welsh*

Named in some genealogies as the child of ARIANRHOD by her brother GWYDION FAB DÔN.

## Nyn(n)-iaw, -yaw
*Welsh*

1 The brother of PEIBAW, with whom he was transformed into an ox by God for his sins. In some genealogies Nynniaw and Peibaw are the sons of BELI and DÔN, and thus the brothers of, among others, GWYDION FAB DÔN, ARIANRHOD, GILFAETHWY and LLUDD[2].
2 The son of BELI and brother of LLUDD, LLEFELYS and CASWALLAWN. In this context Nynniaw is the Welsh version of NENNIUS[2], the brother of LUD and CASSIVELLAUNUS.

# Ochall Oichni

*Irish*

The King of CONNACHT, whose swineherd RUCHT was a great friend of FRIUCH, the swineherd to BODH, King of MUNSTER. The two swineherds, having fallen out with each other and after going through several transformations, were reborn as the bulls FINNBHENNACH and the DONN CUAILNGÈ. See also COPHUR IN DÁ MUCCIDA.

# Odr-as, -us

*Irish*

A maiden who tended a cow. The MÓRRÍGHAN brought her a bull, which she was also supposed to watch over. The bull and the cow followed the Mórríghan into a cave, so Odras also entered that cave but fell asleep inside it. The bull and cow disappeared, so the Mórríghan changed the unfortunate Odras into a pool of water.

# Oenghus

*Irish*

The son of AED ABRAT and brother of LI BAN and FAND[2].

# Oenghus (Mac in(d) O-g, -c)

*Irish*

Usually simply known as Oenghus, his epithet meaning 'Young Lad', Oenghus Mac in Og is the Irish equivalent of the Gaulish MAPONOS and the Welsh MABON. A clever trickster, he gained possession of BRUGH NA BÓINNE from his father, the DAGHDHA, or, some say, from ELCMAR. There he set up his home. Although a god born of primal powers, he is unusually not regarded as a healing deity, but rather as the god of wit, charm and fatal love, as the legends that surround him clearly demonstrate.

The famous *Aislinge Oenguso* relates the story of his forlorn quest for the woman of his dream, CAER[2] the daughter of ETHAL ANUBAL, and his eventual discovery of her. However, Oenghus is possibly best known from his wooing of ÉDÁIN ECHRAIDHE for his foster father MIDHIR, wooing that was successful, and during which he undoubtedly used his various guiles on Édáin Echraidhe. Oenghus fostered DIARMAID UA DUIBHNE, whom he helped when he was besieged in a wood in CONNACHT by FIONN MAC CUMHAILL after GRÁINNE had induced Diarmaid ua Duibhne to elope with her. Oenghus saved Gráinne, whilst Diarmaid ua Duibhne escaped by leaping over the heads of the attackers, a trick no doubt taught him by Oenghus, who later reconciled his foster son and Gráinne with Fionn mac Cumhaill. After the death of Diarmaid ua Duibhne, Oenghus took that hero to live with him at Brugh na Bóinne, and there shared his immortality with him.

An historic king named Oenghus is

recorded as having ruled in Cashel, his death being given as AD 490. Although he probably owes his name to the god Oenghus Mac in Og, he has no other connections with the deity. He was later thought to have resurfaced in the Arthurian legends as King ANGUISH, a name that couples a Gaelic trait with the translation of Oenghus as Angus.

## Ogham
*Irish*

Usually known as Ogham Script, the Irish Celtic alphabet system is said to have been the invention of the god OGHMA, hence the name, but is more likely to have developed during the third and fourth centuries. On first inspection this system of writing appears to be based on the Latin alphabet. However, closer study reveals unique characteristics, such as a mnemonic system that is clearly not Roman in origin. It is thought that some of its elements represent the incorporation of an earlier, now lost, magical script that would have been almost certainly used only by the DRUIDS. Ogham Script is best known as a series of lines or cuts, made on the edges of stones or pieces of wood.

Ogham Script inscriptions have been discovered on the eastern seaboard of the United States, or at least, the inscriptions appear to be Ogham. If they are truly Celtic, they would seem to prove that not only were the Celts excellent coastal sailors but also that they crossed the wide expanse of the north Atlantic.

## Og(h)ma
*Irish*

Usually given the title GRIANAINECH, which means 'Sun-face', Oghma is the Irish equivalent of the Gaulish OGMIOS. One of the TUATHA DÉ DANANN, a strong

champion whose magic words could bind men to follow him, he may have originated as a psychopomp, or heroic guide, of the spirits of the dead. Oghma is perhaps most famous for being accredited with the invention of OGHAM Script, the Irish Celtic alphabet.

Under the tyrannical rule of BRES[1], Oghma was humiliatingly made to collect firewood. Following the installation of LUGH as the leader of the Tuatha Dé Danann, and their success over the FOMHOIRÉ in the Second Battle of MAGH TUIREDH, Oghma is named as one of those who was set to pursue to fleeing remnants of the Fomhoiré forces who were attempting to make off with the magical harp of the DAGHDHA.

## Ogmios
*Gaulish*

A father god, who was regarded as a wise elder. Ogmios, an old man, is usually depicted carrying a club and a bow, attributes that led to his being equated with the Graeco-Roman Hercules. Indeed, a number of carvings from the Romano-Celtic era show a typically Herculean figure with massive muscles, a huge club and wearing a lion's skin. The tip of his tongue is connected by thin chains to the ears of a throng of happy mortals. Ogmios was not simply a god of brute strength, as his Herculean images might portray, for he was the god of eloquence, a skill the Celts believed to be more powerful than force, as well as the god of the binding power of poetry and the poetic word, of charm, of incantation and of image.

Ogmios may have originated as a heroic guide to the spirits of the dead, leading him to be a most powerful deity, one who both binds and liberates, and who conducts the dead into the OTHER-WORLD. His Irish equivalent is OGHMA, who shares many of his attributes.

## Ogyrven
*Welsh*

According to some sources, Ogyrven was the father of CERRIDWEN, to whom he gave his cauldron. He was, perhaps, an early eponymous deity of the alphabet, called *ogyrvens*, as well as the patron of bards and language.

## Oilill
*Irish*

The companion of FERCHESS, who watched EOGABAL and AINÉ[2] leave their SÍDH with a herd of supernatural cattle which they desired. Eogabal was killed by Ferchess, and Ainé was outraged, possibly raped, by Oilill whose ear Ainé hit so hard that it never regrew any skin. Ainé swore to have her revenge, and later caused an argument to break out between EOGAN, one of Oilill's sons, and LUGAID MAC CON, who was killed as a result. Lugaid mac Con's family attacked the followers of Oilill at the Battle of MAGH MUCRIME during which all seven of Oilill's sons were killed.

## Oimelc
*Gaulish*

The Gaulish name for the festival of IMBOLC.

## Oisîn
*Irish*

The son of FIONN MAC CUMHAILL and SAAR or Sabia and father of OSCAR. Oisîn was the greatest poet to have lived in IRELAND, as well as a mighty warrior. Born after his mother had been changed into a deer by a maleficent sorcerer, his name means 'Little Fawn', for that is how he was born. A small tuft of hair grew from his forehead where Saar had licked him, but, because Fionn mac Cumhaill had been the first to embrace the lad, he remained human.

One summer morning, while Oisîn and many members of the FIAN were hunting on the shores of Loch Lena, they saw a beautiful maiden riding a pure white stallion coming towards them. She was NIAMH[2], daughter of the King of TÍR NA MBAN, and she had come to seek the hand of Oisîn whom she had fallen in love with. She cast a spell on Oisîn so that he fell for her, and the two of them rode back to her land, where they were married and lived happily together. One version of the story says that he became the king of Tír na mBan after winning a foot race against Niamh's father, but another says that he rescued the daughter of the King of TIR NA MBÉO, who had been abducted by a giant.

After what seemed like only three weeks, Oisîn sought to visit his father. Niamh tried to dissuade him, but, finding he would not change his mind, she gave him her white steed on which to make the journey, warning him that he must not dismount, otherwise he would never be able to return. When Oisîn arrived back in Ireland he found that everything had changed. He had not been away for just three weeks but for three centuries. The fian were long forgotten, and a new faith was now practised. Disheartened, Oisîn turned to return to his supernatural wife, but on the way he was asked to help a group of peasants struggling with a heavy stone. When Oisîn dismounted he underwent a dramatic transformation, becoming an aged man on the verge of death. The horse vanished in an instant, and Oisîn was taken to St PATRICK whose scribes wrote down all Oisîn said before he died.

## Ol
*Welsh*

One of the seldom mentioned members of the party formed to help CULHWCH. Ol was chosen because he had the ability to pick up any trail, even one that was as much as seven years older than he was, although no indication is given of his age.

## Ollav Fôla
*Irish*

The eighteenth ruler of IRELAND after EREMON, and possibly the only king of Ireland to have reached the highest Druidic rank. Traditionally he reigned *c.*1000 BC. He gave the country a code of legislature and devised a legal system similar to the system of county and crown courts in use today. He was also credited with establishing the triennial fair at TARA, where all kings, vassals, bards, historians and musicians assembled to record the history of the island, create and enforce new laws, settle disputes and so on. He is allegedly buried in the great tumulus at Loughcrew in West MEATH.

## Olwen
*Welsh*

The daughter of the chief giant YSPADDADEN, this maiden, whose alternate name is NIWALEN, appears in the *Mabinogion* story of *Culhwch and Olwen*. Her name appears to mean 'White Track', but it may also come from *olwyn*, a 'wheel'. CULHWCH's step-mother swore that he should only love Olwen, so Culhwch set out to find her, first coming to a royal court, said later to have been that of King ARTHUR, where the gate-keeper GLEWLWYD remarked that he had never, in his long career, encountered such a handsome youth.

The king sent out messengers to look for Olwen, but a year passed without any news. Culhwch then formed a party of gifted companions to help him in his search, these companions being named as CEI, BEDWYR[2], CYNDDYLIG, GWRHYR, GWALCHMAI FAB GWYAR and MENW FAB TEIRGWAEDD, though many others, seldom named, also accompanied him. Setting out, they at length met a shepherd, whose wife turned out to be Culhwch's aunt. She knew Olwen, and, even though she had lost twenty-three of her twenty-four sons to Yspaddaden, she agreed to help Culhwch, telling him that Olwen came to her house every Saturday to wash her hair.

The due day came, and the couple met. Olwen immediately agreed to his suit but told Culhwch that he must obtain the permission of her father. She warned him not to flinch from any conditions set or tasks imposed. Culhwch agreed, and the very next morning his party set out for Yspaddaden's castle. For three days the giant told them to come back the next and then, when they had turned their backs, hurled a poisoned boulder at them. They were too quick and caught the boulder which they hurled back. After three days the giant was severely weakened by his own poison, so he agreed to hear Culhwch. He agreed that he could marry Olwen provided he carried out a number of seemingly impossible tasks. Each of these Culhwch completed, but as Yspaddaden continued to pile condition upon condition, Culhwch rounded up all the giant's enemies and stormed the castle. Yspaddaden was killed, and Culhwch married Olwen, the pair remaining faithful for the rest of their lives.

## Optima
*Welsh*

According to tradition, one of the names

applied to MYRDDIN's mother, the other being ALDAN.

## Oran
*British*

The brother of St COLUMBA. He is alleged to have voluntarily died so that his brother might consecrate the ground on which he wished to build his chapel on the island of IONA with a burial.

## Ord-ollam
*Irish*

A title applied to LUGH in his position as chief protector of the arts and sciences.

## Ordovices
*British*

An ancient northern Welsh tribe that, along with the SILURES of the southeast of WALES, supported CARATACUS against the Roman invaders.

## Orlam
*Irish*

The son of MEDHBHA and AILILL. He was beheaded by CÚ CHULAINN, who made Orlam's charioteer take the severed head back to Medhbha and Ailill. As he stood to attention in front of the grieving king and queen, Cú Chulainn split open his head with a well-aimed, long-range sling shot.

## Oscar
*Irish*

The son of OISÎN. He slew three kings in his first battle, when he also mistakenly killed his friend LINNÉ. Oscar proved his might as a warrior by killing a huge boar that none other, including his grandfather, had been able to catch. He married

AIDEEN, but was soon afterwards killed in the Battle of GABHRA. Aideen died of a broken heart and was buried by OISÎN who was, at least in this version, still in IRELAND at the time of the battle, and not in TÍR INNA MBÉO with NIAMH[2].

## Ossian
*Irish*

A relatively late variant of OISÎN.

## Otherworld(ly)
*General*

In common with most other cultures, the Otherworld is the Celtic land of the dead, but it is far more than simply that. It is, particularly in the Welsh Otherworld of ANNWFN, almost a paradisal fantasy land that has recognizable regions, regions that could, in some ways, be equated with the three regions of the Greek Hades, but even that equation does not really compare with the amazing beauty of the Celtic concept of a land other than their own.

The most usual icon of the Otherworld is a cauldron of plenty, a cauldron that, so most authorities now agree, later inspired the stories of the Holy GRAIL of Arthurian fame. This cauldron appears all over the Celtic lands, from the cauldron of the DAGHDHA in IRELAND, to that of ARAWN in WALES and far beyond.

The Otherworld is certainly a land of the dead, but even the dead are not constrained, for many stories exist of mortals who travel to the Otherworld and subsequently return. It is in this sense, therefore, a transitory realm from which souls are reborn, sometimes as the same person, and sometimes as a completely new person.

It is also the land of the gods, for the Celtic theology is peculiar in having no definition for heaven. The Irish TUATHA

DÉ DANANN inhabit their SÍDH, or earthen barrows, that are, in reality, prehistoric burial chambers. They were awarded this realm by the Sons of MÍL ÉSPÁINE, the first mortals to inhabit Ireland, the passage from worldly to Otherworldly beings signifying the transition of Ireland from a mythical land of the gods to an historical land of mortals.

## Ousel of Cilgwri
*Welsh*

A variation of the BLACKBIRD OF CILGWRI, although the word ousel is actually an archaic name for the European blackbird.

## Owain (Glyndwr)
*Welsh*

An historical character, the son of URIEN of RHEGED, whom he succeeded. He has subsequently passed into the realms of myth and legend, and has countless associations with ARTHUR. Although he certainly lived later than the traditional Arthurian period – he was said to have inflated a heavy defeat on the British about AD 593 – both he and his father have been drawn into Arthurian legend. In this role he is the son of Urien by Arthur's sister, Morgan Le Fay, who appears to have her origins in the goddess

MODRON, whom some Welsh sources name as the mother of Owain.

## Owel
*Irish*

The foster son of MANANNÁN MAC LIR and the father of the goddess AINÉ by a DRUID.

## Owen

1 (*Irish*) One of the warriors of ULSTER who challenged the right of CET to carve the boar of MAC DÁ THÓ, but was quickly silenced by the retort of Cet.
2 (*Welsh*) The son of MACSEN who was said to have met a giant in battle in the valley below DINAS EMRYS. They fought long and hard until each had killed the other.

## Owl of Cwn Cawlwyd
*Welsh*

One of the oldest animals in the world, which conversed with GWRHYR the Interpreter. The expedition mounted by CULHWCH had been taken to the owl by the STAG OF RHEDYNFRC, an animal slightly younger than the owl, which, in turn, took the group on to question the EAGLE OF GWERNABWY.

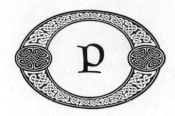

## Pa Gur
*Welsh*

A famous Welsh poem that tells how CEI travelled to Anglesey with a view to killing lions, especially preparing himself for an encounter with the CATH PALUG.

## Padarn Redcoat
*Welsh*

The owner of a coat, known as PAIS PADARN, that was one of the THIRTEEN TREASURES OF BRITAIN[1].

## Pair Drynog
*Welsh*

The cauldron of DRYNOG in which none but the meat of a brave man would boil. It numbered among the THIRTEEN TREASURES OF BRITAIN[1].

## Pais Padarn
*Welsh*

The coat or cloak of PADARN REDCOAT. It rendered the wearer invisible and was included among the THIRTEEN TREASURES OF BRITAIN[1].

## Palug
*Welsh*

The father of the sons who, according to tradition, lived on ANGLESEY and saved and raised the CATH PALUG, the monstrous feline offspring of HÊN WEN.

## Pandrasus
*British*

A Greek king, who captured and enslaved a group of Trojan refugees. They were released after BRUTUS fought and defeated the king, taking the king's daughter IGNOGE as his reluctant wife. He also demanded that Pandrasus supply him with ships, provisions and bullion. So equipped, Brutus left Greece, taking the Trojans with him.

## Parthol-án, -on
*Irish*

A descendant of the biblical JAPHETH. The son of SERA, leader of the second invasion of IRELAND, husband to the adulterous DEALGNAID and father of RURY. His companions became known simply as the 'People of Partholán' or PARTHOLIANS. They defeated the FOMHOIRÉ, forcing them into exile in the Hebrides and on the Isle of MAN. Partholán then set his people to clearing four plains and creating seven lakes, the first landscaping of Ireland. He also built the first guest house, brewed the first beer and established laws and craft. Partholán and all his people, bar one, a man named TUAN MAC STERN, were wiped out by a plague, leaving the island open for NEMHEDH.

## Partholians
*Irish*

The name sometimes given to the people who came to IRELAND under the leadership of PARTHOLÁN.

## Pascen
*Welsh*

A son of URIEN of RHEGED.

## Paschent
*British*

The third son of VORTIGERN, who fled to Germany after his father had been defeated by AMBROSIUS AURELIUS. Paschent returned, but was once again defeated. This time he fled to IRELAND, where he secured the help of King GILLOMANIUS for yet another invasion. Returning to BRITAIN[1], Paschent found Ambrosius Aurelius ill and paid the SAXON woman Eopa to poison him.

## Patrick, St
*Irish*

The patron saint of IRELAND who was, perhaps, born in South WALES late in the fourth century AD. His father, Calpurnius, was a Romano-British deacon. Patrick does not appear to have been the name his parents called him: he is recorded as having carried the name SUCCAT, although this may have been a nickname. According to legend he was captured by pirates when he was sixteen and carried off by them to Ireland, where he was sold to an Antrim chief by the name of Milchru. Six years later he escaped and travelled to FRANCE, where he became a monk. At the age of forty-five he was consecrated a bishop, and in AD 432 he is thought to have been sent as a missionary to Ireland by Pope Celestine I. He landed at Wicklow and from there travelled north to convert his old master Milchru. In County Down he converted another chief, Dichu, and at TARA he preached to LAOGHAIRE, but was unsuccessful in converting him as the official Christian record of that event shows.

From Tara he travelled to Croagh-Patrick in Mayo, then to ULSTER, and as far as Cashel in the south, where he converted King Aenghus about AD 448. Legend says that, during the baptism of Aenghus, the saint accidentally pierced the king's foot with his crozier. Too wrapped up in the ceremony, St Patrick failed to notice what he had done, and Aenghus kept his mouth shut, and presumably his teeth clenched, as he thought it a part of the ceremony.

Patrick addressed himself firstly to the chiefs and made use of the Irish spirit of clanship to break down boundaries. After twenty years travelling the length and breadth of Ireland as a missionary he established his see at Armagh in 454. He died at Saul, the spot Dichu had given him on his arrival in Ireland, and is, in all probability, buried at Armagh. Another tradition states that he ended his days as the Abbot of GLASTONBURY, where he died at the age of 111. His feast-day is 17 March.

The only certainly authentic literary remains of the saint are his spiritual autobiography, *Confession*, and a letter addressed to Coroticus, a British chieftain who had carried off some Irish Christians to be slaves. Both of these are in very crude Latin. Later writers, who obviously wished to preserve some of the Irish mythology and legend in a post-pagan Ireland, connected the saint with a great number of mythological and legendary characters.

## Pebin
*Welsh*

The father of the footholder GOEWIN.

## Pedrawd
*Welsh*

The father of BEDWYR. He later passed into the Arthurian cycle where he became the father of Bedivere, the Arthurian version of Bedwyr.

## Peibaw
*Welsh*

The brother of NYNNIAW[1] who was, along with his brother, turned into an ox by God for his vanity and sins. A traditional Welsh genealogy makes Peibaw and Nynniaw the sons of DÔN, and thus brothers to GWYDION FAB DÔN, ARIANRHOD, GILFAETHWY, AMAETHON, GOFANNON and LLUDD.

## Pen Annwfn
*Welsh*

'Head of Annwfn', the honorific given to PWYLL by his counsellors after they had discovered that he had spent a year in ANNWFN.

## Penardun
*Welsh*

The daughter or sister of BELI, although usually a daughter of DÔN, who, by LLYR, became the mother of MANAWYDAN FAB LLYR, the half-brother of BENDIGEID VRAN and BRANWEN who were Llyr's children by IWERIADD, and of NISIEN and EFNISIEN, whom she bore to EUROSSWYDD. Most sources, however, make Penardun the mother of Bendigeid Vran, Branwen and Manawydan fab Llyr by Llyr, and ignore that god's association with Iweriadd.

## Penarwan
*Welsh*

The wife of OWAIN who was, according to the *Trioedd Ynys Prydein*, unfaithful to him.

## Pendaran Dyfed
*Welsh*

The foster father of PRYDERI.

## Pendragwn
*Welsh*

A combination of the Old Welsh *dragwn*, 'dragon', and the Brythonic *pen*, 'head', which was traditionally used to refer to the head of a tribe, clan or realm, for Pendragwn literally means 'head dragon', the use of 'dragon' signifying a person of the utmost importance, a leader. Thus Pendragwn really means 'head leader'. The title later emerged in the Arthurian legends as Pendragon, a title taken firstly by UTHER and subsequently by ARTHUR.

## Penvro
*Welsh*

An ancient name for Pembroke, the location of GWALES where the seven who had been charged with the burial of BENDIGEID VRAN's severed head stayed for eighty years before one of them opened a door that looked towards CORNWALL. Once that door had been opened, memories of all that had befallen their fellow countrymen came rushing back, and the seven hurried to the WHITE MOUNT in LONDON where they buried the head.

## Peredur
*Welsh*

1 The warrior son of EFRAWG who fought the Battle of ARFDERYDD against

his cousin, the British prince GWEN-DDOLAU. His companion in that battle was GWRGI who was, like himself, a cousin of Gwenddolau. Peredur later resurfaced in the Arthurian cycle as Sir Perceval.

2 The title of a Welsh romance concerning the exploits and quests of PEREDUR[1], which has become included in the *Mabinogion*.

## Phelim (mac Dall)
*Irish*

A variant of FEDLIMID, although it seems likely that the reverse is true.

## Picts
*General*

The name given to the people who inhabited northern BRITAIN[1] in Roman times, their first appearance being recorded near to the close of the third century AD. About the time of the Roman withdrawal they were raiding Britain, and VORTIGERN is thought to have invited the SAXONS to the country to oppose them. GEOFFREY OF MONMOUTH says that they were almost wiped out by King ARTHUR, and would have been had not their priests interceded.

The racial identity of the Picts is almost certainly Celtic, and they called themselves *Priteni* in their own language. It is this name that has, so some say, given rise to Britain. The Irish called them *Cruthin*, a name they also applied to a Pictish race, the *Picti*, who lived in IRELAND. Their name means 'painted folk', which is the name by which the Romans called them. Although the Picts probably preceeded the ancient Britons, BEDE[2] says that they arrived after the Britons and came from Scythia, an area that today lies within the Ukraine in southern Russia. GEOFFREY OF MONMOUTH

stresses that the Picts were defeated by MARIUS, the British king, who is said to have given the Pictish people Caithness. The medieval Irish poet, Mael Mura of Othain, claims that the Picts came from Thrace. There were two main Pict kingdoms, the northern and the southern, the southern being divided into four states, Atholl, Circinn, Fife and Fortrenn.

## Pinner
*British*

The legendary King of ENGLAND who was defeated and killed by MOLMUTIUS as he sought to expand his kingdom.

## Porrex
*British*

An early and legendary prince of BRITAIN[1] who, according to GEOFFREY OF MONMOUTH, was a descendant of BRUTUS. The son of GORBODUC and JUDON, he had a younger brother by the name of FERREX, with whom he quarrelled over the right of succession. Porrex plotted to ambush his brother, but he fled to GAUL from whence he returned with a Gaulish army, but was defeated and killed. As Ferrex had been her favourite, Judon was driven insane by her grief, and, while Porrex slept, she hacked him to pieces. As neither Porrex nor Ferrex had left an heir, the line of Brutus died out when Gorboduc died. After his death, so one tradition says, PRYDEIN came from CORNWALL and conquered Britain, thus leading to the association of Prydein as the eponym of Britain.

## Powys
*Welsh*

An early Welsh kingdom, which was said to have been ruled by legendary kings such as CADELL, CYNGEN and BROCHMAEL.

## Prasutagus
*British*

The husband of BOUDICCA, and thus ruler of the ICENI, who kept a degree of autonomy under the Romans. After his death, however, the Romans plundered the royal possessions, flogged Boudicca and raped her daughters, an act that led Boudicca to rise up against the Romans and lead a successful, though short-lived, campaign against them.

## Preiddeu Annwfn
*Welsh*

*The Spoils of Annwfn*, an early Welsh poem dating from *c*.900, which was allegedly written by TALIESIN. The poem, which obviously uses an earlier legend as its basis, concerns an expedition to the OTHERWORLD to secure a magic cauldron. The *Preiddeu Annwfn* is particularly important to Celtic study because it gives one of the clearest descriptions of the various realms within the Otherworld. There are the glass fort of CAER WYDYR and the paradisal land where a fountain runs with wine and no one ever knows old age or sickness, this region being known as either CAER FEDDWID or CAER SIDDI.

## Priory Oak
*Welsh*

Another name for MERLIN'S TREE in CARMARTHEN.

## Prydein
*British*

Coming from CORNWALL following the death of PORREX, Prydein was said to have conquered the remainder of BRITAIN[1]. It is this legend that has led to his being cited as a possible eponym for the country.

## Pryderi
*Welsh*

The son of PWYLL and RHIANNON. On the night of his birth Rhiannon's ladies-in-waiting fell asleep, and the tiny infant disappeared before he could be named. To save themselves from being blamed, the women smeared Rhiannon with blood and claimed that she had killed the baby and disposed of the body. Pwyll believed her innocent and refused to divorce her. Rhiannon, rather than fight the testimony of the women, did penance by carrying all those who would accept her offer into the castle.

The small baby was discovered by TEYRNON TWRYFT LIANT. He adopted the boy as his own and named him GWRI. A year later, struck by the likeness of the boy to Pwyll, Teyrnon Twryff Liant concluded that the boy he had been looking after was none other than the lost child, so he took him to Pwyll. Pwyll and Rhiannon called the boy Pryderi and placed him in the care of PENDARAN DYFED, under whose guidance he grew up to be handsome, courteous and brave, a great warrior who was loved by his people. He married CIGFA, the daughter of GWYN GOHOYW.

Pryderi was among the seven survivors of the expedition led to IRELAND by BENDIGEID VRAN, and one of those who, after eighty-seven years journeying, buried the severed head of Bendigeid Vran under the WHITE MOUNT in LONDON. On his return to WALES he found that his cousin MANAWYDAN FAB LLYR had been disinherited by CASWALLAWN, the son of BELI. To compensate him for his loss Pryderi gave Manawydan fab Llyr his own mother, Rhiannon, as a wife, along with the seven cantrefs of DYFED.

One night, as Pryderi, Manawydan fab Llyr, Rhiannon and Cigfa were feasting, they heard a huge clap of thunder. This was followed by a cloud, out of which emanated a brilliant, blinding light, which enveloped them. As the light faded, they found themselves quite alone in Dyfed, for all their houses, men and animals had mysteriously disappeared. The four then became hunters, for the woods were well stocked with game and the rivers teemed with fish. For two years they lived quite happily, but Pryderi and Manawydan fab Llyr grew tired of their lonely existence and decided to travel from town to town to earn a living.

Some time later they were in the woods, hunting with their dogs, when the animals disappeared into a CAER. Pryderi, against the better judgement of Manawydan fab Llyr, followed them, meaning to lead them out again, but he too was trapped inside. Manawydan fab Llyr waited until dusk for his cousin to reappear and then returned to Rhiannon to tell her what had happened. She immediately went to the caer and there saw a door that had remained invisible to Manawydan fab Llyr. She, too, entered the caer, whereupon it disappeared, taking Rhiannon, Pryderi and the dogs with it.

Cigfa was very frightened when she realized that only she and Manawydan fab Llyr were left. He, however, behaved honourably towards her, and swore to provide for her in her husband's absence. Having no visible means of doing this, Manawydan fab Llyr became a cobbler, a trade at which he excelled. Within a year he had prospered sufficiently to establish three crofts. These he sowed with wheat, but when the first crop was ripe and he came to reap it, he found that every ear had been stripped clean. The same happened with the second, so he sat and watched over the third. At night a host of mice appeared and started to eat the wheat.

When Manawydan fab Llyr appeared, the mice scattered, but he managed to catch one, which he swore he would solemnly hang the next day for theft. Cigfa tried to dissuade him from this ridiculous act, but Manawydan fab Llyr was adamant that the mouse should pay for its crime. As he was preparing the tiny gallows, a poor clerk came by, the first person other than Cigfa he had seen for a year, and offered Manawydan fab Llyr a sum of money if he would spare the mouse. Manawydan fab Llyr refused. Next a richly dressed priest came by and significantly increased the offer of the clerk, but again the offer was refused. Finally, a bishop accompanied by his entire retinue stopped and offered Manawydan fab Llyr a king's ransom for the life of the mouse. Once more the offer was refused, but the bishop persisted, offering instead to give Manawydan fab Llyr that which he desired more than anything else. Manawydan fab Llyr said that he wanted the return of Rhiannon and Pryderi, and the spell on their land to be lifted. The bishop agreed and revealed himself to be LLWYD FAB CIL COED, the husband of the mouse that Manawydan fab Llyr had captured. He also confessed that it was he who was responsible for the spell, which he had cast to avenge Pwyll's treatment of his friend GWAWL FAB CLUD. Good to his word, Manawydan fab Llyr released the mouse, the spell was immediately broken, Rhiannon and Pryderi appeared, and Dyfed was restored to its former state.

Pryderi's death came about through the trickery of GWYDION FAB DÔN. Pryderi owned a herd of magic swine, which had been given to PWYLL by ARAWN. Gwydion fab Dôn told his master MATH FAB MATHONWY about them and promised to secure them for him. Along with eleven companions, all disguised as bards, Gwydion fab Dôn travelled from GWYNEDD to Dyfed, where he and his companions were warmly received by Pryderi.

Gwydion fab Dôn explained the purpose of his visit to Pryderi and promised the next morning to show him a fair exchange for the swine. After consulting his advisers, Pryderi agreed. That night Gwydion fab Dôn magically created twelve stallions, twelve greyhounds with golden collars and twelve golden shields. Pryderi accepted them and Gwydion fab Dôn hurriedly drove off the swine for he knew that his enchantment would fail after two days.

When it did, Pryderi and his men set out in hot pursuit to meet the army of MATH FAB MATHONWY, who feared for the safety of his kingdom. This was exactly what Gwydion fab Dôn wanted, for the purpose in obtaining the swine was to incite the conflict and thus get Math fab Mathonwy out of the way for long enough to allow him and his brother GILFAETHWY to abduct and ravish the footholder GOEWIN. After two undecisive battles, Pryderi and Math fab Mathonwy called a truce and decided that the argument should be settled in single combat between Gwydion fab Dôn and Pryderi. The two met at MAEN TYRIAWG, where Gwydion fab Dôn used his magic to overcome and kill Pryderi.

## Pwyll
*Welsh*

One of the main characters of the *Mabinogion*. His story is to be found in the first, third and fourth books.

Pwyll, Lord of DYFED, was out hunting one day when he drove the hounds of ARAWN, Lord of ANNWFN, from a stag. To atone for such an insult, Pwyll agreed to spend a year in Annwfn, during which he would kill Arawn's enemy HAFGAN. Arawn then changed their appearance so that each resembled the other, and they parted, each going to the other's realm.

Pwyll acted honourably during his year in Annwfn, for, although he shared a bed with Arawn's wife, who believed him to be her husband, never once did he lie with her. At the year's end, having fulfilled his promise and killed Hafgan, Pwyll returned home to find that Arawn had ruled Dyfed with untold wisdom. Pwyll then explained to his company all that had transpired, which led to his being given the title Pwyll, Pen Annwfn.

Some time later Pwyll first saw the beautiful RHIANNON, daughter of HEFEYDD HÉN. Captivated by her beauty, Pwyll sought her hand and they were betrothed. At the end of the year Pwyll went to Hefeydd's house to be married. However, during the wedding feast a handsome and finely dressed youth came in and asked a boon of Pwyll that he, without thinking, freely granted, only to discover that the youth was GWAWL FAB CLUD, Rhiannon's rejected suitor. The boon requested was for Rhiannon herself.

Although she was furious, Rhiannon was obliged to comply, but she cunningly suggested that they postpone the boon for a year. She then told Pwyll of her plan. On the night in question Pwyll was to hide 100 of his men in the orchard outside the hall. He would enter in the guise of a shabbily dressed beggar during the wedding feast, carrying a large sack that he would ask to be filled with food. She would see that the request was met and would then ask Gwawl fab Clud to tread the food down into the sack and so capture him in it. Pwyll should then summon his men.

The plan went exactly as devised, and Pwyll's men raced into the hall. They gave the sack an almighty kick and carried on doing so in turn until Gwawl fab Clud was forced to plead for mercy. Only when he had promised to withdraw his claim to Rhiannon and never seek revenge was he freed.

Pwyll married Rhiannon and they lived

in contentment, although after three years she still had not borne him a child. His lords advised him to take another wife, but Pwyll refused. Within the year Rhiannon had borne a son. However, while she slept off the efforts of childbirth, her ladies-in-waiting also fell asleep and the baby mysteriously disappeared. In an attempt to cover their guilt, the ladies-in-waiting smeared the sleeping Rhiannon with blood and accused her of murdering the child, who had not even been named. Pwyll refused to accept Rhiannon's guilt, but, as she would not defend herself, he was forced to make her do penance, so she sat outside the castle every day, carrying all those who accepted her offer into the castle on her back.

The baby was found on the doorstep of TEYRNON TWRYF LIANT, who named the boy GWRI. After a year, struck by the child's resemblance to Pwyll, he took the child to the king, who welcomed back his lost son who was named PRYDERI. Pwyll died shortly afterwards, but his wife lived on, later becoming the wife of MANAWYDAN FAB LLYR.

## Pwyll, Pen Annwfn
*Welsh*

'Pwyll, Head of Annwfn', the title given to PWYLL by his lords after they heard of the king's year in ANNWFN and that for the last year DYFED had been ruled over by ARAWN.

## Ráth Cruachan
*Irish*

The location of the royal cemetery RELIGH NA RIGH, in which the historical kings of IRELAND are buried.

## Ráth Luachar
*Irish*

The home of LIA, who kept the treasure bag of the FIAN.

## Red Book of Hergest, The
*Welsh*

A fourteenth-century manuscript that, together with the *White Book of Rhydderch*, contains the *Mabinogion* cycle.

## Red Branch
*Irish*

The collective name given to the heroes at the court of CONCHOBAR MAC NESSA. They were so called because the room they used for their meetings within the palace at EMHAIN MHACHA was coloured red. Other sources say that the name derives from ROSS, who was the forefather of many of the heroes of the Red Branch, the association being made as Ross was usually known with the epithet 'the Red'. This argument certainly bears weight when the genealogy of Ross is considered, but it by no

means encompasses all the heroes of the Red Branch.

## Red Hugh
*Irish*

The name commonly applied to HUGH, the father of MACHA, DITHORBA and CIMBAOTH.

## Regan
*British*

A daughter of King LEIR and sister of GONERIL and CORDELIA. She and Goneril, being the eldest of Leir's daughters, played on the old man's vanity and induced him to give them each a quarter of his kingdom. She married twice, her husbands being MAGLAURUS, Duke of ALBANY, and HENWINUS, Duke of CORNWALL, although some sources make Maglaurus the husband of Regan, and Henwinus the husband of Goneril, or even vice versa. Regan, Goneril, Maglaurus and Henwinus joined forces to usurp the remaining half of Leir's kingdom, allowing the deposed king to retain a retinue of 140 men. Goneril first reduced this to eighty men, then Regan to five, and finally Goneril again to a single man. At this stage Leir went to FRANCE, from where he was to return with his daughter Cordelia and her husband AGANIPPUS, who restored him to the throne for the last three years of his life.

**Religh na Righ**
*Irish*

The royal cemetery of the historical kings of IRELAND. It is situated at RÁTH CRUACHAN.

**Reochaid**
*Irish*

The lover of FINDABAIR. He fought the chiefs to whom Findabair had been variously promised by AILILL and MEDHBHA for agreeing to attack CÚ CHULAINN.

**Rheged**
*Welsh*

A kingdom in the Cumbrian region of northwest BRITAIN[1], which was ruled by URIEN during the late fourth and early fifth centuries AD.

**Rhiannon**
*Welsh*

With a name deriving from RIG ANTONA or 'Great High Queen', Rhiannon is the goddess of horses, who is known as EPONA in Gaul and as ÉDÁIN ECHRAIDHE and MACHA in IRELAND. Her totem animals were the bull and three cranes, animals that have associations with death and rebirth.

The daughter of HEFEYDD HÊN, Rhiannon was extremely beautiful, a beauty that led PWYLL to become enchanted by her. He sought her hand, a union that was agreed to by both Rhiannon and her father. However, at a feast to celebrate their betrothal her rejected suitor, GWAWL FAB CLUD, entered in disguise and claimed her as a boon from Pwyll, which he unwittingly granted.

Rhiannon was furious but was compelled to comply. However, she suggested that the proposed date for the fulfilment of the boon be put off for one year and then concocted a plan with Pwyll. The plan led to Gwawl fab Clud being captured in a sack and kicked viciously by Pwyll's men until he begged for mercy. Pwyll and Rhiannon released Gwawl fab Clud only after he had renounced his claim to Rhiannon and had promised never to seek revenge.

Rhiannon and Pwyll were married, but, as she had not produced a child after three years, Pwyll's advisers beseeched him to take another wife. He refused and within the year Rhiannon had borne a son. As she slept that night, her ladies-in-waiting also fell asleep and the child, who had yet to be named, mysteriously disappeared. Fearing for their own safety, the ladies-in-waiting smeared the sleeping Rhiannon with blood and woke Pwyll, saying that his wife had killed their newborn son. Pwyll refused to accept that his wife could possibly have done such a thing, but, as she would not defend herself, was forced to make her do penance, by carrying all those who accepted her offer into their castle.

The child had meantime been discovered on the doorstep of TEYRNON TWRYF LIANT who took him in, called him GWRI and treated him as his own son. After a year, struck by the child's resemblance to Pwyll, Teyrnon Twryf Liant took the infant to the king, who was overjoyed to be reunited with his son who was called PRYDERI. Pwyll died a short time later.

Pryderi grew into a handsome and brave warrior under the guidance of his foster father PENDARAN DYFED. He succeeded his father and was much loved by his people, eventually marrying CIGFA, the daughter of GWYN GOHOYW.

Pryderi accompanied BENDIGEID VRAN on his expedition to Ireland against King MATHOLWCH, and was one of the seven survivors who returned to BRITAIN[1] carrying the severed head of Bendigeid Vran. In his absence, however, his cousin MANAWYDAN FAB LLYR, the rightful heir of Bendigeid Vran, had been dispossessed by CASWALLAWN, the son of BELI. Pryderi therefore gave Manawydan fab Llyr his mother Rhiannon as his wife along with the kingdom of DYFED.

Rhiannon, together with her son and their hunting dogs, was later trapped in a caer under an enchantment cast by LLWD FAB CIL COED to avenge Pwyll's illtreatment of his friend Gwawl fab Clud, a spell that was later broken after Manawydan fab Llyr and Cigfa had endured much hardship and had finally captured the wife of Llwd fab Cil Coed in the guise of a mouse. As the spell was broken, Rhiannon, Pryderi and their dogs were restored to their former state, as were the lands of Dyfed.

## R(h)ic(c)a
*Welsh*
See RHITTA CAWR.

## Rhitta (Cawr)
*Welsh*
Also RHICCA or RITHO.

A giant who lived on YR WYDDFA FAWR (Mount SNOWDON) and who had a cloak made of beards. He was killed by a king, later named as ARTHUR, whose beard he wanted for the collar to his cloak. He is, through the similarity of their stories, thought to be identifiable with RIENCE.

## Rhiw Barfe
*Welsh*

'The Way of the Bearded One', a path that runs down the hill from BWLCH-Y-GROES, North WALES. It is so called for it is held that the dead RHITTA was thrown down this path to his grave at Tan-y-Bwlch.

## Rhun
*Welsh*

A handsome courtier of ELPHIN's. He was sent to seduce Elphin's wife after Elphin had boasted that his wife was the most virtuous woman alive. TALIESIN had a serving maid take the place of Elphin's wife, and she succumbed to the charms of Rhun who cut off her ring finger to prove the infidelity. When Elphin was confronted with the ring finger he declared that it could not possibly belong to his wife for three reasons: the finger nail was uncut, the ring was too tight and there was flour under the finger nail. His wife cut her nails regularly, wore a ring that was loose, even on her thumb, and never baked.

## Rhydderch (Hael)
*Welsh*

An historical king of Strathclyde, who sometimes apears with the epithet hael, which means 'generous'. He was one of the kings involved in the Battle of ARFDERYDD, and Welsh tradition claims that he was opposed to the side on which MYRDDIN fought, although GEOFFREY OF MONMOUTH, writing about MERLIN, the latinized form of Myrddin, claims that they fought on the same side and that Rhydderch married Myrddin's twin sister GANIEDA.

## Rhygenydd
*Welsh*

The owner of a crock that is sometimes numbered among the THIRTEEN TREASURES of BRITAIN[1]. See also DYSGYL A GREN RHYDDERCH.

## Riangabair
*Irish*

The husband of FINNABAIR and father of three beautiful daughters, one of whom was called ETAN. Also the father of LOEG, the charioteer of CÚ CHULAINN. They entertained Cú Chulainn and Loeg at the start of Cú Chulainn's quest to locate the sons of DOEL, Etan spending the night with the hero.

## Ríb
*Irish*

The brother of EOCHAID AIREMH. He trespassed onto the land of OENGHUS MAC IN OG and MIDHIR and was told to leave by the two gods, who appeared to him in the guise of hospitallers with a haltered pack-horse.

## Rience
*Welsh*

A king who features in a later, Arthurian legend about a cloak made from beards. His story is remarkably similar to a story told in Welsh tradition about a giant, named RHITTA, Rhicca or Ritho, associated with Mount SNOWDON, who also had a cloak made of beards. He is presumably, therefore, the same character. More modern Welsh folklore makes him a robber, whom ARTHUR slew and buried in the neighbourhood of Llanwchllyn.

## Rig Antona
*General*

'Great High Queen', a title that has been variously applied to a large number of Celtic goddesses, but most frequently to those such as EPONA, RHIANNON, MACHA and ÉDÁIN ECHRAIDHE.

## Rigdonn
*Irish*

The father of RUADH.

## Riothamus
*British*

An early king, whom some have sought to make the historic original of King ARTHUR.

## Ritho
*Welsh*
See RHITTA.

## Rivallo
*British*

The son of CUNEDAGIUS, whom he succeeded as King of BRITAIN[1].

## Riwallawn
*Welsh*

A son of URIEN of RHEGED.

## Roc
*Irish*

The steward of OENGUS MAC IN OG. He appears in the *Cath Finntrága* as a smith who helps to repair and manufacture the weapons of the TUATHA DÉ DANANN. Roc had a tryst with the mother of DIARMAID UA DUIBHNE and conceived with her a son who was killed by DÔNN, Diarmaid ua Duibhne's father. Roc discovered the dead boy and cast a Druidic spell over him so that he arose in the form of a monstrous boar, the BEANN GHULBAN, which he placed under bond to kill Diarmaid ua Duibhne.

## Roi-ch, -gh
*Irish*

The wife of ROSS and mother, by him, of
FERGHUS MAC ROICH.

## Rónán
*Irish*

A king of LEINSTER and the father of MAÍL
FOTHARTAIG. His second wife fell in love
with her step-son and attempted to
seduce him but was repulsed. She accused
him of rape, but Rónán at first refused
to believe it. His wife convinced him of
Maíl Fothartaig's guilt, and he had his
son killed.

## Rosmerta
*Gaulish and British*
Also MAIA

Representing material wealth, and thus
a patroness of merchants, this goddess
was associated with the Romano-Celtic
'MERCURY'. Her name appears to mean
'Good Purveyor', and she is sometimes
depicted stirring a churn, although more
normally carrying a basket of fruit, which
has its counterpart in the classical horn of
plenty, the cornucopia.

## Ross (the Red)
*Irish*

A King of ULSTER, whose epithet is
thought by some to have given rise to
the RED BRANCH. Ross married MAGA,
daughter of OENGHUS MAC IN OG, and
became the father, by her, of a giant by
the name of FACHTNA who, in turn,
married NESSA and became the father of
CONCHOBAR MAC NESSA. However,
Maga also married CATHBHADH and
subsequently became the mother; or
grandmother, of several other heroes
of Ulster.

## Roth Fáil
*Irish*

A magic wheel, which was created by
MOG RUITH to enable him to fly through
the air. Known commonly as the 'wheel
of light', it has often been confused with
a mythical flying machine. It was, in fact
merely a solar symbol.

## Ruadh
*Irish*

The son of RIGDONN. On a voyage to
Norway Ruadh found that his three ships
came to a complete stop in the middle of
the ocean, even though the sails were still
filled by the wind. Diving beneath the
ships, he discovered three giantesses
holding them in position. They took him
to their seabed home, where he lay with
each one before both he and his ships were
released. The giantesses told him that they
would bear his son, and he told them that
he would return to visit them on his way
home. Ruadh forgot his promise, however,
and, when the giantesses realized that he
had sailed by, they set off after him with
his son. Ruadh had too big a head start,
and, realizing this, the giantesses gave up
the chase, cut off his son's head, and threw
it after him.

## Ruadh Rofhessa
*Irish*

One of the titles given to the DAGHDHA.
It means 'Mighty and Most Learned
One'.

## Rua(r)dan
*Irish*

The son of BRES[1] and Brig, a daughter of
the DAGHDHA. He was sent by the
FOMHOIRÉ to find out how the wounded
TUATHA DÉ DANANN were healed. He

wounded GOIBHNIU with one of the magical weapons that the smith had made, but Goibhniu returned the compliment and Ruardan died, even though Brig implored Goibhniu to allow DIAN CÉCHT to heal him.

## Rucht
*Irish*

The swineherd of King OCHALL OICHNI of CONNACHT, and a good friend of FRIUCH, who was the swineherd to the god BODB who dwelt in MUNSTER. So strong was their friendship that the populace sought to cause a quarrel between them. As a result of this argument the two swineherds fought each other for several years in a variety of forms – ravens, water-beasts, demons and finally worms. These worms were swallowed by two cows, who later bore two magnificent bulls, one at which was FINNBHENNACH, and the other the DONN CUAILNGÈ. Which bull came from which swineherd is not recorded. See also COPHUR IN DÁ MUCCIDA.

## Rudaucus
*British*

The King of CAMBRIA who formed an alliance with STATER, King of ALBANY, in an attempt to thwart the expansionist ideas of MOLMUTIUS. Together they marched into CORNWALL and confronted Molmutius' army, but both were killed, which left Molmutius as the sole ruler of a united BRITAIN[1].

## Rudiobus
*Romano-Gaulish*

A mysterious horse god, whose name is, perhaps, a Roman corruption of a Gallic name.

## Run
*Welsh*

A son of URIEN of RHEGED.

## Rury
*Irish*

The son of PARTHOLÁN after whom Lake Rury was named, the lake allegedly bursting forth from his grave.

## Saar
*Irish*

Also BLAI and SABIA

The wife of FIONN MAC CUMHAILL and mother of OISÍN, who was born to her after she had been transformed into a deer by a DRUID.

## Sab(i)a
*Irish*

See SAAR.

## Sabrina
*Romano-British*

The Roman form of HABREN, the name given to the river that is known today as the River SEVERN and in which ESTRILDIS and her daughter by LOCRINUS, Habren, were drowned by GWENDOLEN.

## Saingliu
*Irish*

Also DUBSAINGLU OR DUBSAINGLEUD

One of the two famous steeds of the hero CÚ CHULAINN, the name more correctly being Black of Saingliu. Its twin was Grey of MACHA, both foals being born at exactly the same time as Cú Chulainn himself was born.

## Sainred
*Irish*

A son of LIR and thus a brother of MANANNÁN MAC LIR.

## St Michael's Mount
*British*

Situated a short way off the south CORNWALL coast in Mount's Bay and connected to the mainland by a causeway that is usable only at low tide, this rocky island is the legendary home of the early Cornish giant CORMORAN. The island was called DINSUL in the pre-Christian era and was thought to form a part of the lost kingdom of LYONESSE.

## St Michel, Mont
*Gaulish*

A mount situated off the north coast of BRITTANY. It was legendarily inhabited by a giant.

## St Paul's Cathedral
*British*

A familiar landmark on the LONDON skyline, St Paul's Cathedral was designed by Sir Christopher Wren, construction starting in 1675. It is the site that is of particular interest, for here, it is alleged, BLADUD fell from the sky on his wings and met his death, and, later, the Romans established a temple to Apollo and Diana here. Before that, the site was said to have been a Trojan temple, established by BRUTUS himself and subsequently used by LUD, whose name is remembered in Ludgate Hill, the hill that is today crowned by the magnificence of St Paul's Cathedral.

## Salmon of Llyn Llw
*Welsh*

A gigantic fish on whose shoulders CEI and GWRHYR the interpreter travelled. The two heroes were introduced to the Salmon of Llyn Llw by one of the oldest creatures in the world, the EAGLE OF GWERNABWY.

## Salmon of Wisdom
*Irish*
Also known as Salmon of Knowledge.

A fish that was accidentally touched by FIONN MAC CUMHAILL's thumb while he was cooking it for his master FINNÉCES. Thenceforth Fionn mac Cumhaill had only to bite his thumb to learn all that the future held in store.

## Samera
*Irish*

The father of BUAN.

## Samh-ain, -uinn
*General*

One of the four major Celtic festivals, Samhain was celebrated on 1 November. The feast-day is particularly important in the Irish legends because it was the date on which the people of NEMHEDH had to pay their annual tribute of two-thirds of their corn, wine and children to the FOMHOIRÉ. It was also the date of the Second Battle of MAGH TUIREDH, the eve of which saw the DAGHDHA making

love to the MÓRRÍGHAN while she straddled the River UNIUS. Samhain was also the date upon which the terrible AILLÉN MAC MIDHNA annually came to TARA and burnt the court down until he was killed by the eight-year-old FIONN MAC CUMHAILL.

## samildánach
*Irish*

The name for a polymath, a person of great and varied learning and skills. It was used with this meaning as a title for the god LUGH.

## Sawan
*Irish*

The brother of CIAN and GOBBÁN. Sawan was left in charge of the magical cow of Cian while he went into his other brother's forge to have a new weapon made. BALAR had heard of the cow and, while Sawan was tending it, came to him and said that he had overheard his brothers talking and saying that they would leave only rough steel for Sawan's sword, while making their own from the finest steel available. Sawan gave the cow's halter to Balar, who had assumed the guise of a small boy, and rushed into the forge to confront his brothers. No sooner had he entered than Balar resumed his normal form and carried the cow back to TORY Island.

## Saxon
*General*

The general term used for the Teutonic invaders of BRITAIN[1], although the Saxons were only one of the peoples who invaded the country. They were accompanied by the ANGLES (hence the term ANGLO-SAXON) and the JUTES. The invasions by these barbarian peoples, who had neither armour nor cavalry, began sometime between AD 440 and 460. BEDE[2] said that they originated in North Germany (Saxons), Schleswig (Angles) and Jutland (Jutes). Their languages converged into a single tongue, referred to as Anglo-Saxon by Cambridge scholars, and Old English by Oxford scholars. These invaders, whom Bede divided into the three groupings, formed the ancestors of the modern English people.

## Scáth
*Irish*

A mysterious realm to which CÚ CHULAINN was once said to have travelled and where, with the help of the king's daughter, he stole a magic cauldron, three cows and a vast treasure. However, the king wrecked his coracle in mid-ocean, and he had to swim home with his men clinging to him, but minus his booty.

## Scáthach
*Irish*

A prophetess who is described as living to the north of, or beyond, ALBA and of whom CÚ CHULAINN became a pupil to prove his worth. Cú Chulainn fought Scáthach's great rival AÍFE during his time with her and made Aífe his mistress. She bore him a son, CONALL, who also became a pupil of Scáthach.

## Scéla Mucce Maic Dá Thó
*Irish*

*The Story of Mac Dá Thó's Pig*, an early ribald tale on which the later *Fledd Bricrenn* is based. It tells the ludicrous story of MAC DÁ THÓ who owned a massive boar and a wondrously fast dog, the ownership of which was sought by opposing factions. Mac Dá Thó promised the dog to both parties, and then invited both to a feast, at which his pig was to be the roast, Mac Dá Thó hoping to escape the quarrel that was bound to erupt. He did, indeed, escape the fracas, but not until after his pig had been eaten and his dog had fled the scene.

## Sceolaing
*Irish*
See SGEOLAN.

## Scone, Stone of
*British*

The Coronation Stone that is housed under the seat of the coronation chair in Westminster Abbey, LONDON. The stone has had a very chequered history. It was brought to ENGLAND from Scone in SCOTLAND by King Edward I in 1296. Before that the stone had come from IRELAND, where it was known as the Stone of FÁL, or the LIA FÁIL, one of the four wonders the TUATHA DÉ DANANN brought with them.

Legend identifies this stone as the stone that Jacob used for a pillow during his prophetic dream at Bethel (Genesis 28: 18), after which he set it up as a monument and anointed it. His sons are said to have taken it with them to Egypt, from whence it was taken to Spain. It is here that it becomes entangled within the many strands of the creation legends of Ireland, although tradition states that it was brought from Spain to Ireland *c.* 700 BC by the son of a Spanish king. The stone was taken to TARA, where it was first used as a coronation stone because it was said to speak out if a true king sat upon it, but remained silent for a pretender to the throne. From Ireland the stone was sent to DAL RIADA in the fifth century, and from there it was taken to London in 1296. Twice since then it has been removed from Westminster Abbey.

The first time was when Cromwell declared himself Lord Protector upon it in Westminster Hall. The second time was in 1950 when a party of young Scots raided the abbey and attempted to have it installed in a Scottish cathedral, but no cathedral wanted anything to do with it. Finally, with the coronation of Queen Elizabeth II almost due, the thieves relented and revealed its hiding place to the police, who returned it to Westminster Abbey.

## Scoriath
*Irish*

A King of FERAMORC and the father of MORIATH. He entertained the mute MAON at his court before that youth travelled to GAUL, from whence he returned under the name of LABRAIDH LOINGSECH and married his daughter after ousting his usurping uncle COVAC.

## Scotland
*General*

During the fourth and fifth centuries Scotland was divided among three peoples: the Britons, who occupied the Lowlands that had once been Roman territory, and the PICTS and the Scots, who occupied the land north of Hadrian's Wall, the latter having arrived from IRELAND. GEOFFREY OF MONMOUTH asserts that ANGUSELUS ruled Scotland. The *Historia Meriadoci* says that URIEN was the King of Scots.

## Sea of Clear Glass
*Irish*
See ISLANDS OF MAÍL DÚIN.

## Seachran
*Irish*

A giant with whom FIONN MAC CUMHAILL made friends. Seachran took his new friend home to meet his mother and brother, but they were not pleased that he had befriended a mere human. During the feast, Seachran was seized by a huge hairy claw, but he mananged to shake himself free, in the process knocking his mother into a cauldron that had been intended for him. Seachran and Fionn mac Cumhaill fled, but they were pursued by the brother, who killed Seachran but was himself killed by Fionn mac Cumhaill. Seachran was restored to life after Fionn mac Cumhaill chewed his thumb and learnt of a magic ring, which was obtained for him by DIARMAID UA DUIBHNE, the owners of the ring being killed by Seachran's wife.

## Searbhan Lochlannach
*Irish*

A one-eyed giant who was sent to guard a magical rowan tree that had grown by mistake from a berry dropped by one of the TUATHA DÉ DANANN. No one dared go near the giant, for he could only be killed with three blows from his own iron club. He was eventually killed by DIARMAID UA DUIBHNE after FIONN MAC CUMHAILL had demanded his head, or berries from the tree.

## Sédanta
*Irish*
Also SÉTANTA

The boyhood name of CÚ CHULAINN. While still known by this name, he completed his first heroic deed, the defeat of all fifty of the youths in the service of CONCHOBAR MAC NESSA. Later, he was attacked by the fearsome hound of CULANN the smith. He threw his ball down the animal's gaping throat and, before it could recover from the shock, dashed its brains out. Culann complained bitterly about the loss of his dog, so Sédanta promised to act as his guard dog for as long as he had need of one. It was this promise that earned him his popular name, Cú Chulainn, which simply means 'Culann's hound'.

## Segnius
*British and Gaulish*

The duke who welcomed BRENNIUS to his court while the latter was in exile from Britain, and allowed Brennius to marry his daughter a short time before he died, after which Brennius succeeded to the dukedom.

## Seithenyn
*Welsh*

A legendary inhabitant of CANTRE'R GWAELOD and the father of seven sons, one of whom was TUDNO. Some name Seithenyn as the keeper of the sluices, who became so drunk one night that he forgot his duties and allowed the sea to inundate the kingdom.

## Semion
*Irish*

The son of STARIAT who, according to the story told by TUAN MAC CARELL to St PATRICK, settled in IRELAND, and from whom the FIR BHOLG were descended. This, however, is not the usual version, which says that the Fir Bholg came from overseas, and it may be that Semion was undertaking a reconnaisance for them when he was seen by TUAN MAC CARELL.

## Senach
*Irish*

A mysterious being, said by some to have been an ally of MANANNÁN MAC LIR,

against whom CÚ CHULAINN did battle and won.

## Sencha
*Irish*

An historian at the court of CONCHOBAR MAC NESSA. During the feast thrown by BRICRIU, he announced that the dispute over the right of champion to carve the roast should be judged by MEDHBHA and AILILL. Later, he stood by his friend CONAIRE MÓR at DA DERGA's hostel but was so overwhelmed that he only just managed to escape.

## Sequ-ana, -ena
*Romano-Gaulish*

With her totem animal, a duck, Sequana was goddess of the source of the River Seine, which takes its name from her and near which her sanctuary stood.

## Sera
*Irish*

The father of PARTHOLÁN, AGNOMAN[1] and STARN. His name perhaps means 'West', which would indicate that the invasion of IRELAND by Partholán came from a supernatural kingdom.

## Sétanta
*Irish*
See SÉDANTA.

## Setantii
*British*

A Celtic people, once said to have inhabited an area between the River Ribble and Morecambe Bay. Some authorities suggest that this tribe gave their name to Sétanta, or more correctly SÉDANTA, the childhood name of CÚ

CHULAINN, but this appears to be an attempt to claim that that hero had a British ancestry.

## Severn
*British*

The modern name for the River HABREN, which was known as the SABRINA by the Romans.

## Sevira
*British*

The daughter of MAXIMUS and wife of VORTIGERN to whom she bore BRITU.

## Sgáthach
*Irish*

The daughter of EANNA. FIONN MAC CUMHAILL offered to marry her for a year, and her parents agreed to the union. That night, however, as Fionn mac Cumhaill and his men slept, Sgáthach played a magical tune on the harp, and the following morning Fionn mac Cumhaill and his companions found themselves far away from Eanna's home.

## Sgeimh Solais
*Irish*

'Light of Beauty', the daughter of CAIRBRE, whose hand was sought in marriage by a son of the King of the DECIES. The betrothal led the FIAN to demand a tribute from Cairbre, but he swore not to pay it. This led to the Battle of GABHRA, which was to mark the end of the supremacy of the FIAN in IRELAND.

## Sgeolan
*Irish*
Also SCEOLAING or SKOLAWN

One of the two faithful hounds of FIONN MAC CUMHAILL, the other being BRAN[2]. These hounds were in fact Fionn mac Cumhaill's nephews, because their mother, TUIREAN, the sister of Fionn mac Cumhaill, had been turned into a wolf-hound by the supernatural mistress of ILLAN, her husband. She was later restored to her human form, but her sons retained the form of hounds.

## Sgilti
*Welsh*

One of the often neglected members of the party formed to help CULHWCH locate OLWEN. Sgilti was chosen because he was so light-footed that he could march on the ends of the branches in the trees and weighed so little that even the grass did not bend under him.

## Sheela-na-Gig
*General*

The goddess of sexuality, life and death. During medieval monastic times, she came to represent a female demon.

## siabhra
*Irish*

The collective name given to small supernatural beings or sprites.

## Sideng
*Irish*

The daughter of MONGÁN. She was said to have given FIONN MAC CUMHAILL a flat stone to which a golden chain was attached. By whirling this around his head Fionn mac Cumhaill was able to cut his opponents in half with great ease.

## síd(h)
*Irish*

An earthen barrow or burial mound. The sídh are the homes of the TUATHA DÉ DANANN, each leader being provided with one by the DAGHDHA when they were awarded the underground half of IRELAND by the invading and conquering Sons of MÍL ÉSPÁINE. The Welsh counterpart of the sídh is the CAER[1].

Later tradition extended the use of the word sídh from referring just to the home of the gods to referring to the gods themselves. Later still, the word became widely used in folklore to refer to fairies, sprites and any other form of supernatural being.

## Sil
*British*

A mythical king who is only known from a tenuous link with SILBURY Hill in Wiltshire, which is said to have been his burial mound. See also ZEL.

## Silbury
*British*

A huge earthen mound close to the village of Avebury, in Wiltshire. Silbury Hill is a man-made hill measuring 1,640 feet in circumference at its base and 130 feet in height. Radiocarbon dating has dated its foundation at *c*.2660 BC, which makes it a pre-Celtic relic. However, it was obviously important to the Celts, who were well known for taking over the megalithic stone structures at STONEHENGE and Avebury, which are close at hand.

Local legend says that the hill was the tomb of a King ZEL, or SIL, who had been buried on horseback. The top of the hill was allegedly excavated in 1723, when some human remains and an antique bridle were reported to have been discovered, but this now seems suspect. The true purpose of the hill remains a mystery. It was thoroughly investigated throughout the 1960s and 1970s, but, no matter how many tunnels were bored into it, nothing came to light. The hill remains an enigma to this day.

What did come to light was the truly remarkable internal structure of the hill, for it is not merely a heap of earth with grass on top. At its core is a primary mound, 120 feet in diameter, which was built up in layers of clay, flints, chalk, gravel and turf. On and around this, the main bulk of the hill was constructed from radial and concentric walls of chalk blocks filled in with rubble. At this stage the hill took the form of a seven-stepped pyramid and would have glistened white from the chalk. Earth was then heaped onto the terraces and the whole structure grassed over. The amazing internal mechanics have meant that the hill has retained its original shape and size for more than 4,500 years.

## Silé na gCioch
*Irish*

The Gaelic for SHEELA-NA-GIG.

## Silures
*British*

An ancient people who used to inhabit the area of southeast WALES that is known as Siluria. They combined their forces with those of the ORDOVICES from the north of Wales to help CARATACUS against the Romans, but they were finally beaten in AD 51.

## Silvius
*Graeco-Romano-British*

The grandson of AENEAS and father of

BRUTUS, by whom he was accidentally killed. Brutus was exiled for his patricide and finally arrived in BRITAIN[1] with a company of Trojan refugees.

## Simias
*Irish*

A wizard from the mythical city of MURIAS. He was one of the four wizards who taught the TUATHA DÉ DANANN their magic arts before their invasion of IRELAND. Simias was said to have given the Tuatha Dé Danann the inexhaustible cauldron of the DAGHDHA. His three co-tutors were MORFESSA of FALIA, ESIAS of GORIAS and USCIAS of FINDIAS.

## Sinainn
*Irish*

The eponymous goddess of the River Shannon. The daughter of LODAN[2], she was therefore a granddaughter of LIR. She once travelled to a magical well beneath the sea, where she omitted to cast a certain spell. The waters gushed forth in anger and cast her onto the coast of IRELAND, where the River Shannon now has its mouth and where she died.

## Sínech
*Irish*

A relative of MIDHIR with whom that god stayed after he had carried of the reincarnated ÉDÁIN from EOCHAID AIREMH.

## Sirona
*Gaulish*

A somewhat obscure goddess whose name means 'Star' and who was often associated with GRANNUS.

## Sisillius
*British*

A relative of RIVALLO who succeeded GURGUSTIUS as king of BRITAIN[1]. His own son later came to the throne, after a nephew of Gurgustius had reigned for a while. This son, who remains unnamed, was succeeded by GORBODUC.

## Siugmall
*Irish*

A grandson of MIDHIR and FUAMHNACH. He helped his grandmother to dispose of ÉDÁIN ECHRAIDHE and, as a result, was killed alongside her by MANANNÁN MAC LIR. Another version of the story of Midhir and Édáin Echraidhe says that Siugmall was on the side of Midhir, for here he is portrayed as killing EOCHAID AIREMH after that king had compelled Midhir to return the true Édáin Echraidhe to him.

## Skatha
*Irish*

A variant of SCÁTHACH, although it is sometimes used to refer to her realm.

## Skena
*Irish*

The wife of AMHAIRGHIN, the FILI, who died on the journey to IRELAND and was buried as soon as the Sons of MÍL ÉSPÁINE landed.

## Skolawn
*Irish*

The latinization of SGEOLAN, one of the two hounds of FIONN MAC CUMHAILL.

## Smert-ullos, -rios
*Gaulish*

A chthonic deity, a provider of wealth as

well as a protector who kept his foes at bay simply by a display of his amazing strength. The Romans seized on this aspect and sought to equate him with Hercules.

## Smirgat
*Irish*

According to some sources, the name of the woman who became FIONN MAC CUMHAILL's wife towards the end of his life.

## Snowdon, Mount
*Welsh*

The highest mountain in WALES. It was originally known as YR WYDDFA FAWR.

## Sol
*Welsh*

One of the seldom mentioned members of the party formed to help CULHWCH locate OLWEN. He was chosen because he could stand on one foot all day.

## Solomon
*British*

According to Welsh genealogies, the King of BRITTANY and father of CONSTANTINE[1].

## Souconna
*Gaulish*

The eponymous goddess of the River Saône.

## Sovereignty of Ireland, The
*Irish*

A variation of the SPIRIT OF IRELAND, who is usually regarded as MEDHBHA, Queen of CONNACHT.

## Spirit of Ireland, The
*Irish*

Said to have been personified in the most beautiful woman in the land, such as in the case of ÉDAIN ECHRAIDHE, daughter of King AILILL, some say that she was personified as MEDHBHA. Others say that the Spirit of Ireland came to the island in a time before the biblical Flood as one of the people led by CESAIR, that person being BANBHA, wife of the TUATHA DÉ DANANN king MAC CUILL. It was this incarnation of the Spirit of Ireland that AMHAIRGHIN called upon to cause an enchanted wind send by the Tuatha Dé Danann against the Sons of MÍL ÉSPÁINE to drop.

Even though the identity of the Spirit of Ireland may be confused, she remains one of the most important Irish deities, for she embodied the very essence of IRELAND. It was her right to confer the status of king, who had to ritually mate with her, and hers alone to take it away again. This divine right led to her also being known as the SOVEREIGNTY OF IRELAND.

## Sreng
*Irish*

A huge FIR BHOLG warrior, who was sent to parley with the invading TUATHA DÉ DANANN, who put forward BRES[3] as their spokesman. Terms could not be agreed, because the Fir Bholg refused to divide IRELAND in two, so battle could not be avoided, and, although they gained the upper hand on the first day of the First Battle of MAGH TUIREDH, the Fir Bholg were soundly defeated.

## Stag of Rhedynfrc
*Welsh*

Having been directed to this animal by the BLACKBIRD OF CILGWRI, the party helping CULHWCH was passed on to the

OWL OF CWN CAWLWYD, which, in turn, took them to the EAGLE OF GWERNABWY, which finally took them to the SALMON OF LLYN LLW.

## Stariat
*Irish*

The father of SEMION and thus an ancestor of the FIR BHOLG.

## Starn
*Irish*

A son of SERA, the brother of PARTHOLÁN AND AGNOMAN[1] and the father of TUAN MAC STERN.

## Stater(ius)
*Welsh*

According to GEOFFREY OF MONMOUTH, the ruler of DEMETIA or ALBANY. He and RUDAUCUS, King of CAMBRIA, joined forces against MOLMUTIUS, but they were defeated and killed in battle.

## Stonehenge
*British*

The most famous of the large Megalithic stone circles. Standing on Salisbury Plain, Stonehenge was, according to legend, erected as a memorial at the suggestion of MYRDDIN and was allegedly brought over from IRELAND to be re-erected on its present site. Also known as the GIANTS' RING, The name Stonehenge merely dates from medieval times and is not the original name. Archaeological evidence has shown that the ring was built in three stages. In c.2800 BC a ditch and bank along with the heel stone were all that stood on the site, but c.2000 BC blue-stone pillars, perhaps originating in the Priseli Hills, WALES, were brought to the site, transported up the Avon and

erected. The ring was completed c.1500 BC when sarsen trilithons were erected.

## Stradawl
*British*

The wife of COEL.

## Sualtam
*Irish*

The husband of DEICHTINE and father of SÉDANTA, the hero who later became better known as CÚ CHULAINN.

## Succat
*Irish*

Possibly the childhood name of St PATRICK, although it is possible that Succat was nothing more than a nickname.

## Sucell-os, -us
*Gaulish*

The 'Good Striker', a smith god who is usually depicted as a mature man holding a long-handled mallet, sitting on, or with one leg on, a wine barrel and in the company of a dog, his totem animal. His consort appears to have been NANTOSVELTA. Some authorities feel that Sucellos may have originated as a chthonic fertility god, and, although he is usually assimilated with the Roman Silvanus, some believe that he is more closely equatable with 'DIS PATER'.

## Suibhne Geilt
*Irish*

A King of DÁL NARAIDI, who is perhaps best known as SWEENEY THE MAD. He was said to have lost his sanity at the Battle of Moira, an historic battle fought in AD 637, whereafter he became a 'wild man' roaming the woods. His life story is told in the *Buile Suibne*, a story that some feel might have been the foundation for the story of MYRDDIN.

## Sul(is)
*British*

The goddess of wisdom, who was of such importance that the Romans named the city of BATH in her honour, the Roman name for that city being AQUAE SULIS, or 'Waters of Sulis'. Sul's consort was a sun god, whose carved face, bristling with the rays of the sun, was found during excavations beneath the present pump room in Bath. Some have suggested that the story of BLADUD's magical flight from Bath to LONDON might have derived from a solar myth, now long forgotten, featuring this deity.

Sul is known only at Bath, which suggests that she was a local deity, manifesting herself in the copious hot springs of the city. Her importance in the region is reflected by the fact that the Romans did not obliterate her memory when they built a temple in Bath, but instead amalgamated their temple with the one already in existence. The Romano-Celtic deity so produced is known as SULIS MINERVA, a combination of Sul and the Roman goddess Minerva. This deity was highly revered throughout the Roman Empire, respect that is confirmed in an inscription found on the base of a long-lost statue. This inscription tells of the visit of a Roman state augurer from Rome, who came to Bath to consult the deity and make use of her oracular powers. The inscription further says that his request, whatever that might have been, was answered.

The assumption usually made about the assimilation of Sul and the Roman Minerva is not correct, for dedications to Sul on her own reveal her to be a chthonic UNDERWORLD goddess, similar in many respects to the classical Hecate, whose association is with blessing, cursing and prophecy. These are not attributes of the Roman Minerva. It seems more likely that, following the arrival of the Romans, the true aspect of Sul was lost, her attributes being replaced by more Minervan ones.

## Sulis Minerva
*Romano-British*

The goddess created by the amalgamation of the Roman goddess Minerva with the local goddess SULIS at BATH, the city being named AQUAE SULIS by the Romans in honour of the important Celtic solar deity they found there. Sulis Minerva presided over the therapeutic properties of the hot baths within her city. She also presided over curses and cursing. As an UNDERWORLD goddess she was also associated with prophecy, an oracle being established in her temple at Bath, an oracle that was on one occasion visited by a Roman state augurer. Her prophetic powers came from the Underworld, where all the latent powers of the earth flow together, and the past and the future are as one time.

## Sun Tear
*Irish*

The daughter of FIACHNA[2], who gave her to LOEGHAIRE[2] for his help in freeing the wife of Fiachna from GOLL.

## Sweeney the Mad
*Irish*

The literal translation of SUIBNE GEILT.

## Tadhg
*Irish*

The son of CIAN. He met the divine CLIODNA, who was accompanied by three magical and brightly coloured birds, which feasted on the apples that grew on the eternal apple trees of TÍR TAIRNGIRI and whose song was so sweet that they could soothe the sick and wounded to sleep.

Other sources name Tadhg as the son of NUADHA and the father of MUIRNE, whose hand was sought in marriage by CUMHAILL. He foresaw that he would lose his fortress if he allowed the marriage, so he refused, whereupon Cumhaill abducted her. In the ensuing battle Cumhaill was killed, but not until after Muirne had conceived a son, DEIMNE, who became better known as FIONN MAC CUMHAILL.

## Tailtiu
*Irish*

The battle at which the Sons of MÍL ÉSPÁINE beat the TUATHA DÉ DANANN for the second time, here killing the three Tuatha Dé Danann kings MAC CÉCHT, MAC CUILL and MAC GRÉINE and so becoming the rulers of IRELAND. The conquered Tuatha Dé Danann were compensated with the underground half of the realm. The battle was fought at Teltin, now Telltown.

## Taín Bó Cuailngè
*Irish*

Translated as *The Cattle Raid of Cooley*, this great prose saga preserves a picture of the Irish Iron Age traditions, and it thus represents an essential reference source to the Celtic researcher. Although it is preserved in the *Book of Leinster* (*c.*1150), the *Taín Bó Cuailngè* is obviously far older than that.

The basis of the *Taín Bó Cuailngè* is the quest by MEDHBHA to obtain the DONN CUAILNGÈ, the great brown bull that is the property of ULSTER and that she desired so that her possessions might rival those of AILILL, who owned the great white bull FINNBHENNACH. Medhbha raised a huge army and marched against Ulster, whose warriors had been afflicted by a curse laid on them by MACHA. However, one warrior, the mighty CÚ CHULAINN, remained immune to that curse, and he single-handedly held off the forces of CONNACHT for many weeks, killing hundreds but receiving terrible wounds himself.

Finally, while Cú Chulainn was fighting the sons of CALATIN, Medhbha managed to penetrate deep into Ulster and bring back the Donn Cuailngè. Triumphantly, she took the bull to her camp where it fought Finnbhennach and totally annihilated the white bull before trotting off. Cú Chulainn died after failing to recognize the presence of the MÓRRÍGHAN, and Medhbha and Ailill had to return to Connacht with less than they started out with, for the Donn Cuailngè had returned to Ulster and of Finnbhennach there were but a few scraps left.

## Taise
*Irish*

The daughter of the King of Greece (here a mythical land) who loved FIONN MAC CUMHAILL but was intercepted by her father's guards as she tried to come to him. She was rescued by GOLL and OSCAR who brought her to FIONN MAC CUMHAILL, but what happened after that is not recorded.

## Taliesin
*Welsh*

The magically born child of CERRIDWEN, who lived in Penllyn with her husband. TEGID VOEL and with their children, who number either two or three, the former number being the most usual. These children were the fairest maiden in all the world – CREIRWY – and the most ugly and disadvantaged man ever to have been born – AFAGDDU. Some sources name a third son, MORFRAN AB TEGID, but it is usually thought that he and Afagddu are one and the same.

Cerridwen sought to compensate her son for his disadvantages by brewing a potion of Inspiration and Science in a vast cauldron, a brew that had to boil for a year and a day simply to produce the three drops that would bestow the gifts she sought for her son. Having collected together all the necessary ingredients, she set GWION BACH, the son of GWREANG, to stir the mixture and gave the blind man MORDA the job of kindling the fire beneath the huge pot. She ordered them never to cease with their allotted task or they would have her to answer to.

Every day Cerridwen added more herbs to the brew. Towards the end of the year three drops of the fluid fell onto the thumb of Gwion Bach, who immediately sucked it to cool it and thus ingested the full potency of the brew. He at once knew that his life was in danger and fled. The cauldron then split in two and the remainder of the potion, poisonous now that the three divine drops had been produced, ran into a stream and poisoned the horses of GWYDDNO GARANHIR.

When Cerridwen returned to find her year's work spoiled, she immediately suspected Morda and struck him around the head with a log until one of his eyes fell out onto his cheek. As he still protested his innocence, Cerridwen realized that it was Gwion Bach she was after. Setting off in hot pursuit, she soon started to gain on the fleeing boy. Sensing her approach he turned himself into a hare, but she countered by becoming a greyhound. Gwion Bach leapt into the air and, changing into a fish, dived into a river. Cerridwen followed as an otter. Once more Gwion Bach sensed her approach, and he jumped out of the water and changed into a bird. She did the same and became a hawk. At length Gwion Bach flew over a barn and dropped onto the threshing floor, there changing into a grain of wheat among the thousands that were strewn all over. Cerridwen landed and changed herself into a hen and soon afterwards swallowed Gwion Bach.

Cerridwen soon found that she was pregnant and nine months later gave birth to a beautiful baby boy. Cerridwen could not bring herself to kill him, so she placed him in a leather bag and threw him into the river. The bag caught on the fish weir of Gwyddno Garanhir where it was found by ELPHIN. The first thing he saw as he opened the bag was the baby's forehead, at which he exclaimed 'Taliesin' which means 'radiant brow', and thus the child received his name.

Much later, Taliesin was said to have rescued his foster father Elphin when the latter had been imprisoned by MAELGWYN, an episode which forms the subject matter of Thomas Love Peacock's novel *The Misfortunes of Elphin* (1829).

This is the traditional view of the magical conception of Taliesin, although an alternative story says that Taliesin was magically created by GWYDION FAB DÔN, and that he was originally a god.

Taliesin became famed for his poetic prowess. URIEN of RHEGED was said to have once been poetically addressed by Taliesin, but it appears that the poet was not a resident of RHEGED and possibly has a southern Welsh origin. *The Book of Taliesin*, which was possibly compiled in the fourteenth century, is thought to contain some authentic poems by Taliesen, whose historicity is now regarded as without doubt, living perhaps in the sixth or seventh century. The manuscript for this work is now in the National Library of WALES, Aberystwyth.

Taliesin numbers amongst the seven survivors of the expedition led by BENDIGEID VRAN to IRELAND against King MATHOLWCH. Later, this story was to be refined in the *Preiddeu Annwfn*, which said that he was one of the seven who survived an expedition into the OTHERWORLD to secure a magical cauldron.

Both Welsh tradition and the *Vita Merlini* make Taliesin a contemporary of MYRDDIN, representing the two talking with each other. The verse ascribed to Taliesin is somewhat difficult to understand, being constructed in an obscure manner. This has led some commentators to ascribe the verse to Myrddin, saying that it only later came to be attributed to Taliesin. Other sources add that Taliesin had a son named ADDAON, who was subsequently killed by LLONGAD GRWRM FARGOD EIDYN.

## Taltiu
*Irish*
Also TELTA

The wife of EOCHAIDH MAC ERC, who had her palace at Telltown (TAILTIU), where she was buried, and where, even in medieval IRELAND, a great annual fair was held in her honour.

## Tanaros
*Gaulish*

The god of thunder and lightning, although this name may simply be a misspelling of TARANIS

## Tara
*Irish*

For many centuries the most sacred place in IRELAND Tara was the site in County MEATH of the royal court of the King of Ireland, although some contend that Tara is really the name of the great hall and that the name of the court has been lost. Tara became the religious and political centre of Celtic Ireland, where, until the mid-sixth century, a new king's ritual marriage with the SPIRIT OF IRELAND was celebrated and feasted at a ceremony known as the FEIS TEMHRACH.

Situated approximately 23 miles northwest of Dublin, Tara sits on a hilltop that was undoubtedly a sacred site long before the arrival of the Celts. Today, only a few mounds, ditches and earthworks distinguish the hill from many others in the vicinity. An oblong enclosure, some 759 feet long and 46 feet wide, with a series of entrances on either side, was the great banqueting hall of Tara. Here the legendary TARBFEIS took place until St PATRICK outlawed it.

The court features in many of the Irish legends. It is the capital of the TUATHA DÉ DANANN to which came the invading

Sons of MÍL ÉSPÁINE; the court of CORMAC MAC AIRT; the court of EOCHAIDH AIREMH to which MIDHIR came to relaim ÉDÁIN ECHRAIDHE; the court where FIONN MAC CUMHAILL, at the age of eight, killed the monstrous AILLÉN MAC MIDHNA who annually came at SAMHAIN and burned the court down; the location of the feast from which GRÁINNE eloped with DIARMAID UA DUIBHNE; the court of CONCHOBAR MAC NESSA and thus the location of the RED BRANCH; and the alleged burial place of the head and one of the hands of CÚ CHULAINN.

## Taran-is, -os
Gaulish

One of the three most important Celtic deities of GAUL, the other two being ESUS and TEUTATES. Human sacrifices are reported to have been made to all three gods. The god of the wheel and a Druidic father god, whose attributes were thunder and the oak tree, both of which were important Druidic entities, Taranis is also the god of the seasons and the stars. Associated with the powers of change, the Romans assimilated him with their god Jupiter, although he is possibly more correctly equated to the shadowy Dis Pater, a primal god of the UNDERWORLD.

## Tarbfeis
Irish

The legendary bull feast that was held at TARA following the death of a king. A bull would be roasted and a chosen man would eat the flesh of the bull and drink a broth made from its blood and bones. During his sleep a DRUID would chant an incantation over him, and the sleeping man would see the next king of IRELAND in a dream. This rite was finally outlawed by St PATRICK.

## Tarvos Trigaran-os, -us
British and Gaulish

The 'Three-horned Bull', images of which have been found on both sides of the English Channel. It is possible that he has his Irish equivalent in the DONN CUAILNGÈ. See also DÔNN[2].

## Tasha
Irish

A supernatural maiden who fell in love with FIONN MAC CUMHAILL when he and his men came to the help of her father. In return for the help of the FIAN, Tasha was allowed to accompany Fionn mac Cumhaill to IRELAND, where they were married.

## tawlbwrdd
Welsh

A backgammon board, although sometimes said to be a chess board, which was counted among the THIRTEEN TREASURES of BRITAIN[1]. It had a ground of gold, and men of silver, who would play themselves. It has its Irish equivalent in the game of FIDCHELL.

## Tea
British

The daughter of the biblical king Zedekiah, whom the Scots said came to IRELAND in 585 BC with two companions, bringing with her the LIA FÁIL, or stone of FÁL. She married an Irish king, possibly EREMON, and the hill of his court was named Temair after her. This hill is none other than TARA. The story itself is of Scottish invention and has very little to do with the traditional Irish mythology on which it is undoubtedly based.

## Teach-Dhoinn
*Irish*

The Gaelic for TECH DUIN.

## Tech Duin
*Irish*

The island off the southwest coast of IRELAND on which it is believed that DÔNN[1], the discourteous leader of the Sons of MÍL ÉSPÁINE, was buried after he had drowned and to which he still welcomes dead warriors.

## Tegau E(u)fron
*Welsh*

The wife of CARADOC VREICHVRAS who had three treasures: a mantle (clouk), a cup and a carving knife. Depending on which list is consulted, her treasures are sometimes included in the THIRTEEN TREASURES OF BRITAIN[1].

## Tegid Voel
*Welsh*

The husband of CERRIDWEN and father, by her, of CREIRWY and AFAGDDU. Some sources name a third son as MORFRAN AB TEGID, but it is generally believed that this son is none other than Afagddu, which is a derisive nickname. Tegid Voel is described as being of gentle lineage, his home being on an island in the middle of LLYN TEGID, from which he takes his name.

## Teirgwaedd
*Welsh*

The father of MENW FAB TEIRGWAEDD.

## Teirtu
*Welsh*

The owner of a magical harp that would play itself when so commanded.

## Telta
*Irish*
See TALTIU.

## Tenuantius
*British*

The son of LUD and brother of ANDROGEUS. He and his brother were still too young to succeed their father on his death, so the throne passed to Lud's brother, CASSIVELLAUNUS, who, in an attempt to thwart any possibility of trouble, made Androgeus the Duke of KENT and Tenuantius the Duke of CORNWALL. Together with their uncle, the two brothers twice helped to defeat JULIUS CAESAR as he made exploratory raids into BRITAIN[1]. However, the third attack by Julius Caesar was more successful, because Androgeus betrayed his uncle and brother to the Romans. The Romans besieged Cassivellaunus and Tenuantius near CANTERBURY, now Androgeus changed sides again and acted as a mediator. Cassivellaunus agreed to pay Rome a tribute, after which Julius Caesar returned to Rome and took Androgeus with him.

Tenuantius ascended to the throne after the death of his uncle, and he reigned in peace because he honoured the tribute to Rome. He was succeeded in turn by his own son CUNOBELINUS, who had been raised in Rome in the household of the emperor Augustus.

## Ternova
*British*

A variant of TROIA NOVA. It is mentioned

in the myth of the magical King BLADUD.

## Tethra
*Irish*

A shadowy figure who was said to refer to the fish he herded as his cattle. His only real appearance in the Irish legends is during the Second Battle of MAGH TUIREDH, in which he was reported to have fought alongside the FOMHOIRÉ, possibly even being numbered among their rulers. His war sword, which recounted all it had done when unsheathed, was captured by OGHMA.

## Teutates
*Gaulish*

A tribal deity, possibly a god of war, who was one of the three main gods of Celtic GAUL, the other two being ESUS and TARANIS. The Romans sought to equate Teutates, whose name comes from a Celtic root meaning 'warlike', with Mars.

## Teyrnon Twryf Liant
*Welsh*

The owner of the most beautiful mare in the world, a mare that foaled every year on 1 May, but whose colts always mysteriously vanished. Unable to withstand the loss any longer, Teyrnon Twryf Liant hid himself in the stable and watched his mare foal. As he stood and gazed on the wonderful colt a huge clawed hand reached into the stable and took hold of the animal. Teyrnon Twryf Liant jumped up and severed the arm at the elbow so that it fell into the stable along with the colt. He rushed outside to see if he could identify the thief, but nothing was in sight. As he came back into the stable he found a baby boy, whom he took in to his wife. They named

him GWRI. A year later, having learnt of the mysterious disappearance of the newborn baby boy of PWYLL and RHIANNON and struck by the infant's likeness to the king, he concluded that this must be their lost baby. Teyrnon Twryf Liant took the child to the king. Amid great celebrations Rhiannon renamed the child PRYDERI.

## Thirteen Treasures
*Welsh*

The treasures or curiosities that MYRDDIN was said to have procured and then sailed away with, never to be seen again, in his glass boat. These mystical items altered from source to source, but most common among them were:

- **Dyrnwyn**: the sword of RHYDDERCH HAEL, which would burst into flames from the cross to the point if any man, save Rhydderch, drew it.
- **Mwys Gwyddno**: the hamper of GWYDDNO, which had the power to turn any meat placed on or in it, into sufficient to feed a hundred people.
- **Corn Brangaled**: the horn of BRANGALED, which could provide any drink desired.
- **Cadair, neu car Morgan Mwynfawr**: the chair or car of MORGAN MWYNFAWR, which would carry a person seated in it wherever they wished to go.
- **Hogalen Tudno**: the whetstone of TUDNO, which would sharpen none but the weapon of a brave man.
- **Llen Arthur**: the veil of ARTHUR, which rendered the wearer invisible. (This item is a later addition to the list.)
- **Cyllel Llawfrodedd**: a DRUID sacrificial knife said by some to have belonged to a character named LLAWFRODEDD.
- **Pais Padarn**: the cloak of PADARN REDCOAT, which would make the wearer invisible.

- **Pair Drynog**: the cauldron of DRYNOG in which none but the meat of a brave man would boil. Some sources name this as the cauldron that had once belonged to the giant DIWRNACH.
- **Dysgyl a gren Rhydderch**: the platter of RHYDDERCH upon which any meat desired would appear. Some sources name the owner of the magical dish as RHYGENYDD, and some also include a crock that was also said to have belonged to Rhygenydd. This would, however, appear to be a confusion.
- **Tawlbwrdd**: a chess or, more accurately, a backgammon board with a ground of gold and men of silver who would play themselves. This is sometimes named as the GWYDDBWLL board belonging to GWENDDOLAU.
- **Mantell**: a robe that would keep the wearer warm no matter how severe the weather. This is sometimes confused with Llen Arthur, and is then said to render the wearer invisible. Some say that it had once belonged to TEGAU EUFRON.
- **Modrwy Eluned**: the ring of ELUNED, which conferred invisibility on the wearer. An unnamed stone also belonging to Eluned is sometimes mentioned in the list.
- The halter of CLYDNO EIDDYN.

## Thitis
*Welsh*

One of the nine sisters of MORGEN.

## Ti(g)ernmas
*Irish*

A mythical king, the fifth in line after EREMON. Tigernmas is alleged to have introduced the worship of CENN CRÚIACH into IRELAND and to have been the first to mine and smelt gold in Ireland. Tigernmas and three-quarters of his people were said to have been killed while worshipping Cenn Crúiach on the eve of SAMHAIN.

## Tír fó -Thuinn, -Thiunn
*Irish*

'The Land under the Waves', a supernatural underwater kingdom that appears in the story of DIARMAID UA DUIBHNE, who was taken there to help its king but held there against his will and rescued by FIONN MAC CUMHAILL.

## Tír (in)na mBan
*Irish*

An OTHERWORLDLY realm that was entirely populated by women, which led to it popularly being known as the LAND OF WOMEN. The island was visited by BRÂN who thought that he and his companions only remained there a year. They found out that they had, in fact, stayed for hundreds of years when they attempted to return home.

## Tír (in)na mBéo
*Irish*

A paradisal OTHERWORLDLY realm, euphemistically called the LAND OF THE LIVING, where sickness and old age were unknown and where the people perpetually feasted. It is the land to which CONNLA[2] was taken and became king.

## Tír (in)na n-Oc, -Og
*Irish*

The OTHERWORLDLY realm known as the LAND OF THE YOUNG or LAND OF YOUTH. This was the realm to which OISÍN travelled and married NIAMH[2] with whom he lived for 300 years, although to him it seemed like just three weeks.

### Tír Tairngiri
*Irish*

The OTHERWORLDLY land, known as the LAND OF PROMISE, which was ruled by MANANNÁN MAC LIR, although MIDHIR was also regarded as a god of this realm, for on one occasion that god lured CORMAC MAC AIRT to the kingdom.

### Togodumnus
*British*

The son of CUNOBELINUS and brother of CARATACUS whom he fought alongside in an attempt to thwart the Roman invasion led by CLAUDIUS. Although they delayed the invasion they were eventually beaten.

### Tollen, St
*British*

A saintly figure who was said to have defeated GWYNN AP NUDD, the Welsh Lord of the Dead on GLASTONBURY TOR. See also COLLEN.

### Tonwenna
*British*

The wife of MOLMUTIUS and mother, by him, of BRENNIUS and BELINUS. The two warring brothers were finally reconciled after Tonwenna had appealed to them to make their peace.

### Topa
*Irish*

The manservant to PARTHOLÁN, who was seduced by DEALGNAID, Partholán's wife, and is therefore possibly the father of RURY.

### Tor Môr
*Irish*

The precipitous headland on TORY Island on which BALAR built a tower in which he confined his daughter ETHLINN, and where she was visited by CIAN and conceived LUGH.

### Torach
*Irish*

An alternative name, sometimes used to refer to TORY Island, the stronghold of the FOMHOIRÉ.

### Torc Triath
*Irish*

The king of boars. He corresponds to the giant boar TWRCH TRWYTH, which appears in the *Mabinogion* and against which CULHWCH was sent by YSPADDADEN in his quest to win the hand of OLWEN.

### Torna Éices
*Irish*

A FILI who lived in ULSTER and was said to have been the foster father of NÍAL NOÍGIALLACH.

### Tory
*Irish*
Also TORACH

The precipitous island off the coast of Donegal that was the stronghold of the FOMHOIRÉ. The people of NEMHEDH once stormed the island and succeeded in killing one of the two FOMHOIRÉ kings of the time, CONANN. The other king, MORC, however, killed all but thirty of the attackers, who were then forced to flee from IRELAND.

## Totnes
*British*

The town in south Devon where BRUTUS and his Trojan refugees were said to have landed, their immigration being opposed by GOGMAGOG and the other giants who lived in BRITAIN[1]. It is also the town where AMBROSIUS AURELIUS was said to have landed from BRITTANY and where he was proclaimed king.

## Toutates
*Gaulish*
See TEUTATES.

## Tremeur
*British*

According to the legends surrounding CUNOMORUS, Tremeur was either the son of Cunomorus and TREPHINA, or of Trephina and JONAS. One tradition makes him the offspring of the first couple, also calling him GILDAS JUNIOR, while another makes his parents the second coupling, and gives him the alternative name of Judwal.

## Trend(h)orn
*Irish*

A servant in the employ of CONCHOBAR MAC NESSA. He was sent by that king to spy on DERDRIU and the sons of UISNECH after they had returned to IRELAND from their exile in SCOTLAND, the express purpose of his mission being to report whether the beauty of Derdriu had been diminished in her absence. He was spotted by NAOISE, who put out one of his eyes with an expertly thrown chess piece, but Trendhorn completed his mission and reported to Conchobar mac Nessa that Derdriu was still the most beautiful woman alive.

## Trenmor
*Irish*

The father of CUMHAILL and thus grandfather of FIONN MAC CUMHAILL.

## Treon
*Irish*

The father of the giantess BEBHIONN, whom he had betrothed, against her will, to AEDA[2].

## Trephina
*Welsh*

The daughter of WAROK and wife of CUNOMORUS.

## Trí Dé Dána
*Irish*

The triad of the gods of craftmanship. They were CREIDHNE, GOIBNIU and LUCHTAINE. During the Second Battle of MAGH TUIRECH, one of the few occasions when they actually worked together, they forged and repaired the weapons of the TUATHA DÉ DANANN. However, the honorific, which means 'Three Gods of Dan', is also sometimes applied to BRIAN, IUCHAR and IUCHARBA. See also COLUM CUALLEINECH.

## Tri-Novantes
*British*

The tribal name given to the Britons said to be inhabiting LONDON and the territory to the north of that city at the time of JULIUS CAESAR's second incursion into BRITAIN[1] in 54 BC. Fearing the ambitions of CASSIVEL-LAUNUS, the Tri-Novantes placed themselves under Roman protection along with other British tribes. Cassivallaunus, having agreed to pay tribute to Rome in return for independence, also agreed to uphold the separate independence of the Tri-Novantes. Later, during the revolt led by BOUDICCA in the first century AC, the Tri-Novantes joined forces with her ICENI people, but were supressed by the Romans after they had defeated Boudicca.

## Tri-Novantum
*Romano-British*

A later name given to TROIA NOVA, or 'New Troy', the city legendarily founded by BRUTUS and today known as LONDON. The TRI-NOVANTES, who inhabited the city and the land to the north at the time of JULIUS CAESAR's second exploratory visit to BRITAIN[1], take their name from this ancient name for the capital city of Britain.

## Triads
*Welsh*

The common name for the *Trioedd Ynys Prydein*.

## Trioedd Ynys Prydein
*Welsh*

*The Triads of the Island of Britain*, one of the oldest extant Welsh manuscripts, dating from the sixth century, consists of political lyrics, war songs, songs praising chiefs and elegies on the same, religious, hymns and pseudonymous poems, variously ascribed to MYRDDIN and TALIESIN. The *Triads*, as they are popularly known, were written by Celtic bards of the time, and are outstanding and essential source texts for Celtic research. They undoubtedly inspired many of the later writers, such as GILDAS and NENNIUS[1], who adapted the text to suit their own purposes.

## Troia Nova
*British*

BRUTUS gave the name to the city he founded on the River Thames. It was later known as TRI-NOVANTUM and is better known today as LONDON.

## Troynovant
*British*

See TROIA NOVA.

## Troynt
*Welsh*

A little used variant of TWRCH TRWYTH.

## Trwyn yr Wylfa
*Welsh*

A hill on whose summit the people of HELIG AP GLANOWG were alleged to have fled when the sea inundated their kingdom, one of the lost kingdoms of WALES that is now said to lie about 2 miles off the coast at Penmaenbach.

## Tuag (Inbir)
*Irish*

A beautiful maiden who was kept in seclusion so that no man might see her. However, she had been seen by MANANNÁN MAC LIR who was instantly besotted. He sent a DRUID named FER FÍDAIL, the son of FOGABAL, in the guise of a woman to gain access to her. However, Fer Fídail fell in love with Tuag and spent three nights with her, before causing her to fall into an enchanted sleep in which state he carried her down to the shore, where he left her while he went to look for a boat. Manannán mac Lir sent a huge wave to drown the maiden and afterwards summarily disposed of Fer Fídail.

## Tuan mac Carell
*Irish*

The son of CARELL, who was conceived after his wife ate the salmon that was the final animal incarnation of TUAN MAC STERN, who had come to IRELAND as one of the companions of PARTHOLÁN.

## Tuan mac Stern
*Irish*

The nephew of PARTHOLÁN. He came with that leader to IRELAND and was the sole survivor of the plague that wiped out those people. He lived alone for twenty-three years after the death of the people of Partholán before he hid in the hills and witnessed the arrival of NEMHEDH and his companions. There then started a series of transformations to Tuan mac Stern that are typical of Celtic mythology.

One night he fell asleep as an old man. The next morning he awoke as a stag, young in both body and heart. He remained in that form, as the king of all the deer of Ireland, during the occupation of Nemhedh and his people. As they died out, so Tuan mac Stern once again fell asleep in old age. This time he woke up as a wild boar, once more rejuvenated.

Now he witnessed the arrival of the FIR BHOLG and remained in the shape of the boar while those people were the inhabitants of Ireland. Again old age set in, and this time he was rejuvenated as an eagle, in which form he saw the arrival of the TUATHA DÉ DANANN and then the Sons of MÍL ÉSPÁINE. While they were in occupation, he once again reached old age and was reborn as a salmon.

This salmon was caught by a fisherman and taken to the home of CARELL whose wife ate him whole. He gestated in her womb for nine months before being reborn as a human boy, but now having the name TUAN MAC CARELL. It is in this incarnation that he met St PATRICK and told that saint the history of Ireland. See also FINNEN.

## Tuatha Dé (Danann)
*Irish*

Literally translated as the 'People of the Goddess Dana', the Tuatha Dé Danann are the true gods of Celtic IRELAND. They are recorded in the *Leabhar Gabhála Éireann* as the remnants of the people of NEMHEDH, who fled to unnamed northern lands, although some have suggested that these lands were the Hebrides, or even the Orkney or Shetland Islands. Returning as the fifth of the six invasions Ireland endured in its mythological history, they followed the FIR BHOLG who were also a people formed from the residue of the people of Nemhedh. However, the Tuatha Dé Danann had, during their longer absence from Ireland, learned all manner of magical skills and brought with them four magical items. These were the stone of FÁL given to them by the wizard MORFESSA in FALIA, the invincible spear of LUGH, given to them by ESIAS in GORIAS, the inescapable sword of NUADHA, given to them by USCIAS in FINDIAS, and the inexhaustible cauldron of the DAGHDHA, their leader, given to them by SIMIAS in MURIAS.

When confronted by the Fir Bholg, the Tuatha Dé Danann demanded that the kingship of the country be handed to them or they would fight for it. The Fir Bholg chose the latter and were utterly defeated at the First Battle of MAGH TUIREDH, although the Tuatha Dé Danann's king, Nuadha, lost an arm in the fight and so had to abdicate. The few survivors of the Fir Bholg fled into exile among the FOMHOIRÉ.

The new king chosen by the Tuatha Dé Danann was not the best decision they had ever made, for they chose the

tyrannical BRES[1] who was half Tuatha
Dé Danann and half Fomhoiré. His
tyranny was soon put to an end, and
Nuadha, having had a silver arm fitted,
was restored to the throne. Bres defected
to the Fomhoiré and raised an army
against the Tuatha Dé Danann, who
prepared for the battle. Shortly before the
battle was due to began, Lugh arrived at
TARA, the Tuatha Dé Danann's capital,
and Nuadha, recognizing the superiority
of the polymath, stepped down in his
favour.

The Second Battle of Magh Tuiredh
was now fought, this battle being against
the Fomhoiré army led by Bres. The battle
was decided in single combat between
Lugh and the giant BALAR. Lugh won with
a well-aimed slingshot, which went
straight through Balar's single eye and
continued out of the back of his head to
decimate the Fomhoiré horde.

The number of Tuatha Dé Danann
deities has never been fully established.
Notable among them were Lugh, OGHMA,
the Daghdha, the three kings MAC CUILL,
MAC CÉCHT and MAC GRÉINE along with
their goddess wives BANBHA, FÓDLA and
ÉRIU, the last of which gave her name to
EIRE. The Tuatha Dé Danann were finally
defeated by the sixth and last invasionary
party to land in Ireland, the Sons of
MÍL ÉSPÁINE. The final battle was that
of TAILTIU, after which the Tuatha Dé
Dannan negotiated with their conquerors
to retain at least a part of their realm.
They were given the underground half,
and the Daghdha provided each of the
Tuatha Dé Danann with a SÍDH, or
earthen barrow. There the Tuatha Dé
Danann are said still to live.

## Tudno
*Welsh*

A famous Welsh saint, who is said to
have been one of the seven sons of
SEITHENYN and who hailed from the lost
kingdom of CANTRE'R GWAELOD.

## Tudwal Tudglyd
*Welsh*

The owner of a whetstone that was
counted among the THIRTEEN TREASURES
of BRITAIN[1].

## Tuireann
*Irish*
Also TYREN

The daughter of BODB and sister of SAAR.
She married ILLAN but was turned into a
wolf-hound by her husband's supernatural
lover while she was pregnant. She gave
birth to two hounds, BRAN[2] and SGEOLAN,
who became the faithful hunting dogs
of FIONN MAC CUMHAILL, her brother-in-
law. Her human form was restored to her
after Illan had promised his mistress that
he would renounce her.

## Tu(i)renn
*Irish*

The son of OGHMA and the father of
BRIAN, IUCHAR and IUCHARBA.

## Tulchainde
*Irish*

The DRUID to CONAIRE MÓR. He loved
DIL, the daughter of LUGMANNAIR, and
persuaded her to elope with him from the
Isle of FALGA (Isle of MAN), but she set
the condition that her two beloved oxen,
FEA and FERNEA, should accompany
them. Unable to do this himself, for the
oxen would have sunk their boat,
Tulchainde enlisted the help of the
MÓRRÍGHAN, who magically transported
the beloved oxen over the water to MAGH
MBREG, to where Dil and Tulchainde had
travelled.

## Turbe (Trágmar)
*Irish*

The father of the smith god GOIBHNIU, although some sources say he was the father of GOBBAN SAER. He appears to have had a connection with the sea, because he was said to hurl his axe at the sea when it was in full flood and forbid it to come beyond the point where the axe fell.

## Twrch Trwyth
*Welsh*

A fierce boar, which had originally been a king who was transformed by God for his wickedness. Almost certainly a recollection of an earlier boar deity, the boar being a cult animal among the Celts, he corresponds directly to TORC TRIATH, the king of the boars in Irish mythology.

In the story of *Culhwch and Olwen*, one of the tasks that YSPADDADEN set CULHWCH was to obtain the razor and comb (alternatively said to be a comb, razor and shears) from between the ears of this monstrous boar in order to barber Yspaddaden in preparation for Culhwch's marriage to OLWEN. The boar had already killed a great number of men before Culhwch caught up with it. Running it down, MABON snatched the razor while CYLEDYR THE WILD obtained the shears. The boar evaded them for a while, but they managed to find it again and procure the comb. They then forced the boar to jump off a cliff into the sea, when it swam away, never to be seen again.

## Ty Gwydr
*Welsh*

Literally a 'house of glass'. MYRDDIN's home was thought to be one, being said to stand either on BARDSEY Island, or on a boat, in which he sailed away with the THIRTEEN TREASURES.

## Tylwyth Teg
*Welsh*

The collective name for the people of GWYNN AP NUDD, although not necessarily referring to the dead themselves. The Tylwyth Teg are more akin to the fairies of popular folklore than to anything else, but they are possibly best described as spirits awaiting rebirth.

## Tyren
*Irish*
See TUIREANN.

## Tyronoe
*Welsh*

One of the nine sisters of MORGEN.

## Uar-gaeth-sceo Luachair-sceo
*Irish*

One of the ridiculous names given by the MÓRRÍGHAN when she was asked to identify herself by CÚ CHULAINN. The other, equally tongue-twisting name she gave was FAEBOR BEG-BEOIL CUIMDIUIR FOLT SCENBGAIRIT SCEO UATH. Cú Chulainn failed to recognize that the woman he was questioning was the Mórríghan, a mistake that ultimately led to his death.

## Uathach
*Irish*

The daughter of SCÁTHACH and brother of CUARE and CET. She fell in love with CÚ CHULAINN and taught him how he might get the better of her mother and thus how he might marry Uathach without a dowry.

## Uchtdelbh
*Irish*

'Shapely Bosom', the wife of MANANNÁN MAC LIR, with whom AILLÉN, son of EOGABAL and brother of AINÉ², fell in love. Ainé came to the rescue of her brother who was suicidal, as she herself loved Manannán mac Lir. Together they went to the home of the god, where Ainé smothered Manannán mac Lir with kisses and Aillén made it apparent that he loved Uchtdelbh. As Manannán mac Lir was well satisfied with the love he was being shown by Ainé, he gave Uchtdelbh to Aillén.

## Ugainy
*Irish*

A legendary king of IRELAND who also ruled over the greater part of western Europe. He was said to have married a princess of GAUL and had two sons, LOEGHAIRE[1] and COVAC, who fought over the right to succeed him.

## Uí Liatháin
*Irish and Welsh*

An Irish dynasty that is recorded as having ruled over the Welsh kingdom of DEMETIA (DYFED), possibly being expelled during the fifth or sixth century by AGRICOLA. It has been suggested that they brought with them a great number of the Irish legends, which gradually became interwoven with the native Welsh legends, a suggestion that attempts to explain the resemblance of a great many of the Welsh and Irish legends.

## Uí Néill
*Irish*

The name by which the descendants of NÍAL NOÍGIALLACH were known.

## Uí Tarsig
*Irish*

A division of the GALIÓIN, of which FIONN MAC CUMHAILL was the most prominent member.

## Uigreann
*Irish*

A warrior of the court of CONN CÉTCH-ATHLACH. He fought CUMHAILL after he had abducted MUIRNE and refused to give her back. He was later killed by FIONN MAC CUMHAILL, who was, according to some sources, in turn killed by Uigreann's sons.

## U(i)sne(a)ch
*Irish*

A member of the RED BRANCH, he was the husband of ELVA, the daughter of CATHBHADH and MAGA, and the father of NAOISE, ARDÁN and AINNLE, the cousins of CÚ CHULAINN, who were collectively known as the sons of Uisnech.

## Ulaidh
*Irish*

The original Irish name for ULSTER, one of the four original Irish kingdoms. Ulaidh was a huge realm that covered all of northern IRELAND, including Donegal, and had its capital at EMHAIN MHACHA. It was subsequently divided by NÍAL NOÍGIALLACH after he had conquered it.

## Ullan
*Irish*
See ILLAN.

## Ulster
*Irish*

Originally known as ULAIDH, and one of the four early kingdoms of IRELAND. Ulster was created by the FIR BHOLG as one of the five CÓIGEDH, or provinces, into which they divided the land, the other provinces being LEINSTER, MUNSTER, CONNACHT and MEATH in the centre of all of them. Ulster was the traditional enemy of Connacht. The Fir Bholg were later replaced by the TUATHA DÉ DANANN, the true gods of Irish Celtic mythology. They, in turn, were defeated by the Sons of MÍL ÉSPÁINE, who are regarded as the traditional ancestors of the royal house of Ulster.

## Umall
*Irish*

A little used variant of CUMHAILL.

## Undersea Island
*Irish*
See ISLANDS OF MAÍL DÚIN.

## Underworld
*General*

'The Land of the Dead', the realm to which all those who have died pass. The Celtic idea of the Underworld really exists within the OTHERWORLD, for it is not the dark, foreboding place of other pagan cultures, but rather a discernible realm where all go. It is also the home of the gods, for the Celts had no concept of a realm that would equate to heaven, the sole domain of the gods.

## Undry
*Irish*

The inexhaustible cauldron of the DAGHDHA.

## Unius
*Irish*

The river in which the DAGHDHA made love to the MÓRRÍGHAN while she stood with one foot on each bank on the eve of the feast of SAMHAIN as she washed the bloody corpses and armour of those about to die in the Second Battle of MAGH TUIREDH to be fought the following day. In return for the sexual favours of the Daghdha, the Mórríghan promised to help the TUATHA DÉ DANANN in the coming battle.

## Uri-en, -an
*British and Welsh*

An historical ruler (*c.*570) of the kingdom of RHEGED, a Brythonic kingdom in the northwest of ENGLAND. He was assassinated by a former ally, possibly around 590, after he had defeated the Bernicians. Urien was the father of OWAIN, and of three sons named RIWALLAWN, RUN and PASCEN. A Welsh legend makes Urien the father of Owain by the daughter of ARAWN.

## Uscias
*Irish*

Hailing from the mythical city of FINDIAS, Uscias was one of the four wizards who taught their magic to the TUATHA DÉ DANANN before they came to IRELAND. He is said to have equipped them with the invincible sword of NUADHA. His co-tutors were MORFESSA of FALIA, ESIAS of GORIAS and SIMIAS of MURIAS.

## Uthecar
*Irish*

The father of CELTCHAR.

## Uther
*British*

The son of CONSTANTINE[1] and the brother of CONSTANS and AMBROSIUS AURELIUS. He succeeded Ambrosius Aurelius, who is sometimes named as his father. Infatuated with EIGYR, the wife of GORLOIS, Uther managed to fulfil his desires with Eigyr through the intervention of MYRDDIN, their union occurring on the night that Gorlois was killed in battle by Uther's troops. Later, Uther married Eigyr, but was killed in battle and allegedly buried at STONEHENGE.

Later tradition makes King ARTHUR the child born of the magical union between Uther and Eigyr. This, however, postdates the origin of Uther by a considerable time and is simply the invention of later writers. That Uther once lived is now thought fairly certain, but that he ever fell in love with Eigyr or used magic to enable him to lie with her is pure invention.

## Vendotia
*Welsh*

The Latin name for the North Welsh kingdom of GWYNEDD. It has its root in VENDOTII, the name of the people who inhabited the kingdom.

## Vendoti(i)
*Welsh*

The ancient British people who inhabited VENDOTIA. GEOFFREY OF MONMOUTH names their king as CADWALLON.

## Venetii
*Gaulish*

A Gaulish tribe noted for the skill of its mariners and still considered to be in existence during the sixth century. Tradition states that TREPHINA, the daughter of their leader WAROK, married CUNOMORUS.

## Vindonnus
*Gaulish*

The continental version of FIND and one that formed the basis of such place names as Vienna or Uindopona.

## Vivionn
*Irish*
See BEBHIONN.

## Votadini
*British*

A north British tribe of which CUNEDDA was said to have been the ruler just before he emigrated to WALES in about AD 430.

## Vortigern
*British*

A British king, whose latin name was Uurtigernus, who is first mentioned in the writings of BEDE[2]. However, Vortigern means 'overlord', so it appears that this is a title rather than a proper name. Vortigern is generally accepted as an historical character, although the extent of his realm remains a mystery. NENNIUS[1] supports this suposition by saying that he ascended in AD 425. It seems possible that he may have married a daughter of the rebel Roman Emperor MAXIMUS, and is credited with sons named VORTIMER, CATIGERN, PASCHENT and FAUSTUS.

GEOFFREY OF MONMOUTH says that he was a king of BRITAIN[1] who instigated the assassination of CONSTANTINE[1] and installed CONSTANS, the son of the murdered king, as his puppet. Later he killed Constans and took the throne for himself. Vortigern is reputed to have invited the SAXONS to Britain to repel the PICTS. His reign was interrupted for a while while his son VORTIMER ruled in his stead, but he returned after his wife poisoned his son. He fled to WALES after the slaughter of the the British princes on

Salisbury Plain. In Wales he tried to build himself a tower, but each night the stones disappeared. He consulted a local magician, MYRDDIN, who ascribed this to the presence of DRAGONS. Vortigern was burned to death in his tower by AMBROSIUS AURELIUS, the rightful heir, who had the help of his brother UTHER.

## Vortimer
*British*

The son of VORTIGERN and brother, according to some sources, of CATIGERN, PASCHENT and FAUSTUS. He was King of BRITAIN[1] for a short while when his father was either deposed or had abdicated in his favour, but he was poisoned by his step-mother, after which his father regained the throne. Vortimer had said that after he died he should be buried in the place at which the SAXONS, whom he had opposed, most commonly landed. A statue of him should also be erected there to frighten the invaders away. GEOFFREY OF MONMOUTH says that his wishes were not complied with, but the Welsh *Trioedd Ynys Prydein* say that his bones were buried in the chief British ports. A similar tradition said that a statue of him was erected at Dover. Although his father is almost universally regarded as historical, many commentators regard Vortimer as pure fiction.

## Vran
*Welsh*

The shortened and popular version of BENDIGEID VRAN.

## Wales
*General*

Although nowadays a single country, as indeed it was sometimes portrayed in the Celtic legends, it was, at that time, a patchwork of minor kingdoms, including GWYNEDD, DYFED and POWYS. Many of the most major Arthurian sources have a Welsh origin, and even the Continental romances owe much to Welsh tradition. There seems little doubt that ARTHUR and many of his knights have a Welsh provenance. They then progressed south into CORNWALL, which, to this day, has a very strong Welsh character.

## Warok
*Welsh*

The chief of the VENETII. His daughter, TREPHINA, married CUNOMORUS.

## Wessex
*General*

The kingdom of the West SAXONS in BRITAIN[1], which was said to have been founded about AD 500 and which covered present-day Hampshire, Dorset, Wiltshire, Berkshire, Somerset and Devon. By 829 Wessex had become the dominant kingdom in Britain and for the first time united the country under its rule as a single nation.

## White Book of Rhydderch, The
*Welsh*

An early fourteenth-century manuscript, which, together with the *Red Book of Hergest*, contains the MABINOGION cycle. It is today housed in the National Library of WALES, Aberystwyth.

## White Mount
*British*

Called BRYN GWYN in Welsh, the White Mount is one of the most important pagan sites in LONDON, for it is the location of the burial of the severed head of BENDIGEID VRAN by PRYDERI, MANAWYDAN FAB LLYR, GLIFIEU, TALIESIN, YNAWAG, GRUDDIEU and HEILYN. The head was buried with its face towards FRANCE so that it would forever act as a magical guardian of the country. Later tradition says that King ARTHUR dug up the interred head because he wanted to be the sole guardian of BRITAIN[1]. The White Mount was one of the four major Druidic sites of London, and it is also the burial place of the founder of London, BRUTUS, as well as of the fifth-century BC monarch MOLMUTIUS. Today, little is actually visible of the White Mount, for the White Tower within the Tower of London was built on it.

## White Stag
*General*

Unsurprisingly, a white stag features in a

number of Celtic stories, for the Celts (along with many other cultures) held the white stag as an especially mystical animal that was thought to have originated in the OTHERWORLD.

## Wild Hunt
*General*

A supernatural hunt that survives in folklore to this day. The ghostly figures of the riders in the hunt may be seen riding by. In ENGLAND the Wild Hunt was said to have been seen in both Devon and Somerset. Most famously it was said to have been led by King ARTHUR who rode in procession to GLASTONBURY either at noon or on clear nights that were lit by a full moon.

## Winchester
*British*

The city in Hampshire that claims to be the oldest cathedral city in ENGLAND. The foundation of the city is attributed to HUDIBRAS, the ninth ruler of BRITAIN[1] after BRUTUS, sometime in the ninth

century BC. Hudibras called the city Caer Gwent, the White City. It was later enlarged by MOLMUTIUS. Later still Winchester became the administrative centre of England and a place where kings were both crowned, and buried.

## Wisdom, Salmon of
*Irish*
See SALMON OF WISDOM.

## Women, Land of
*Irish*

The literal translation of TÍR INNA MBAN, the OTHERWORLDLY kingdom that was inhabited entirely by beautiful women.

## Wrnach
*Welsh*

The giant owner of a sword that CULHWCH had to obtain as one of the tasks imposed by YSPADDADEN if Culhwch were to marry OLWEN. CEI obtained it by trickery and killed Wrnach.

## Ychdryt Varyvdraws
*Welsh*

One of the seldom mentioned members of the party that helped CULHWCH locate OLWEN. He was chosen as he could project his beard above the heads of his comrades and thus provide them with shelter in bad weather.

## Yder
*British*

A mythical giant, who was said to have done battle with three other giants that lived on Brent Knoll in Somerset. He killed the giants, but was mortally wounded himself and died shortly afterwards.

## Yesu
*British*

A variant of ESUS, which some have fancifully sought to link with the name of Jesus Christ in an attempt to assert that the Messiah came to BRITAIN[1].

## Ygern-a, -e
*British*

The anglicized version of EIGYR, the original name of IGRAINE, wife of GORLOIS, Duke of CORNWALL.

## Ynaw-ag, -c
*Welsh*

One of the seven survivors of the expedition mounted by BENDIGEID VRAN against King MATHOLWCH of IRELAND to rescue BRANWEN. The other six who survived the slaughter were PRYDERI, MANAWYDAN FAB LLYR, GLIFIEU, TALIESIN, GRUDDIEU and HEILYN. They brought Branwen back to WALES, having exterminated the Irish except for five pregnant women, who hid in a cave, but Branwen died of a broken heart when she thought of the wholesale destruction brought about on her behalf. Ynawag and his companions also carried the severed head of Bendigeid Vran back with them and, after a much delayed journey, buried it in accordance with the king's instructions under the WHITE MOUNT in LONDON.

## Ynys Enlli
*Welsh*

The Welsh name for BARDSEY Island.

## Ynys Fanaw
*Welsh*

The Welsh name for the Isle of MAN, the legendary home of LLYR.

## Ynys Witrin
*British*

'The Glassy Isle', the original name of GLASTONBURY.

## York
*British*

A city in Yorkshire. Its legendary founder, in 944 BC, was EBRAUC, the sixth king after BRUTUS. In AD 71 The Romans captured the city from the BRIGANTES, called it Eboracum and made it their northern headquarters.

## Yr Wyddfa (Fawr)
*Welsh*

The original name for Mount SNOWDON, that probably signified 'The Great Tomb', referring to a large cairn that once stood on its summit. This also gave rise to the name CLOGWYN CARNEDD YR WYDDFA, 'The Precipice of the Carn on Yr Wyddfa'. Another name is CARNEDD Y CAWR, 'The Giant's Carn', and this poses the question: who was this giant buried atop the ancient peak in WALES? The cairn itself was demolished in the nineteenth century and made into a kind of tower, which existed for some years before the present building was erected. According to Sir John Rhys in his CELTIC FOLKLORE (1901), this was the reputed grave of RHITTA CAWR, a giant sometimes known as RHICCA, who killed kings and clothed himself in a garment made from their beards.

## Ys
*Gaulish*

A legendary city of BRITTANY. It was supposed to have become submerged thanks to DAHUT or AHES, the daughter of GRADLON. It has been suggested that this character, Dahut, may have, in some small way, contributed to the legend of Morgan Le Fay, for she was said to have been a fairy referred to locally as a MARI-MORGAN.

## Ysbaddad(d)en
*Welsh*
See YSPADDADEN.

## Yseudydd
*Welsh*

A servant of GWENHWYFAR, who appears in some sources as one of the members of the party formed to help CULHWCH locate OLWEN. His companion was YSKYRDAW, also a servant of GWENHWYFAR. They were chosen because they could run as fast as their thoughts.

## Yskyrdaw
*Welsh*

A servant to GWENHWYFAR and companion of YSEUDYDD, whom he accompanied on the quest led by CULHWCH to locate OLWEN.

## Yspaddad(d)en
*Welsh*
Also YSBADDADEN

The chief giant, or PENKAWR, and father of OLWEN. A huge being, forks had to be placed under his eyelids in order to prop them open, a trait that has led some to claim that he is the analogue of the Irish BALAR. Yspaddaden features in the story of *Culhwch and Olwen*, in which he set CULHWCH a series of seemingly impossible tasks, subsequently imposing innumerable conditions if Culhwch was to gain the hand of Olwen. Finally, unable to endure any more of the giant's conditions, Culhwch rounded up all Yspaddaden's enemies and stormed his castle. Yspaddaden was killed by GOREU during the attack.

**Ywerit**
*Welsh*

According to some Celtic sources, the father of BENDIGEID VRAN.

## Zel

*British*

A mythical king who is said to have been buried on horseback within the hill that appears to carry his derivative name of SIL, the hill itself being known as SILBURY Hill. Zel, or Sil, appears to have been a crude attempt to explain the existence of the hill, although when the hill was excavated in 1723 human remains and an antique bridle were allegedly discovered.

# Appendix 1
## Some Celtic Genealogies

Note· Because some of the names mentioned within these genealogies are non-Celtic, not all will have entries within the main text.

### 1. KING ARTHUR

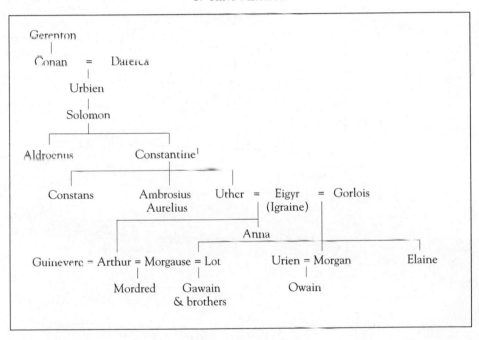

## 2. House of Llyr

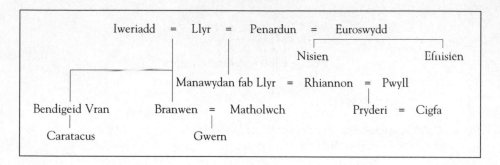

## 3. Bride

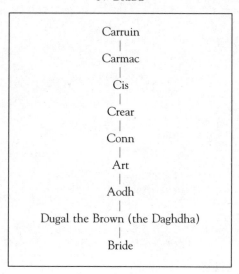

## 4. Conaire Mór

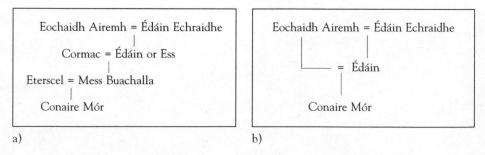

a)                                    b)

## 5. Conchobar mac Nessa and the Red Branch

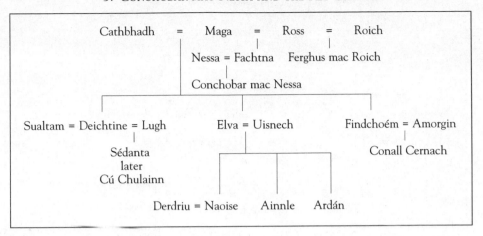

## 6. Cunomorus

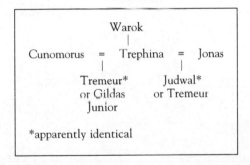

## 7. House of Dôn

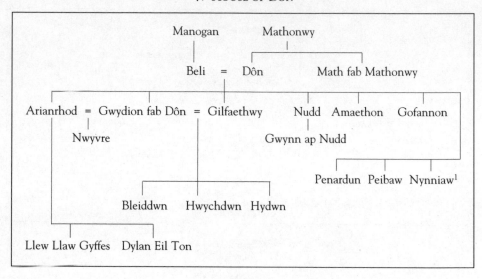

## 8. Eliseg

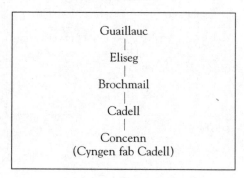

## 9. Myrddin

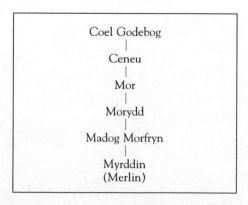

10. ANGLO-SAXON INVADERS

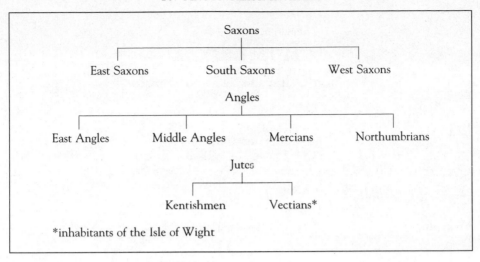

*inhabitants of the Isle of Wight

# Appendix 2
## Non-Celtic Deities and Heroes

Following are brief descriptions of the non-Celtic deities, heroes and places named in the main text. They are included here to enable comparisons to be made with the characters or places with which they have been assimilated. Names in SMALL CAPITALS have entries within the main text.

**Aegyptus**
*Greek*

The eponymous ruler of Egypt. He suggested a mass marriage between his fifty sons and the fifty daughters of Danaus, his brother.

**Anchises**
*Graeco-Roman*

The father of AENEAS by Aphrodite (Roman Venus).

**Andromeda**
*Greek*

The beautiful daughter of Cepheus and Cassiopeia, who was saved from a sea monster by the hero Perseus, who used the severed head of the Gorgon Medusa to turn that sea monster into stone.

**Aphrodite**
*Greek*

Called Venus by the Romans, Aphrodite was the Greek goddess of love, feminine beauty, marriage and fertility, and patroness of prostitutes. By Anchises she became the mother of the semi-divine AENEAS.

**Apollo**
*Graeco-Roman*

The twin of Artemis and the most popular of all the Greek gods, he was the god of prophecy and divine distance, of beneficent power and righteous punishment. He presided over law and made men aware of their guilt, also cleansing them of it. He was god of music, poetry and dance, archery, pastoral life and agriculture. Apollo also protected animals from disease, and was the patron of farmers, poets and physicians. In later times he also became recognized as the god of light and the sun.

**Ariadne**
*Greek*

The daughter of Minos who helped Theseus to escape from the Minotaur and later married the god Dionysus, who placed her crown in the heavens as the constellation Corona Borealis.

**Artemis**
*Greek*

The twin sister of Apollo, she was called Diana by the Romans. Artemis was the virgin goddess of the hunt, protectress of children and young animals, protectress of the hunted and vegetation, the goddess of chastity and, later, goddess of the moon.

## Asclepi -os, -us
*Graeco-Roman*

The son of Apollo and god of medicine. The iconography of a serpent entwined around a caduceus is still used as a medical symbol worldwide. His medical skills enabled him to bring the dead back to life, a trait that cheated the god Hades, who persuaded Zeus to strike him down with a thunderbolt and then place him in the heavens as the constellation Ophichus, so that he could do no more harm.

## Augustus
*Roman*

The Great Emperor of the Roman Empire (63 BC – AD 14), the son of Gaius Octavius, senator and praetor, and Atia, the niece of JULIUS CAESAR. He became Gaius Julius Caesar Octavianus through adoption by Julius Caesar in his will (44 BC), and later received the name Augustus ('Sacred', 'Venerable') in recognition of his services and position (27 BC). By the naval victory at Actium he became the sole ruler of the Roman world.

## Cassiopeia
*Greek*

The wife of Cepheus and mother, by him, of Andromeda. She once boasted that her daughter was more beautiful than the Nereids (sea-nymphs), a claim that led Poseidon to demand the sacrifice of Andromeda. The unfortunate princess was saved by Perseus. After her death Cassiopeia was placed in the heavens by Poseidon, hanging upside down in a chair for half the time as final and eternal punishment for her boast.

## Centaur
*Greek*

A mythical creature, half-horse, half-man, which was portrayed in early art as having the head, arms, torso and forelegs of a man, and the hindquarters of a horse. Later, the forelegs also became equine.

## Cornucopia
*Graeco-Roman*

The 'horn of plenty', said to have been one of the horns of the goat that nursed the infant Zeus. This horn had the power to refill itself with food and drink eternally.

## Danaides
*Greek*

The collective name for the fifty daughters of Danaus by ten different wives. Aegyptus suggested that these fifty young women should marry his fifty sons. The Danaides fled but were located and the marriage went ahead. On the wedding night forty-nine of the Danaides murdered their new husbands. Only one, Hypermnestra, spared her husband.

## Danaus
*Greek*

The brother of Aegyptus and father of the fifty Danaides. He instructed his daughters that they should murder their husbands, the fifty sons of Aegyptus, on their wedding night. Forty-nine complied with these instructions, although Hypermnestra spared her new husband's life.

## Diana
*Roman*

Initially a woodland deity, the Romans rapidly assimilated Diana with the Greek goddess Artemis.

## Dis Pater
*Roman*

The richest of all the Roman gods, the god of death, who is the equivalent of the Greek god Hades. The more common name for the Roman god of the dead, Pluto, is a euphemism that means 'wealth'.

## Hades
*Greek*

The name Hades has a dual role in Greek mythology, for it is the name both of the god of the dead and of the realm over which the god presides. The realm was divided into three distinct regions: that to which the righteous went after death (Elysium), that for those who had led an indifferent life (Asphodel) and that to which sinners were sent (Tartarus).

## Hecate
*Greek*

An extremely powerful goddess, who was worshipped in heaven, on earth and in Hades. Originally a moon goddess, Hecate was the patroness of rich men, sailors and flocks, and the bestower of the wealth and blessings of daily life. Later, she came to be regarded as a dread divinity, triple-headed and triple-breasted, who lived in the deepest region of Hades, where she presided over witchcraft and the black arts, becoming patroness of witches and sorceresses and protectress of graveyards and crossroads.

## Hercules
*Roman*

The Roman name for the Greek semi-divine hero Heracles, the son of Zeus by the mortal Alcmene. Hercules had to contend with the wrath of Hera, Zeus' wife, throughout his life, during which he completed twelve immense labours, sailed with Jason and the Argonauts and accomplished many other feats of strength and courage before his untimely death, after which he was reconciled with Hera and welcomed into the domain of the gods.

## Janus
*Roman*

One of the few uniquely Roman gods, who was looked upon as the creator of the world. The god of doorways and passage and of buildings in general, and of beginnings and endings of days, months and years. He was usually depicted with two faces, one facing forwards, the other facing backwards.

## Jupiter
*Roman*

Identified with the Greek Zeus, Jupiter was the god of the sky, the sun, the moon and all the heavenly bodies. Originally an agricultural deity, Jupiter later developed to become the protector of Rome and the Roman Empire.

## Mars
*Roman*

The equivalent of the Greek Ares. Originally an agricultural deity, Mars developed into the god of war when the Roman Empire expanded. He became one of the three protector deities of Rome and in popularity second only to Jupiter.

## Medusa
*Greek*

Originally a beautiful maiden, Medusa was transformed into a hideous monster by Athene after she had lain with Poseidon in a temple sacred to Athene. One glance from Medusa had the power to petrify human flesh. She was killed by Perseus, who used her severed head to turn to stone the sea-monster about to devour Andromeda.

## Mercury
*Roman*

The god of eloquence, skill, trading and thieving, and messenger to the gods. He was identified with the Greek Hermes, whose role he echoes.

## Midas
*Greek*

The king who was once given the power to turn everything he touched into gold, but who soon found the gift to be a curse and asked for the power to be taken away again. He later insulted Apollo, who made his ears turn into those of an ass, a secret he kept from everyone except his barber who told the secret to some reeds, which passed it on when the wind rustled them.

## Minerva
*Roman*

The goddess of education and business, who later developed into the goddess of war, at which time she became assimilated with the Greek Athene.

## Neptune
*Roman*

The god of the sea and fresh water. The equivalent of the Greek Poseidon.

## Perseus
*Greek*

The son of Zeus by the mortal Danaë. Perseus is best known as the killer of the Gorgon Medusa. He then used the monster's severed head to rescue the maiden Andromeda from a sea-monster.

## Serapis
*Graeco-Romano-Egyptian*

A composite god invented and introduced by Ptolemy I in an attempt to unite the Greeks, the Romans and the Egyptians. Revered as a healing deity, Serapis combined the attributes of Zeus, Hades and Asclepios with the Egyptian god Osiris.

## Silvanus
*Roman*

An agricultural deity, associated with the mysterious forces in woods, fields and flocks.

## Thórr
*Norse-Teutonic*

The god of thunder and lightning, war and agriculture. The oldest and strongest of Odínn's sons, Thórr was represented as a handsome, red-bearded warrior, benevolent towards man, but a mighty adversary of evil. His most famous attribute was the massive hammer with which he protected the other gods.

## Troy
*Greek*

Once thought of as a purely legendary city, the historicity of Troy was established between 1871 and 1873 when the German archaeologist Heinrich Schliemann excavated a site on the coast of

Asia Minor and uncovered the city. The city, the home of AENEAS and his father Anchises, was sacked by the Greeks in the ten years of the Trojan War. Aeneas survived and travelled to Rome where he became regarded as the legendary founder of the Roman people.

**Valkyrie**
*Norse-Teutonic*

The twelve warlike handmaidens of Odínn, who were alleged to hover over battlefields and select those to be killed, and then conduct them to Valhalla to spend eternity in the company of Odínn.

**Venus**
*Roman*

The goddess of love. The Roman equivalent of the Greek goddess Aphrodite.

**Vesta**
*Roman*

The daughter of Saturn, goddess of the hearth and household, of fire and purity and the patron of bakers. Supreme in the conduct of religious ceremonies, Vesta's temple in Rome was the site of the eternal sacred flame, which was tended by the Vestal Virgins.

**Yggdrasil**
*Norse-Teutonic*

The world tree, a giant evergreen ash at the centre of the cosmos, whose roots reach down to the UNDERWORLD, and whose branches reach into the heavens. It is tended by the three Norns who live either beneath its branches or within its root system.

# Bibliography

The books listed below contain information that is relevant to the study of the Celts, their religion and their way of life, although some of them cover a much wider period in history. It is by no means a complete list of all the books that have been published on the subject of the Celts. Works marked * are to be regarded as essential core reference texts.

**Anderson, A.R.** *Alexander's Gate, Gog and Magog and the Inclosed Nation* (Cambridge, Mass., 1932)

**Ashe, Geoffrey** *The Glastonbury Tor Maze* (Gothic Image, Glastonbury, 1979)

—, *Kings and Queens of Early Britain* (Methuen, London, 1982)

—, *Mythology of the British Isles* (Methuen, London, 1990)

**Atkinson, R.J.C.** *Stonehenge and Avebury* (H.M.S.O., London, 1959)

**Automobile Association/Ordnance Survey** *Leisure Guide: Cornwall* (Automobile Association, Basingstoke, 1988)

—, *Leisure Guide: Wessex* (Automobile Association, Basingstoke, 1988)

—, *Leisure Guide; Snowdonia and North Wales* (Automobile Association, Basingstoke, 1989)


**Barber, Chris,** *Mysterious Wales* (David & Charles, Newton Abbot, 1982)

**Barber, W.T.** *Exploring Wales* (David & Charles, Newton Abbot, 1982)

**Baring-Gould, S. and Fisher, J.** *Lives of the British Saints* (Cymrroddorion Society, London, 1907–13*)

**Bartrum, P.C.** (ed.) *Early Welsh Genealogical Tracts* (University of Wales Press, Cardiff, 1966*)

**Bede** (trans. Leo Shirley-Price) *A History of the English Church and People* (Penguin Books, Harmondsworth, 1955*)

—, (trans. John Stevens) *The Ecclesiastical History of the English Nation* (J.M. Dent & Sons Ltd, Everyman's Library 479, undated)

**Beresford Ellis, Peter** *Celtic Inheritance* (Frederick Muller, London, 1985)

**Berry, Claude** *Portrait of Cornwall* (Robert Hale, London, 1984)

**Blight, J.T.** *Ancient Stone Crosses in Cornwall* (Simpkin, Marshall & Co., London, 1872)

**Branston, Brian** *The Lost Gods of England* (Thames & Hudson, London, 1957)

**Briggs, Katharine M.** *A Dictionary of British Folk-Tales* (Routledge & Kegan Paul, London, 1971)

—, *A Dictionary of Fairies* (Allen Lane, London, 1976)

**Bromwich, Rachel** *Trioedd Ynys Prydein: The Welsh Triads* (University of Wales Press, Cardiff, 1978)

**Butler, Alban** *Lives of the Saints* (12 volumes) (Burns, Oates and Washbourne, London, 1926–38*)

**Byrne, John Francis** *Irish Kings and High Kings* (Batsford, London, 1987)


**Carr-Gomm, Philip** *The Elements of the Druid Tradition* (Element Books Ltd., Shaftesbury, 1991)

—, *The Druid Way* (Element Books Ltd., Shaftesbury, 1993)

**Cavendish, C.** (ed.) *Mythology; An Illustrated Encyclopedia* (Black Cat, London, 1987)

**Chadwick, N.K.** *The Age of Saints in the Early Celtic Church* (Oxford University Press, Oxford, 1961)

—, *Early Brittany* (University of Wales Press, Cardiff, 1969)

—, *The Celts* (Penguin Books, Harmondsworth, 1970)

**Chippindale, Christopher** *Stonehenge Complete: Archaeology, History, Heritage* (Thames & Hudson, London, 1983)

**Coghlan, Ronan** *Pocket Dictionary of Irish Myth and Legend* (Appletree Press, Belfast, 1985)

**Cotterell, Arthur** *A Dictionary of World Mythology* (Windward, London, 1979)

**Croker, T. Crofton** *Fairy Legends and Traditions of the South of Ireland* (John Murray, London, 1825–28*)

**Cross, T.P. and Slover, C.H.** *Ancient Irish Tales* (Harrap, London, 1937)

**Crossley-Holland, Kevin** *Folk Tales of the British Isles* (Folio Society, London, 1985)

—, *British Folk Tales* (Orchard Books, London, 1987)

**Cunliffe, B.** *The Celtic World* (The Bodley Head, London, 1979)

**D'Arbois de Jubainville, H.** (trans. R.I. Best) *The Irish Mythological Cycle* (Hodges & Figgis, Dublin, 1903*)

**Dames, Michael** *The Silbury Treasure* (Thames & Hudson, London, 1976)

—, *The Avebury Cycle* (Thames & Hudson, London, 1977)

**Davidson, Hilda Ellis** *The Lost Beliefs of Northern Europe* (Routledge, London, 1993)

**Davies, T.R.** *A Book of Welsh Names* (Sheppard Press, London, 1952)

**Delaney, Frank** *Legends of the Celts* (Hodder & Stoughton, London, 1989)

**Dillon, Myles** *Early Irish Literature* (University of Chigaco Press, 1948*)

—, (ed.) *Irish Sagas* (Stationery Office, Dublin, 1959)

**Dillon, M. and Chadwick, N.K.** *The Celtic Realms* (Weidenfeld & Nicolson, London, 1967)

—, *The Celts* (Weidenfeld & Nicolson, London, 1967)

**Ditmas, E.M.R.** *Traditions and Legends of Glastonbury* (Toucan Press, Guernsey, 1979)

**Dixon-Kennedy, Mike** *Arthurian Myth & Legend: An A–Z of People and Places* (Blandford, London, 1995)

**Dunn, Joseph** *The Ancient Irish Epic Tale, Taín Bó Cuailnge* (David Nutt, London, 1914*)

**Ebbutt, M.J.** *Hero-Myths and Legends of the British Race* (Harrap, London, 1910)

**Evans-Wentz, J.D.** *The Fairy Faith in Celtic Countries* (Oxford University Press, London, 1911)

**Faraday, L. Winifred** (trans.) *The Cattle-Raid of Cuailnge* (David Nutt, London, 1904*)

**Farmer, D.H.** *The Oxford Dictionary of Saints* (Clarendon Press, Oxford, 1978)

**Field, J.** *Place Names of Great Britain and Ireland* (David & Charles, Newton Abbot, 1980)

**Gantz, Jeffrey** (trans.) *The Mabinogion* (Penguin Books, Harmondsworth 1976*)

—, (trans.) *Early Irish Myths & Sagas* (Penguin Books, Harmondsworth, 1981)

**Garmonsway, G.N.** (ed.) *Anglo-Saxon Chronicle* (J.M. Dent, London, 1933*)

**Geoffrey of Monmouth** (trans. J.J. Parry) *Vita Merlini* (University of Illinois Press, Urbana, 1925*)

—, (trans. L. Thorpe) *History of the Kings of Britain* (Penguin Books, Harmondsworth 1966*)

**Gibbs, R.** *The Legendary XII Hides of Glastonbury* (Llanerch, Lampeter, 1988)

**Gildas** (trans. Michael Winterbottom) *De Excidio* (Phillimore, Chichester, 1978*)

**Giles, J.A.** *History of the Ancient Britons* (W. Baxter, Oxford, 1854*)

Glassie, Henry (ed.) *Irish Folk Tales* (Penguin Books, Harmondsworth, 1987)

Graves, Robert *The White Goddess* (Faber & Faber, London, 1961)

Gray, Louis Herbert (ed.) *The Mythology of all Races* (13 volumes) (Marshall Jones Company, Boston, Mass., 1918*)

Green, Miranda J. *The Gods of Roman Britain* (Shire Publications, Princes Risborough, 1983)

—, *The Gods of the Celts* (Alan Sutton, Gloucester, 1986)

Gregory, Augusta *Cuculain of Muirthemne: The Story of the Men of the Red Branch of Ulster arranged and put into English* (Colin Smythe, Gerrard's Cross, 1970)

Grinsell, L.V. *Legendary History and Folklore of Stonehenge* (Toucan Press, Guernsey, 1975)

—, *The Druids and Stonehenge* (Toucan Press, Guernsey, 1978)

Guest, Lady Charlotte (trans.) *The Mabinogion* (J.M. Dent, London, 1906*)

Handford, S.A. (trans.) *The Conquest of Gaul (The Gallic Wars by Julius Caesar)* (Penguin Books, Harmondsworth, 1963)

Harbison, Peter *Guide to the National Monuments of Ireland* (Gill & Macmillan, Dublin, 1970)

Hawkes, Jacquetta *Prehistoric Britain* (Harvard University Press, Cambridge, Mass., 1953)

Hawkins, Gerald S. *Stonehenge Decoded* (Fontana, London, 1970)

Henderson, William *Notes on the Folklore of the Northern Countries of England* (W. Satchell, Peyton, London, 1879)

Hodgkin, R.G. *A History of the Anglo-Saxons* (2 volumes) (Oxford University Press, Oxford, 1935*)

Hole, Christina *English Folklore* (B.T. Batsford, London, 1940)

Holweck, F.G. *A Biographical Dictionary of Saints* (Herder, St Louis, 1924)

Jackson, Kenneth Hurlstone *The Oldest Irish Tradition: A Window on the Iron Age* (Cambridge University Press, 1964)

—, (trans.) *A Celtic Miscellany* (Penguin Books, Harmondsworth, 1970)

Jacobs, Joseph (coll.) *Celtic Fairy Tales* (David Nutt, London, 1892)

—, *More Celtic Fairy Tales* (David Nutt, London, 1894)

[N.B. The two above titles are available as a single volume facsimile reprint under the title *Celtic Fairy Tales*, published by Senate, an imprint of Studio Editions, 1994]

Jones, G. and Jones, T. (trans.) *The Mabinogion* (Dent, London, 1949*)

Joyce, P.W. *Old Celtic Romances* (Talbot Press, Dublin, 1961)

Kavanagh, Peter *Irish Mythology: a Dictionary* (Goldsmith, Kildare, 1988)

Kendrick, T.D. *British Antiquity* (London, 1950)

Kightly, Charles *Folk Heroes of Britain* (Thames & Hudson, London, 1984)

Kinsella, Thomas *The Tain* (Oxford University Press, Oxford, 1970*)

Knott, E. and Murphy, G. *Early Irish Literature* (Routledge & Kegan Paul, London, 1966)

Lethbridge, T.C. *Gogmagog, the Buried Gods* (Routledge & Kegan Paul, London, 1957)

—, *Legends of the Sons of God* (Routledge & Kegan Paul, London, 1957)

Lloyd, John Edward *A History of Wales* (Longman, London, 1939)

Loomis, R.S. *Celtic Myth and Arthurian Romance* (Columbia University Press, New York, 1927)

—, *The Grail: from Celtic Myth to Christian Symbol* (University of Wales Press, Cardiff, 1963)

Mac an tSaoi, M. (ed.) *Dhá Scéal Artúraíochta (Visit of Grey Ham)* (Dublin Institute for Advanced Studies, Dublin, 1946*)

Mac Biocaill, G. *Ireland Before the Vikings* (Gill & Macmillan, Dublin, 1972)

MacCana, Proinsias *Celtic Mythology* (Hamlyn, London, 1970)

MacCulloch, John Arnott *The Religion of the Ancient Celts* (Edinburgh, 1911)

——, *Celtic Mythology* (Marshall Jones Company, Boston, Mass., 1918, republished Constable & Co., London, 1992)

Mackenzie, Donald A. *Scotland: the Ancient Kingdom* (Blackie, Edinburgh, 1930)

MacNeill, Maire *The Festival of Lughnasa* (Oxford University Press, Oxford, 1962)

Maltwood, K.E. *A Guide to Glastonbury's Temple of the Stars* (reissued, James Clarke, Cambridge, 1964)

Matthews, Caitlín *Mabon and The Mysteries of Britain* (Arkana, London, 1987)

Matthews, J. *Boadicea* (Firebird Books, Poole, 1988)

——, *Fionn mac Cumhail* (Firebird Books, Poole, 1988)

Matthews, J. and C. *The Aquarian Guide to British and Irish Mythology* (Aquarian Press, Wellingborough, 1988)

Matthews, J. and Stewart, R.J. *Legendary Britain* (Blandford, London, 1989)

Michell, John *The Travellers Key to Sacred England: A Guide to the Legends, Lore, and Landscape of England's Sacred Places* (Harrap Columbus, London, 1989)

Morris, J. (ed. and trans.), *British History and the Welsh Annals* (Phillimore, Chichester, 1980*)

Murphy, Gerard *Saga and Myth in Ancient Ireland* (C.O. Lochlainn, Dublin, 1955)

Murray, Margaret *The God of the Witches* (Oxford University Press, London, 1952)

Neeson, Eoin *Irish Myths and Legends*, I and II (Mercier, Cork, 1973)

O'Driscoll, Robert (ed.) *Celtic Consciousness* (Canongate, Edinburgh, 1982)

O'Faolain, Eileen *Irish Sagas & Folk Tales* (Oxford University Press, Oxford, 1954)

O'Hogain, Daithi *The Hero in Irish Folk History* (Gill & Macmillan, Dublin, 1985)

O'Kelly, Claire *Newgrange* (John English, Wexford, 1971)

Oman, Charles *England before the Norman Conquest* (Methuen, London, 1939)

O'Rahilly, Cecile *The Tain* (Dublin Institute of Advanced Studies, 1967*)

O'Rahilly, T.F. *Early Irish History & Mythology* (Dublin Institute of Advanced Studies, 1946*)

Osborn, Marijane (trans.) *Beowulf* (University of California Press, 1983*)

O'Sullivan, Sean *Folk Tales of Ireland* (Routledge & Kegan Paul, London, 1966)

——, *The Folklore of Ireland* (B.T. Batsford, London, 1974)

——, *Irish Folk Custom & Belief* (Mercier, Cork, 1977)

O'Sullivan, T.D. *The 'De excidio' of Gildas* (Brill, Leiden, 1978*)

Pears Encyclopedia of Myths and Legends (4 volumes) (general editors, Mary Barker and Christopher Cook), vol 2. *Western & Northern Europe: Central & Southern Africa*, Sheila Savill (Pelham Books, London, 1978)

Pennick, Nigel and Jackson, Nigel *The Celtic Oracle* (Aquarian Press, Wellingborough, 1992)

Pepper, Elizabeth and Wilcock, John *Magical and Mystical Sites: Europe and The British Isles* (Phanes Press, Grand Rapids, Michigan, 1993)

Piggot, S. *The Druids* (Penguin Books, Harmondsworth, 1974)

Porter, J.R. and Russell, W.M.S. (ed.) *Animals in Folklore* (The Folklore Society, London, 1978)

Raftery, Joseph (ed.) *The Celts* (Mercier, London, 1964)

Reader's Digest *Folklore, Myths and Legends of Britain* (Hodder & Stoughton, London, 1973)

Rees, A. and B. *Celtic Heritage* (Thames & Hudson, London, 1974)

Rhys, John *Celtic Folklore* (Clarendon Press, Oxford, 1901*)

Ritson, Joseph, *Folklore & Legends* (W.W. Gibbings, London, 1891)

Rolleston, T.W. *Myths and Legends of the Celtic Race* (Harrap, London, 1911*, republished Senate, London, 1994*)

**Ross, Anne** *Everyday Life of the Pagan Celts* (Carousel Books, London, 1967)

—, *Pagan Celtic Britain* (Cardinal, London, 1974)

**Rutherford, W.** *The Druids* (Aquarian Press, Wellingborough, 1983)

**Senior, M.** *Myths of Britain* (Orbis, London, 1979)

**Seymour, St John D.** *Irish Witchcraft and Demonology* (Hodges, Figgis & Co., Dublin, 1913)

**Simms, George Otto** *St Patrick* (The O'Brien Press Ltd, Dublin, 1991)

**Smyth, Daragh** *A Guide to Irish Mythology* (Irish Academic Press, Dublin, 1988)

**Spence, L.** *The Minor Traditions of British Mythology* (London, 1948)

**Squire, Charles** *Celtic Myth & Legend* (Gresham Publishing, London, undated)

**Stewart, R.J.** *The Prophetic Vision of Merlin* (Arkana, London, 1986)

—, *Cuchulainn* (Firebird Books, Poole, 1988)

—, *Where is Saint George?* (Blandford, London, 1988)

—, *Celtic Gods, Celtic Goddesses* (Blandford, London, 1990)

**Strachan, John** (ed.) *Stories from the Tain* (Hodges, Figgis & Co., Dublin, 1908)

**Tatlock, J.S.P.** *The Legendary History of Britain* (University of California, Berkeley, 1950)

**Thom, Alexander** *Megalithic Sites in Britain* (Clarendon Press, Oxford, 1967)

—, *Megalithic Lunar Observatories* (Clarendon Press, Oxford, 1971)

**Thorpe, Lewis** (trans.) *The History of the Kings of Britain* (Penguin Books, Harmondsworth, 1966*)

**Treharne, R.F.** *The Glastonbury Legends* (Cresset, London, 1967)

**Vendryes, J. et al.** *Lexique étymologique de l'irlandais ancien* (Paris, 1959)

**Waddell, L.A.** *The British Edda* (Chapman & Hall, London, 1930)

**Wentz, E.** *The Fairy Faith in Celtic Countries* (Colin Smythe, Gerrards Cross, 1977)

**Weston, Jessie L.** *From Ritual to Romance* (Doubleday, Garden City, 1957)

**Westwood, Jennifer** *Albion: A Guide to Legendary Britain* (Paladin, London, 1987)

**Whitlock, Ralph** *The Folklore of Wiltshire* (B.T. Batsford, London, 1976)

—, *The Folklore of Devon* (B.T. Batsford, London, 1977)

**Wright, Neil** (ed.) *Historia Regu Britanniae* (D.S. Brewer, Cambridge, 1985*)

**Yeats, W.B.** *Fairy and Folk Tales of Ireland* (Colin Smythe, Gerrard's Cross, 1977)

—, *The Fairy Faith in Celtic Countries* (Colin Smythe, Gerrard's Cross, 1977)